THE

PATIENT FERMENT

—— OF THE ——

EARLY CHURCH

Maynard Weaver
1434 Canterbury Ct
Goshen IN 46526
Phone 535-9212

To Mike and Phyllis, with gratitude for vigorous discussions and shared life at Prairie Street, In Christ,

Alan Kreider

THE
PATIENT
FERMENT
—— OF THE ——
EARLY CHURCH

The Improbable Rise of Christianity
in the Roman Empire

ALAN KREIDER

Baker Academic

a division of Baker Publishing Group
Grand Rapids, Michigan

Published by Baker Academic
a division of Baker Publishing Group
P.O. Box 6287, Grand Rapids, MI 49516-6287
www.bakeracademic.com

Printed in the United States of America

Library of Congress Cataloging-in-Publication Data
Names: Kreider, Alan, 1941– author.
Title: The patient ferment of the early church : the improbable rise of Christianity in the Roman Empire / Alan Kreider.
Description: Grand Rapids, MI : Baker Academic, 2016. | Includes bibliographical references and index.
Identifiers: LCCN 2015043726 | ISBN 9780801048494 (pbk.)
Subjects: LCSH: Church history—Primitive and early church, ca. 30–600.
Classification: LCC BR162.3 .K74 2016 | DDC 270.1—dc23
LC record available at http://lccn.loc.gov/2015043726

16 17 18 19 20 21 22   7 6 5 4 3 2 1

For Kim and Sally Tan
who embody patient ferment

Contents

ACKNOWLEDGMENTS

To write a book like this is to be indebted to many people. I owe much to Michael Green, whose *Evangelism in the Early Church* first seized my imagination, and much more to Ramsay MacMullen, whose formidable erudition and penetrating gaze have challenged me since I first read *Christianizing the Roman Empire*. On many occasions he has been kind to me, and I have at times thought of my research as an inner conversation with him. Other scholars whose learning and generosity have meant a great deal to me are Paul Bradshaw and Everett Ferguson. Four scholars—three Germans and an American—have written works that at important stages shaped my thinking: Georg Kretschmar, Norbert Brox, Wolfgang Reinbold, and Rodney Stark. To all of these I am indebted. As I was writing, two friends—Christopher Rowland and Eoin de Bhaldraithe, O.Cist.—faithfully read my chapters and broadened my horizons. Others who read chapters include Andy Alexis-Baker, David Boshart, Shana Peachey Boshart, Andy Brubaker-Kaethler, Matt Cordella, Leslie Fairfield, Everett Ferguson, Brian Haymes, Jay Freel Landry, Stuart Murray Williams, Gerald Schlabach, and Wilbert Shenk. In my attempt to think clearly about Augustine's approach to patience, Gerald Schlabach was particularly helpful, providing perceptive insights and concrete suggestions. In the later stages of my writing, a "Patient Ferment Group" met monthly at the welcoming table of James and Barb Nelson Gingerich to eat delicious meals and scrutinize my chapters. I am grateful to James and Barb and to the faithful table companions whose encouragement and criticisms helped me greatly: Ryan Harker, Rachel Miller Jacobs, Loren Johns, Eleanor Kreider, David B. Miller, and Mary Schertz. Barb also gave initial editorial scrutiny to each chapter as it emerged, and Ryan helped me with classical Greek. Kim and Sally Tan are friends whose lives have inspired me and who for years have believed in my project and supported it; at long last I am able to dedicate this book to them, with deep gratitude.

Of course, I could not have written this book without the support of institutions: Mennonite Board of Missions (now Mennonite Mission Network) supported me as I studied early Christianity; Anabaptist Mennonite Biblical Seminary provided me with a Faculty Scholarship Development Grant and with an excellent library (whose assistant director, Karl Stutzman, has done wonders in tracking down obscure publications); and the hospitable sisters at St. Benedict's Monastery, St. Joseph, Minnesota, have five times given me an ideal setting for research as a scholar in their Studium program.

Most of all I owe gratitude to my wife, Eleanor, one of whose manifold gifts is her knowledge of early Christianity. As I worked on this book, I found joy in talking with her at length, knowing that the enthusiasms that we discussed are shared. Eleanor read and critiqued many drafts of these chapters and was patient even when there were no discernible signs of ferment! How can I adequately express thanks to her, and to all these dear people? Perhaps in part by absolving them of responsibility for the perversities that remain!

ABBREVIATIONS

Ancient Sources

Ad Quir.	Cyprian, *Ad Quirinum tes-timonia adversus Judaeos* [*To Quirinus: Testimonies against the Jews*]		2nd ed. Steenbrugge: Abbatia Sancti Petri, 1961
		Cult. fem.	Tertullian, *De cultu femi-narum* [*On the Dress of Women*]
Adv. Jud.	Tertullian, *Adversus Judaeos* [*Against the Jews*]	Demetr.	Cyprian, *To Demetrianus*
An.	Tertullian, *On the Soul*	Dial.	Justin, *Dialogue with Trypho*
Apol.	*Apology*	Did.	*Didache*
Autol.	Theophilus, *Ad Autolycum* [*To Autolycus*]	Did. apost.	*Didascalia apostolorum*
		Diogn.	*Epistle to Diognetus*
		Dom. or.	Cyprian, *De dominica ora-tione* [*On the Lord's Prayer*]
Bapt.	Tertullian, *On Baptism*		
Cels.	Origen, *Against Celsus*	Don.	Cyprian, *To Donatus*
1–2 Clem.	1–2 Clement, Epistles	Ep.	*Epistle*
Cod. theod.	*Codex theodosianus*	Epit.	Lactantius, *Epitome of the Divine Institutes*
Comm.	*Commentary*		
Comm. Dan.	Hippolytus, *Commentarium in Danielum* [*Commentary on Daniel*]	Exh. cast.	Tertullian, *De exhortatione castitatis* [*Exhortation to Chastity*]
Comm. Rom.	Origen, *Commentarii in Romanos* [*Commentary on Romans*]	Fug.	Tertullian, *De fuga in perse-cutione* [*On Flight in Time of Persecution*]
Conf.	Augustine of Hippo, *Confessions*	Hab. virg.	Cyprian, *De habitu virginum* [*The Dress of Virgins*]
Const.	*Apostolic Constitutions*	Haer.	Irenaeus, *Adversus haereses* [*Against Heresies*]; Hip-polytus, *Refutatio omnium haeresium* [*Refutation of All Heresies*]
Cor.	Tertullian, *De corona militis* [*The Crown*]		
CPL	*Clavis Patrum Latinorum.* Edited by Eligius Dekkers.		

Herm. Mand.   Shepherd of Hermas, Mandate

Herm. Sim.   Shepherd of Hermas, Similitude

Herm. Vis.   Shepherd of Hermas, Vision

Hist. eccl.   Eusebius, *Ecclesiastical History*; Socrates, *Ecclesiastical History*

Hom. Exod.   Origen, *Homiliae in Exodum* [*Homilies on Exodus*]

Hom. Ezech.   Origen, *Homiliae in Ezechielem* [*Homilies on Ezekiel*]

Hom. Gen.   Origen, *Homiliae in Genesim* [*Homilies on Genesis*]

Hom. Jer.   Origen, *Homiliae in Jeremiam* [*Homilies on Jeremiah*]

Hom. Jos.   Origen, *Homiliae in Josuam* [*Homilies on Joshua*]

Hom. Judic.   Origen, *Homiliae in Judices* [*Homilies on Judges*]

Hom. Lev.   Origen, *Homiliae in Leviticum* [*Homilies on Leviticus*]

Hom. Luc.   Origen, *Homiliae in Lucan* [*Homilies on Luke*]

Hom. Num.   Origen, *Homiliae in Numeros* [*Homilies on Numbers*]

Hom. Sam.   Origen, *Homiliae in Samuelum* [*Homilies on 1 Samuel*]

Idol.   Tertullian, *On Idolatry*

Inst.   Lactantius, *The Divine Institutes*

Laps.   Cyprian, *De Lapsis* [*The Lapsed*]

Leg.   Athenagoras, *Legatio pro Christianus* [*Plea for Christians*]

Marc.   Tertullian, *Against Marcion*

Mart.   Origen, *Exhortation to Martyrdom*

Mart. Pol.   Martyrdom of Polycarp

Mort.   Cyprian, *On Mortality*

Nat.   Tertullian, *Ad nationes* [*To the Heathen*]

Oct.   Minucius Felix, *Octavius*

Off.   Cicero, *De officiis* [*On the Duties*]

Or.   *De oratione* [*On Prayer*]

Or. Graec.   Tatian, *Oratio ad Graecos* [*Address to the Greeks*]

Orat. paneg.   Gregory Thaumaturgus, *Oratio panegyrica in Origenem* [*Address of Gratitude to Origen*]

Paed.   Clement of Alexandria, *Christ the Educator*

Paen.   Tertullian, *On Repentance*

Pan.   Epiphanius, *Panarion* [*Refutation of All Heresies*]

Pat.   Augustine, *On Patience*; Cyprian, *On the Good of Patience*; Tertullian, *On Patience*

Peregr.   Lucian, *De morte Peregrini* [*The Passing of Peregrinus*]

Pol. Phil.   Polycarp, *Letter to the Philippians*

Praescr.   Tertullian, *The Prescription of Heretics*

Protr.   Clement of Alexandria, *Protrepticus* [*Exhortation to the Greeks*]

Ps.-Clem.   Pseudo-Clementine Epistles

Quis div.   Clement of Alexandria, *Quis dives salvetur* [*Salvation of the Rich*]

Scap.   Tertullian, *To Scapula*

Serm.   *Sermo(nes)* [*Sermon(s)*]

Spect.   Tertullian, *De spectaculis* [*The Shows*]

Strom.   Clement of Alexandria, *Stromata* [*Miscellanies*]

Test.   Tertullian, *De testimonio animae* [*The Soul's Testimony*]

Trad. ap.   [Hippolytus?], *Traditio apostolica* [*The Apostolic Tradition*]

Unit. eccl.   Cyprian, *The Unity of the Catholic Church*

Ux.   Tertullian, *Ad uxorem* [*To His Wife*]

Virg.	Tertullian, *De virginibus velandis* [*The Veiling of Virgins*]	*Vit. Cypr.*	Pontius of Carthage, *Vita Cypriani* [*Life of Cyprian*]
Vit. Const.	Eusebius, *Vita Constantini* [*Life of Constantine*]	*Zel. liv.*	Cyprian, *De zelo et livore* [*On Jealousy and Envy*]

Modern Sources

ACW	Ancient Christian Writers. 1946–
ANF	*Ante-Nicene Fathers*, edited by Alexander Roberts and James Donaldson. 1885–87. 10 vols. Repr. Peabody, MA: Hendrickson, 1994
BJP	Paul Bradshaw, Maxwell E. Johnson, and L. Edward Phillips, *The Apostolic Tradition: A Commentary*. Hermeneia. Minneapolis: Fortress, 2002
CCL	Corpus Christianorum: Series Latina
CIL	*Corpus Inscriptionum Latinarum*. Berlin, 1862–
CSEL	Corpus Scriptorum Ecclesiasticorum Latinorum
FC	Fathers of the Church. Washington, DC: Catholic University of America Press, 1947–
FRLANT	Forschungen zur Religion und Literatur des Alten und Neuen Testaments
HTR	*Harvard Theological Review*
HTS	Harvard Theological Studies
JECS	*Journal of Early Christian Studies*
JRS	*Journal of Roman Studies*
JSNTSup	Journal for the Study of the New Testament Supplement Series
JTS	*Journal of Theological Studies*

LCC	Library of Christian Classics. Philadelphia: Westminster, 1953–
LCL	Loeb Classical Library
LNTS	Library of New Testament Studies
NPNF[1]	*Nicene and Post-Nicene Fathers*, Series 1, edited by Philip Schaff. 14 vols. 1886–1889. Repr. Peabody, MA: Hendrickson, 1994
NPNF[2]	*Nicene and Post-Nicene Fathers*, Series 2, edited by Philip Schaff and Henry Wace. 14 vols. 1890–1900. Repr. Peabody, MA: Hendrickson, 1994
PG	Patrologia Graeca, edited by J.-P. Migne. 162 vols. Paris, 1857–1886
PL	Patrologia Latina, edited by J.-P. Migne. 217 vols. Paris, 1844–1864
RAC	*Reallexikon für Antike und Christentum*
SC	Sources chrétiennes. Paris: Cerf, 1943–
SL	*Studia Liturgica*
StPatr	Studia Patristica
TTH	Translated Texts for Historians
VC	*Vigiliae Christianae*
VCSup	Supplements to Vigiliae Christianae

INTRODUCTION

The growth of the Christian church in the Roman Empire is mysterious. Scholars who spend their entire lives studying this phenomenon continue to find it surprising. Why did this minor mystery religion from the eastern Mediterranean—marginal, despised, discriminated against—grow substantially, eventually supplanting the well-endowed, respectable cults that were supported by the empire and aristocracy? What enabled Christianity to be so successful that by the fifth century it was the established religion of the empire?

Some have addressed this question by emphasizing the clash of ideas. During the church's early centuries, Christians developed their thinking to a formidable extent. They learned to deploy their ideas in differing ways as they engaged in conversation and debate with adherents of other religions. A classic book in this tradition is Michael Green's *Evangelism in the Early Church* (1970). Other scholars, in the footsteps of Edward Gibbon, eighteenth-century English ancient historian, have emphasized the "causes" of the Christians' triumph—their intolerant zeal, their teaching about the afterlife, their miraculous powers, their austere morals, and their organization. In particular, Ramsay MacMullen in his *Christianizing the Roman Empire* (1984) has added to Gibbon's list a sixth cause, force—in the early centuries the psychological force of exorcism and miracle, and in the fourth and fifth centuries the physical force of state-sponsored destruction and compulsion.

What do I have to add to these two approaches? Four things.

First, patience. Patience was not a virtue dear to most Greco-Roman people, and it has been of little interest to scholars of early Christianity. But it was centrally important to the early Christians. They talked about patience and wrote about it; it was the first virtue about which they wrote a treatise, and

1

they wrote no fewer than three treatises on it. Christian writers called patience the "highest virtue," "the greatest of all virtues," the virtue that was "peculiarly Christian." The Christians believed that God is patient and that Jesus visibly embodied patience. And they concluded that they, trusting in God, should be patient—not controlling events, not anxious or in a hurry, and never using force to achieve their ends. I introduce patience in chapter 2, and it recurs throughout the book. As we ponder patience, we will come closer to understanding the resilience and distinctive lifestyle of the early Christians that led to their growth in numbers.

2·   Second, habitus—reflexive bodily behavior. The sources rarely indicate that the early Christians grew in number because they won arguments; instead they grew because their habitual behavior (rooted in patience) was distinctive and intriguing. Their habitus—a term I have learned from French sociologist Pierre Bourdieu—enabled them to address intractable problems that ordinary people faced in ways that offered hope. When challenged about their ideas, Christians pointed to their actions. They believed that their habitus, their embodied behavior, was eloquent. Their behavior said what they believed; it was an enactment of their message. And the sources indicate that it was their habitus more than their ideas that appealed to the majority of the non-Christians who came to join them. In this book habitus first appears in stories that I tell in chapter 3, and it characterizes distinctive forms of individual and group witness that I present in chapters 4 and 5. Like patience, habitus permeates the rest of the book.

3.   Third, catechesis and worship. The early Christians were uncommonly committed to forming the habitus of their members. So they emphasized catechesis—careful formation and teaching—in preparation for baptism. The Christians were vastly more serious about catechesis than were the members of other religions of their time—and for good reason. They believed that impatient habits (unlike those of Jesus Christ) were deeply engrained in people who were raised in Greco-Roman societies. From experience they knew that if people were to develop patient reflexes, they needed time, the friendship of mentors, and the opportunity to grow in patient ways of living that were normal for Christians. After being shaped by catechesis, people who became Christians were baptized and then were sustained by the worship of Christian communities. Prayers and the Eucharist—the heart of the worship services—were not open to catechumens (those who were receiving catechesis before baptism) and certainly not open to outsiders. Nevertheless, worship was essential for the church's mission. In it the Christians glorified God and were renewed in their patient habitus. Chapters 6 and 7 will enable us to appreciate the formative power of the churches' catechesis and the sustaining power of their worship. Both, in my view, were essential to the church's growth.

Fourth, ferment. Early Christians did not write explicitly about ferment, but I find it a useful metaphor to describe the way their patient growth occurred. It operated reticently, by what theologian Origen called God's "invisible power." It was not susceptible to human control, and its pace could not be sped up. But in the ferment there was a bubbling energy—a bottom-up inner life—that had immense potential. We will see this ferment throughout the book. And in chapters 9 and 10, as I consider the emperor Constantine I and the formidable theologian Augustine, I will ask what happened to the ferment of patience when Christians attempted to control change and force its pace.

As I have written the book, I have been aware of the boldness of what I am doing. In our era, many have pronounced the death of the grand narrative. Scholars know that it is wise to restrict their attention to narrow topics that they can study with unimpeachable craft. I understand this caution and am somewhat surprised to find myself tracing the growth of the Christian church across four centuries, using patience as a guide.

My broad study has its limits. First, I have given too little attention to the complex interactions between gentiles and Jews in the early centuries. In chapter 8 I deal with a church order that shows how a cluster of messianic communities in Syria dealt with these interactions, but the topic is vastly bigger than that. Second, I have been too grand in writing about the growth of "the early church," for in many places there were competing churches. I am aware of the "fractionation" of early Christianities in Rome and many other places, and I know that "heretical" churches continued to exist for centuries. I wish I had been able to deal more with the "gnostic" groups' habitus and means of growth, but the character of their literature does not make this an easy study—people whom many call "gnostics" did not write church orders or treatises on patience! And third, to my great regret I have had to limit myself to the Roman Empire and to exclude the engrossing story of the growth of the church in the Persian Empire. In 2007 I spent three months doing initial research into that story, and I concluded that it was too rich and varied to be included in this book as it was taking shape.

So the book has its limits, but it is nevertheless bold. It covers a broad time span—between the New Testament and the consolidation of the imperial church in the fifth century. I do not limit myself to the convention of scholars by writing about either Christianity's early centuries or the Christianity of late antiquity. Further, the book draws on many academic disciplines: history, theology, liturgy, ethics, and missiology. Readers must decide whether my synoptic approach is irresponsible or illuminating.

A word about my own subjectivity. How does who I am shape this book? I am an American male, a Mennonite Christian, and a Harvard PhD with a dissertation/book on an aspect of the English Reformation. In the 1970s the Mennonite church called me to work as a missionary in England, and I lived there for thirty years, doing many things. I pastored a small church and served as the director of the London Mennonite Centre and later of the Centre for Christianity and Culture at Regent's Park College, Oxford. I participated in the Anabaptist Network and was active in the peace movement. I am married to Eleanor Kreider, whose passion for liturgy led her to take a course at Notre Dame that carefully examined the church orders. She shared her discoveries with me. In the mid-1980s I began to study the early church seriously. Since then I have taught early Christianity in several countries—where I have found interest especially in the Global South—and have written a small cluster of books and articles. In 2000, Eleanor and I moved back to our native Indiana, where I have taught church history and mission at Anabaptist Mennonite Biblical Seminary. Now, in my retirement, in this book I am drawing together my teaching about early Christianity.

Does my subjectivity shape the book? Of course it does, and that dynamic can be bad or good, or both! For example, in reading the early Christian writers closely I have been astonished to discover the widespread presence of the theme of peace in the life and mission of the church. And I have asked myself: Why have others not seen this? Why did I not see this earlier? And why do I see it now? Is it because of subjectivity on my part? Or have others ignored peace because of their subjectivities? And what essential things do I persist in ignoring and misreading? Readers must judge.

PART 1

GROWTH AND PATIENCE

1

THE IMPROBABLE GROWTH
OF THE CHURCH

In the first three centuries the church was growing. Contemporaries commented on this; the second-century AD Epistle to Diognetus observed that Christians "day by day increase more and more."[1] At the turn of the third century, in Carthage in North Africa, the theologian Tertullian with extravagant exaggeration referred to the Christians as "a great multitude of men—almost the majority in every city."[2] Fifty years later, in his Sunday homilies in Caesarea in Palestine, the great Origen made confident statements about the church's worldwide growth:

> Behold the Lord's greatness. . . . Our Lord Jesus has been spread out to the whole world, because he is God's power. . . . The power of the Lord and Savior is with those who are in Britain, separated from our world, and with those who are in Mauretania, and with everyone under the sun who has believed in his name. Behold the Savior's greatness. It extends to all the world.[3]

1. *Diogn.* 6.9, trans. E. R. Fairweather, *Early Christian Fathers*, ed. C. C. Richardson, LCC 1 (1953), 218.
2. Tertullian, *Scap.* 2, trans. R. Arbesmann, FC 10 (1950), 154.
3. Origen, *Hom. Luc.* 6.9, trans. J. T. Lienhard, FC 94 (1996), 27. Other passages with a similarly expansive view are Clement of Alexandria, *Strom.* 6.18; Tertullian, *Apol.* 25.23, 25; *Fug.* 6.2; *Praescr.* 20.5; *Did. apost.* 6.8.1.

No one disputes that the early church was growing, but its growth is hard to measure. For a long time scholars assumed that Christian growth was so rapid that in the early fourth century, on the eve of the emperor Constantine's accession, five to six million people—between 8 and 12 percent of the imperial populace—were Christian. The most confident statement of this approach was given in the 1990s by a sociologist, Rodney Stark, who calculated that for the church to reach this level, it grew across the first three centuries by 40 percent per decade.[4] Stark's confidence has attracted wide assent but also withering criticism, not least from ancient historian Ramsay MacMullen, who has demanded solid, archaeological evidence and posited a much smaller Christian number by AD 310.[5] Debates and speculations will continue as scholars study particular areas in detail. For now, we can safely assume three things:

- Christian numbers were growing impressively in the first three centuries.
- This growth varied tremendously from place to place. In certain areas (parts of Asia Minor and North Africa) there were considerable numbers of Christians. But in other areas there were few believers. And some cities, such as Harran in Mesopotamia, were known to be virtual "Christian-free" zones.[6]
- By the time of Constantine's accession, the churches not only had substantial numbers of members; they extended across huge geographical distances and demanded the attention of the imperial authorities.

It is not surprising that this movement—both growing and worldwide—was buoyant and confident.

We tend to assume this growth and to forget how surprising it was. Nobody had to join the churches. People were not compelled to become members by invading armies or the imposition of laws; social convention did not induce them to do so. Indeed, Christianity grew despite the opposition of laws and social convention. These were formidable disincentives. In addition, the possibility

4. Rodney Stark, *The Rise of Christianity: A Sociologist Reconsiders History* (Princeton: Princeton University Press, 1996), 6.

5. Ramsay MacMullen, *The Second Church: Popular Christianity, A.D. 200–400*, SBL Writings from the Greco-Roman World Supplement Series 1 (Atlanta: Society of Biblical Literature, 2009), 102–4, 173nn17–18. See also Jan N. Bremmer, *The Rise of Christianity through the Eyes of Gibbon, Harnack and Rodney Stark* (Groningen: Barkhuis, 2010), 50–51, 64–65.

6. Robin Lane Fox, *Pagans and Christians* (San Francisco: Harper & Row, 1986), 28. For a parallel case, Aphrodisias in Asia Minor, see Laura Hebert, "Pagans and Christians in Late Antique Aphrodisias," in *Conversion to Christianity from Late Antiquity to the Modern Age*, ed. Calvin B. Kendall, Oliver Nicholson, William D. Phillips Jr., and Marguerite Ragnow (Minneapolis: Center for Early Modern History, University of Minnesota, 2009), 85–114.

of death in persecution loomed over the pre-Constantinian church, although few Christians were actually executed.[7] In many places baptismal candidates sensed that "every Christian was by definition a candidate for death."[8] More generally, as Kate Cooper has pointed out, Christians knew that they, as members of a "dubious group," were vulnerable to being "turned in" by their neighbors or by others who wanted to see them deprived of privileges.[9] In the 240s Origen commented about the "disgrace among the rest of society" that Christians experienced.[10] Christians had to be cautious.

Nevertheless the churches grew.[11] Why? After 312, when the emperor Constantine I aligned himself with Christianity and began to promote it, the church's growth is not hard to explain. But before Constantine the expansion is improbable enough to require a sustained attempt to understand it. The growth was odd. According to the evidence at our disposal, the expansion of the churches was not organized, the product of a mission program; it simply happened. Further, the growth was not carefully thought through. Early Christian leaders did not engage in debates between rival "mission strategies." The Christians wrote a lot; according to classicist Robin Lane Fox, "most of the best Greek and Latin literature which remains [from the later second and third centuries] is Christian."[12] And what they wrote is surprising. The Christians wrote treatises on patience—three of them—that we will study in this

7. Candida Moss (*The Myth of Persecution: How the Early Christians Invented a Story of Martyrdom* [New York: HarperOne, 2013]) has rightly noted the development of the "idea of the persecuted church" in the fourth century, but she has not appreciated the importance of persecution in the experience of the pre-Constantinian Christians. She does not take into account the nonapologetic church orders and catechetical materials that deal matter-of-factly with death "for the name of the Lord" as a possibility that any believer might have to deal with (*Trad. ap.* 19.2, BJP 102; Cyprian, *Ad Quir.* 3.16–18; *Did. apost.* 5.6.2, "if we are called to martyrdom" (trans. and ed. Alistair Stewart-Sykes, *The Didascalia Apostolorum: An English Version with Introduction and Annotation* [Turnhout: Brepols, 2009], 204).

8. Gustave Bardy, *La conversion au christianisme durant les premiers siècles* (Paris: Aubier, 1949), 170.

9. Kate Cooper, "Christianity, Private Power, and the Law from Decius to Constantine: The Minimalist View," *JECS* 19, no. 3 (2011): 339.

10. Origen, *Cels.* 3.9, trans. H. Chadwick (Cambridge: Cambridge University Press, 1965), 134; cf. Tertullian, who in *Fug.* 3.2 (trans. E. A. Quain et al., FC 40 [1959], 282) reports that when Christians attend their meetings, "we arouse the curiosity of the pagans, and we fear lest we stir their opposition."

11. To get a sense of the church's growth in five areas of the ancient world according to recent scholarship, see the articles by Mark Humphries ("The West [1]: Italy, Gaul, and Spain"), Éric Rebillard ("The West [2]: North Africa"), Raymond Van Dam ("The East [1]: Greece and Asia Minor"), David Brakke ("The East [2]: Egypt and Palestine"), Lucas Van Rompay ("The East [3]: Syria and Mesopotamia"), in *The Oxford Handbook of Early Christian Studies*, ed. Susan Ashbrook Harvey and David Hunter (Oxford: Oxford University Press, 2008), 283–386.

12. Lane Fox, *Pagans and Christians*, 270.

book. But they did not write a single treatise on evangelism. Further, to assist their growing congregations with practical concerns, the Christians wrote "church orders," manuals that provided guidance for the life and worship of congregations. The best treatment of how a second-century Christian should persuade a pagan to become a believer was published in London in 1970![13]

In places where we would expect to find instructions to engage in mission—for example, a growing church's catechetical materials preparing people for baptism—we look in vain for references to evangelization. The best surviving summary of catechetical topics, Cyprian's *To Quirinus* 3, contains 120 precepts for catechumens in Carthage, but not one of them admonishes the new believers to share the gospel with the gentiles. Early Christian preachers do not appeal to the "Great Commission" in Matthew 28:19–20 to inspire their members to "make disciples of all nations"; they assume that the "apostles" (Jesus's eleven plus Paul) had done this in the church's earliest years and that it had already been fulfilled in the church's global expansion.[14] When writers referred to the Matthew 28:19–20 text, it was to buttress the doctrine of the Trinity or to address the issue of baptism, not to inspire missionary activity.

To be sure, the Christians continued to use the word *apostolos*, but it had lost its connection to mission. Except for the very early Didache (11.2, 5) in which traveling "apostles" were a part of the community's life, Christian writers thought of apostles as bishops who in succession protect the apostolic truth, not as missionaries who embody and carry out the apostolic task.[15] In the mid-third century the large and influential church in Rome had a substantial staff containing scores of presbyters, deacons, subdeacons, acolytes, exorcists, readers, and doorkeepers—but not a single apostle.[16] Nor did it or any other church known to us have accredited "evangelists" or "missionaries."[17]

Of course there were no missionary societies at that period and no parachurch mission agencies. Surprisingly, there are only two missionaries whose names we know. The Alexandrian teacher Pantaenus's journey from Egypt to India appears legendary, but there seems to be more history behind Origen's

---

13. Michael Green, *Evangelism in the Early Church* (London: Hodder & Stoughton, 1970), chaps. 3, 5–6.

14. Martin Goodman, *Mission and Conversion: Proselytizing in the Religious History of the Roman Empire* (Oxford: Clarendon, 1994), 106–8; Norbert Brox, "Zur christlichen Mission in der Spätantike," in *Mission im Neuen Testament*, ed. Karl Kertelge, Quaestiones Disputatae (Freiburg-im-Breisgau: Herder, 1982), 196–98.

15. Einar Molland, "Besass die alte Kirche ein Missionsprogramm und bewusste Missionsmethoden?," in *Kirchengeschichte als Missionsgeschichte*, vol. 1, *Die alte Kirche*, ed. Heinzgünter Frohnes and Uwe W. Knorr (Munich: Chr. Kaiser, 1974), 56–57.

16. Eusebius, *Hist. eccl.* 6.43.11.

17. Molland, "Besass die alte Kirche ein Missionsprogramm?," 59.

student Gregory, who in the mid-third century returned to his native Pontus in what is today northern Turkey.[18] There simply are no others. The bearers of the faith are nameless. There are no iconic missionary heroes/heroines, no self-conscious successors to Paul, until the fifth century when Patrick, the evangelist of Ireland, shows what had not been present in earlier centuries.[19]

Most improbable of all, the churches did not use their worship services to attract new people. In the aftermath of the persecution of Nero in AD 68, churches around the empire—at varying speeds in varying places—closed their doors to outsiders. By the end of the second century, most of them had instituted what liturgical scholars have called the *disciplina arcani*, the "discipline of the secret," which barred outsiders from entering "private" Christian worship services and ordered believers not to talk to outsiders about what went on behind the closed doors.[20] Fear motivated this closing—fear of people who might disrupt their gatherings or spy on them. By the third century, some churches assigned deacons to stand at the doors, monitoring the people as they arrived. They admitted catechumens to the opening part of worship, the service of the word with its readings and sermon, but not pagans; and to the service of the Eucharist that followed they admitted neither pagans nor catechumens—only the baptized members of the community and believers from other churches with letters of recommendation.[21] It is not surprising that pagans responded to their exclusion from Christian worship by speculation and gossip.[22] The baptized Christians, on the other hand, knew how powerful the worship services were in their own lives—early fourth-century North African believers said simply, "We cannot go without the Lord's supper." They knew that worship services were to glorify God and edify the faithful, not to evangelize outsiders.[23]

And yet, improbably, the movement was growing. In number, size, and geographical spread, churches were expanding without any of the probable

18. Eusebius, *Hist. eccl.* 5.10; 6.6; 6.13.2; Wolfgang Reinbold, *Propaganda und Mission im ältesten Christentum: Eine Untersuchung zu den Modalitäten der Ausbreitung der frühen Kirche*, FRLANT 188 (Göttingen: Vandenhoek & Ruprecht, 2000), 288–95.

19. Patrick, *Confessio* 40; Dale T. Irvin and Scott Sunquist, *History of the World Christian Movement* (Maryknoll, NY: Orbis Books, 2003), 1:239.

20. Edward Yarnold, SJ, *The Awe-Inspiring Rites of Initiation: Baptismal Homilies of the Fourth Century* (Slough, UK: St. Paul Publications, 1971), 50–51.

21. Athenagoras, *Leg.* 1.3; *Did. apost.* 2.39; Gregory of Pontus, *Canonical Epistle* 11; Origen, *Cels.* 3.51. For letters of commendation, see AnneMarie Luijendijk, *Greetings in the Lord: Early Christians and the Oxyrhynchus Papyri*, HTS 60 (Cambridge, MA: Harvard University Press, 2008), chap. 4.

22. Minucius Felix, *Oct.* 9.3.

23. *Acts of the Abitinian Martyrs* 12; in *Donatist Martyr Stories: The Church in Conflict in Roman North Africa*, trans. and ed. Maureen A. Tilley, TTH 24 (Liverpool: Liverpool University Press, 1996), 36–37.

prerequisites for church growth. The early Christians noted this with wonder and attributed it to the patient work of God.[24] Teaching catechumens in
Caesarea around 240, Origen observed that throughout history God had been
faithful to Israel, sending them prophets, turning them back from their sins.

> [God] was always patient by sending those who cure; up till the Chief-healer came,
> the Prophet who surpassed prophets, the Healer who surpassed healers. They
> forsook and killed the one who had come. . . . God selected another nation. See
> how great the harvest is, even though there are few workers. But also in another
> way God plans always that the net is thrown on the lake of this life, and all kinds of
> fish are caught. He sends out many fishers, he sends out many hunters, they hunt
> from every hill. See how great a plan it is concerning the salvation of the nations.[25]

This was *patient ferment*. The patient God was at work, Origen affirmed, and
God used not influential or powerful people but obscure fishers and hunters
to achieve a huge end. There is an inexorability about this process that the
eminent German theologian Adolf Harnack likened to "a steady fermenting
process."[26] Ferment refers to the "mysterious, bubbling life forces," micro-
organisms at work collaboratively in ways that transcend human understanding.[27] As Origen spoke, the ferment was happening. It was brewing, but not
under anyone's control. It was uncoordinated, it was unpredictable, and it
seemed unstoppable. The ferment was spontaneous, and it involved ordinary
ingredients that at times synergized into a heady brew. The churches grew in
many places, taking varied forms. They proliferated because the faith that
these fishers and hunters embodied was attractive to people who were dissatisfied with their old cultural and religious habits,[28] who felt pushed to explore
new possibilities, and who then encountered Christians who embodied a new
manner of life that pulled them toward what the Christians called "rebirth"
into a new life.[29] Surprisingly, this happened in a patient manner.

---

24. Brox, "Zur christlichen Mission," 207.
25. Origen, *Hom. Jer.* 18.5.3, trans. J. C. Smith, FC 97 (1998), 195–96.
26. Adolf Harnack, *Die Mission und Ausbreitung des Christentums in den ersten drei Jahr-
hunderten*, 4th ed. (Leipzig: Hinrichs, 1924), 1:226, "gleichsam ein stätiger Gärungsprozess";
Adolf Harnack, *The Mission and Expansion of Christianity in the First Three Centuries*,
trans. J. Moffatt, 2 vols. (New York: Putnam's, 1904), 1:258; cited in Reinbold, *Propaganda
und Mission*, 296.
27. Sandor Ellix Katz, *The Art of Fermentation: An In-Depth Exploration of Essential Concepts and Processes from around the World* (White River Junction, VT: Chelsea Green, 2012), 19.
28. Like a number of scholars today, I take "habits" seriously and understand them in light
of the concept of *habitus*. See chap. 3 for a discussion of this term.
29. Justin, *1 Apol.* 61.3–4, 10, trans. E. R. Hardy, *Early Christian Fathers*, ed. C. C. Richardson, LCC 1 (1953), 282–83; Cyprian, *Don.* 3–4.

2

THE GOOD OF PATIENCE

In the 250s Cyprian, the bishop of Carthage in North Africa, had a plateful of problems. Within the church he was involved in conflicts: with confessors, with lapsed rich people, and even with the bishop of Rome. Outside the church he and other Christians faced waves of hostility from the imperial authorities. And there was no one—inside the church or outside it—who had not been seared by an epidemic that had terrified all of North Africa, killing innumerable people. Some Christians were disheartened and losing hope; others, having received violent treatment by their non-Christian neighbors, wanted revenge against people who had tormented them. The world seemed out of control.

Amid it all, Cyprian, as bishop, wanted to keep the Christians true to their tradition. This, at its heart, meant embodying the Christian good news, bearing it in their bodies and actions, living the message visibly and faithfully so that outsiders would see what the Christians were about and, ideally, would be attracted to join them. So in 256 Cyprian wrote a treatise of encouragement for his people. "Beloved brethren," he wrote, "[we] are philosophers not in words but in deeds; we exhibit our wisdom not by our dress, but by truth; we know virtues by their practice rather than through boasting of them; we do not speak great things but we live them."[1]

1. Cyprian, *Pat.* 3, trans. G. E. Conway, FC 36 (1958), 265; Cyprian's phrase "non eloquimur magna sed uiuimus" is identical to that in Minucius Felix, *Oct.* 38.6 (SC 291:186, trans. G. H. Rendall, LCL 250 [1931], 432).

"We do not speak great things but we live them." A striking phrase! And it is not original with Cyprian. Fifty years earlier the North African Christian controversialist Minucius Felix uses the identical phrase in his *Octavius*. We don't know where Minucius Felix got the phrase. Did it originate with him, or were both he and Cyprian quoting a slogan that was popular among North African Christians? Were they reflecting Jesus's Sermon on the Mount (Matt. 7:24)? We cannot be sure. But by the way Cyprian uses this phrase, he tells his readers that the challenge the Christians face in the mid-third century is to live their faith, making it visible, demonstrating the gospel to the watching world.

Cyprian relates the faith that the Christians are to demonstrate to a particular virtue—*patience*. Their faith is a patient faith: "Therefore, as servants and worshipers of God, let us show by spiritual homage the patience that we learn from the heavenly teachings. For that virtue we have in common with God."[2] Christians, said Cyprian, are to be visibly distinctive. They are to live their faith and communicate it in deeds, and their deeds are to embody patience. *Patientia*: when Christians make this virtue visible and active, they demonstrate the character of God to the world. In order to encourage embodied witness, witness that is true to God and true to the Christian tradition, Cyprian wrote *De bono patientiae* (*On the Good of Patience*), one of three treatises on patience written in the early Christian centuries[3] that help us understand the changing character of the early church's ferment.[4]

In expounding patience, Cyprian was writing in a deep Christian tradition. Fifty years before him, Tertullian, also in Carthage, had written *On Patience*, the first treatise by a Christian on a particular virtue. And it was significant that Tertullian chose to give such prominence to patience.[5] In what way was

2. Cyprian, *Pat.* 3 (Conway, 265).
3. The three treatises are Tertullian, *On Patience* (*De patientia*; ca. 204); Cyprian, *On the Good of Patience* (*De bono patientiae*; ca. 256); and Augustine, *On Patience* (*De patientia*; ca. 417).
4. Translating *patientia* is problematic. The Latin-speaking Christians (like the later Vulgate) used *patientia* to render the two Greek words *makrothymia* and *hypomonē* (e.g., Tertullian, *Pat.* 12.9). Thereby they resemble contemporary Spanish translators of the Bible who elide into *justicia* the two Hebrew words *tsedekah* and *mishpat*. In the late fourth century, John Chrysostom proposed a distinction between the two Greek words: *makrothymia* as the stance of the powerful person who chooses not to use power to avenge himself; *hypomonē* as the stance of the powerless person who has no choice but to be nonviolent. See Richard C. Trench, *Synonyms of the New Testament* (Grand Rapids: Eerdmans, 1953), 195–96. Contemporary translators of the Latin and Greek text into English at times vary the translations according to context, such as rendering *patientia* as "forbearance" or "endurance" as well as "patience." In German translations, *patientia* can be rendered as *Gelassenheit* as well as *Geduld* (Michel Spanneut, "Geduld," *RAC* 9 [1976]: 264). As a general rule, I find it helpful to translate *patientia* as "patience," in the conviction that the multivalence of the word enriches our understanding of the authors' intentions.
5. Robert L. Wilken, *The Spirit of Early Christian Thought: Seeking the Face of God* (New Haven: Yale University Press, 2003), 283.

it significant? Why, we may wonder, did the early Christians write and think
so much about patience? Their churches were growing steadily—wouldn't it
have made sense for them to think about something more buoyant or more
practical than patience? If they had advocated a holy impatience—a *just*
impatience—might their churches have grown even more rapidly? On the
other hand, is it possible that the early Christians considered patience to be
crucial to their churches' life and growth? What, for a church that was both
persecuted and growing, was the good of patience?

Justin: Patience in Rome

Second-century Christian writers may help us answer these questions. We
begin in Rome with the philosopher-catechist Justin, who wrote in Greek. In
the 150s Justin (martyred 165) wrote a reasoned defense of Christianity—an
Apology—directed to the emperor Antoninus Pius. In it he contends that the
Christians are growing in numbers because their lives embody "the fair commands of Christ." In the Christians who follow Jesus their critics encounter
a "good hope" that attracts them.[6]

The teachings of Jesus, according to Justin, are not only essential for Christians to learn mentally; they are indispensable guides for the Christians' daily
living. Justin notes that his community doesn't consider people true Christians
if they simply quote Christ's teachings but don't live them.[7] Jesus himself had
insisted on this: "Not everyone who says to me, Lord, Lord . . . but only the
one who does the will of my Father" (Matt. 7:21). Further, Justin believes
that the effectiveness of Christian witness depends on the integrity of the
believers' lifestyles. So the church baptizes only people who live the things
that Christ teaches, and allows them to participate in the eucharistic services
only if they "live as Christ handed down to us."[8]

To help his readers know the sayings of Christ that are important to his
circle of believers, Justin in chapters 15 and 16 of his *Apology* quotes extensively Jesus's sayings (generally from the Sermon on the Mount or Sermon
on the Plain). He lists them under four categories: continence (sexual ethics);
affection for all people (enemy-loving and sharing with the needy); patience
(and freedom from anger); and speaking the truth (and not swearing oaths).[9]

6. Justin, *1 Apol.* 14.3, trans. E. R. Hardy, *Early Christian Fathers*, ed. C. C. Richardson,
LCC 1 (1953), 242–89.
7. Justin, *1 Apol.* 16.8.
8. Justin, *1 Apol.* 61.2; 66.1 (Hardy, 282, 286).
9. In including patience in this list, Justin may have drawn on earlier concerns of the church
in Rome: see 1 Clem. 13.1; Ignatius, *To the Romans* 10; Herm. Mand. 8.9. See especially Herm.

According to Justin, patience is central to the life of his community in Rome. Justin uses various sayings of Jesus to illustrate the significance of patience for members of his community: turning the other cheek when someone hits them in the face; giving their tunics to someone who takes their cloak; avoiding the incendiary sin of anger; and, if they are compelled to go one mile, going two miles. When people see Christians behaving like this, Justin comments, people are intrigued; they "wonder" at the God whom the Christians say motivates their behavior.[10] So it is important for Christians not to quarrel like other people, and it is essential that they live their "good works" visibly in the sight of others. Then, when Christians live with integrity and visibility, "by our patience [*hypomonēs*] and meekness [Christians will] draw all men from shame and evil desires."[11] According to Justin, patience attracts people.

But how does patience work? As an example, Justin points to the area of business. "Many who were once on your side . . . have turned from the ways of violence and tyranny, overcome by observing the consistent lives of their [Christian] neighbors, or noting the strange patience [*hypomonen xenen*] of their injured acquaintances, or experiencing the way they did business with them."[12] What did that mean in practice? Were Christian business people slower than others to evict renters whose payments had fallen in arrears? Were they counterculturally reluctant to force destitute people to repay them money that they owed for food or clothing? Were they unusually willing not only to lend without interest but to forgive debts entirely? Were the Christians ready to explain their behavior in light of the Christian message? We cannot know the details. But Justin makes certain things clear: Christians were involved in business; because of Jesus's teachings, they were committed to a lifestyle of "strange patience"; and as business people Christians behaved in patient ways that their pagan contemporaries found intriguing. In fact, some pagans found the Christians' behavior unsettling enough to convert to Christianity, or as Justin puts it, to "change sides," turning away from their "ways of violence and tyranny" and joining the Christian community. It is likely that this kind of process didn't happen only in business; there were many other areas of everyday life in which Christians, by embodying patience, motivated people

---

Mand. 5.2.3: "But patience [*makrothymia*] is great and mighty; it has a forceful power that flourishes in a spacious arena; it is cheerful, glad, and free of anxiety, glorifying the Lord at all times, having no bitterness in itself but remaining always meek and mild. This patience, therefore, dwells with all those who hold on to the faith intact" (trans. B. D. Ehrman, LCL 25 [2003], 2:259).

10. Justin, *1 Apol.* 16.2 (Hardy, 252).

11. Justin, *1 Apol.* 16.3 (Hardy, 252); C. Munier, *Saint Justin Apologie pour les Chrétiens* (Fribourg: Éditions Universitaires, 1995), 58.

12. Justin, *1 Apol.* 16.4 (Hardy, 252; Munier, 58).

to become believers.[13] The good of patience had many dimensions, and according to Justin one of these was that it drew people to the faith.

Clement of Alexandria: Patience—a Way of Living

We move our attention from imperial Rome to the sophisticated world of Alexandria in Egypt, where Clement, the leading Christian teacher, lived two generations after Justin (ca. 160–215). In Clement's view, patience comes to believers in the course of the "great change" of conversion that brings them from unfaith to faith. Patience is a part of a rich ecosystem whose virtues reflect the character of God and are mutually supportive.[14]

In this ecosystem, patience is indispensable. It is necessary in times of persecution, in which the Christian "show[s] himself masculine in patience and endurance—in his life, behavior, words, and practice—night and day."[15] The Christian's models are Daniel and Jonah: although imprisoned with lions, Daniel received from God the capacity of endurance and the ability to be a witness in "language, life and behavior" in the heart of a hostile empire, and Jonah was sustained in the threatening environment of the fish's belly.[16] But patience is not only necessary in times of persecution; it is also an aspect of the Christian's daily living. A mature Christian (whom Clement calls a "gnostic") "forms the habit of doing good." And this becomes a way of living that leads "those he holds dearest"—his relatives and family—toward "repentance and conversion."[17]

In all their activities Christians are "filled with joy uttering and doing the precepts of the Lord," teaching their children never to lose hold of God's commandments and hope.[18] Christians have God's laws inscribed on their hearts: "You shall not kill . . . you shall love your neighbor as yourself," and "to him that smites you on the one cheek, offer also the other. . . . You [must] patiently endure [*hypomenein*] the severity of the way of salvation."[19] At times this approach may lead to martyrdom; if it does so, the martyrs will

---

13. See also Justin, *1 Apol.* 14.3 (Hardy, 249–50): "We who hated and killed one another and would not associate with men of different tribes because of [their different] customs, now after the manifestation of Christ live together and pray for our enemies and try to persuade those who unjustly hate us, so that they, living according to the fair commands of Christ, may share with us the good hope of receiving the same things [that we will receive] from God, the master of all."

14. Clement, *Strom.* 2.31.1; 2.46.1, trans. J. Ferguson, FC 85 (1991), 179, 190.

15. Clement, *Strom.* 2.81.3 (Ferguson, 213).

16. Clement, *Strom.* 2.104.1 (Ferguson, 226).

17. Clement, *Strom.* 7.12.80, trans. J. E. L. Oulton and H. Chadwick, LCC 2 (1954), 144.

18. Clement, *Strom.* 7.12.80 (Oulton and Chadwick, 144).

19. Clement, *Protr.* 10, trans. G. W. Butterworth, LCL 60 (1919), 232–33.

confirm the truth of their words by their deeds, demonstrate patience to their executioners, and express love to the Lord.[20]

Origen: Persistent Patience—the Core of the Christian Witness

The theologian Origen (d. ca. 254) viewed patience more somberly than Clement. After following in Clement's footsteps as a teacher in Alexandria, in the 230s Origen moved to Caesarea in Palestine, where as a theologian and catechist he tried to articulate a faith that would be comprehensible to his contemporaries. Origen was the son of a martyr. Conflict with neighbors and authorities, and the potential of torture and death, formed his thought world. Understandably, patience (*hypomonē*) was a theme that recurred as he taught aspiring intellectuals and eager catechumens. According to his student Gregory of Pontus, Origen insisted on embodying the views that he articulated; he "stimulated us by the deeds he did more than by the doctrines he taught."[21] As he formed his students to be "lovers of virtue," Origen gave primary attention to patience, which according to Gregory was "that virtue peculiarly ours"—it distinguished Christians from other people.[22] Although Gregory did not spell out what it was about patience that Origen commended,[23] reading Origen's writings gives some clues.

At the heart of patience, according to Origen, is Jesus Christ, who embodied patience; he is the exemplar of patience, "patience itself."[24] Throughout Christ's life patience was evident in many ways, and especially in his passion, in which "he manifested a courage and patience superior to that of any of the Greeks."[25] In embodying patience, Christ perfectly expressed the way that God works to bring God's mission to completion. God, in dealing with Israel across the centuries, was never in a hurry. God instructed the people, sent them prophets, and "was always patient by sending those who cure." In the fullness of time, God sent "the Chief-healer, the Prophet who surpassed prophets, the Healer who surpassed healers." The people rejected and killed Jesus, but they did not frustrate God's purposes. God's mission is unhurried

---

20. Clement, *Strom.* 4.4. See further Annewies van den Hoek, "Clement of Alexandria on Martyrdom," StPatr 26 (1993): 324–41.

21. Gregory Thaumaturgus, *Orat. paneg.* 9, trans. S. D. F. Salmond, *ANF* 6:31.

22. Gregory Thaumaturgus, *Orat. paneg.* 12 (Salmond, 6:33).

23. Henri Crouzel comments that Gregory called *hypomonē* "ours" because "it is a virtue most distinctively Christian, that of the martyrs." See *Grégoire le Thaumaturge*, ed. H. Crouzel, SC 148 (Paris: Cerf, 1969), 65.

24. Origen, *Hom. Jer.* 17.4.2, trans. J. C. Smith, FC 97 (1998), 183.

25. Origen, *Cels.* 7.55, trans. H. Chadwick, *Origen: Contra Celsum* (Cambridge: Cambridge University Press, 1965), 441.

and unstoppable. With persistent patience God fished in wider waters, so that "the net [will be] thrown on the lake of life, and all kinds of fish are caught." In this way, Origen teaches, God's plan for the salvation of the nations will be realized.[26]

When people seek to follow Christ, according to Origen, God forms them into people who embody this patience. Christ's followers are not in a hurry; they listen carefully when the word is read and preached, and they patiently call to account straying Christians who attend worship services irregularly.[27] Patient believers trust God. When they are subjected to penitential discipline, they "patiently bear the judgment made about them, whether they have been rightly or wrongly deposed."[28] Their reflexes are nonviolent—when others treat them violently, they never exact an eye for an eye but respond in silence and patience, and even offer words of blessing.[29]

As he taught in the 230s and 240s, Origen sensed that the world was a place ominous and dangerous for Christians. He knew that some pagans wanted to limit their freedom, even to eliminate them. So Origen determined to form the catechumens—apprentice Christians—in Caesarea so that they would not wilt in persecution. He knew that when Christians are not properly trained, persecution can destroy them, emptying them "of all [their] reserves and [making them] suddenly naked and empty." These believers can survive only if they have been formed so they embody the virtue of patience, "so that by our patience [the pagans'] shamelessness may be overcome." To Origen, patience was a source of hope; he was encouraged by Paul's Epistle to the Romans (5:3–4): "Tribulation produces patience, indeed patience produces assent to belief, and assent to belief produces hope."[30]

Origen envisioned the world as a great theater filled with spectators, all of them watching to see how the Christians respond to persecution. In the theater a wide variety of people, including neighbors, scorn the believers and "shake their heads at us as fools."[31] The way Christians play their part in this "spectacle" is critical to their witness. God is with them—they must never forget that; when they are under torture, "the eye of God is present with those who endure." Jesus, Origen states, laid down his soul for the Christians; so "let us, then, lay ours down, nor shall I say for him, but for ourselves—for

---

26. Origen, *Hom. Jer.* 18.5.3 (J. C. Smith, 195); also *Hom. Jer.* 16.1.
27. Origen, *Hom. Jos.* 20.1; *Hom. Gen.* 10.3.
28. Origen, *Hom. Ezech.* 10.1.4, trans. T. P. Scheck, FC 62 (2010), 129.
29. Origen, *Selecta in Psalmos*, Hom. 1 on Ps. 38 (PG 12:1394).
30. Origen, *Hom. Judic.* 7.2, trans. E. A. D. Lauro, FC 119 (2010), 97; also Origen, *Mart.* 41.
31. Origen, *Mart.* 18–19, trans. R. Greer, *An Exhortation to Martyrdom*, Classics of Western Spirituality (New York: Paulist Press, 1979), 53–54.

those who will be built up by our martyrdom."[32] Origen believes that patience—Christians treating their neighbors well and behaving courageously in the arena—is at the core of the church's witness.

Tertullian: Patience—the Character of God and the Lifestyle of Hope

We move next to North Africa, where a succession of Latin writers established a tradition of the theology of patience.[33] The founder of this was the theologian and controversialist Tertullian, who in 204 wrote *On Patience*. This work, the first treatise by a Christian on a single virtue, is important.[34] In it Tertullian establishes a biblical and theological basis for the central role that patience had been playing and would continue to play in the life of the Christian communities. And he writes to help the believers think Christianly about their lives so that they would differentiate themselves from their neighbors who did not grasp the power and profundity of a patient lifestyle, and even more from philosophers who were unwilling to recognize patience as a virtue.[35]

Why did Tertullian's learned contemporaries dismiss patience as a virtue? Of course, they were not always dismissive. At times, people in the upper reaches of the highly vertical Greco-Roman society used patience to indicate a gritty resolve. For these people, patience could connote the attitude of a noble soul who chooses to endure difficulties, resisting inevitabilities as he pursues an honorable cause. But in general, when ancient Latin writers used the term *patientia*, they didn't have heroes in mind; they were thinking of subordinates and victims. Patience seemed an appropriate attitude for people of no account who were on the receiving end of actions or experiences. For these people—powerless, poverty stricken, and often female—*patientia* was ignominious. Patience was the response of people who didn't have the freedom to define their own goals or make choices. Notably patience was a response of slaves, for whom it was an inevitability, not a virtue.[36]

---

32. Origen, *Mart.* 23, 41 (Greer, 57, 72).

33. Michel Spanneut, "La Non-violence chez les pères Africains avant Constantin," in *Kyriakon: Festschrift Johannes Quasten*, ed. Patrick Granfield and Josef A. Jungmann (Münster: Aschendorff, 1970), 1:36.

34. For Tertullian's *De patientia*, I have used the translation of Emily Joseph Daly, FC 40 (1959), 193–222; the Latin text is in *Tertullien: De la patience*, ed. J.-C. Fredouille, SC 310 (Paris: Cerf, 1984).

35. Wilken, *Spirit of Early Christian Thought*, 283.

36. Robert A. Kaster, "The Taxonomy of Patience, or When Is *Patientia* Not a Virtue?," *Classical Philology* 97, no. 2 (2002): 135–38.

But Tertullian didn't draw primarily on pagan philosophy or conventional usage.[37] As a member of the North African Christian community, when he used *patientia* he drew upon the word's deep rooting in the biblical tradition, and he made it central to the life of the North African Christian subculture.[38] In Tertullian's view, for the Christians *patientia* has nothing to do with social location; for all Christians, whether poor or more comfortably off, whether slave or free, it is "the highest virtue."[39] It is so even for Tertullian himself, but Tertullian breaks his flow to confess his inadequacy to write about patience; alas, he is irascible, "ever suffering from the fever of impatience." And because Tertullian, typical of early Christians, believes that there must "be no discrepancy between words and deeds," he hesitates to write about patience. Characteristically, Tertullian overcomes his hesitation—because patience is indispensable. In the strongest terms, Tertullian states that patience is at the heart of being a Christian. To be a Christian means that one has accorded to patience "pre-eminence in matters pertaining to God."[40]

Above all this is why, for Tertullian, patience is preeminent; it is rooted in the character of God. According to Tertullian, God is the exemplar of patience. God is promiscuously generous; he shares the wonders of creation, the brilliance of the sun and seasons, with everyone—the just and the unjust alike (Matt. 5:45). God endures ungrateful, greedy people who worship idols. God does not compel belief, but "by his patience he hopes to draw them to himself."[41] And the means by which God seeks to attract people is incarnation. "God allows himself to become incarnate"[42]—a self-positioning of patience.

How odd Jesus's story is, and how different from the exploits of Cicero's exemplar Hercules. Tertullian recounts the narrative of Jesus, whose labors (unlike Hercules's) did not include killing, capturing, and stealing[43] but who instead kept a low profile, who bore reproaches, who would not hear of forcing

37. Simon Price, "Latin Christian Apologetics: Minucius Felix, Tertullian, and Cyprian," in *Apologetics in the Roman Empire: Pagans, Jews, and Christians*, ed. Mark Edwards, Martin Goodman, Simon Price, and Christopher Rowland (Oxford: Oxford University Press, 1999), 119. Yet cf. Jean-Claude Fredouille, who argues that the patience Tertullian praises is a virtue "more stoic than properly Christian," in SC 310 (Paris: Cerf, 1984), 30. In contrast, Marcia L. Colish (*The Stoic Tradition from Antiquity to the Early Middle Ages* [Leiden: Brill, 1990], 2:26) contends that for Tertullian "the model for Christian patience is to be found in the patience of God and the long-suffering of Christ, not in the teaching of the schools."

38. Tertullian (e.g., in *Pat.* 12.9) uses the Latin word *patientia* to render both the New Testament Greek nouns *makrothymia* and *hypomonē* as they occur in 2 Cor. 6:4–7.

39. Tertullian, *Pat.* 1.7 (Daly, 194).

40. Tertullian, *Pat.* 1.1, 1.6 (Daly, 193–94).

41. Tertullian, *Pat.* 2.3 (Daly, 195).

42. Tertullian, *Pat.* 3.2 (Daly, 195).

43. Spanneut, "Geduld," 250.

people, who ate at anyone's table, who declined to call for massive angelic intervention, who rejected the avenging sword, who healed the servant of his enemy, and thereby "cursed for all time the works of the sword."[44] As Jesus went to the cross he was scorned, spat upon. "Patience such as this no mere man had ever practiced!"[45] Tertullian recognizes that the story of Jesus doesn't attract everybody; some pagans find it a reason to reject the faith. But for Christians the story of Jesus, together with "the words Our Lord used in his precepts," are evidence that "patience is the very nature of God."[46]

Of course, Tertullian recognizes that there was a long human history before Jesus. The fall of Adam and Eve was marked by human impatience, which was "the original sin in the eyes of the Lord."[47] Subsequently, humans committed repeated acts of impatience, which they backed up by the demand "an eye for an eye and a tooth for a tooth."[48] In Tertullian's view, such behavior was unsurprising; the absence of patience is characteristic of a world in which "there was not yet faith." But when Jesus came, he—"the Lord and teacher of patience"—changed things by uniting "the grace of faith with patience."[49] For Jesus patience was not only a fundamental teaching—a *praeceptum universum*; it also was a practice—a *disciplina*.[50] And the practice of patience, undergirded by the teaching of patience, prohibits humans from committing injury, even lawful injury, in any area of human experience. So in keeping with the teaching of Jesus, Christians will not call others "you fool!"[51] They will not be concerned about the loss of property, which the Lord did not seek, and which they may gladly lose from theft or violence. "Patience to endure, shown on occasions of loss, is a training in giving and sharing."[52] And, according to Jesus's teaching, believers will not inflict physical injury upon enemies. When they are offended, under pressure, and tempted to retaliate, they recall Jesus's Sermon on the Mount teachings that they have memorized, probably as they prepared for baptism. Tertullian admonishes his readers: "If one tries to provoke you to a fight, there is at hand the admonition of the Lord: 'If someone strike [you] . . . on the right cheek, turn to him the other also.' [And if someone] burst out in cursing or wrangling, recall the saying: 'When men reproach you, rejoice.'"[53]

44. Tertullian, *Pat.* 3.2–8 (Daly, 195–97).
45. Tertullian, *Pat.* 3.10 (Daly, 197).
46. Tertullian, *Pat.* 3.11 (Daly, 197).
47. Tertullian, *Pat.* 5.21 (Daly, 202).
48. Tertullian, *Pat.* 6.4 (Daly, 204).
49. Tertullian, *Pat.* 6.4–5 (Daly, 204).
50. Tertullian, *Pat.* 7.1.
51. Tertullian, *Pat.* 6.5 (Daly, 204).
52. Tertullian, *Pat.* 7.9 (Daly, 206).
53. Tertullian, *Pat.* 8.2–3 (Daly, 207).

Tertullian urges Christians, who live by Jesus's precepts, to wear their oppressors out with patience: "Let wrong-doing grow weary from your patience."[54]

But how can Christians live this patience? How can they take seriously this "precept [that] is unequivocally laid down: evil is not to be rendered for evil"?[55] Their hopeful expectation of the resurrection enables this. According to Tertullian, the key to the believers' patient lifestyle is their confession that in the resurrection of Jesus, God has vindicated his teachings and way, and as a result they expect that they too will be resurrected. Tertullian asserts, "If we believe in the resurrection of Christ, we believe in our own, also, since it was for us that he died and rose again." Christians don't need to fear death or be weighed down by grief, for death is only "the beginning of a journey," and those who have gone ahead will be missed but need not be mourned. Death inevitably leads to "lonesomeness," but patience alleviates it.[56] The Christians' lifestyle is rooted in hope.

In contrast, impatience is hopeless. According to Tertullian, impatient actions do not produce what they promise. Instead, impatient actions make things worse, bringing about massive misfortunes. "Now, nothing undertaken through impatience can be transacted without violence, and everything done with violence has either met with no success or has collapsed or has plunged to its own destruction."[57] Patience, on the other hand, brings new possibilities. Patience is the source of the "practices of peace," which bring reconciliation week by week in the Christian worship services (Matt. 5:24). Patience brings to Christians the life of the Beatitudes and the life of love that Paul celebrates in 1 Corinthians 13, which is the "highest sacrament of the faith" (*summum fidei sacramentum*).[58] Indeed, patience brings good to all aspects of human experience:

> In poverty patience supplies consolation; upon wealth it imposes moderation; the sick it does not destroy, nor does it, for the man in health, prolong his life; for the man of faith it is a source of delight. It attracts the heathen, recommends the slave to his master, the master to God. It adorns a woman, perfects a man. It is loved in a child, praised in a youth, esteemed in the aged. In both man and woman, at every age of life, it is exceedingly attractive.[59]

Patience, Tertullian was convinced, is an inextricable part of the work of God: it is a "child of God's nurturing" and the "inseparable companion" of

---

54. Tertullian, *Pat.* 8.2 (Daly, 207).
55. Tertullian, *Pat.* 10.3 (Daly, 210).
56. Tertullian, *Pat.* 9.2–3 (Daly, 209).
57. Tertullian, *Pat.* 10.8 (Daly, 211).
58. Tertullian, *Pat.* 12.8–9 (Daly, 215).
59. Tertullian, *Pat.* 15.3 (Daly, 220).

the Holy Spirit. Of course, patience is precious but its existence is precarious; Tertullian treasures patience but senses that it can be evanescent. As a charismatic who addresses readers who are open to the work and gifts of the Holy Spirit, he cautions them; if they do not live lives of patience, the Spirit will go away. Without patience, which is "its companion and assistant," the Spirit will "feel very uncomfortable" and leave them.[60]

Tertullian concludes with contrasts. In this life people who live without God's patience experience oppressive, exploitive human relationships, and posthumously they encounter judgment and punishment—"fire beneath the earth."[61] However, people who live with patience, who believe in the resurrection and are empowered by the Spirit, offer their lives to God as a response to his gracious gift of patience to them.[62]

What a remarkable treatise Tertullian's *Patience* is.[63] We can read it as an essay on a virtue, which it clearly is, or as an essay on ethics. But it may be more illuminating for us to see it as a treatise on mission that helps us understand the "combination of relaxation and urgency" that characterized the early Christians' approach to mission.[64] Tertullian wrote the treatise at a time when the North African Christians were living under pressure; the violent scenes in the Carthage amphitheater recorded by the *Passion of Perpetua and Felicity* are contemporaneous with *Patience*.[65] Tertullian is closely in touch with this persecution, and he knows acutely how numerically insignificant the Christians were.[66] But he doesn't seem worried about this. He is not concerned about the future. He believes that God is at work and that patience is God's means of drawing people to himself.[67] By the patient teaching and work of Christ, God has disclosed his character to the world. And God's patient character has deep consequences for the Christians.

Tertullian knows that some—no doubt many—outsiders will reject the patience that Christ lived and taught and that Christians are learning. He is

60. Tertullian, *Pat.* 15.7 (Daly, 221).
61. Tertullian, *Pat.* 16.4 (Daly, 221); also 10.3 (Daly, 210).
62. Tertullian, *Pat.* 16.5 (Daly, 221–22).
63. *Patience* is the most concentrated treatment of patience in Tertullian's writings, yet he also refers to patience in many other places, as in *Or.* 4.2–5; *Marc.* 4.16; 5.36; *Scorpiace* 12; *Scap.* 2; *Bapt.* 12.
64. George A. Lindbeck, *The Church in a Postliberal Age*, ed. James J. Buckley (Grand Rapids: Eerdmans, 2002), 82.
65. Kossi Adiavu Ayedze, "Tertullian, Cyprian, and Augustine on Patience: A Comparative and Critical Study of Three Treatises on a Stoic-Christian Virtue in Early North African Christianity" (PhD diss., Princeton Theological Seminary, 2000), 151–52.
66. Cf. Tertullian, *Nat.* 1.7; trans P. Holmes, *ANF* 2:115: the Christians, obviously a minority movement, are "besieged, and attacked, and kept prisoners actually in our secret congregations."
67. Tertullian, *Pat.* 2.3 (Daly, 195).

not surprised by their rejection; he believes that God in his patience allows this. But other outsiders, Tertullian observes, look at the Christians and their patient approaches to life and are intrigued. Patience, he asserts, "attracts the heathen."[68] And it poses questions for them. Why, the pagans wonder, do Christians live as they do? For this reason, Christians don't need to feel frantic. As we shall see in later chapters, Christians do what they can to share their faith and to bring people through baptism into the life of God's people. But Christians are not impatient. They entrust all things, including their own lives and the salvation of all people, to the God who patiently is making all things new.

Cyprian: Patience—Walking in the Footsteps of Christ

We now turn to Cyprian, the bishop of Carthage, Tertullian's city, the pre-eminent city of Roman Africa. In Cyprian's day, fifty years after Tertullian, the churches were much stronger numerically and more developed institutionally than they had been when Tertullian was writing. In many ways, though, Cyprian's decade—he was bishop from 248 until his martyrdom in 258—was a traumatic time. In 250–51 Emperor Decius issued an edict requiring all inhabitants of the empire to sacrifice to the gods. In response to this, Cyprian went into exile. Some Christians stayed at home, burned incense to the emperor, and survived; others refused and were imprisoned. A few were executed. Tension between believers who had suffered and those who had lapsed (the *confessores* and the *lapsi*) was intense. In 252, soon after the end of the persecution, an outbreak of plague traumatized Carthage, and many people, including Christians, died. As the decade progressed, there were also strains between churches in Africa and the church in Rome about matters of discipline and ethics.

In this setting, Cyprian wrote a second treatise on patience. Why did he think that was necessary? There were lots of virtues about which no Christian writer had yet written—why not a treatise on prudence, justice, or fortitude? Hadn't Tertullian's treatise on patience been exhaustive and well argued? Hadn't he said the right things? Cyprian in his treatise makes it clear that he values Tertullian's work. According to his secretary, reported later by Jerome, Cyprian every day asked to see Tertullian's writings, saying, "Hand me the master."[69] Although he did not necessarily say this specifically of Tertullian's *Patience*, that must have been on Cyprian's desk as he wrote his own treatise.

---

68. Tertullian, *Pat.* 15.3 (Daly, 220).
69. Jerome, *On Illustrious Men* 53, trans. T. P. Halton, FC 100 (1999), 74.

Every page of Cyprian's writing shows his deep affinities with the theology, ethics, and missiology of Tertullian. And in specific ways Cyprian restates and underscores what Tertullian's treatise said.

So around 256 Cyprian wrote a new statement on patience. No doubt he knew that a new treatise by him *as bishop* would have more clout with the African Christians than Tertullian's earlier one. Perhaps he sensed that he could write more simply than Tertullian. Certainly he knew that the church was in a different place than it had been fifty years earlier. Especially in the decade prior to Cyprian's writing, Christians had been through severe testing; some believers were tired, some were losing hope, some were in danger of lapsing into impatient practices, even engaging in acts of violent revenge against their enemies. In the face of these developments, Cyprian may have sensed that patience—the characteristic virtue of the church—was under pressure. But patience would help his people live as Christians in their pressure-filled situation. So Cyprian set out to renew their conviction that there was something *good* in patience. He followed in Tertullian's tradition by writing a treatise on patience, but he changed its title; instead of *On Patience (De patientia)*, Cyprian's title was *On the Good of Patience (De bono patientiae)*.[70] Cyprian believed that patience was good; he had to show people what that good was and demonstrate why it mattered.

Like Tertullian, Cyprian begins his treatise by reaffirming a hallmark of early Christianity—holism. Christians and their communities must live a life of integrity with no discrepancy between words and deeds. Outsiders will judge the Christians not so much by what they say (most people won't listen to them anyway) as by what they are and do. As Cyprian puts it near the start of his treatise, "We know virtues by their practice rather than through boasting of them."[71] If patience is not *good* in the lived experience of humans, it isn't worth talking about.[72]

Cyprian joins Tertullian in asserting that patience is an attribute of God. In fact, patience is a virtue that Christians "have in common with God."[73] Quoting the same Sermon on the Mount text that Tertullian cites at the beginning of his *Patience*, Cyprian affirms that God "makes the day to rise and the sun to shine equally over the good and the evil" (Matt. 5:45).[74] God, Cyprian notes, is generous to all people; he reliably blesses them all—just

---

70. I use G. E. Conway's translation of *De bono patientiae*, in FC 36 (1958), 257–87; the Latin text is in *Cyprien de Carthage: À Donat; et, La vertu de patience*, ed. J. Molager, SC 291 (Paris: Cerf, 1982).

71. Cyprian, *Pat.* 3 (Conway, 265).

72. This (*Pat.* 3) is the context for Cyprian's use of the famous slogan "We do not speak great things but we live them." See note 1 above.

73. Cyprian, *Pat.* 3 (Conway, 265).

74. Cyprian, *Pat.* 4 (Conway, 265).

and unjust alike—with winds that blow, fountains that flow, harvests that are abundant. To be sure, people do things that grieve and anger God; they visit the temples, engage in idolatrous rites, and worship images. God in patience endures all these things. Patiently, God waits for the time when humans will be converted from idolatry, malice, and crime to fullness of life.[75]

Cyprian builds on Tertullian by pointing to the role of Jesus in bringing about people's conversion. Jesus's "precepts for salvation" (*praecepta in salute*) are central in this. These precepts come from the wellspring of Jesus's ethical teaching, the Sermon on the Mount, which Cyprian cites extensively:

> You have heard that it was said, "Thou shalt love thy neighbor and shalt hate thy enemy." But I say to you, Love your enemies and pray for those who persecute you, so that you may be the children of your Father in heaven, who makes his sun rise on the good and the evil. . . . For if you love those who love you, what reward shall you have? Do not even the publicans act thus? . . . You, therefore, will be perfect as your heavenly Father is perfect. (Matt. 5:43–48)[76]

As he quotes this passage, Cyprian offers his readers a "heavenly birth" in which they can "become like God" (*simile Deo*). As God perfects them, "the patience of God the Father" abides in them and enables them to live patiently—"to possess among our virtues what can be put on a par with the divine merits!"[77]

But following Tertullian, Cyprian immediately goes on to state that these words are hollow unless they are lived. That's how Jesus lived: he "did not teach by words only, but he also fulfilled it by his deeds." One of the miracles that proved his divinity was his "habitual forbearance," by which he "exemplified his Father's patience." With this in mind, Cyprian recounts the events of Jesus's life: his incarnation; his baptism; his conflict with the devil, in which "he did not carry the fight beyond words"; his practice of foot washing, in which he taught by example the attitude that "a fellow servant ought to have toward his companions and equals"; and his receiving the kiss of Judas. According to Cyprian, all of Jesus's behavior—his entire missional style—was patient:

> But what wonderful equanimity in bearing with the Jews, and what wonderful patience in persuading the unbelieving to accept the faith, in winning the ungrateful by kindness, in responding gently to those who contradicted Him, in enduring the proud with mercy, in yielding with humility to persecutors, in

75. Cyprian, *Pat.* 44 (Conway, 266).
76. Cyprian, *Pat.* 5 (Conway, 267).
77. Cyprian, *Pat.* 5 (Conway, 267).

wishing to win over the murderers of the prophets and those persistently rebellious against God even to the very hour of His passion and cross![78]

And this culminates in his passion, in which Jesus does not proclaim his majesty but silently perseveres in his death in which "a full and perfect patience" is realized.[79]

At this point Cyprian moves beyond Tertullian. As he reflects on the consequences that Jesus's teaching, life, and passion will have for the North African Christians, Cyprian shifts his emphasis from obeying Christ's precepts to walking in Christ's footsteps. It is essential for the success of the church's mission that the believers embody the gospel, and as they do this they find that Christ's precepts are indispensably life giving. Christ's example is paramount. Cyprian quotes 1 John 2:6: "He who says that he abides in Christ ought himself also to walk just as He walked."[80] For Cyprian this is holy ground; according to Simone Deléani, following Christ is the heart of Cyprian's spirituality.[81]

Cyprian knows that this emphasis on following Jesus is important for his people because severe, multiple crises threatened to engulf them. They face not only the personal crises of work and death that affect everybody; they also face crises that affect them in particular because they are Christians: loss of land, prison, sword, beasts, fire, crucifixion. To believers facing these crises, Cyprian offers patience as their "helper and companion."[82] Cyprian knows that some of the Christians are tired. Nevertheless he urges them to persevere in hope and to express their hope in lives that are a foretaste of the future that they hope for: "Patient waiting is necessary that we may fulfill what we have begun to be."[83] And the way believers express their hope is by performing good works. Quoting a Pauline text that he loved (Gal. 6:10–9), Cyprian encourages his people: "While we have time, let us do good *to all men*, but especially to those who are of the household of faith. And in doing good let us not grow tired, for in due time we shall reap."[84] Cyprian urges his people, exhausted and disheartened though some may be, not to withdraw. They must not stop doing good work to outsiders as well as to their fellow believers.

---

78. Cyprian, *Pat.* 6 (Conway, 269).
79. Cyprian, *Pat.* 7 (Conway, 270).
80. Cyprian, *Pat.* 9, where Cyprian likewise cites 1 Pet. 2:21–23: "Christ also has suffered for you, leaving you an example so that you may follow in his steps" (Conway, 271).
81. Simone Deléani, *Christum sequi: Étude d'un thème dans l'oeuvre de Saint Cyprien* (Paris: Études Augustiniennes, 1979), 110.
82. Cyprian, *Pat.* 12 (Conway, 275).
83. Cyprian, *Pat.* 13 (Conway, 276).
84. Cyprian cites Gal. 6:10 before 6:9. See Cyprian, *Pat.* 13 (Conway, 276); Pontius of Carthage, *Vit. Cypr.* 10.

But the Christians must stop doing bad works! Cyprian urges them not to commit "acts of the flesh and the body whereby the soul is stormed and captured." Adultery, deceit, and homicide are temptations that lurk, always ready to seduce wavering believers, and they are mortal sins. The believers' antidote to them is patience. "Let patience be strong and stable in the heart, and then the sanctified body and temple of God will not be corrupted by adultery, innocence dedicated to justice will not be infected by the contagion of deceit, and the hand that has held the Eucharist will not be sullied by the blood stained sword."[85]

But a deeper problem is lurking. Cyprian is aware that some Christians are not only tired; they want revenge. They are eager to retaliate against people who had attacked them during the persecutions. Such thinking must have affected quite a few people. According to Cyprian, "a very great number [*plurimos*], either because of the weight of their pressing injuries or because of resentment toward those who attack them . . . wish to be revenged quickly."[86]

It is hard to know what is going on here. Is Cyprian dealing with Christians who, in the tradition of the North African *catervae* (youth gangs), want to arm themselves for self-protection and even for retaliation?[87] Whoever these people were, in the final four chapters (21–24) of *On the Good of Patience* Cyprian takes them seriously. "I must warn you," he says. Whatever persecutions the Christians have experienced, and whether it has been Jews or pagans or heretics who have mistreated them, Christians must not avenge themselves. Cyprian places himself among them: "We should not hasten to revenge their pain with an angry speed." Why not? It is not, as he has argued throughout the treatise, because Christ's precepts have taught all believers to turn the other cheek; it is also not because "following Christ" entails living lives of voluntary suffering. Instead, Cyprian looks forward to judgment. Addressing people who are tempted to resort to violence, Cyprian appeals to the Lord of the Apocalypse (Rev. 22:10–12), who orders his people "to wait and to endure with a strong patience the day of future vengeance."[88]

This is a new theme. Throughout *On the Good of Patience*, Cyprian has made much of the Sermon on the Mount and the imitation of Christ, but in this passage at the end of the treatise "his ethic of non-retaliation is not grounded in the 'love of the enemies,' but in the eschatological intensity of

---

85. Cyprian, *Pat*.14 (Conway, 277).
86. Cyprian, *Pat.* 21 (Conway, 283).
87. Brent D. Shaw, *Sacred Violence: African Christians and Sectarian Hatred in the Age of Augustine* (Cambridge: Cambridge University Press, 2011), 20–27. I have found no evidence of Christian *catervae* (gangs) before the fourth century.
88. Cyprian, *Pat.* 21 (Conway, 283–84).

God's vengeance."[89] On the day of reckoning, Jesus Christ, the Judge and the Avenger, will come in power to vindicate his suffering people with fire.[90] When Christ "revenges himself, [he] is destined to revenge us, the people of his Church and the number of all the just from the beginning of the world."[91] Since Christ's day has not yet come, Cyprian urges Christians, as they anticipate the day, to live patiently. They are not to defend themselves before the Lord's time. Instead, as always, they are to keep the precepts of the Lord. Why? Not because their behavior will be an attractive expression of God's character, and not because there is something self-evidently good in patience. Rather, because the eternal consequences of not keeping the precepts are terrifying. When the day of wrath comes, impatient Christians who do not do what Christ taught will be punished along with the impious and the sinners. Cyprian's treatise ends with a bang.[92]

However, just before these final four chapters, in chapters 17–20 Cyprian writes a first conclusion to the treatise that sums up his main themes. In these chapters the virtue of patience is expansive and beneficent. Patience commends Christians to God and saves Christians for God. It enables Christians to endure the unavoidable crises of life—"loss of wealth, burning fevers, torments of wounds, the death of dear ones"—with strength and faith that appear remarkable to their pagan neighbors. "Nothing else distinguishes the unjust from the just more than this, that in adversities the unjust man complains and blasphemes because of impatience, while the just man is proved by patience."[93] Patience is a distinctive sign of the Christian; it enables believers to live "in the way of Christ" amid the crises of their lives. Patience will "temper anger, bridle the tongue, govern the mind, guard peace . . . extinguish the fire of dissension, restrain the power of the wealthy, teach us to pardon our offenders quickly and to ask pardon of others." In his peroration Cyprian shows his stature as a rhetorician: "It is this patience which strongly fortifies the foundations of our faith. It is this patience which sublimely promotes the growth of hope. It directs our action, so that we can keep to the way of Christ while we make progress because of His forbearance. It ensures our perseverance as sons of God while we imitate the patience of the Father."[94]

89. Ayedze, "Tertullian, Cyprian, and Augustine," 213.
90. Cyrian, *Pat.* 22 (Conway, 285).
91. Cyprian, *Pat.* 24 (Conway, 286).
92. Cyprian's emphasis on divine vengeance is also evident in *Demetr.* 17: "Our certainty of the vengeance which is to come makes us patient" (trans. R. J. Deferrari, FC 36 [1958], 182).
93. Cyprian, *Pat.* 17 (Conway, 280).
94. Cyprian, *Pat.* 20 (Conway, 283).

This buoyant patience animates Cyprian's *On the Good of Patience*, but not only that—it also animates the missional expansion of the early church.[95] It is not the crabbed, judgment-awaiting obedience of chapters 21–24 that explains the church's growth; it is life in "the way of Christ," distinctive and hopeful. Christians, as Cyprian knew well, were growing in numbers because they were distinct from the "unjust"—living patiently in relation to their neighbors and enemies, doing good to them, and waiting for them to come to faith.

Lactantius: Patience—the Supreme Virtue and a Key to Worship and Mission

We conclude this chapter with Lactantius (ca. 250–ca. 325), the third protagonist in the tradition of patient theology. Like Tertullian and Cyprian, Lactantius was a North African. In a small town there, he studied with a grammarian who taught him elegant Ciceronian Latin, and soon he moved to the provincial capital of Carthage, where he himself taught rhetoric. Early in his life he converted from paganism to Christianity. Soon after the turn of the fourth century he moved to Asia Minor, where the emperor Diocletian hired him to practice and teach his exquisite Latin rhetoric at the court in Nicomedia. There he met articulate and powerful pagans, who were moving toward a decisive showdown with the empire's Christian minority. In this setting—a world of religious tension and the early stages of persecution—Lactantius wrote his magnum opus, the *Divine Institutes*, whose seven books contained a coherent apology for Christianity in light of the culture of his pagan peers and the literature that had shaped their thinking.

In 303, when the Great Persecution broke out, Lactantius left the court and traveled to the West, possibly to Italy. There, as early as 310, the new emperor Constantine invited Lactantius to tutor his son Crispus, and so Lactantius moved to the capital of Trier in northern Europe. In Trier he produced a revised edition of the *Divine Institutes*, which he read aloud at court; his audience at times included Constantine, to whom he dedicated the work and whose religious policies it may have influenced.[96] In both the original version of the *Divine Institutes* and in its revisions, the theme of patience is prominent.

---

95. *On the Good of Patience* is the most concentrated treatment of patience in Cyprian's writings, yet he refers to patience in many other places: *Ad Quir.* 3, in which 3 of 120 "heads" (topics taught to catechumens) have to do with patience (3.35, 45, 106); *Demetr.* 17, 20; *Zel. liv.* 15–16; *Mort.* 9–10; *Dom. or.* 15.

96. The passages I cite from Lactantius's *Divine Institutes* come from the translation of Anthony Bowen and Peter Garnsey, *Lactantius: Divine Institutes*, TTH 40 (Liverpool: Liverpool University Press, 2003).

In the seven books of the *Divine Institutes*, Lactantius presented a systematic argument for Christianity that dealt with a wide range of themes. Patience was only one of these, and Lactantius dealt with it in a concentrated way in only one chapter (book 5, chap. 22). Unlike his African predecessors Tertullian and Cyprian, he did not write a treatise specifically devoted to patience, but patience was supremely important to him. In the *Divine Institutes* he refers to *patientia* over 150 times. There is no other virtue that he mentions as often or praises as fulsomely: patience is "the greatest of all virtues"; it is "the supreme virtue"; and, he adds, "there is no truer virtue than patience."[97] Lactantius is willing to share the greatness of patience with other virtues. In his study of patience in early Christian writings, Michel Spanneut observed that Lactantius "ultimately mixed every virtue with patience."[98] Spanneut did not note what is manifest in Lactantius's work—that patience profoundly shapes his understanding of mission.

Like Tertullian and Cyprian, Lactantius grounds his understanding of patience in the character and work of God. He does this especially when dealing with the coming of Christ. "People," he notes, "prefer example before talk, because talk is easy and example is hard."[99] This is why God chose to send not disembodied words from heaven but an incarnate Son in a mortal body.

In classical thought, perfect virtue endured pain with patience in accordance with justice and duty; further, perfect virtue was fearless in the face of impending death and endured it bravely when it came. Therefore someone who teaches perfection has a double duty—to "teach it all by precept and to substantiate it in action."[100]

So God sent Jesus Christ, both God and man, to speak precepts of salvation and to perform deeds that opened the road to justice for all who would follow him toward eternal life. Speaking and acting in this way brought Christ to the cross. "Why," Lactantius asks, "did he not at least suffer some decent form of death?"[101] Because, Lactantius claims, only in dying by crucifixion could Christ help "the lowest in society." By coming in humility and suffering, Christ brought "hope of salvation to all who had to die the sort of death that is common among the lowest in society, in case there were even one who could not imitate him." Further, Christ suffered as he did so that his body would be "kept whole" for the resurrection and so that, as his body was lifted up on the

---

97. Lactantius, *Inst.* 6.18.16; 6.18.30; 6.18.19 (Bowen and Garnsey, 370–71).
98. Spanneut, "Geduld," 266.
99. Lactantius, *Inst.* 4.23.8 (Bowen and Garnsey, 265).
100. Lactantius, *Inst.* 4.24.7 (Bowen and Garnsey, 267).
101. Lactantius, *Inst.* 4.26.29 (Bowen and Garnsey, 272).

cross, "God's sufferings would be visible to all nations."[102] By means of the incarnation and the cross, the Father displays his way of enacting justice and enabling patience among humans, whom he calls to be his children.

Patience as lived by God's children is shaped by God's action in Christ. Jesus's followers ponder his life, for he came to "teach virtue and patience not only by words, but also by deeds."[103] Looking at him, they will "bear with equanimity . . . ills whether imposed or accidental."[104] They will be content with what they have, speak the truth, charge no interest on loans, control their emotions, and refuse to create an enemy.[105] Above all, unlike those who follow the political philosopher Cicero, when they are offended they will not retaliate. Cicero had stated, "A good man is one who would help those he could and would harm no one unless provoked by mistreatment."[106] To this Lactantius responds indignantly, "What need was there to add 'unless provoked by mistreatment,' pinning vice onto a good man like an awful tail, and denying his patience, which is the greatest of all virtues."[107]

Lactantius has learned to live patiently. As a convert from paganism to Christianity, he has identified himself with a community that characterizes itself by patience. The community draws together people of widely varied backgrounds, "people of every sex, race and age" who walk "the heavenly path" together.[108] With them he has learned to be hospitable, to ransom captives, to maintain orphans and widows, and to care for the sick. With them he has learned to repudiate all violence and killing, including the impatient acts of aborting, exposing unwanted infants, and killing in warfare.[109] He has learned to trust God and not to be in a hurry.

Patience has also transformed his view of religious competition—on the part of both the pagan religious establishment, which as he wrote had begun to persecute the Christians, and the endangered Christian minority. However threatening the current situation may have seemed to him, Lactantius writes calmly and deliberately. In his view God was doing something big and inexorable: from east to west "every sex, every generation, every family and district" are being drawn to God without compulsion; "truth has its own power to

102. Lactantius, *Inst.* 4.26.30–34 (Bowen and Garnsey, 272).
103. Lactantius, *Epit.* 43, trans. W. Fletcher, *ANF* 7:239.
104. Lactantius, *Inst.* 5.22.3 (Bowen and Garnsey, 326).
105. Lactantius, *Inst.* 6.18.7, 10, 32 (Bowen and Garnsey, 369, 371).
106. Cicero, *Off.* 3.76; cited by Lactantius, *Inst.* 6.18.15 (Bowen and Garnsey, 370).
107. Lactantius, *Inst.* 6.18.16 (Bowen and Garnsey, 370).
108. Lactantius, *Inst.* 6.3.16 (Bowen and Garnsey, 335).
109. Lactantius (*Inst.* 6.20.17) contends that "killing a human being is always wrong because it is God's will for man to be a sacred creature"; in 6.20.15–26 he inveighs against soldiering, capital punishment, and the smothering of newborn babies (Bowen and Garnsey, 375).

prevail."[110] So persecution is hopeless, doomed to fail. "There is no need for violence and brutality; worship cannot be forced."[111] Lactantius goes on: "If you want to defend religion by bloodshed, torture and evil, then at once it will not be so defended; it will be polluted and outraged. There is nothing that is so much a matter of willingness as religion, and if someone making sacrifice is spiritually turned off, then it's gone, it's nothing."[112] Persecution, like all killing, is self-destructive. In contrast, Lactantius points to the steady growth of the Christian church. "Worship of God increases the more they try to suppress it," and this continues amid terrible tortures in settings where the "invincible patience" of Christians is manifest.[113] Persecution also fails, according to Lactantius, because it offends the moral sensibilities of the on-lookers, who, repelled by the cruelty, become new recruits to Christianity.[114]

To his pagan readers Lactantius utters an invitation. Worship cannot be compelled; instead, it is

> achieved by talk rather than blows, so that there is free will in it. [Pagan think-ers] must unsheathe the sharpness of their wits: if the reasoning is sound, let them argue it! We [Christians] are ready to listen if they would tell; if they keep silent, we simply cannot believe them, just as we do not yield when they use violence. Let them copy us, and so bring out the reason in it all; we use no guile ourselves, though they complain we do; instead, we teach, we show, we demonstrate.[115]

Simultaneously, Lactantius challenges his Christian readers to be true to their patient approach to mission. They can do this confidently, without thinking that everyone, coerced by state power, must worship their God: "We . . . make no demand that our God, who is everyone's God willy nilly, be worshipped by anyone unwillingly, and we do not get cross if he is not worshipped. We are confident of his supreme power."[116] Christians must be willing to listen to their critics ("we are ready to listen") and to engage with them in rigorous debate. Lactantius has written his *Divine Institutes* to help the Christians do this well. But the deeper challenge to Christians, Lactantius was convinced, was to live their faith. They must live with trust in God and fidelity to Christ, whom God sent to embody and impart virtue,

---

110. Lactantius, *Inst.* 5.13.1, 5 (Bowen and Garnsey, 306).
111. Lactantius, *Inst.* 5.19.11 (Bowen and Garnsey, 320).
112. Lactantius, *Inst.* 5.19.23 (Bowen and Garnsey, 321).
113. Lactantius, *Inst.* 5.13.4; 6.17.7 (Bowen and Garnsey, 320, 366).
114. Lactantius, *Inst.* 5.22.18–19 (Bowen and Garnsey, 328).
115. Lactantius, *Inst.* 5.19.11–12 (Bowen and Garnsey, 320).
116. Lactantius, *Inst.* 5.20.9 (Bowen and Garnsey, 524).

so that they will have something solid to teach, show, and demonstrate. Lactantius must have known the struggles that many Christian communities had at precisely this point. But he, like Justin, Tertullian, and Cyprian, also knew Christian communities that were living what they proclaimed. When Christians offered the world not just theological statements but embodied virtue, when they backed up their assertions "not only in words but also in examples drawn from reality," they attracted people who felt an irresistible pull to join them.[117]

Conclusion: The Many-Dimensioned Good of Patience

With Lactantius we have completed our overview of early Christian writings about patience. The authors, living in different places and milieus, have different accents. But their writings contain themes that define patience and that recur and fit together, constituting a gestalt of patience. In broad terms, these themes are as follows:

- *Patience is rooted in God's character*: God is patient, is working inexorably across the centuries to accomplish his mission, and in the fullness of time has disclosed himself in Jesus Christ.
- *The heart of patience is revealed in the incarnation of Jesus Christ*: Jesus's life and teaching demonstrate what patience means and beckon those who follow him to a patient lifestyle which participates in God's mission.
- *Patience is not in human control*: People who live a patient lifestyle trust God and do not try to manipulate outcomes; they live incautiously, riskily.
- *Patience is not in a hurry*: Patient Christians live at the pace given by God, accepting incompleteness and waiting.
- *Patience is unconventional*: It reconfigures behavior according to Jesus's teachings in many areas, especially wealth, sex, and power.
- *Patience is not violent*: It accepts injury without retaliating in kind, because violence is not God's calling to them and cannot bring fundamental change.
- *Patience gives religious freedom*: It does not compel religious beliefs and observances.
- *Patience is hopeful*: It entrusts the future confidently to God.

117. Lactantius, *Inst.* 5.17.8 (Bowen and Garnsey, 314).

In subsequent chapters we will explore how the early Christians gave expression to patience in their lives and communities. At times they embodied patience halfheartedly; Cyprian was not the only leader who encountered believers who behaved in exasperating ways. Nevertheless, throughout the early centuries the Christian churches continued to grow numerically. Arguably, a significant reason for this growth was the Christians' patience. Justin Martyr bears witness to this. When he stated that the Christians' "strange patience" caused pagans to become believers, he was on to something.[118]

118. Justin, *1 Apol.* 16.4 (Hardy, 252).

3

PUSH AND PULL

Religion in the Roman Empire was huge, multifaceted, and unavoidable. It expressed itself in a myriad of situations, at home and in the forum, in the streets and at the baths, in places of beauty and in times of danger, on occasions of celebration and mourning. It was infinitely varied, constantly incorporating new divinities, and (almost) "infinitely tolerant."[1] Why in such a world did Christianity attract converts? It was hardly to be predicted that a faith that emanated from a widely despised and mistrusted region—Palestine—could make significant headway elsewhere in the Roman world; and it was deeply improbable that this faith of Jewish origin would by the early fourth century become a major world religion whose adherents were a significant slice of the imperial populace.

Why would anyone become a Christian? For two centuries at least, the Christians were a small movement. In certain places they were no doubt growing at a rapid pace. Nevertheless, they were statistically insignificant, marginal to the life of most Romans.[2] There were good reasons not to become

1. Mary Beard, John North, and Simon Price, *Religions of Rome*, 2 vols. (Cambridge: Cambridge University Press, 1998), 1:41; Ramsay MacMullen, *Christianizing the Roman Empire (A.D. 100–400)* (New Haven: Yale University Press, 1984), 14.

2. Rodney Stark, *The Rise of Christianity: A Sociologist Reconsiders History* (Princeton: Princeton University Press, 1996), 6–7. Ramsay MacMullen (*The Second Church: Popular Christianity, A.D. 200–400*, SBL Writings from the Greco-Roman World Supplement Series 1 [Atlanta: Society of Biblical Literature, 2009], 102–3) rightly makes the statistics considerably more modest without altering the general contours of Stark's model.

Christian. Disincentives were strong: if you became a Christian, you could be gossiped about, be made sport of by workmates, get in trouble with your master, be suspect to your neighbors. At times becoming a believer could get you jailed, sent to the mines, or killed. And there was a luxuriant variety of other religious options to choose from. There were public cults, family cults, private cults, healing cults, and oracles. These were sufficiently satisfying to the majority of people that they did not look further. Most people didn't become Christians.[3]

But some people did become Christians. What motivated them? People who study shifts in religious adherence pay attention to the "push" and the "pull" that are at play in every conversion.[4] What in the existing religious options so dissatisfied some people that it *pushed* their adherents to explore new options? And then what was it in Christianity that so attracted people, that it *pulled* them to explore something that might be very costly? John North, an expert on paganism in the Roman world, has put the issue like this: "There was a steady drift of pagans away from their traditional attachments and a great deal of peaceful co-existence and discussion; but . . . the survival of pagan practice depended on their success in retaining members, generation by generation. It remains, of course, a serious question why pagans did so drift away from traditional attachments."[5]

In this chapter we cannot survey the immense range of pagan observances. Instead, we will look at three samples of pagan piety that have left us with usable documentation: a public cult, a private association, and an oracular shrine. These samples were scattered across the empire—the public cult from the Capitol in Rome; the private association from the village of Lanuvium southeast of Rome; and the shrine, the renowned oracular site of Claros in Asia Minor. Each of these samples of piety appealed to many people. We will try to understand what gave them their viability across time; but we will also

3. Of course some Christians also became pagans. Conversions went both ways. The fourth-century emperor Julian "the Apostate" is the best known. But already in AD 112, Pliny the Younger in his famous *Ep.* 10.96 to Trajan refers to "those who had been [Christians], but had ceased to be such, some three years ago, some a good many years, and a few even twenty" (trans. J. Stevenson, *A New Eusebius*, rev. ed. [London: SPCK, 1987], 19). The third century shows examples of gentile Christians who were serious in their exploration of Judaism; see Walter Ameling, "The Christian *Lapsi* in Smyrna, 250 AD (*Martyrium Pionii* 12–14)," VC 62 (2008): 133–60. At Cyprian's execution, "one of the officers [the *Tesserarius*], a former Christian, offered him his clothes, as if he might wish to change his garments for drier ones" (Pontius, *Vit. Cypr.* 16, trans. M. M. Müller and R. J. Deferrari, FC 15 [1952], 22).

4. See, e.g., Robert Brenneman, *Homies and Hermanos: God and Gangs in Central America* (New York: Oxford University Press, 2012), 89–90.

5. John North, "Pagans, Polytheists and the Pendulum," in *The Spread of Christianity in the First Four Centuries: Essays in Explanation*, ed. W. V. Harris (Leiden: Brill, 2005), 137.

try to understand the dysfunctions, dissonances, and frustrations that might *push* some people to explore new options. In dialogue with each sample, we will look at a correlative Christian group (church), each of them from third-century North Africa, where our evidence is densest. Of each we will ask: what in the Christian grouping might *pull* people, address their concerns, speak to their longings, cause them to join new groups—often at considerable personal cost? In a competitive religious environment, what could the Christian groups offer that could overcome the massive disincentives to becoming a *Christianus* or a *Christiana*?

Can Humans Change? The Realities of Habitus

The most formidable disincentive to major religious change is always our social formation. Floating on the surface of our consciousness are our ideas and convictions. We are thinking creatures, and we may believe that ideas determine our identity and that decision making shapes our ethical behavior. If we have been informed by Marx and Freud, however, we will realize that socioeconomic structures and psychological realities also shape us profoundly. All of us are shaped by poverty or wealth or power-relationships, and our experiences of our parents are potent. Without negating these realities, French reflexive sociologist Pierre Bourdieu points us to another motivator that he believes is deeper which he calls *habitus*.[6]

Bourdieu contends that the knowledge that truly forms us is more profoundly a part of us than our intellectual knowledge. It is "corporeal knowledge," a "system of dispositions" that we carry in our bodies.[7] This knowledge is trained in ways that are non-explicit. It is formed by social conventions, including the ways we do everyday tasks—Bourdieu points to our table manners, the way we use knives and forks—that at an early age we learn are acceptable and that become second nature to us.[8] Habitus is reinforced by story, the little stories of our family and community as well as the big stories that undergird our culture. Habitus is further formed by example, by our parents, peers, and role models—people who have authority in our life. Above all, habitus is formed by repetition, by the sheer physicality of doing things over and over

6. Bourdieu draws upon insights originating with Aristotle and developed by Aquinas. See Omar Lizardo, "Habitus," in *Encyclopedia of Philosophy and the Social Sciences*, ed. Byron Kaldis (Los Angeles: Sage, 2013), 1:405–7.
7. Pierre Bourdieu, *Pascalian Meditations*, trans. Richard Nice (Stanford, CA: Stanford University Press, 2000), 130–35.
8. Pierre Bourdieu, *The Logic of Practice*, trans. Richard Nice (Stanford, CA: Stanford University Press, 1980), 69.

so that they become habitual, reflexive, and borne in our bodies. According to Bourdieu, "We learn bodily. . . . The most serious social injunctions are addressed not to the intellect but to the body, treated as a 'memory pad.' . . . There are things that cannot be done in certain circumstances ("that's not done") and others that cannot *not* be done."[9] This is knowledge that is not taught but inhaled; it is learning that we acquire without being aware that we are learning. As philosopher James K. A. Smith puts it, following Bourdieu, "Habitus is acquired, is learned, by incarnate pedagogies that in oblique, allusive, cunning ways work on the body and thus orient the whole person."[10] Learning habitus involves bodily movement—kinesthetics—and the engagement of the imagination—poetics.[11] It is habitus that constitutes our profoundest sense of identity; that forms our deepest convictions, allegiances, and repulsions; and that shapes our response to ultimate questions—what will we live for, die for, and kill (or not kill) for.[12]

For Bourdieu habitus is profound. At times he seems to think that habitus is a part of the human self that is virtually hardwired: "it cannot be touched by voluntary, deliberate transformation."[13] If so, this would make many forms of change impossible—including religious conversion. However, elsewhere Bourdieu cautiously admits that a transformation of habitus is possible.[14] And on the basis of the three samples in this chapter, I will argue that profound religious conversions did happen in the early centuries of our era. The protagonists in our stories indicate this by showing—at times in situations which they could not control, in which they had little time to think and ponder and discuss, in which they were responding to intimidating powers and unimaginable dangers—that they were behaving in unconventional ways that did not reflect their original formation. They were behaving unconventionally with their bodies. They were manifesting what Jennifer Glancy has called "corporal nonconformity."[15] They were able to do this because they were participants in a movement that, at least for a time, addressed the issues of religious change seriously.

9. Bourdieu, *Pascalian Meditations*, 141, 146.

10. James K. A. Smith, *Imagining the Kingdom: How Worship Works* (Grand Rapids: Baker Academic, 2013), 98.

11. Ibid., 15.

12. Tertullian, *Apol.* 39.7.

13. Bourdieu, *Outline*, in Richard Jenkins, *Pierre Bourdieu*, rev. ed., Key Sociologists (London: Routledge, 2002), 75. The extent to which humans are "hardwired" is an ongoing issue among neuroscientists, who debate the extent to which humans have "neuroplasticity."

14. Bourdieu, *Pascalian Meditations*, 149.

15. Jennifer A. Glancy, *Corporal Knowledge: Early Christian Bodies* (Oxford: Oxford University Press, 2010), 48.

The early Christian leaders appreciated the sheer difficulty of religious change. They attempted to change not just the thinking but the bodily deportment and reflexes of pagans en route to becoming Christians. This was difficult. The Christian leaders recognized that, even after catechesis and baptism, there were profound continuities in the social reflexes of their people. Their wiring was almost hard. But not quite. Change was much more difficult than historians and theologians in the grip of "mentalism" (Bourdieu's term) think. But it was not impossible.[16] Corporal nonconformity could be taught. As we shall see in chapters 6–7, Christian communities worked to transform the habitus of those who were candidates for membership—tinkering with their wiring, or even attempting a more far-reaching rewiring—by two means: catechesis, which rehabituated the candidates' behavior by means of teaching and relationship (apprenticeship); and worship, the communities' ultimate counterformative act, in which the new habitus was enacted and expressed with bodily eloquence.[17] The communities were able to attempt this rewiring because something had happened in the lives of the candidates that had shaken them, jarred them loose, given them a vision of an alternative way to view God, themselves, and the world. We will look at examples of this in three genres of religion—public, private, and crisis.

Public Religion

Rome, AD 69—Rebuilding the Capitol

The first example of public religion comes from Rome in the middle of the first century AD. The civil wars of 68–69 had destroyed the Capitol—the temple at the apex of the Capitoline Hill devoted to protecting the Roman deities Jupiter, Juno, and Minerva. In a classic text of Roman religion, the historian Tacitus tells the story of the rebuilding of the temple.[18]

Tacitus's account records the steep verticality of Roman society.[19] The inspiration behind the temple's rebuilding came from no less than the apogee of imperial society, Emperor Vespasian himself. To oversee the task, Vespasian commissioned a man who was in the equestrian order but "whose influence and reputation put him on an equality with the nobility." When the time came for the dedication of the site, the *praetor* (president of the liturgy), a

---

16. Bourdieu, *Pascalian Meditations*, 136.
17. Smith, *Imagining the Kingdom*, 183.
18. Tacitus, *Histories* 4.53, trans. C. H. Moore, LCL 151 (1931), 98–103.
19. For an emphasis on verticality, see Ramsay MacMullen, *Roman Social Relations, 50 B.C. to A.D. 284* (New Haven: Yale University Press, 1974), 94.

distinguished civil servant, was guided by the *pontifex* (chief priest), also a Roman aristocrat; the positions of both *praetor* and *pontifex* were purchasable for imposing sums.[20] Participating in the service were the six Vestal Virgins, all daughters of aristocratic Roman families.[21] The account does not say where the money and precious metals for the reconstructed temple came from, but they likely were from the private wealth of the Roman elite: "it was the rich who paid for paganism."[22] The aristocrats' love of status (*philotimia*) led to their benefactions (*euergetism*, "good-deedism").[23] At the climax of the dedication liturgy, when the foundation stone was pulled into place, everyone pulled together—"the magistrates, the priests, senators, knights, and a great part of the people." The people, it seems, were necessary, for the public liturgy was to be a vehicle for the piety of the entire city; but the account states explicitly that not all the people were there, and the bulk of those missing from "the great part" were probably the mass of people living at "bare bones subsistence" or below.[24] In any case, the event was choreographed by the aristocracy and in the interest of the aristocracy. In the dedication of the Capitoline temple, it was the Roman elite that mattered, the 2 percent at the top of a society marked by steep verticality. Roman *religio* confirmed and rationalized that verticality.

The ultimate purpose of the temple being dedicated, like all Roman religion, was to protect the empire and the city. The means of protection was ritual, precisely and punctiliously performed. In Tacitus's account we see the advice of the specialist diviners (the *haruspices*), the control of space and building materials, and the exact performance of the purifying sacrifice of pig, sheep, and ox (*suovetaurilia*). These were to make sure that when the gods and humans engaged in exchange, the gods would not be offended by inadequate human religious performance; the gods would provide protection from disasters such as war, famine, and the plague because the people had performed appropriate rites in an appropriate manner: *Do, ut des*—"I, the mortal, give, so that you, the immortal, might give in return."[25] Since a liturgical faux pas could anger the gods, who in retribution would bring about

20. James B. Rives, *Religion in the Roman Empire* (Malden, MA: Blackwell, 2007), 115.

21. Beard, North, and Price, *Religions of Rome*, 2:202.

22. Ramsay MacMullen, *Paganism in the Roman Empire* (New Haven: Yale University Press, 1981), 112.

23. Christine Trevett, *Christian Women and the Time of the Apostolic Fathers (AD c. 80–160): Corinth, Rome and Asia Minor* (Cardiff: University of Wales Press, 2006), 13n.

24. Walter C. Scheidel and Steven J. Friesen, "The Size of the Economy and the Distribution of Income," *JRS* 99 (2009): 84, 89.

25. Roger Beck, "The Religious Market of the Roman Empire: Rodney Stark and Christianity's Pagan Competition," in *Religious Rivalries in the Early Roman Empire and the Rise of Christianity*, ed. Leif E. Vaage (Waterloo, ON: Wilfrid Laurier University Press, 2006), 244.

communal disaster, the services had to be performed with verbal formulae and ritual movements that were strictly monitored, so that there would be an "orthopraxy of cult."[26] "That constant presence, the anger of the gods," was triggered by how people worshiped, not by how they lived.[27]

So it is not surprising that the dedication ceremony, according to Tacitus, was precisely controlled. At one point, when "one enthusiastic and joyful effort" on the part of everyone lifted the stone to the correct place, there was a hint of emotion. But the event as a whole was affectively cool; the account emphasizes self-control and emotional restraint. The tone did not become lighter until the very end of the ceremony, in the food and festivities that inevitably followed (which Tacitus does not describe), when the wine flowed and the sacrificed pig, sheep, and ox enabled many people to eat as they otherwise could not afford to do.

What sort of habitus did Roman public religion such as the dedication of the Capitol form in the participants? Certainly it was a habitus of belonging; the participants knew that they were members of the civic community of Rome, their involuntary community of birth. Also, it was a habitus of deference, in which the participants were grateful to their benefactors and respectful of the verticality of society, with its steep social gradation and virtual exclusion of women from cultic activity. Further, it was a habitus of fear, concerned that the gods would be angered if the participants contravened the social order or offered imprecise worship. Of course, the habitus of the Roman was shaped by much more than the large, public cultic festivals scattered throughout their year, such as the one Tacitus records for us. In a well-developed polytheistic system such as Rome's, there were countless other religious activities. The Roman religious world was tolerant, and many Roman citizens cobbled together religious lives as they participated in a wide range of religious observances; at times they took part in the "mysteries"—for example, the cults of Cybele or Mithras—which could be as unbridled as the temple dedication was minutely controlled. Further, the Roman's habitus was shaped by all manner of experiences—societal, familial, economic—in which religion played a peripheral if persistent role. Religion's role in the formation of habitus was complex.

We cannot prove this, of course. But it seems probable that a Roman here and there who took part in events such as the dedication of the Capitol was bored with it, felt critical of it, and found others to complain to. We can imagine that such people said bits of the following: "Nothing happened in that ritual; it was dull and preprogrammed. It was performed by 'them'—the

26. Rives, *Religion in the Roman Empire*, 48.
27. Robin Lane Fox, *Pagans and Christians* (San Francisco: Harper & Row, 1986), 95.

elite, the so-called *honestiores* who are putting it on ostensibly for the entire community but in reality for their own benefit—while we *humiliores*, who after all are the vast bulk of the people, are passive; we 'attend, admire, applaud, and consume.'[28] Our presence makes no difference. Of course we get meat and drink out of it, but it doesn't change our lives or give us hope. Does this even satisfy the gods? Does it really protect the empire?" Thinking of this sort, by even a tiny minority of attendees, may have been sufficient to push a few nonconformists toward the Christians when they encountered them.

Carthage, AD 203—"Games" in the Arena

Our second example of public religion comes more than a century later from Carthage, the leading city of Roman Africa. In May 203 the proconsul Hilarianus scheduled a public event—a day of games and spectacles to be performed in the city's amphitheater to celebrate the birthday of the emperor's son, Caesar Geta. The amphitheater was a wonder of Roman engineering that, hardly by accident, replicated the verticality of society.[29] In the amphitheater's higher section, the populace, seated according to wealth and influence, filled the stands overlooking the arena. At the upper section's visual center were the benefactors—the local *decurions*, magistrates, and landowners—who sponsored the games as an act of benevolence, *euergetism*, that both entertained the public and bolstered their own authority and prestige. In the lower section, far below in the arena, were the victims—animals, gladiators, and criminals—who would fight to entertain the populace. Some of the gladiators and all of the criminals would die. Gladiators, of course, were expensive, but criminals were cheap. According to an imperial law of 176, a procurator was allowed to sell condemned criminals to provincial landowners for use in games that they sponsored at one-tenth the price of a gladiator.[30] So Hilarianus could have sold local prisoners, including Perpetua and her friends, at a cut rate, making money for himself, saving money for the local sponsors, and enabling the killing to happen as economically as possible—and of course simultaneously titillating the crowds and warning them not to do what the criminals had done.

So on May 7, 203, Carthaginians went to the amphitheater to participate in a public event. They were people behaving normally, thousands of them,

28. Beck, "Religious Market," 248.

29. Candida R. Moss, *Ancient Christian Martyrdom: Diverse Practices, Theologies, and Tradition* (New Haven: Yale University Press, 2012), 137–38.

30. *Senatusconsultum* of 176 or 177, in *CIL* 2:6278; discussed in Kate Cooper, "A Father, a Daughter, and a Procurator: Authority and Resistance in the Prison Diary of Perpetua of Carthage," *Gender and History* 23, no. 1 (2011): 696–97.

acting according to local custom and habitus. They went to the arena to be entertained, to pay honor to the emperor and the local aristocrats, to get food and drink, to watch their equivalent of football on New Year's Day. They anticipated no surprises. The animals would gore each other, the gladiators would fight skillfully and die well, and the dehumanized criminals would cringe before being dispatched by an animal's teeth or the executioner's sword. The day's events would confirm the society's vertical values and degrade those who in some way threatened them.

Into this world came something unanticipated. As the onlookers peered into the arena, they—benefactors and ordinary citizens—saw criminals who were not hardwired as the dominant society was. They saw people—Christians— who embodied uncommon allegiances and responded with inexplicable reflexes. As a result, the Christians behaved in ways that subverted the carefully choreographed planning of the birthday party and profoundly challenged the values on which it was based. Because of the Christians' presence, the liturgy of the games did not bind all of society together—there was a group, bound together by a *superstitio*, that embodied an unsettling alternative. According to an account of the day's activities that has survived in the *Passion of Saints Perpetua and Felicitas*, the crowds who observed this were emotionally engaged; they oscillated between intrigue, fury, attraction, and revulsion. The Christians involved did not view the onlookers' fascination as strange. In the words of the theologian Origen fifty years later, the Christians viewed it as an occasion on which they intentionally [went] "in procession before the world."[31]

The *Passion of Saints Perpetua and Felicitas* (henceforth *Passion*) is a lengthy account of public witness of these women and other members of a Christian community in the Carthage amphitheater.[32] The largest portion of the account (chaps. 3–10) is devoted to Perpetua's prison memoir and visions—the most substantial example of writing by a Christian woman until the 380s. Saturus, the community's catechist, contributes chapters 11–13, including a vision, and chapter 15 deals with Felicitas. The *Passion* concludes with six chapters in which an anonymous narrator retells the story of the public events in the amphitheater in which Perpetua and Saturus were not writers but protagonists.

The six Christians named in chapters 16 to 21 were members of a Christian community in the small town of Thuburbo Minus, thirty-five miles west of

---

31. Origen, *Mart.* 42; Robin Darling Young, *In Procession before the World: Martyrdom as Public Liturgy in Early Christianity* (Milwaukee: Marquette University Press, 2001), 14.

32. I use the translation of Maureen A. Tilley, "The Passion of Saints Perpetua and Felicity," in *Religions of Late Antiquity in Practice*, ed. Richard Valantasis, Princeton Readings in Religions (Princeton: Princeton University Press, 2000), 387–97; the Latin text is in *The Acts of the Christian Martyrs*, trans. and ed. Herbert A. Musurillo (Oxford: Clarendon, 1972), 106–31.

Carthage.[33] According to the *Passion*, all of them were catechumens preparing for baptism, which they received while in prison,[34] except for their catechist Saturus, who joined them in captivity. All were young (*adolescentes*); Perpetua was twenty-one. Two of them, including Felicitas, were slaves. Except for Perpetua, they were apparently all from society's lower orders, *humiliores*. Perpetua in contrast was *honeste nata* (well born). It is not likely that she was from an elite family; the procurator's humiliating beating of her father tells against that.[35] But the lucidity of her writing and the confidence of her bearing point toward her being at least from the lower reaches of the province's upper class.[36]

The final day's activities begin with the Christians marching into the amphitheater.[37] They had already spent some weeks in prison; this would have given them time to plan how they would behave when in the spotlight. It is likely that they decided to defy conventional stereotypes by behaving confidently, without cringing—they would march into the arena purposefully and joyously. Perpetua, whose gaze "stared down the spectators," could have planned to behave in this way, or her behavior could have been reflexive.[38] The prisoners may have decided that, if they got the chance, they would behave undeferentially toward the procurator Hilarianus. We know that when the Christians fervently prayed for Felicitas to give birth, she did so *statim*, immediately, two days before the events in the amphitheater;[39] they wanted Felicitas to be with them as they gave not solitary witness but witness together.

But there were things the Christians could not prepare for. As they filed into the amphitheater, they didn't know what to expect. They had to improvise. So when the choreographers demanded that they put on costumes, the male Christians as priests of the god Saturn and women Christians as priestesses of the goddess Ceres, their objection must have been instinctive. They would not be deprived of their own identity; they would not be cast as pagan hierophants in the religious dimension of the games. Perpetua spoke for them all: "Now we came here of our own will, so our freedom might not

33. See the Greek recension of the *Passion of Perpetua* 2.1, in Brent D. Shaw, "The Passion of Perpetua," *Past and Present* 139 (May 1993): 10n.

34. *Passion* 3.5.

35. *Passion* 6.5.

36. Walter Ameling, "*Femina Liberaliter Instituta*—Some Thoughts on a Martyr's Liberal Education," in *Perpetua's Passions: Multidisciplinary Approaches to the "Passio Perpetuae et Felicitatis,"* ed. Jan N. Bremmer and Marco Formisano (Oxford: Oxford University Press, 2012), 84; Shaw, "Passion of Perpetua," 11; cf. Cooper, "A Father, a Daughter," 696.

37. *Passion* 18.1.

38. *Passion* 18.2 (Tilley, 395).

39. *Passion* 15.5.

be constrained."[40] In the face of their noncooperative approach, the tribune relented. Later when Perpetua and Felicitas were both stunned after being tossed by the cow (the female animal that had been provoked to kill them, as women), Perpetua woke up, went to Felicitas, raised her up, and the two stood side by side—a patrician and a slave reflexively and highly visibly expressing Christian horizontality.[41]

The Christians communicated corporeally, bodily. They could not control what was going on around them, but they could be themselves. They were rarely given the opportunity to make speeches, and even when someone invited them to speak, they were likely to refuse.[42] Their word was in their bodies, individually and communally. They were in the arena, a world in which customarily each person would fend for himself or herself, fighting alone against gladiators or animals; but the Christians in contrast embodied commonality. In the amphitheater they were in a societal and architectural setting that loudly asserted verticality, but their bodies expressed horizontality. In a world that gave prime place to genetic family, they called each other "sister" and "brother," whom they indicated by habitual gestures to be primary family—family they loved passionately and were willing to die for. According to the Dutch historian of the ancient world Jan Bremmer, "We will never be able to understand the rise of Christianity if we do not take into account such intense feelings, as we never hear of them in members of other contemporary pagan cults and religions."[43]

The *Passion* records occasions in which crowds of outsiders, the *populus*, interact with the Christians. Early in the account, when Hilarianus sentenced the prisoners, a huge crowd gathered in the forum to watch.[44] A later occasion occurred on the night before the games. As the Christians celebrated their *libera*, their last meal, the *populus* was present looking on. The Christians, for whom this was an *agapē* meal of worship and fellowship, looked up, saw the outsiders, and addressed them—expressing their joy in suffering, warning them of God's judgment, and inviting them the next day to recognize them in the amphitheater. The outsiders apparently found the emotional tugs of this occasion to be bewildering, and—the *Passion* reports—"many of them came to believe."[45]

40. *Passion* 18.5 (Tilley, 395).
41. *Passion* 20.6.
42. See, e.g., Mart. Pol. 10.2.
43. Jan N. Bremmer, "Felicitas: The Martyrdom of a Young African Woman," in Bremmer and Formisano, *Perpetua's Passions*, 42.
44. *Passion* 6.1.
45. *Passion* 17.1–3 (Tilley, 395).

On the following day in the amphitheater, three of the Christian men for unspecified reasons began to warn the "onlooking *populus*."[46] When all the Christian prisoners filed past Procurator Hilarianus, the Christians, instead of expressing fear of death or respect for the emperor's representatives, used gestures that everyone could see. The gestures indicated what they saw as the outcome of the justice of God and their own patience—"What you do to us, God will do to you." This time the Christians' visual communications enraged the crowd, who demanded that the people who threatened of judgment be scourged by a line of gladiators.[47]

But soon the crowd's mood shifted again. When Perpetua and Felicitas were stripped naked and the provoked cow tossed them, the crowd recoiled in horror. These two women were suffering, Perpetua delicate and young, and Felicitas "immediately post-partum with milk still leaking from her breasts."[48] So at the crowd's demand the two women were brought back and dressed.

When the men suffered, the crowd's response was less sympathetic. When the catechist Saturus bled profusely after an attack by a leopard, the crowd responded with the rhythmic chant, "*Saluum lotum! Saluum lotum!* Had a great bath! Had a great bath!"[49] At the very end, after most of the Christians had been seriously wounded by the animals, the crowd's interest was clearly still lively, for they asked that all the Christians be brought to a central spot where they could see clearly as the gladiator's sword finished them off. They saw the executions; but they also saw the Christians mustering the strength of body and will to stand up, gather themselves as a group in the specified spot, and give a final embodied witness. These disparate people, women and men, slave and free, poor and advantaged, "kissed each other so that they might bring their martyrdom to completion with the kiss of peace."[50] Exhausted and in pain though they were, in extremis the prisoners did reflexively, virtually on autopilot, what they had been habituated to do in their services of worship—they exchanged the kiss of peace, embodying a love that transcended social barriers.

How did the pagan onlookers respond to the Christians' public witness? Probably most of them viewed the Christians' behavior in the amphitheater as distasteful, indicative of wild-eyed, uncultured enthusiasm. But the *Passion* reports that some members of the crowd found that the Christians had jarred them loose from former ways of thinking and living. The account tells

46. *Passion* 18.7 (Musurillo, 126).
47. *Passion* 18.8–9 (Tilley, 295–96).
48. *Passion* 20.2 (Tilley, 396).
49. *Passion* 21.2 (Musurillo, 128); Shaw, "Passion of Perpetua," 9.
50. *Passion* 21.7 (Tilley, 397).

us of one specific person who became a believer—the adjutant Pudens, the soldier who as commandant of the jail dealt with the prisoners intimately. Soon after the Christians were put in jail, Pudens began to treat them well because he observed that they had a "great power" (*magnam virtutem*) among them[51]—the power of courage, of visions and prayer, of the aura of God. Some weeks later Pudens had become a Christian.[52] And at the very end of the *Passion*, in the Christians' last minutes in the amphitheater before the sword dispatched them, Pudens managed to be with them. The catechist Saturus admonished Pudens, "Remember me, and remember the faith." Saturus asked Pudens for his ring, dipped it in his own blood, and gave it back to Pudens as a memento, a tangible expression of the faith they had begun to share.[53]

How was this habitus—this distinctive, reflexive, embodied expression of the faith—formed? What was it that shaped the African Christians so that they embodied the faith under pressure? There is so much about these Christians that we do not know: the content of the catechesis that Saturus taught them; the influence that big-city Carthage had on the thought and practice of believers in Thuburbo Minus; the willingness or unwillingness of churches in either town to allow catechumens to participate in the worship of churches that still met in houses.[54]

Of course, if we try to determine how the Christians learned, it's easier to talk about how ideas were transmitted than how habitus was formed. Walter Ameling writes helpfully on the transmission of ideas.[55] He contends that the teaching that happened was primarily not written but oral. He indicates that Perpetua and others quoted the Bible in a generalized way, which they had probably learned orally and memorized inaccurately. He finds Perpetua picking up phrases from Tertullian's writing, probably from oral communication, which she then used in her own writing. Perpetua also absorbed some of Tertullian's theological ideas—the imitation of Christ, the blessed reality of the afterlife, the presence of Christ to the suffering Christian, God's willingness

51. *Passion* 9.1 (Musurillo, 118).
52. *Passion* 16.4.
53. *Passion* 21.5–6 (Musurillo, 131).
54. In the *Passion of Perpetua* (10.13; 12.5; 21.8), the kiss of peace is a reflexive practice of Christians who have been baptized only recently while in prison, indicating the probability that they have become habituated to the practice as catechumens. Apparently this reflects a situation where the church's eucharistic meal was in the evening, with real food, at which catechumens seem to have been present. This scene differs from the morning, token-food Eucharist of the *Apostolic Tradition* 18.3, which restricts the kiss to the "faithful." See Paul F. Bradshaw, *Reconstructing Early Christian Worship* (Collegeville, MN: Liturgical Press, 2010), 23.
55. Walter Ameling, "*Femina Liberaliter Instituta*," 78–102.

to answer prayers in visions—but again these may be theological ideas that were widely shared among the African Christians. A telltale incident occurs at the time of Perpetua's baptism in prison. Able to request one baptismal favor from the Holy Spirit, she chooses *sufferentiam carnis*, patient endurance in the flesh—a theme of Tertullian's but also, as we have seen, an emphasis of the North African church (3.5).[56]

How, in the world of Perpetua, does patient endurance move from the realm of ideas to the embodied world of habitus? Let me propose four clues. One clue is role models who embody the message in attractive ways and impart it to others. In this account, the catechist Saturus stands out as a "spiritual leader" who encouraged Perpetua.[57] He came to the prison late—by his own choice to be with his catechumens and suffer death with them. In Perpetua's first vision and again in the arena, Saturus was the first one to move forward into suffering; according to Perpetua he "had been the builder of our strength," and he was still relating to her in that way at the end of her life (4.5; 21.8). So his and Perpetua's authoritative influence lay not only in their visions; it lay in the lives that embodied their visions. A second clue: the formation of habitus comes through the recitation of certain phrases that people can repeat day by day, and especially when they are in trouble. In the *Passion*, the phrase "I am a Christian" has tremendous importance.[58] As such it is typical of North African martyr accounts in general, where it becomes a leitmotif connoting an entire way of life, an entire value system, that was fundamentally contrary to the way of life embodied in the amphitheater.[59] A third clue: Christians can learn to embody distinctive approaches to difficult situations—even torture—by preparing themselves. Maureen Tilley has argued that Tertullian helped people in his network to get ready for prison by means of fasting and other ascetic practices.[60] In the *Passion* we watch as the Christians prayed and fasted in

---

56. Tertullian, *Paen.* 13; *Or.* 29.1; cf. Ameling, "*Femina Liberaliter Instituta*," 100. Perpetua and the *Passion* in general do not use the Latin word *patientia*.

57. Jan N. Bremmer, *The Rise of Christianity through the Eyes of Gibbon, Harnack and Rodney Stark* (Groningen: Barkhuis, 2010), 44.

58. *Passion* 3.2; 6.4.

59. Maureen A. Tilley, "The Ascetic Body and the (Un)Making of the World of the Martyr," *Journal of the American Academy of Religion* 59, no. 3 (1991): 470; Jan N. Bremmer, "'Christianus sum': The Early Christian Martyrs and Christ," in *Eulogia: Mélanges offert à Antoon A. R. Bastiaensen à l'occasion de son soixante-cinquième anniversaire*, ed. G. J. M. Bartelink, A. Hilhorst, and C. J. Kneepkens (The Hague: Nijhoff, 1991), 11–20.

60. Tilley, "Ascetic Body," 472–43. An example from Tertullian: "I am not so sure that the wrist which is always surrounded by a bracelet will be able to bear the hardness of chains with resignation; I have some doubts that the leg which now rejoices to wear an anklet will be able to bear the tight squeeze of an ankle chain; and I sometimes fear that the neck which is now

preparation for events that would test their toughness to the breaking point.[61] And a final clue: the worship of the Christian community, repeated week by week, shaped the worshipers' habitus by giving them kinesthetic as well as verbal habits. The *Passion* provides very little information about this, but it does mention two rites that were formative. The first of these we glimpse in the prisoners' last meal, which for the prisoners became a worship service at table, which for North African Christians in this period was both *agapē* and Eucharist.[62] The other, the kiss of peace, was "one of the most prevalent features of early Christianity." It is not surprising that the kiss keeps recurring throughout the *Passion* and is present at its conclusion—a reflexive ritual gesture in which the martyrs embody their faith and enact it in a way that subverts verticality.[63]

The mid-second-century author of the Epistle to Diognetus wrote this about the converting power of patient, embodied witness: "Do you not see how they are thrown to wild animals to make them deny the Lord, and how they are not vanquished? Do you not see that the more of them are punished, the more do others increase?"[64] Justin Martyr and Tertullian wrote in the same vein.[65] Historians have come to a similar judgment: "Every public execution was a great and often successful advocating opportunity for the church."[66] It was not primarily what the Christians said that carried weight with outsiders; it was what they did and embodied that was both disconcerting and converting. It was their habitus—their reflexes and ways of life that suggested that there was another way to perceive reality—that made the Christians interesting, challenging, and worth investigating.[67]

---

laden with strings of pearls and emeralds will give no room to the executioner's sword" (*Cult. fem.* 2.13.4, trans. E. A. Quain, FC 40 [1959], 148).

61. M. Therese Lysaught, "Witnessing Christ in Their Bodies: Martyrs and Ascetics as Doxological Disciples," *Annual of the Society of Christian Ethics* 20 (2000): 247–48.

62. Andrew McGowan, "Rethinking Agape and Eucharist in Early North African Christianity," *SL* 34 (2004): 165–76.

63. *Passion of Perpetua* 10.13; 12.5; 21.8; Michael Philip Penn, *Kissing Christians: Ritual and Community in the Late Ancient Church* (Philadelphia: University of Pennsylvania Press, 2005), 2.

64. *Diogn.* 7.8, trans. E. R. Fairweather, *Early Christian Fathers*, ed. C. C. Richardson, LCC 1 (1953), 219.

65. Tertullian, *Apol.* 50.15; Justin, *2 Apol.* 6.6 (5.6); Lactantius, *Inst.* 5.22.18–19.

66. Wolfgang Reinbold, *Propaganda und Mission im ältesten Christentum: Eine Untersuchung zu den Modalitäten der Ausbreitung der frühen Kirche*, FRLANT 188 (Göttingen: Vandenhoek & Ruprecht, 2000), 314. Cf. Everett Ferguson's assessment that the martyrdoms were "the best advertising available"; see his article "Early Christian Martyrdom and Civil Disobedience," *JECS* 1 (1993): 76.

67. A Maryknoll priest, William Frazier, has observed, based on twentieth-century experience, that "the way faithful Christians die is the most contagious aspect of what being a Christian means." Cited in David Bosch, *Transforming Mission* (Maryknoll, NY: Orbis Books, 1991), 122.

Private Associations

The second genre is the private religious association. The religious life of the Roman Empire in the second century was complex, with a wide range of religious organizations that provided services that complemented each other. Civic cults, such as those we have been examining, had observances throughout the year that followed a schedule of customary festivities and imperial holidays; participation in these was widespread and had immense social and cultural power. But people also looked to other categories of organizations to meet their social and religious needs. One of these categories was that of the private clubs or associations, commonly called *collegia* or *hetaeria*. These took many forms. Some were primarily social, for craft or professional groups—shop owners, firemen, sailors; some focused on providing respectable burials for members; some were especially focused on the worship of a particular god. Whatever their primary intents, the associations almost always combined social, burial, and religious functions. They had deep attractions: they provided their adherents with face-to-face relationships and a vastly greater sense of participation and responsibility than the public cults could offer. Because the associations were private, the imperial authorities at times viewed them as places where subversive movements festered. Early in the second century Trajan for a time banned all *collegia*.[68] Subsequent imperial authorities were willing to allow their existence, but they kept a wary eye on them and restricted them to one meeting per month.[69] Despite this restriction, in the second and third centuries the *collegia* were flourishing across the Roman Empire.

The private associations have been seen as the area of Roman social organization that provided the closest parallel to Christian assemblies.[70] But questions about the associations arise. What was their role in their local societies and their attraction to their neighbors? What areas of dissonance and dissatisfaction within them at times pushed people to explore other groupings, including the Christians? And what relationships and activities within the Christian groups at times pulled association members toward them? Let us look at two examples with certain parallels: a second-century society in Lanuvium and a Christian community in Carthage, both of which addressed the personal and status-indicative issue of burial.

68. Pliny the Younger, *Ep.* 10.96.7.
69. "Regulations of the Worshippers of Diana and Antinoüs," AD 136, Lanuvium, in *Associations in the Greco-Roman World: A Sourcebook*, ed. Richard S. Ascough, Philip A. Harland, and John S. Kloppenborg (Waco: Baylor University Press, 2012), 195.
70. Robert Wilken, *The Christians as the Romans Saw Them* (New Haven: Yale University Press, 1984), 47.

A Burial Society in Lanuvium, AD 136

The Association of Diana and Antinoüs was founded in AD 136 in the town of Lanuvium thirty kilometers southeast of Rome. We know of it because in that year a marble plaque with an inscription of the association's constitution was placed in a wall of the town's temple of Antinoüs, where all the town's residents could see it—and from which archaeologists could retrieve it to inform us.[71] The plaque tells about the association's founding. A local patron, Lucius Casennius, wanted to foster the worship of Diana, the goddess of the hunt, and Antinoüs, a hero and lover recently deified by Emperor Hadrian. Working with other family members, he bequeathed a small endowment to a *collegium* to provide annually 800 *sestertii* (HS), approximately a laborer's income for 200 to 266 days.[72] This benefaction enabled the *collegium* to honor Diana and Antinoüs and also to pay for the funerals of its members. It further subvented the *collegium*'s monthly meetings, lubricating their friendships and conviviality with food and good wine.

According to the constitution, it was not hard to join the *collegium*. A prospective member must first read the constitution; with that knowledge he could join the association "so as not to find cause for complaint later or bequeath a lawsuit" to his heir. It was sufficient preparation for the prospective member to know what he was getting into, so he must be able to read; he could be either slave or free, but he had to be a male. The constitution prescribes no behavior that the candidate must master or ideas that he must learn, and it specifies no initiation rite that he must undergo. But the candidate, whether free or slave, must have money. The Lanuvium association's entry fee was lower than some, but even so, at HS 100 plus an amphora of good wine, it was substantial. According to one recent study, 65 percent of the populace across the Empire were either at or below the subsistence level and thus could not afford to join a burial society that cost this much.[73] The new member also committed himself to pay

71. The translation of the constitution is from Ascough, Harland, and Kloppenborg, *Associations in the Greco-Roman World*, 194–98. For its Latin text, see Andreas Bendlin, "Associations, Funerals, Sociality, and Roman Law: The *Collegium* of Diana and Antinoüs in Lanuvium (*CIL* 14:2112) Reconsidered," in *Aposteldekret und antikes Vereinswesen: Gemeinschaft und ihre Ordnung*, ed. Markus Öhler (Tübingen: Mohr Siebeck, 2011), 210–12; I discovered Bendlin's study too late to use it in this chapter. For comment on the Lanuvium association, see Wilken, *Christians as the Romans Saw Them*, 35–40.

72. A sestertius was equivalent to between one-quarter and one-third of a laborer's daily pay. See Ramsay MacMullen and Eugene N. Lane, eds., *Paganism and Christianity, 100–425 C.E.: A Sourcebook* (Minneapolis: Fortress, 1992), 67.

73. See Scheidel and Friesen, "Size of the Economy," 84, who provide an "optimistic" scenario of the civilian gross income distribution in the Roman Empire as a whole (table 9). According to their estimates, 10 percent of the populace were constantly food-insecure (i.e., they lived below the subsistence level); 55 percent lived perilously close to a "bare bones" subsistence level (in bad years they could fall below subsistence); 19 percent were poor but relatively secure;

monthly dues of one-third *sestertius*, which somewhat added to the burden. If the member kept up with his monthly dues, when he died the association would pay his funeral expenses to the hefty sum of HS 300 (about three months' wages), and mourning members of the association would march in his procession and stand by his pyre. If he died more than twenty miles from Lanuvium and the association learned of this, it would send members to take care of his funeral, paying their expenses. And if he died more than twenty miles from Lanuvium without the association having been informed of his death and a local person buried him, the association was to pay this person the costs of the obsequies—provided that seven Roman citizens had verified the accounts to be sure that no fraud has been committed. The constitution provides less information about the *collegium*'s social and religious life than about its burials. It specifies monthly dinners and gives dates and memorial and religious associations of six of these. When a slave in the association is freed, he is to contribute a celebratory amphora of good wine to the monthly meeting. Yearly a chairman (*magister*) was chosen to preside at these based on a rota of the association's members. Four members were to assist by providing amphoras of good wine,[74] loaves of bread, four sardines per member, and hot water. The chairman was to preside benevolently, making sure that the conversation at the meals was "in peace and good cheer." Those chosen as rotating directors of the association, like its secretary and sergeant-at-arms, were to be immune from dues and to receive double portions in the association's occasional distributions. The constitution's final clauses prescribe its religious activities. On solemn days the association's directors, dressing themselves in white, were to make solemn offerings with incense and wine, and on the feasts of Diana and Antinoüs they were to place oil in the public baths in the gods' honor.

A particular characteristic of the constitution is its self-protective feel. The founders were aware that there were many ways things could go wrong.

- *Nonpayment of dues*: Members were to pay their monthly dues, but in some years they could not do so. They were at the mercy of an

---

around 12 percent were a "middling" sector; and under 2 percent constituted an economic elite. In towns there was typically a broader distribution of wealth than in the countryside, and between one-eighth and one-quarter of the urban populace were in the "middling" category, but "subsistence-level households must have formed a solid majority even in urban settings" (ibid., 84, 85, 90). Cf. Bruce W. Longenecker, "Socio-Economic Profiling of the First Urban Christians," in *After the First Urban Christians: The Social Scientific Study of Pauline Christianity Twenty-Five Years Later*, ed. Todd D. Still and David G. Horrell (London: T&T Clark, 2009), 44–45.

74. Three times the Lanuvium constitution requires the provision of "good wine," which may indicate that the association had some members who were struggling economically and might find it hard to provide wine that was good enough.

agricultural economy dependent on harvests. According to the constitution, if a member failed to pay dues for six consecutive months, he would be dropped from the rolls; when "the common lot of humankind befalls him, his claim to burial shall not be considered," and his burial would be the best that his relatives, if he had any, could arrange. At worst, the dying ex-member would be thrown into a mass burial pit where there might be "predatory post-mortem attacks of dogs and birds."[75] Punishment for a richer member's default was less drastic. If a chairman (*magister*) in his year of rotation defaulted on paying for the association's dinner, he would pay a fine of ten days' wages (HS 30).

- *Withholding the corpse of a slave*: Even if slaveholders "unreasonably" withheld the body of a slave belonging to the association, the association would hold obsequies for the slave—"a funeral with an image of him will be held."

- *Fraud*: The founders had a well-developed fear of fraud. When members were sent to supervise the obsequies of a member twenty miles from Lanuvium, they were ordered to render an account "in good faith." If the association found them "guilty of any fraud" they were to pay a fourfold fine. Security must be given that no one would claim excessive sums. "Let no bad faith attend!"

- *Misbehavior at dinner*: The constitution specified several kinds of misbehavior, and for each it prescribed a fine suitable to the offense. For a member causing a disturbance at dinner by moving from one seat to another, the fine was HS 4; for "speaking abusively of another" or "causing an uproar" the fine was HS 12. The largest fine (HS 20) was levied on those who spoke insultingly of the president.

The constitution of the Association of Diana and Antinoüs provided, in its marble plaque which all of Lanuvium's literate people could read, a structure for an organization that addressed recognized needs in the town's small society—burial, conviviality, and religion. Religion, about which the constitution is least explicit, seems to have suffused all of the association's activities. The association addressed these needs in ways that were reasonable. At times, as in its treatment of slaves, it may have bent local values in the direction of compassion; it rejoiced in their manumission, and it provided obsequies for slave members despite their masters' "unreasonable" blockage. But in general,

---

75. John Bodel, "Dealing with the Dead: Undertakers, Executioners and Potter's Fields in Ancient Rome," in *Death and Disease in the Ancient City*, ed. Valerie M. Hope and Eireann Marshall (London: Routledge, 2000), 129.

its rules represented local common sense; they embodied the local habitus. For example, the constitution treats all members on the basis of strict equality. The constitution also recognizes its members' propensities, as humans, to fraudulence in finance and, as people who enjoy draining an amphora of wine, to turbulence at dinners; and it controls these in ways that seem justifiable.

In all of this, the association of Diana and Antinoüs stood with other institutions in the small-town life of Lanuvium. For locals who had sufficient resources to join and pay their dues, it provided useful resources. It was one of many religious and social institutions in society that worked together to sustain the life of local people and to form their habitus. We do not have information about how the people in Lanuvium viewed the association. Nevertheless, we do know that in other cities some people struggled with the limitations of comparable associations. As a result of this, they were ready to consider alternative assemblies, formed by a cluster of teachings and reflexes rooted in Jesus Christ, which affirmed that a habitus, venerable and apparently immutable though it was, not only should be changed but could change.

The Christian Association in Carthage: Tertullian, Apology 39

In North Africa, more than a half century after the founding of the Lanuvium burial association, the Christian theologian Tertullian wrote his *Apology*. In it Tertullian ranges widely, dealing with many issues and concerns; but throughout he is interested not only in the Christians' ideas but also in the ways they embodied them. At the heart of the *Apology* is chapter 39, in which Tertullian describes the local assemblies in which the Christians gather.[76] The words that he uses for these—*factio, corpus, secta*—are words commonly used for private associations such as the *collegium* in Lanuvium.[77] Tertullian presents the Christian assemblies in terms that non-Christian readers would recognize; he attempts to establish common ground. But Tertullian is also interested in differentiating the Christian assemblies from the *collegia*. He does this especially by looking, not at the written constitutions of the groups, but at the configuration of activities, customs, and reflexes that constitutes the groups' habitus. The ways Christians behave, Tertullian is convinced, are their most articulate statements. As he puts it on the last page of his *Apology*, Christians "teach by deeds."[78] So how did the Christian associations look when compared to the pagan associations?

76. For the Latin text and English translation of Tertullian's *Apology*, see T. R. Glover, LCL 250 (1931), 2–227.
77. Wilken, *Christians as the Romans Saw Them*, 46.
78. Tertullian, *Apol.* 50.16 (Glover, 227).

In chapter 39 Tertullian presents the Christian association's *negotia*— its proceedings. At the heart of these proceedings are meetings specifically dedicated to religious activities. Tertullian does not say how often these took place, but the meetings were certainly more frequent than in the typical *collegium* whose meetings took place monthly or on "festive days" or members' birthdays. The Carthage Christians' meetings are vastly more intense than those in Lanuvium. At their core is prayer, in which the members together approach God, struggle with God, and even "do violence [*vis*]" to God that he may grant their requests. In their prayers they implore God not only for their own concerns but also for the concerns of the world—for example, for the emperor, for peace on earth, and for "postponement of the end."[79] They read "the books of God," which, Tertullian says, gives them perspective on "the nature of the times" and increases their hope and confidence. Central to their teaching is the *disciplina praeceptorum*, "discipline of the precepts," by which Tertullian indicates that they are internalizing the teachings of Christ.[80] Their gatherings are marked by the maintenance of discipline—teaching about behavior, the correction of misbehavior, even the exclusion of those who do not live according to the community's standards (not of those who cannot pay their monthly dues). Overseeing these meetings are the "presidents," who are chosen, not as in a pagan association by rota or "for a price," but because of their maturity and character. In contrast to the pagan associations (and Tertullian likes to point out these contrasts), "nothing that is God's goes for a price."[81]

This pricelessness governs the Christian associations' handling of money. Like the Lanuvium burial association, the Carthage Christians must solicit money on a monthly basis; in contrast to the civic cults, these private associations do not have rich benefactors who support their activities, and they rely on regular donations from the ordinary people who are their members. The pagan associations precisely stipulate the entrance fees and monthly maintenance fees that are equal for all members. The Christian assemblies, according to Tertullian, have a different approach. They do not restrict membership to people who can meet certain financial requirements, and they do not make continuing membership contingent upon paying a set monthly fee.[82] Instead, their emphasis is on the members' voluntary contributions; members pay

79. Tertullian, *Apol.* 39.2 (Glover, 175).
80. Tertullian, *Apol.* 39.3 (Glover, 175). See *praecepta* elsewhere in Tertullian, where they clearly refer to the teachings of Christ: e.g., *Or.* 3.4; 9.1, 26; *Pat.* 3.11; 7.1; 10.3.
81. Tertullian, *Apol.* 39.4 (Glover, 175).
82. Tertullian does not here describe the demanding formational requirements that Christian candidates [catechumens] must meet; for these, see chap. 6 below.

if they can and pay only as much as they can afford. "Nobody," Tertullian insists, "is compelled." What the Christians contribute is placed in an *arca*, a "chest," from which monies are disbursed (evidently by the community's leaders) to sustain the ministries of the association. Among these ministries, burying people figures prominently; like the Lanuvium association, the Christian assembly is a burial association.

But according to Tertullian, the Christians do not bury only members who pay their subscriptions; they also bury members who could never pay or who have ceased to be able to pay—the "poor." The presidents respond to these poor people, not by lopping them off the membership rolls if harvests fail or if they lose their jobs, but by providing care for them. The respectful burial of all members, poor as well as those who are less precariously situated, is only one part of the Christian assembly's vision of care for its members, who find themselves with a wide variety of needs.[83] The Christians further provide for other people in need—"for boys and girls who lack property and parents, and then for slaves grown old and ship-wrecked mariners; and for any who may be in mines, islands or prisons," and so on. The social ministries of the Christian assemblies are wide-ranging, reflecting their memberships, which, even in times of persecution, seem to be growing in size and in socioeconomic diversity.[84]

The Christians' economic behavior, Tertullian contends, is visible to their neighbors. "*Vide*," the neighbors say, "look!" The Christians' meetings may be private, but their effects can be seen in people's lives. According to Tertullian, the neighbors are attracted to this and attribute it to the Christians' love for each other: "how they love one another . . . and how they are ready to die for each other." Tertullian sees the Christians' behavior as the product of conversion, which has made them "brothers." The apologist Tertullian cannot resist claiming that the Christians' behavior differs from that of the pagans. The Christian brotherhood (*fraternitas*) is upheld by the community's resources, whereas in pagan circles the family's resources "as a rule dissolve the fraternal tie."[85]

The primary meeting of the Christian associations was a meal. In this they resembled the pagan associations, but their secretive quality led to wild rumors. Their neighbors were suspicious of the cannibalism and sexual license that

---

83. Until the fourth century, the Christian assemblies do not seem to have owned burial properties; private Christian patrons provided burials for Christians. In the charitable activity of burying the poor, Christian women often took the lead. See Carolyn Osiek, "Roman and Christian Burial Practices," in *Commemorating the Dead: Texts and Artifacts in Context; Studies of Roman, Jewish, and Christian Burials*, ed. Laurie Brink and Deborah Green (Berlin: de Gruyter, 2008), 245, 263.

84. Tertullian, *Apol.* 39.5–6 (Glover, 175–77).

85. Tertullian, *Apol.* 39.7–10 (Glover, 177).

they thought went on in the meal, and the Christians may inadvertently have encouraged this by calling their meal "love"—*agapē* (*dilectio*).[86] In Carthage around AD 200 these *agapē* meals were "the central liturgical event of the community." They took place in the evenings at least weekly and were occasions on which the community ate the sacral food called "eucharist" and experienced the intensification of its common life.[87] Tertullian reports that these were real meals in which participants ate ordinary, nontoken food in modest quantities according to circumstance and in order to meet need: "With God there is greater consideration for those of lower degree."[88] Before the meal there was a prayer of blessing, and after the meal there was a time of spontaneous worship that may have been a Christian adaptation of the Roman after-dinner *symposium*.[89] According to Christian conventions, no one during the meal was to eat or drink too much, because during the *symposium* lucidity might be required of any member who was asked to contribute to the worship: "Each [member], from what he knows of the Holy Scriptures, or from his own heart, is called before the rest to sing to God." In this face-to-face setting the Spirit might empower any member to contribute to the upbuilding of the entire community regardless of their education or wealth. This multivoiced participation intensified the sense of family identity and gave substance to the notion that the community was a family of "brothers." After the prayer that brought the *symposium* to a conclusion, the Christians made their way home knowing that they had "dined not so much on dinner as on discipline."[90]

Did what Tertullian describes in this famous passage amount to a habitus shift for Carthaginian people? Did the Christian assembly provide a matrix within which the character and reflexes of people could be transformed? Throughout his *Apology* Tertullian claims that it did. The Christian assembly, in contrast to the pagan private associations, was a setting in which people are corrected, reformed.[91] "We are from among yourselves," Tertullian exults. "Christians are made, not born."[92] Christians are no longer like pagans; their habitus is changed.

How did this change happen? In chapter 39 Tertullian indicates that it took place in a particular setting—the Christian associations (churches). These

---

86. As in Jude 12.
87. McGowan, "Rethinking Agape and Eucharist," 168–69; Paul F. Bradshaw and Maxwell E. Johnson, *The Eucharistic Liturgies: Their Evolution and Interpretation* (Collegeville, MN: Liturgical Press, 2012), 31.
88. Tertullian, *Apol.* 39.16 (Glover, 181).
89. Bradshaw and Johnson, *Eucharistic Liturgies*, 31–32.
90. Tertullian, *Apol.* 39.16–19 (Glover, 181).
91. Tertullian, *Apol.* 3.3–4.
92. Tertullian, *Apol.* 18.4 (Glover, 91).

differed from pagan associations in part by the sheer density of their common life. They met much more frequently—not monthly but at least weekly, and often throughout the week as well. The Christian assembly was not one of a palette of social commitments of an urban Roman; it was the center of the Christians' lives. It was not one aspect of a varied religious life; it *was* their religious life. The Christians were creating an alternative community that had nonconformist approaches to common social problems and that imparted to its participants a powerful sense of individual and group identity. This had immense formative power.

The church's members, whatever their social origin, sensed themselves to be a new family—brothers and sisters. "How much more fittingly are those both called brothers and treated as brothers who have come to know one Father God, who have drunk of one spirit of holiness, who from one womb of common ignorance have come with wonder to the one light of truth!"[93] The community members were of varied social origins and wealth. Many, probably most, of the family were poor. "Most of us are poor," the contemporary North African apologist Minucius Felix asserted.[94] Of course, some family members were literate and had some financial resources. But by welcoming the 65 percent of the empire's population who were living near or below the subsistence level, the Christian churches opened themselves to growth in a way that would have seemed grossly irresponsible to the founders of the Lanuvium association.

Of course, the Christian family was not defined by the vertical values of the wider society; it was horizontal in its solidarity, making all its members brothers. And sisters too—its membership, unlike the Lanuvium association, included women as well as men. As we shall see in chapter 6, entering the church was difficult, but the difficulty was not financial; it was ethical and moral. It required a period of formation that lasted for considerable periods of time and that changed the candidates' thought and reflexes. This ethical and formational process was as open to poorer people as to wealthier ones. Once admitted, the members knew they belonged to a community in which their contributions were important and whose sharing mechanisms would be there to feed and clothe them if they lost their livelihoods. We do not know to what extent the prospect of economic security was a "pull" for prospective Christians, but it must have been this for some.[95]

93. Tertullian, *Apol.* 39.9 (Glover, 177).
94. "*Plerique pauperes*," in Minucius Felix, *Oct.* 36.2, trans. G. H. Rendall, LCL 250 (1931), 425.
95. Wayne Meeks, *The Origins of Christian Morality: The First Two Centuries* (New Haven: Yale University Press, 1993), 213.

The Christian association's meetings evidently had another appeal—the sense of the presence of God. Tertullian's writing captures the expectant, nonroutine aura of the Christian meetings. The meetings were occasions in which members prayed, "massing their forces" to wrestle with God in prayer. As Tertullian comments in his treatise *On Prayer* (29), the Christians did not distinguish between spiritual and economic/social topics in their prayers; they prayed passionately for divine provision and protection as they encountered sickness, temptation, poverty, and demonic possession. In their precarious daily lives they sensed themselves able to survive only if God was real to them and answered their prayers. In their *agapē*/eucharistic meals they shared food in God's presence, and then after the meal, in the symposium, they experienced the rich and varied work of the Spirit through many of the members. "Each one" could bring a Scripture passage, a testimony, a song. This was the setting in which members uttered prophecies and spoke of visions which in North Africa were a "normal part of the Christian life."[96] The community's worship was designed to empower all members and to give them a sense of their worth that expressed itself in courageous living and bold testimony. According to their reports, in their times of worship the Holy Spirit could do surprising things, moving them by evidences of the numinous in their midst. Worship was the energizing core of the Christians' life, the source of their buoyancy that contrasted so strongly with the protective defensiveness of the Lanuvium *collegium*. Amid conventional North African society, Christians were able to embody an alternative habitus because they were convinced that they experienced God's energizing reality.

But what the outsiders saw was not their worship. It was their habitus. According to Tertullian, the outsiders looked at the Christians and saw them energetically feeding poor people and burying them, caring for boys and girls who lacked property and parents, and being attentive to aged slaves and prisoners. They interpreted these actions as a "work of love." And they said, "*Vide*, look! How they love one another."[97] They did not say, "*Aude*, listen to the Christians' message"; they did not say, "*Lege*, read what they write." Hearing and reading were important, and some early Christians worked to communicate in these ways too. But we must not miss the reality: the pagans said *look*! Christianity's truth was visible; it was embodied and enacted by its members. It was made tangible, sacramental. Some people—a minority in society, no doubt, but a small number that was growing—were drawn by

---

96. Cecil M. Robeck Jr., *Prophecy in Carthage: Perpetua, Tertullian, and Cyprian* (Cleveland: Pilgrim Press, 1992), 2.

97. Tertullian, *Apol.* 39.7 (Glover, 177).

this to approach the Christians to inquire about their faith. Attracted by the Christians' habitus, people may have asked about their own associations' approach to poor people. (Is it right to cut people off when they experience economic reverse? If I lose my livelihood, what will happen to me when I die?) Moved by the Christians' embodied love for each other, people may have asked about the possibility of experiencing this themselves. Intrigued by Christians in whom God's powerful presence is evident, people may have wondered whether they could experience God too. Could they approach the secretive church to get in on a good thing? The Carthaginian Christians' habitus drew people toward faith.

Religion in Response to Crisis

The third genre of religion entails activities that enable people to hear the words of gods or God as they apply to the welfare of a city. A way of illustrating this is to examine how pagans and Christians responded to a threat—a plague—that affected the entire society. The epidemics that broke out in the Roman Empire in the second and third centuries were a huge threat, and the ways people responded to these are illuminating.

In ancient society (and into the early modern world) a plague, although often dormant, loomed in the fears of people. At times these fears were actualized when outbreaks of plague spread through entire societies with catastrophic results. In our period the two great plagues were the Antonine Plague of 166–72 and the so-called Plague of Cyprian of 251–ca. 270. It's not clear what these plagues' diseases were, or how many deaths they resulted in. Scholars speculate that the former plague was an outbreak of smallpox, and the latter of measles. In a world without good hygiene and antibiotics, both plagues killed many people. How many died in the plagues is a matter of debate. Some scholars maintain that the Antonine Plague killed 2 percent of the imperial population; others argue for a death toll of 25 percent or more.[98] A death toll somewhere between the two extremes is reasonable. But even if the death toll were "only" 2 percent of the population, across the empire more than a million people would have died, and a vastly larger number of people would have been seriously ill. Pagans and Christians agreed that the suffering

---

98. Cf. Christer Bruun, "The Antonine Plague and the 'Third-Century Crisis,'" in *Crises and the Roman Empire: Proceedings of the Seventh Workshop of the International Network Impact of Empire (Nijmegen, June 20–24, 2006)*, ed. Olivier Hekster, Gerda de Kleijn, and Danielle Slootjes (Leiden: Brill, 2007), 201–17. Also Walter C. Scheidel, "A Model of Demographic and Economic Change in Roman Egypt after the Antonine Plague," *Journal of Roman Archaeology* 15 (2002): 97–114.

was immense. An utterance of the oracle at Claros in the 160s conveys the distress of the plague:

> Woe, Woe! A strong calamity attacks on the ground—a pervasive, unyielding plague is slaying—(with) on the one hand, a punishing sword in hand, and on the other hand, raising the lately wounded ghosts of the bitterly lamented mortals. And it distresses the entire land of the enclosed city, cutting down animals, making an end of an entire generation; oppressing with defilement, it forces mortals out.[99]

How should people respond to this "pervasive, unyielding plague"? To this question, pagans and Christians gave different answers.

Pagan—the Oracles of Apollo

In Asia Minor as well as other parts of the empire, in times of crisis people turned to oracles for advice and comfort. Although no oracular texts survive from the plague of the 250s, many do from the Antonine Plague of the 160s, and these are illuminating.[100] Cities sought advice about how to cope with the crisis of the plague by sending delegations to famous oracular shrines at Claros, Didyma, and Delphi. Located in situations of natural beauty, each of them possessed an aura of divine immediacy. The inquiring visitors came to them from great distances, frequented their altars, marveled at the colossal statues of Apollo and other gods, and conversed with priests. At the right moment, on auspicious nights while a priest was sacrificing to the gods on a great altar, a prophet entered into a sacred space under the earth, where he heard the allusive and ambiguous words of Zeus's spokesman Apollo. The prophet reported these words to a *thespode* (poet), who converted them into intricately constructed poetry that addressed the questions that the delegates had brought to the oracle. After the delegates had paid substantial fees, they returned to their city with divine guidance for their situations.[101]

The delegates came to a shrine such as Claros with urgent questions: Why has this disastrous plague struck our city? What can we do to rid ourselves of the problem? Since the delegates customarily attributed a disaster to the anger of the gods, they wanted to know which god had been angered and what their city had done to elicit the divine anger. The oracles' answers customarily

99. R. Cagnet, G. Lafaye, et al., eds., *Inscriptiones Graecae ad Res Romanas Pertinentes, Inscriptiones Asiae II* (Paris: E. Leroux, 1927; reprint, Chicago: Aries, 1975), 4:492, trans. Ryan Harker.
100. Lane Fox, *Pagans and Christians*, 231.
101. Ibid., 169–77.

pointed to humans who had given insufficient attention to a god, or to cultic acts that people had performed inaccurately or perfunctorily, or to something that was polluting the society or profaning it. Christians were uncomfortably aware that pagans often attributed problems to the presence of Christians: "Many are complaining and are blaming us because wars are arising more frequently, because the plague, famine are raging."[102] This analysis could lead to persecution.

But the oracles often pointed to other causes and solutions. In response to the Antonine Plague in the 160s, the oracle of Claros ordered inquirers from the small town of Caesarea Trochetta in Lydia to respond to the plague by performing acts of purification and liturgy. "It is necessary," the oracle informed them, "to draw pure water from seven carefully prepared fountains" and then to sprinkle this on their houses. Meanwhile, in the middle of the plain outside the town, it was necessary for them to erect a large statue of Apollo armed with a threatening bow that he brandished in his right hand. When they had done these things, the oracle reassured them, the plague would be shot away.[103] Nearby, also in the 160s, when leaders of the famous city of Pergamum came to Claros for advice about how to respond to "the painful plague," the oracle poetically urged them to undertake specific measures. After dividing the young men of the town into four groups, the leaders were to organize a week of sacrifices and libations to the gods:

> For seven consecutive days, offer thigh-cuts on the altar
> of Athena, burning a calf—two years old, pure, unmated—
> and three bulls to Zeus and to Heavenly Bacchus.
> In like manner, for the son of Coronis [Asclepius] as well, making the
> accustomed thigh-cuts of a bull, prepare a sacrificial feast beforehand;
> and the young men, as many as you are, being dressed in military
> cloaks,
> not without your fathers—pouring a drink-offering upon one another,
> ask for a good remedy for the pestilence from the immortal ones.[104]

The oracle ordered the Pergamum leaders to inscribe this response on pillars where the entire populace could see it. Like the oracle's response to Caesarea Trochetta, the response to Pergamum did not explain the plague; it provided remedies. The remedies were symbolic and cultic and fitted in with

---

102. Cyprian, *Demetr.* 2, trans. R. J. Deferrari, FC 36 (1958), 168.

103. Cagnet, Lafaye, et al., *Inscriptiones Graecae*, 4:492, trans. Ryan Harker. See Lane Fox, *Pagans and Christians*, 232.

104. Cagnet, Lafaye, et al., *Inscriptiones Graecae*, 4:360, trans. Ryan Harker. See Lane Fox, *Pagans and Christians*, 232–33.

the customs, social structures, and deep reflexes of both communities. The oracular pronouncements did not suggest novel approaches to the crisis, nor did they propose unconventional ethical behavior—ethics were not within the purview of the gods. In Asia Minor the crisis of the Antonine Plague left the habitus of the communities intact.

Carthage—the Sermon of Cyprian

In Carthage in the 250s, eighty years after the Antonine Plague, the Christian community responded to a renewed outbreak of plague very differently from the pagans of Caesarea Trochetta and Pergamum. Led by Bishop Cyprian, the Christian community responded to the crisis not by cultic acts to appease the gods but by practical deeds to help suffering people. These deeds not only consciously reaffirmed the Christians' habitus; they applied it in new circumstances and intensified it. The insight to do this did not, as in Asia Minor, come from consulting an external oracle. The insight came from within.

In the half century before Cyprian's time in the 250s, the church in Carthage had grown substantially, but it was still a minority in the city as well as in North Africa as a whole. When the plague struck in 251, the church was embattled and battered. The Christians had just emerged from the first empire-wide persecution of the church, which the emperor Decius had begun in 249 with a decree requiring all people in the empire, including all Christians, to offer sacrifices to the gods. In many places, including North Africa, the churches underwent harrowing experiences. A few Christians were executed. Many members "lapsed," surviving by signing documents stating that they had done honor to the gods.[105] By the end of 250 the persecution was effectively over, but in its wake relationships were severely damaged. There was painful disunity among Christians, many of whom had sacrificed (the *lapsi*) but now wanted to be readmitted to the church's life. And at times there was deep alienation between Christians and local pagans who had threatened or endangered them. These people, in the Christians' view, were their enemies.

At this moment, just as Cyprian and other church leaders were attempting to deal with these enormous problems, the plague broke out, threatening pagans and Christians alike. It made people violently ill—vomiting, diarrhea, fevers, putrefaction—and then it killed many of them.[106] People who were still uninfected often attempted to avoid contagion by fleeing Carthage. If

---

105. Graeme Clarke, "Third-Century Christianity," in *The Cambridge Ancient History*, ed. A. Bowman, A. Cameron, and P. Garnsey, 2nd ed. (Cambridge: Cambridge University Press, 2005), 12:625–26.

106. For a graphic description, see Cyprian, *Mort.* 14.

they needed to remain in the city, they at times tried to protect themselves by throwing into the streets bodies of plague victims, some of whom were apparently still alive. "Many diseased and dying people . . . asked the pity of the passers-by."[107] It was a crisis for the entire urban community of Carthage. How should the church respond?

Cyprian, the leading bishop in North Africa, was aware of the difficulties that the churches were having in responding to the plague. He knew that pagan activists in Carthage were blaming the Christians for the outbreak.[108] He also knew that in the crisis of the plague, as well as during the recent persecution, many Christians were wobbly—seduced by luxury and "standing less firmly."[109] They needed the guidance of divinely inspired words but of course did not turn to an oracular shrine to receive these. Instead Cyprian responded to the crisis by calling the entire Christian community together to listen collectively to the words that were already present in their midst. As he drew on the texts and traditions of the church and applied these to the people's behavior, Cyprian assumed that the Christians could hear the voice of God. And he believed that if they genuinely listened to God, the Christians would respond to the plague in a way that was marked by courage and patience. These, he said, constitute "the difference between us and others who know not God."[110]

We don't know where in Carthage the believers gathered. This extraordinary meeting, drawing from various local assemblies, must have put a strain on the largest of the spaces in which the Christians met.[111] We also do not know what the gathered Christians did. Did they pray? Did they celebrate the Eucharist? What his biographer Pontius tells us is that Cyprian gave the assembly an address that was both prophetic and pastoral and that addressed the believers' situation in time of plague. Pontius gives us notes which summarize some of the speech's main points.[112] According to Pontius, Cyprian did not attempt to explain the plague. As Cyprian later wrote, some Christians were upset when they observed that "the power of this disease attacks our people

107. Pontius, *Vit. Cypr.* 9, trans. M. M. Müller and R. J. Deferrari, FC 15 (1952), 13.

108. Cyprian, *Ep.* 59.6.1, ed. and trans. G. W. Clarke, *The Letters of St Cyprian of Carthage,* 3, ACW 46 (1986), 73–74.

109. Cyprian, *Mort.* 1, trans. R. J. Deferrari, FC 36 (1958), 199.

110. Cyprian, *Mort.* 11, 13 (Deferrari, 207, 209).

111. According to Peter Oakes, "The essence of 'house church' . . . is the meeting of Christians in someone's own home (which may also be a workshop), rather than in a building specially constructed for worship. . . . The early Christian groups [may be called] 'house churches' even when they meet in apartment blocks" (*Reading Romans in Pompeii: Paul's Letter at Ground Level* [Minneapolis: Fortress, 2009], 92).

112. For Cyprian's sermon, see Pontius, *Vit. Cypr.* 9, trans. M. M. Müller and R. J. Deferrari, FC 15 (1952), 13–14.

equally with the pagans."[113] Cyprian would have none of this; in his sermon he simply reminds the people that Jesus, in the Sermon on the Mount, had said that God sends the rain on the just and the unjust, and by extension the plague could also descend on everybody without distinction. The question for Cyprian was not why the plague had broken out but how Christians should respond to it. And Cyprian, acting under pressure in this critical moment in his community's history, drew reflexively on his community's texts and tradition—and on his own favorite themes.

Cyprian's first point, according to Pontius, reminded the people of the blessings of mercy. He pointed to examples from the Bible that indicated that charity merited God's favor. He may also have reminded the people of the tradition, now two centuries old, of Christian congregations creating "an organization, unique in the classical world, that effectively and systematically cared for its sick."[114] So the Christians had the charitable institutions (the community's financial chest [*arca*], attentive and active women, and deacons) as well as the habitus that equipped them to assist each other in time of need. People with this tradition, this habitus of mutual aid, will not leave their suffering fellow believers to die without bread and water; they will not throw them into the streets.

According to Pontius, Cyprian then went further, no doubt stretching his hearers. Cyprian drew on biblical texts that were at the heart of his theology of patience (see chap. 2 above). He especially gave voice to the words of Jesus, whose "advice and encouragement" in the Sermon on the Mount spoke to them in their desperate crisis. Drawing on these resources, he urged his people to respond to this time of danger and suffering by imitating God. "It [is] not at all remarkable if we cherish only our own brethren with a proper observance of love." Instead, Christians should do "more than the publican or the pagan." They should overcome evil with good and exercise "a divine-like clemency, loving even their enemies . . . and praying for the salvation of their persecutors." For doesn't God make the sun to rise and rain to fall upon all people, not merely on his own friends? And shouldn't "one who professes to be a son of God imitate the example of his Father"? Cyprian's flock were deeply schooled in Jesus's teaching that they should love their enemies. And Cyprian extended this teaching by applying it to the provision of crisis nursing for our brothers but "not only our brothers." Let us imagine the rhetorician Cyprian as he warmed to his point: You Christians, you are my people and

---

113. Cyprian, *Mort.* 8 (Deferrari, FC 36:204).
114. Gary B. Ferngren, *Medicine and Health Care in Early Christianity* (Baltimore: Johns Hopkins University Press, 2009), 114.

flock, you know the mercy of God, and you demonstrate this by providing visits, bread, and water for other believers who are suffering. I praise God for your faithfulness. Now I am calling you to broaden your view, to exercise "a divine-like clemency" by loving your pagan neighbors. Visit them, too; encourage them; provide bread and water for them. I know that in recent months some pagans have been involved in persecuting you. Pray for them; "pray for their salvation," and help them. You are God's children: the descendants of a good Father should "prove the imitation of his goodness."[115]

Pontius tells us that Cyprian in his sermon dealt with other "important matters" that he did not have room for in his biography.[116] One may speculate. Did Cyprian remind the people of a theme that is central to his pastoral teaching—that they as believers could die without fear?[117] Did Cyprian develop yet another favorite theme—that the believers' conversations with pagans will flourish when their lives are consistent with their words? "No occasion should be given to the pagans to censure us deservedly and justly, on the ground that we grieve for those who we say are living with God, as if entirely destroyed and lost. . . . It profits nothing to show forth virtue in words and destroy truth in deeds."[118]

What Pontius does tell us is that Cyprian responded to the crisis of the plague by urging the people to live lives marked by the habitus of patience—trusting God, living without being able to control the outcome, living unhurriedly, living unconventionally, loving their enemies. We do not know how his hearers responded. No doubt their response was uneven. But according to Pontius some of them got the point: through their care for the pagans as well as fellow believers, the Christians did good for *all* kinds of people, "not merely for those of the household of the faith."[119] Sociologist Rodney Stark suggests how this may have worked out. Drawing from the letter that Bishop Dionysius of Alexandria wrote in AD 260, two years after Cyprian died, concerning the responses of Christians to the plague in Egypt, Stark reconstructs the "elementary nursing" that Christians provided to plague victims; he also speculates that the Christians' response to the plague markedly increased

115. Pontius, *Vit. Cypr.* 9 (Müller and Deferrari, 14).

116. Pontius, *Vit. Cypr.* 10 (Müller and Deferrari, 14).

117. In *Mort.* 26 (Deferrari, 220), Cyprian looks to paradise, "our country," where patriarchs, apostles, and martyrs are already present, along with our relatives and loved ones who have died; that is where "the merciful [enjoy] their reward who have performed works of justice by giving food and alms to the poor, who in observing the precepts of the Lord have transferred their earthly patrimony to the treasuries of heaven."

118. Cyprian, *Mort.* 20 (Deferrari, 215–16).

119. Pontius, *Vit. Cypr.* 10, citing Gal. 6:10.

Christian numbers vis-à-vis pagans.[120] The Christian witness was embodied. Its eloquence was in behavior that the Christians may or may not have explained but that definitely posed questions for the pagans who observed it. It may have led to a flock of new inquirers and catechumens. The church's all-embracing response to the crisis also led the church henceforth to broaden its medical care to nonbelievers.[121]

But the crisis left at least one Christian asking questions. Cyprian's biographer Pontius speculated that if Christian worship had not been closed to outsiders, and "if the pagans could have heard [Cyprian in full flight] . . . they probably would have believed at once."[122] Might there be a more direct and efficient way to communicate the gospel, more centered on public worship and star preachers and less on embodiment by the community? In these thoughts, Pontius was perhaps being impatient. Certainly he was ahead of his time, a forerunner of the fourth and fifth centuries.

Conclusion

In the second and third centuries pagans and Christians were neighbors. In this chapter we have seen them as they responded to real-life situations and as they developed public, private, and oracular institutions to enable them to respond well. Most people remained in the religions that Greco-Roman civilization provided for them. When dissatisfied, they were able to give time and money to other religious groupings that appealed to them. Into this tolerant world, Christianity came with its exclusive adherence. Further, it came with its habitus, which in day-to-day living and especially when under pressure was different from pagan norms.

The Christians' behavior could be deeply unsettling, jarring the people out of conventional pathways. Pagans and Christians responded to similar situations in ways that were different—sometimes because of their theological reflections and often because of the ways they behaved and embodied their faiths. A few people—initially a tiny number of courageous people but soon a larger group—looked at the Christians, who were often most eloquent when they were not in control of situations, and intuited that another way of

120. Eusebius, *Hist. eccl.* 7.22. My account owes much to Stark, *Rise of Christianity*, 89–91; see also his influential earlier article, "Epidemics, Networks, and the Rise of Christianity," *Semeia* 56 (1992): 159–75. For an evaluation of Stark's work on epidemics, see Steven C. Muir, "'Look How They Love One Another': Early Christian and Pagan Care for the Sick and Other Charity," in Vaage, *Religious Rivalries*, 213–31.
121. Ferngren, *Medicine and Health Care*, 121.
122. Pontius, *Vit. Cypr.* 10 (Müller and Deferrari, 14).

living was possible and that the Christian way of living was worth so much that they would give up everything to seek it. These people, who felt *pulled* to investigate the Christian communities seriously, also often were those who experienced the pagan groupings to be unsatisfying, and thus felt impelled—*pushed*—into the unexplored terrain of the Christian churches. This process happened gradually, by a process of fermentation. In the coming chapters we will see how it worked.

PART 2

FERMENT

4

CHRISTIANS AS AGENTS OF GROWTH

Fermentation is an intriguing process. It is gradual. Except for a stray bubble that emerges now and then, nothing seems to be happening. Until late in its operation, it is unimpressive. And yet it has a cumulative power that creates and transforms. As Michael Pollan, who writes insightfully about food, observes, "A ferment generates its own energy from within. It not only seems alive, it is alive. And most of this living takes place at a scale inaccessible to us without a microscope."[1]

So it was with early Christianity. On the plane of the emperors, senates, and legions, Christianity was a minor *superstitio*. To the people who mattered, it was of little significance. And yet, for those with eyes to see and intuitions to perceive, a new energy was emerging, something reticently alive and inexorable in operation.

How did this Christian ferment work? In this chapter and the next, we will look at the ingredients of this fermenting process. What was it that enabled the Christian groups to grow, unstoppably, despite disincentives? And what

1. Michael Pollan, *Cooked: A Natural History of Transformation* (New York: Penguin Press, 2013), 295.

was the synergy between these ingredients? We will see that the growth happened despite an evident lack of planning and control.[2]

The early Christians had a perspective that they called "patience." They believed that God was in charge of events; they knew they were not. So they were not surprised that the church's growth was uneven, that there were certain areas where there were concentrations of Christians and other areas where there were no believers at all. Christian leaders didn't think or write about how to systematize the spread of Christianity; they were not concerned to cover the world evenly with evangelistic efforts.[3] Instead the Christians concentrated on developing practices that contributed to a habitus that characterized both individual Christians and Christian communities. They believed that when the habitus was healthy, the churches would grow. Their theology was unhurried—a theology of patience. It is characteristic of their approach that the carriers and embodiers of the growth were marginal, humble, and often anonymous, women as well as men, individuals as well as communities. In this chapter we will look at individuals, Christians who participated in patient ferment by scattering.

Missionaries on the Move: Migration Mission

Extraordinary Christians—the Twelve

According to early Christian tradition, exemplary men took the lead in the spread of Christianity. In the New Testament, after his resurrection Jesus summoned his disciples and gave them his call to "make disciples of all nations" (Matt. 28:19). According to the *Didascalia apostolorum*, a third-century Syrian church order, his disciples gathered together and decided to share the missionary task among themselves: "[We] . . . divided the world among ourselves into twelve parts, and [went out] to the nations so that we could preach the word in all the world."[4] This scenario was a commonplace in early Christian writings. According to Tertullian, Jesus's disciples, the apostles, went forth into the world and preached to the nations. "They then in like manner founded churches in every city, from which all the other churches, one after

---

2. For a study of early Christianity's expansion in light of Adolf Harnack's "constant process of fermentation," see Wolfgang Reinbold, *Propaganda und Mission im ältesten Christentum: Eine Untersuchung zu den Modalitäten der Ausbreitung der frühen Kirche*, FRLANT 188 (Göttingen: Vandenhoek & Ruprecht, 2000), 298, 306. I owe much to Reinbold's valuable study.

3. Tertullian's statement in *Fug.* 6.2 that "we preach throughout the whole world" is an overstatement that does not fit in with the known priorities of Tertullian or other Christian leaders.

4. *Did. apost.* 6.8.1, trans. and ed. Alistair Stewart-Sykes, *The Didascalia Apostolorum: An English Version with Introduction and Annotation* (Turnhout: Brepols, 2009), 229–30.

another, derived the tradition of the faith."[5] According to a common early Christian understanding, in the distant past what later came to be called the "Great Commission" had already been carried out by extraordinary Christians, the Twelve. Thereafter it was ordinary Christians who continued the ferment.

Ordinary Christians

Ordinary Christians—they were the key. Except for Pantaenus and Gregory, whom we mentioned in chapter 1, it was anonymous Christians, not the officially constituted leaders of the Christian communities, who were primarily responsible for Christianity's spread. Lay Christians traveled to new areas and established churches. What caused ordinary Christians to get involved in this? Often it was work. Christians followed their business opportunities or the imperatives of their jobs by moving from their home areas to new areas as merchants, artisans, doctors, prisoners, slaves, and (by the third century) soldiers. As they traveled, they often moved in existing networks of family, profession, and faith (not least communities of Jews). Taking their faith with them, in new places they founded Christian cells.[6] One scholar has called this process "migration mission."[7] According to Per Beskow, this "seems to have been the ordinary means of spreading the Gospel."[8]

What theologies animated these carriers of faith? Had anyone prepared them for missionary activities? Many of them must have been instructed prior to their baptisms, but the catechetical programs we know of have little to do with equipping believers to plant new churches. We also do not know how these participants in migration mission behaved vis-à-vis the people they met in their new settings. It is fair to assume that their approaches were variations of the ordinary behavior of Christians involved in the life of local churches.

5. Tertullian, *Praescr.* 20.5, trans. P. Holmes, ANF 3:252. For further patristic citations, see Norbert Brox, "Zur christlichen Mission in der Spätantike," in *Mission im Neuen Testament*, ed. Karl Kertelge, Quaestiones Disputatae 93 (Freiburg-im-Breisgau: Herder, 1982), 194–99.

6. Rodney Stark and William Sims Bainbridge, "Networks of Faith: Interpersonal Bonds and Recruitment to Cults and Sects," *American Journal of Sociology* 85 (1980): 1376–95; Rodney Stark, *The Rise of Christianity: A Sociologist Reconsiders History* (Princeton: Princeton University Press, 1996), 20, 55–57.

7. John Howard Yoder, *As You Go: The Old Mission in a New Day* (1961), in Yoder, *Theology of Mission: A Believers Church Perspective*, ed. Gayle Gerber Koontz and Andy Alexis-Baker (Downers Grove, IL: IVP Academic, 2014), 404–6.

8. Per Beskow, "Mission, Trade and Emigration in the Second Century," *Svensk Exegetisk Årsbok* 35 (1970): 104–14. See also W. H. C. Frend, "A Note on the Influence of Greek Immigrants on the Spread of Christianity in the West," in *Mullus: Festschrift Theodor Klauser*, ed. Alfred Stuiber and Alfred Hermann (Münster: Aschendorff, 1964), 125–29; Giovanni Battista Bazzana, "Early Christian Missionaries as Physicians: Healing and Its Cultural Value in the Greco-Roman Context," *Novum Testamentum* 51 (2009): 232–51.

As we shall see shortly, it is likely that women were key participants in this process just as they were at later stages of Christianity's early expansion. Egyptian papyri indicate that in the early centuries Christian women were far more geographically mobile than non-Christian women.[9] Recent research has also shown that in fifth- and sixth-century evangelizations of Armenia and Georgia, obscure women, often slaves, took the lead in establishing Christian cells, demonstrating what Andrea Sterk has called "the missionary success of the lowly."[10] Something like this may have happened earlier. In second-century Syria, for example, when itinerant prophets visited villages in which there were ostensibly no Christians, they discovered that "a single believing woman" was already there, living in a household in a pagan environment. At times such women may have formed the sleeper cells of future church communities.[11]

Itinerant Prophets

Although typically these itinerant Christians were ordinary laypeople, at times they were people who had prophetic gifts and wonderworking powers. These people figure prominently in the Didache, in which the community developed means of testing their messages. Did a prophet "behave like the Lord"? Did he "practice what he preaches"? Did he "say in the Spirit, 'Give me money, or something else'"?[12] These tests, which mirror the concern for a lived faith that many early Christian writers express, helped the community distinguish authentic prophets from charlatans. And some of them may have been rogues. That's what second-century pagan writer Celsus thought: the Christian prophets were deceivers—roaming about, begging, and prophesying with oracular obscurity in words that were "meaningless and nonsensical."[13]

Was it possible to be more sympathetic to the itinerant prophets than Celsus was? In his *Letters to Virgins*, "Clement," an anonymous second-century

9. AnneMarie Luijendijk, *Greetings in the Lord: Early Christians and the Oxyrhynchus Papyri*, HTS 60 (Cambridge, MA: Harvard University Press, 2008), 119.

10. Andrea Sterk, "'Representing' Mission from Below: Historians as Interpreters and Agents of Christianization," *Church History* 79, no. 2 (2010): 302; A. Sterk, "Mission from Below: Captive Women and Conversion on the East Roman Frontiers," *Church History* 79, no. 1 (2010): 1–39; Cornelia Horn, "St. Nino and the Christianization of Pagan Georgia," *Medieval Encounters* 4 (1998): 242–64.

11. Ps.-Clem. 2.5.1, trans. Hugo Duensing (from Syriac into German), "Die dem Klemens von Rom zugeschriebenen Briefe über die Jungfräulichkeit," *Zeitschrift für Kirchengeschichte* 63 (1950–51): 166–88.

12. Did. 11.8–12, trans. C. C. Richardson, in *Early Christian Fathers*, ed. C. C. Richardson, LCC 1 (1953): 177.

13. Origen, *Cels.* 7.9, trans. H. Chadwick, *Origen: Contra Celsum* (Cambridge: Cambridge University Press, 1965), 403.

Syrian writer who styled himself after the first-century Clement of Rome, attempted to be more friendly. "Clement" made it clear that the itinerant prophets were not primarily evangelists. And they didn't have a standard approach; it varied from town to town.

When they visited a town in which there was a small community of believers, the prophets focused their attention on building up the local church. They addressed the needs of the Christians—the orphans and widows and those who were harassed by evil spirits. Where people were ill, "Clement" provided the itinerants with instructions about how to exorcise them acceptably, "without disturbance and talkativeness . . . but as men who have received the gift of healing from God . . . confidently, to the praise of God." But "Clement" did not see the itinerants' exorcism, healing, and care of the poor as evangelistic tools; instead, these were resources that the itinerants offered to Christian brothers and sisters to establish local congregations as places where compassion ruled and healing could be expected to take place.[14]

When the itinerants entered another kind of town, one in which there was "only one Christian woman and no other believers," "Clement" reports that their approach was even less evangelistic. They didn't seem to have been surprised to find an isolated Christian woman in the town. She may have represented a widespread phenomenon in which believers, possibly especially women believers, were scattered by economic forces that they could scarcely comprehend. As an isolated Christian, the solitary woman may have been praying for believers to join her in life and prayer. This is precisely what our itinerants failed to do. They didn't show concern to encourage the Christian sister spiritually or to assist her in bringing good news to the townsfolk. Why not? Possibly because women were reputed to have irresistible sexual allure; or possibly because the itinerants "saw their honour defined particularly in relation to the sexual purity of females."[15] In any event, "Clement" was worried about protecting the prophets' reputation rather than supporting their isolated sister. If they visited her, what might unbelievers think? Their dealings with the isolated Christian woman must be transparently chaste; there must not be a whiff of sexual impropriety! So not only were the itinerants not to stay with her; they were not even to pray with her, not even to read the Scriptures with her. Let them "flee from there as from a snake, as from sin."[16] Poor evangelists! And who knows? As happened elsewhere, the woman—patiently, unbothered by the male Christians—might find other ways to build a believing community.

14. Ps.-Clem. 1.12.5 (Duensing, 178).
15. Margaret Y. MacDonald, *Early Christian Women and Pagan Opinion: The Power of the Hysterical Woman* (Cambridge: Cambridge University Press, 1996), 252–53.
16. Ps.-Clem. 2.5.1 (Duensing, 182).

The itinerant prophets could be more relaxed when they entered a third kind of town—one in which there were no Christians at all. But once again, according to "Clement," their primary concern was not to propagate the gospel but to maintain their reputation for unimpeachable behavior: "Let our behavior be to the praise of God." They were "in no situation to assimilate to the pagans, as believers are not similar . . . to the godless." So when the itinerants performed exorcisms or healings, they did these only for members of the Christian communities. These were not for the pagans. In fact, according to "Clement" the itinerants had no desire to interact with the pagans: we "do not sing to the heathen, do not read them the Scriptures." Their desire was rather to protect their own purity as "an example for those who are already believers and for those who one day will believe."[17] So the itinerants knew that pagans were becoming Christians, even though they did not interact with them. How then did they think that the churches were growing? The itinerants must have assumed that it was the local Christians' unimpeachable reputation, coupled with rumors of life and healing in their congregations, that attracted the outsiders.

Christians at Home

The non-itinerant Christians had a characteristic approach to their day-to-day life, which was to keep a low profile. They were known to be "silent in the open, but talkative in hid corners."[18] They did not want to cause a stir or to find public places to preach their message. Even when martyrdom offered their leaders the opportunity to address the masses, the leaders were diffident. In second-century Smyrna when the proconsul urged the Christian bishop Polycarp to "try to move the people," the bishop responded dismissively, "As for the mob, I do not think they deserve to listen to a speech of defense from me."[19] A few years later in Gaul, when the governor gave Bishop Pothinus of Lyon a chance to tell the crowd gathered at a tribunal about the Christian God, Pothinus said only, "If you are worthy, you will know."[20] Polycarp and Pothinus evidently thought that it was their behavior as martyrs, not the words they might speak, that would convey the Christian faith to the watching world. In general this is a principle: the churches did not seek attention but instead propagated the gospel by other means. What were these?

17. Ps.-Clem. 2.6.2–4 (Duensing, 183–84).
18. Minucius Felix, *Oct.* 8.3, trans. G. H. Rendall, LCL 250 (1931), 335.
19. Mart. Pol. 10, trans. and ed. Herbert A. Musurillo, *The Acts of the Christian Martyrs* (Oxford: Clarendon, 1972), 11.
20. Eusebius, *Hist. eccl.* 5.1.29 (trans. Musurillo, *Acts,* 71).

Domesticity

The church of the early centuries was rooted in the *domus*, both the physical space and the cluster of people who lived there, both kin and not kin.[21] Christians lived in ordinary places scattered throughout their cities and towns. Like all urbanites they lived and worshiped in dwellings, many of which were within enormous *insulae*—architectural "islands"—multistoried buildings that held apartments of a wide variety of sizes. According to recent archaeological studies, most of these apartments were small, the homes of the people who were predominantly poor. A few were medium sized, for people whose fortunes had looked up, and a very few were capacious, the exquisitely decorated, multiroomed dwellings of the rich. In such *insulae* many ranks of society lived close to one another.[22] The neighbors watched each other and saw each other's comings and goings. When an ambitious and successful stonemason moved from a smaller to a larger unit, which not only housed his family but was a place for his business, people noticed. They would also see when a Christian church began to meet in his apartment. As time went on, some congregations grew, and they could then move their meetings from the stonemason's flat to the larger apartments of a wealthier member. An example of what was happening comes from mid-third-century Caesarea (Palestine), in which the Christian community was meeting in what was or had been the house of a prosperous person. The multiroomed apartment gave opportunity for misbehavior: "Some do not even patiently wait while the texts are being read in church. Others do not even know if they are read, but are occupied with mundane stories in the furthest corners of the Lord's house."[23] This was still a house, a domestic building, but it was a large one. This pattern, with Christians meeting in domestic spaces, continued to be dominant in the Christian movement for a full century after Constantine's accession to the throne. Throughout Christianity's first four centuries, the church was primarily a domestic phenomenon.[24]

21. Kate Cooper, "Closely Watched Households: Visibility, Exposure, and Private Power in the Roman *Domus*," *Past and Present* 197 (2007): 5.

22. My understanding of the built environment in which the early Christians lived owes much to Peter Oakes, *Reading Romans in Pompeii: Paul's Letter at Ground Level* (Minneapolis: Fortress, 2009), chaps. 1–2. Also see Edward Adams, *The Earliest Christian Meeting Places: Almost Exclusively Houses?*, LNTS 450 (London: Bloomsbury T&T Clark, 2013), 7–10.

23. Origen, *Hom. Exod.* 12.2, trans. R. E. Heine, FC 71 (1981), 369. See also Origen's *Hom. Jer.* 19.13.4, trans. J. C. Smith, FC 97 (1998), 212: "No one who enacts the Passover as Jesus wishes is in a room below. But if someone celebrates with Jesus, he is in a great room above, in a furnished room made clean, in a furnished room adorned and prepared."

24. Kim Bowes, "Early Christian Archaeology: A State of the Field," *Religion Compass* 2, no. 4 (2008): 581; Bradly S. Billings, "From House Church to Tenement Church: Domestic Space

There could not be many secret meetings in an *insula*. As Christians went to gatherings in the small flat of a craftworker, or in the bigger apartment of a merchant, people observed their movements. The watchers saw that the Christians, unlike members of the pagan associations, met often. In second-century Rome, Justin reported that "we are constantly together."[25] It's not clear what Justin meant by this, but it is likely that by AD 200 a Roman domestic church had its main meeting, the weekly Eucharist, on Saturday night or Sunday morning. "You have a festival day every eighth day!" exulted Tertullian.[26] But the church also had morning sessions for catechesis and prayer, evening meetings for meals, and possibly quick visits to bring food for a meal, to find hospitality for a friend, or to look in the church's storehouse for a tunic or a pair of shoes for one's child or friend. The church's meeting and social rooms, sandwiched within the large apartment buildings, functioned as "inconspicuous community centers."[27]

Architectural forms are powerful. They determine the ethos of the people who live and worship within them; and the domestic spaces in which the early Christians met were instrumental in enabling the Christians to develop their characteristic habitus. The Christians were familial: they related in a face-to-face manner to people they knew and loved. The Christians were socially active: they had intensive, embodied forms of care for members and others. Outsiders, meanwhile, who were barred from the church apartment because of the Christians' concern for security and secrecy, looked at the Christians' comings and goings and responded at times with salacious rumors and at times with inquisitiveness and envy.

Participation in Daily Life

As we have seen, Christians lived among non-Christian neighbors generally in tight circumstances. Privacy was scarce. In the course of daily life the

---

and the Development of Early Urban Christianity—the Example of Ephesus," *JTS* 62, no. 2 (2011): 542, 552, 563. In Bowes's view, the famous "house church" in Dura-Europos in Syria was one of a kind and not characteristic of a category of church buildings (*domus ecclesiae*) between domestic dwellings and basilicas. According to Paul Post in "Dura Europos Revisited: Rediscovering Sacred Space," *Worship* 86, no. 3 (2012): 222–43, the Dura building may not even have been the home of a local congregation. For a contrasting approach, which builds a missional scenario on the *domus*, see Reidar Hvalvik, "In Word and Deed: The Expansion of the Church in the Pre-Constantinian Era," in *The Mission of the Early Church to Jews and Gentiles*, ed. Jostein Ådna and Hans Kvalbein (Tübingen: Mohr Siebeck, 2000), 281–82.

25. Justin, *1 Apol.* 67, trans. E. R. Hardy, LCC 1 (1953): 287.
26. Tertullian, *Idol.* 14, trans. S. Thelwall, *ANF* 3:70.
27. Richard Krautheimer, *Rome, Profile of a City, 312–1308* (Princeton: Princeton University Press, 1980), 33.

Christians ascended and descended stairs, bought items from street vendors, and carried food to meetings and to friends' houses. The believers, whose dress was often simple and unostentatious, did not immediately reveal their identity to passersby, but their identity could emerge as relationships developed. Sometimes this came as a surprise: "'A good man,' they say, 'this Caius Seius, only that he is a Christian.'"[28] At times breakthroughs occurred when Christians offered to pray for sick neighbors. But if the early Christians had strategies for converting people, they did not teach these or write about them. As Origen put it in a Sunday sermon: "You catechumens—who gathered you into the church? What goad compelled you to leave your houses and come together in this assembly? We did not go to you from house to house. The Almighty Father put this zeal into your hearts by his invisible power."[29] Instead of urging the Christians to go from house to house, or recommending that they replace their evangelistic methods with something more effective, Origen expressed his patient trust in God's "invisible power."

How then did the church grow? Scholars have seen the church's growth as coming about through something modest: "casual contact."[30] Contact could come about in innumerable ways through the translocal networks of family and profession in which most people participated. Masters interacted with slaves; residents met neighbors; and above all believers networked with relatives and work colleagues. In all these relationships, "affective bonds" were formed.[31] The most reliable means of communicating the attractiveness of the faith to others and enticing them to investigate things further was the Christians' character, bearing, and behavior. The habitus of the individual Christian was crucial.

Women as Carriers of the Faith

As Christians across the centuries have told the story of the early church, they have accorded the central roles to men. The intellectuals and the writers were men; they are called "church fathers," and their writings have been called

---

28. Tertullian, *Apol.* 3.1, trans. T. R. Glover, LCL 250 (1931), 19.
29. Origen, *Hom. Luc.* 7.7, trans. J. T. Lienhard, FC 94 (1996), 31.
30. E. Glenn Hinson, *The Evangelization of the Roman Empire: Identity and Adaptability* (Macon, GA: Mercer University Press, 1981), 49. See also Everett Ferguson, "Some Factors in the Growth of the Early Church," *Restoration Quarterly* 16 (1973): 45; Brox, "Zur christlichen Mission," 221; Ramsay MacMullen, *Christianizing the Roman Empire (A.D. 100–400)* (New Haven: Yale University Press, 1984), 40–41.
31. John Lofland and Rodney Stark, "Becoming a World-Saver: A Theory of Conversion to a Deviant Perspective," *American Sociological Review* 30 (1965): 862–75.

"patristics." Lists of leaders of communities were always lists of men. The early centuries have been what historian Christine Trevett has called a "no (wo)man's land of Christian history."[32] But this is not how early Christianity appeared to its contemporaries, and the careful work of scholars—especially women scholars—has helped us see the growth of the church with new eyes. As the worldwide Christian movement gained in membership, women played an indispensable part in the story.

Writing about Women

Alas, it is hard to write about the women believers. The sources that survive are few and fragmentary. They often come from Christianity's enemies, who do their best to discredit Christianity by associating the Christians with groups in society who in their view were contemptible. More seriously, except for Perpetua (whom we met in chap. 3) who left a visionary prison diary, Christianity's writers were virtually all men. And as Kate Cooper and other scholars have pointed out, the men who wrote about women did so from their own perspectives and for their own ends, using the women as rhetorical instruments in their own intra-male games of ecclesiastical and doctrinal hardball.[33] We have little evidence about women, and the evidence we do have is often tainted. Of course, the sources rarely permit us to speak about women either individually or statistically en masse. Judith Lieu has with reason contended that even when the writers ostensibly talk about the practice of women, they in fact tell us far more about "the rhetoric of language" of their male counterparts. Can we then talk about the social experience of the early Christian women? Not, Lieu concludes, without hazard.[34]

But is this a hazard worth risking? When male scholars, after centuries of deleting women, begin once again to include women in the story, it is right for scholars—particularly women scholars—to be suspicious. But must that suspicion deter us from the search for Christian practices? Must it make us so cautious that we engage in an analysis of rhetoric but do not attempt to discern the habits and reflexes that underlie the rhetoric? I don't think so; the

---

32. Christine Trevett, *Christian Women and the Time of the Apostolic Fathers (AD c. 80–160): Corinth, Rome and Asia Minor* (Cardiff: University of Wales Press, 2006), 5.

33. Kate Cooper, "Insinuations of Womanly Influence: An Aspect of the Christianization of the Roman Aristocracy," *JRS* 82 (1992): 155; Elizabeth A. Clark, "Thinking with Women: The Uses of the Appeal to 'Woman' in Pre-Nicene Christian Propaganda Literature," in *The Spread of Christianity in the First Four Centuries: Essays in Explanation*, ed. W. V. Harris (Leiden: Brill, 2005), 43.

34. Judith M. Lieu, *Neither Jew nor Greek? Constructing Early Christianity* (New York: T&T Clark, 2003), 97.

evidence, read carefully and with due suspicion, is strong enough to be useful. Indeed, it seems to indicate that the Christianity of the first three centuries, like the church that in the twentieth century has become global, was what eminent woman missiologist Dana Robert has called a "women's movement."[35]

Early Christianity as a Women's Movement

It was not that the women—except in exceptional cases—occupied official leadership positions in the movement. Women were almost never bishops; only in exceptional cases were they "apostles" and presbyters; and only occasionally—at a few times and in a few areas—did they serve as deacons or "deaconesses."[36] No, the significance of women in the early centuries was not in their institutional leadership but in their sheer number. It may be hard to prove this, but I am convinced that from an early date the majority of Christians were women.[37] Further, the Christian women produced "stars," saints and martyrs such as Blandina and Perpetua who inspired and unsettled Christians and pagans alike.[38] But perhaps the women's greatest significance was their energetic involvement as community builders, providers of service, and practitioners of humble evangelism. In all this they inspired the entire Christian movement. Christine Trevett has put it well: "[Women were] in the frontline," understood in terms both "of a favourable position from which to evangelize and of vulnerability to attack."[39]

I recognize that the argument for the number and prominence of women is controversial. Eminent scholars differ, especially about essentialism—which Judith Lieu calls "biologism." Lieu contends that it is wrong to adopt "a highly contentious biologistic perspective" that claims that women have a

35. Dana L. Robert, "World Christianity as a Women's Movement," *International Bulletin of Missionary Research* 30, no. 4 (2006): 180.

36. On women as bishops, see Ute Eisen, *Women Officeholders in Early Christianity* (Collegeville, MN: Liturgical Press, 2000), 205–9; as presbyters, see Kevin Madigan and Carolyn Osiek, *Ordained Women in the Early Church* (Baltimore: Johns Hopkins University Press, 2005), 163–98; as apostles, see Eisen, *Women Officeholders*, 49–55; as deacons and deaconesses, see Madigan and Osiek, *Ordained Women*, 24–27, 107–18.

37. Carolyn Osiek and Margaret Y. MacDonald, *A Woman's Place: House Churches in Earliest Christianity* (Minneapolis: Fortress, 2006), 12; Robin Lane Fox, *Pagans and Christians* (San Francisco: Harper & Row, 1986), 309–10; Stark, *Rise of Christianity*, 98; Reinbold, *Propaganda und Mission*, 309. For more skeptical views, see Lieu, *Neither Jew nor Greek?*, 90; Trevett, *Christian Women*, 13.

38. W. H. C. Frend, "Blandina and Perpetua: Two Early Christian Heroines," in *Les Martyrs de Lyon (177)*, Colloques internationaux du Centre national de la recherche scientifique 575 (Paris: Éditions CNRS, 1978), 167–77; Brent D. Shaw, "The Passion of Perpetua," *Past and Present* 139 (May 1993): 14.

39. Trevett, *Christian Women*, 119.

predisposition to be religious that is gendered, not primarily socially constructed.[40] This could be, but there is evidence to the contrary. Across the centuries and around the world, in a kaleidoscopic variety of religions, one finds women preponderantly present. Scholars today are becoming alert to the impressive presence of women in contemporary religious life. An example is Rodney Stark's recent article about religious participation in the twentieth century.[41] Basing his work on the 1995–96 World Values Surveys, which provide comparative data for forty-nine countries, Stark discovered that in every country, when people were asked, "Are you a religious person?" a higher proportion of women than men answered yes. Ratios varied: proceeding alphabetically, in Armenia the ratio of females to males was 1.27:1; in Austria it was 1.15:1; in Belarus it was 1.45:1; and so on.[42] Stark notes that "these results were fully replicated when based on other measures of religiousness."[43] And he finds similar ratios in non-Christian countries such as Japan, China, and Azerbaijan.[44] The evidence of this data tallies with my observation of renewal movements within Christianity and of "New Religious Movements." Repeatedly, in all of these, women have outnumbered men.

But how about historically, in the ancient world? Of course, for the ancient world I cannot offer my personal observations. And I can offer only one statistic. In 305 during the Great Persecution, in Cirta in North Africa, imperial officials raided a house church and (conveniently for our purposes) compiled a list of its possessions. On this list the examiners found, along with chalices, candleholders, and other liturgical equipment, a stock of clothing. The church had what was evidently a clothes store, to which members contributed clothing that other members could claim when they needed it. The clothing included "eighty-two women's tunics . . . , sixteen men's tunics, thirteen pairs of men's shoes, forty-seven pairs of women's shoes."[45] In the same decade, church leaders meeting in Elvira in Spain issued canons dealing with their concerns; among these was Canon 15: "No matter the large number of girls, Christian maidens are by no means to be given in matrimony to pagans lest youth, bursting forth in bloom, end in adultery of the soul."[46]

40. Lieu, *Neither Jew nor Greek?*, 86.
41. Rodney Stark, "Physiology and Faith: Addressing the 'Universal' Gender Difference in Religious Commitment," *Journal for the Scientific Study of Religion* 41, no. 3 (2002): 495–507.
42. Ibid., 497–98.
43. Ibid., 496.
44. Ibid., 499.
45. *Gesta apud Zenophilum* 3, in *Optatus: Against the Donatists*, trans. and ed. Mark Edwards, TTH 27 (Liverpool: Liverpool University Press, 1997), 154.
46. Canons of Elvira 15, trans. Samuel Laeuchli, *Power and Sexuality: The Emergence of Canon Law at the Synod of Elvira* (Philadelphia: Temple University Press, 1972), appendix, 128.

In Elvira as in Cirta, and as in Rome in the early third-century episcopacy of Callistus, there were evidently more women than men.[47] Why was this? Except when husbands compelled them to become Christians as part of a household conversion—which seems to have been rare—women did not have to become believers. They chose to join, despite the disincentives that all people faced, and despite the churches' patriarchal structures and practices. It could be that women felt freer when they became Christians than they had been as pagans. Indeed, at times they may have sensed that they were indispensable collaborators in the creation of a new world. When women became Christians, life in some respects may have become more complicated for them. It also became richer.

What Motivated the Women?

When women became Christians, and when in certain intangible but potent ways they took the lead in the growth of the church, why did they do so? Stark points to benefits that accrued to women who joined the churches—the greater fidelity of Christian husbands and the Christian church's repudiation of killing (abortion and infanticide).[48] Can we go further? Why were women more likely than men to join Christian communities? Two English sociologists, Tony Walter and Grace Davie, have proposed that the tendency of women in many societies to be more religiously active than men (which they accept) results from women's greater experience of being physically vulnerable and not in control of their life circumstances—not least through their experience of childbirth. Women also tend to be more present to children in sickness and to old people who are dying.

Do birth and death "entail some encounter with the sacred"?[49] Here we are in the domain of mystery. Nevertheless, to me it makes sense to see unprominent people—believing women, who cannot control things—not as the bit-part players that the surviving texts would make them appear to be. No, they were on center stage, not only because there were more of them, but also because they played crucial parts in shaping the plot.

47. Peter Lampe, *From Paul to Valentinus: Christians in Rome in the First Two Centuries* (Minneapolis: Fortress, 2003), 118–22.

48. Stark, *Rise of Christianity*, 117–22. The number of women in the Christian communities may also have been augmented by the Christians' adopting and raising children who had been exposed on local dumps. The Greek name Kopreus means "off the dung-heap" (Lane Fox, *Pagans and Christians*, 343).

49. Tony Walter and Grace Davie, "The Religiosity of Women in the Modern West," *British Journal of Sociology* 49, no. 4 (1998): 648.

Women in Action

Where do we see women active in church life? In their dispersion. Earlier in this chapter we encountered one such woman, the isolated believing woman in a Syrian village from whom the itinerant evangelists fled lest they be compromised.[50] How, one wonders, did this woman get there? Was she converted there, or was she as a believer transported there as a result of warfare, or as a slave in a large household that migrated under the authority of a pagan *paterfamilias*? And what happened to her after the evangelists left town? Did she die there, as an isolated Christian? Did she lose her faith? Or did she somehow find Christian companionship—through meeting other dispersed Christians or through sharing her lifestyle and patient hope with others who found her strangely impressive?

Women also formed groups. The texts make it clear that Christian women were able to enter households that were inaccessible to Christian men. Clement of Alexandria observed that in third-century Egypt it was "through [women] the Lord's teaching was introduced to the women's section of the household without incurring slander."[51] Possibly our "isolated believing woman" was able to find or foster Christian friendship in this way. From the third-century church order *Didascalia apostolorum*, we know that the Syrian women were able to enter establishments fluidly, with a low-key subversiveness.[52] Out of such relationship building, carried on by women essentially acting on their own, groups came into being such as the one that the pagan philosopher Celsus found.

Writing in the 180s, Celsus noted with distaste that Christians formed groups to which they attracted riffraff, including women: "wool-workers, cobblers, laundry-workers, and the most illiterate and bucolic yokels." To him these were people of no account, who in a hierarchical world knew that they were the dregs of society and that they had no views worth expressing or being listened to. If they spoke up in the presence of their "elders and more intelligent masters," they would be whipped. But when in private they got hold of children and "stupid women," the Christians became articulate, saying that "the people must not pay any attention to their father and school-teachers, but must obey them. . . . The Christians alone, they say, know the right way to live."[53]

50. Ps.-Clem. 2.5.1.

51. Clement of Alexandria, *Strom.* 3.6.53, trans. E. A. Clark, *Women in the Early Church* (Collegeville, MN: Liturgical Press, 1983), 53.

52. *Did. apost.* 3.12.4.

53. Origen, *Cels.* 3.55 (Chadwick, 165–66).

How, one wonders, had these Christians—no doubt poor people, women, and others of no account—received the good news? How had they learned that they had personal dignity? How had they discovered that there was a "right way to live" that conflicted creatively with the wisdom of conventional, violent, vertical society? How had they learned to live in this way? According to Celsus, they learned these things in their workplaces. Women and children learned about "perfection" in unlikely places—"the wool-dresser's shop, or . . . the cobbler's or the washerwoman's shop." "And by saying this," Celsus concludes derisively, "they persuade them." Celsus doesn't tell us who the persuaders were, but in light of their easy entry into the wool-dresser's shop, they may well have been women. He also does not tell us what these messengers to the wool-dresser's shop persuaded their hearers to believe about God, Christ, prayer, or the future. But he does tell us that the messengers brought hope of a new world and that they imparted energy to seek this world in companionship with marginal people. Together they had found "the right way to live," an alternative *habitus* that relativized the world of their masters and gave their lives meaning.

Slaves and Women in Mixed Marriages

Other women were members of households as slaves or as wives in mixed marriages. Slave women had little power vis-à-vis the household's *paterfamilias*, who could not only command her service but also order her to share his bed. A young woman slave who had met Christians and learned of the church's rejection of adultery would have found this agonizing. Similarly, the Christian wife of a pagan might find life uncomfortable. Ancient custom assumed that wives would follow their husband's family cults.[54] A mixed marriage was a sign that something unusual had happened: either a woman had committed the surprising and unsettling act of becoming a Christian, or a Christian woman, finding it impossible to find a suitable husband among the Christian men, had married a pagan.[55] In these circumstances how were Christian wives to live? They learned the admonition of 1 Peter 3:1 that they should behave submissively toward their pagan husbands, who may be "won over without a word by their wives' conduct."[56] The Syrian *Didascalia* urged believing women to "demonstrate religion through modesty and gentleness"; in this way "those who are of the heathen may be turned and grow into faith."[57]

54. Lane Fox, *Pagans and Christians*, 83.
55. I have found only one mention of a Christian husband with a wife who "is not yet a believer" (*Trad. ap.* 41.12 [BJP, 198]).
56. Trevett, *Christian Women*, 199.
57. *Did. apost.* 1.10.3, trans. Stewart-Sykes (2009), 116.

The wife's desire to be evangelically compliant to her husband could conflict with her commitment to Christian principles and her desire to observe the rites and habitus of her religion. Aline Rousselle imagines a scene that evokes for us the pain of a Christian woman married to a pagan: "The woman, her legs apart, still in the position in which she had delivered her child, was forced to remain silent and excluded from the decision as to whether he [or she] should be accepted into the family, or left to die or become a slave."[58] What conflicting emotions and grief she must have felt when her husband exercised his *patria potestas*! As head of household he had the legal right to determine whether the child would live or die, while she longed for the child, agreed with her church that the exposure of infants is a grave sin, and wanted to please her husband—for his salvation.[59]

But there was much more than submission in a mixed marriage. Around AD 205 Tertullian wrote *To His Wife* to persuade Christian women, no doubt upper-class women, that marrying a pagan was a bad idea.[60] In it he provides a precious window into the tugs and pulls of life in a mixed marriage.[61] Tertullian depicts a frustrated Christian woman whose husband (a "servant of Satan," Tertullian styles him) obstructs her "performance of Christian duties and devotions." Her husband frustrates her attempts to participate in the cluster of practices that constitute the habitus of the Christian community. The community holds a *statio*, a twice-weekly meeting for penitence and prayer; her husband responds by scheduling visits to the baths.[62] The community holds a fast; he arranges for a feast at the identical time. He has power to hinder his wife from living the life of a normal Carthaginian Christian woman. He can impede her attempts to be mobile, to go about to serve the poor, to enter the houses of strangers, to stop in "at every hovel in town in order to visit the brethren." Can she participate in the community's devotional life? Only with difficulty—the husband keeps her from being present at evening devotions, participating in the all-night Paschal vigil, attending the Lord's Supper. Could she take part in the community's charitable practices? Once

58. Aline Rousselle, *Porneia: On Desire and the Body in Antiquity* (Oxford: Blackwell, 1988), 4; cited in Trevett, *Christian Women*, 192.

59. Cornelia B. Horn and John W. Martens, *"Let the Little Children Come to Me": Childhood and Children in Early Christianity* (Washington, DC: Catholic University of America Press, 2009), 20–21.

60. Georg Schöllgen, *Ecclesia Sordida? Zur Frage der sozialen Schichtung frühchristlicher Gemeinden am Beispiel Karthagos zur Zeit Tertullians* (Münster: Aschendorff, 1984), 210.

61. For what follows, see Tertullian, *Ux.* 2.4–8, trans. W. P. Le Saint, ACW 13 (1956), 29–32.

62. John F. Baldovin, *The Urban Character of Christian Worship: The Origins, Development and Meaning of Stational Liturgy*, Orientalia Christiana Analecta 228 (Rome: Pontificio Istituto Orientale, 1987), 143.

again, the husband is uncooperative. When the wife wants to go to prison to kiss the chains of a martyr, to greet a brother with the kiss of peace, to wash the feet of members of the community, to feed and provide accommodation for traveling Christians, the husband says no.

And yet, according to Tertullian, the husband does bend to some extent. The wife had managed to get the fragments of presanctified bread that she eats before breakfast; this indicates that she had attended a recent eucharistic meal in her church. Further, he watches his wife. When she is at home with him in their *domus*, he observes her as she does things that Christians do: she makes the sign of the cross on her bed and body; she exorcises ("blows away, with a puff of breath") something unclean; she gets up in the middle of the night to say prayers. Some husbands, Tertullian informs us, scoff at these practices; some make mental note of them for use "if ever their wives displease them." A mixed marriage is hard work; in a marriage like this it is difficult to "pray to Christ." Tertullian has experience with these difficulties.[63] So, to discourage women believers from entangling themselves with pagan husbands, he makes his account bleak.

But Tertullian is of two minds. He recognizes that "by an act of the divine condescension" something good can happen. Apparently the husband's struggle is not with Christian doctrine; he does not need a careful explication of the oneness of God or a discussion of the anger of the gods. Instead, as Tertullian says repeatedly, the husband is troubled by "the distinctive religious observances of [Christians'] daily life," by "these practices of ours," by "our way of life." In short, the pagan husband's problem is the Christians' habitus.

But the habitus can be a conduit instead of a blockage. When the wife performs these observances, visibly, in the husband's presence, "the patronage of divine grace, at least in part" is present, and the husband can experience "a feeling of awe." In one compact sentence,[64] Tertullian (who is arguing against women believers marrying pagans) presents what can happen missionally in a mixed marriage. The unbelieving husband, he reports, has sensed the *magnalia*, the miraculous power of God; he has seen evidence of the truth; he has watched his wife as she has become a better person; and—to cap it all—he has become a "candidate for God." The "servant of Satan" is becoming a child of God. In fact, Tertullian says, "men like this are rather easily won over, once the grace of God has brought them into contact with the faith." For all the "chilling negativity" of some of Tertullian's views of

---

63. Tertullian, *Nat.* 1.4; *Apol.* 3.3; cf. Cyprian in *Ad Quir.* 3.90, who urges a Christian woman to stay with her pagan husband; but if she needs to depart, she should remain unmarried.

64. Tertullian, *Ux.* 2.7.2, ed. C. Munier, SC 273 (1980), 142: "Sensit magnalia, uidit experimenta, scit meliorem factum; sic et ipse Dei candidatus est timore."

women,[65] for all his squeamishness about mixed marriages, Tertullian had evidence that in mixed marriages Christian wives wooed husbands and that they were primary recruiters of new believers.

Conclusion

An unmixed marriage, Christian with Christian—this according to Tertullian enabled believers to live life in its fullness. This is not what we expect from the ascetic Tertullian, who said harsh things about marriage.[66] But here it is—Tertullian celebrating the knitting together of "two who are one," who together serve the same Master. Nothing divides them. And together they are able to live the Christian habitus: "Unembarrassed they visit the sick and assist the needy. . . . They attend the Sacrifice without difficulty. . . . They need not be furtive about making the Sign of the Cross, nor timorous in greeting the brethren."[67] They are a small community, a microcosm of the Christian assembly in which believers are formed into the body of Christ, and a part of the ferment of God's work in the world. As we leave this couple in the context of individual Christians as agents of growth, we anticipate the larger community that demonstrates God's patient work more fully than any individual or married couple could. To the larger community we turn in the coming chapter.

65. Elizabeth A. Clark, "Devil's Gateway and Bride of Christ: Women in the Early Christian World," in *Ascetic Piety and Women's Faith: Essays on Late Christian Antiquity*, Studies in Women and Religion 20 (Lewiston, NY: Edwin Mellen, 1986), 25, 29; e.g., Tertullian, *Cult. fem.* 1.1.1–2.

66. Tertullian, *Exh. cast.* 10, trans. W. P. Le Saint, ACW 13 (1956), 58: "How much better a man feels when he happens to be away from his wife."

67. Tertullian, *Ux.* 2.8.8, trans. W. P. Le Saint, ACW 13 (1956), 35.

5

COMMUNITIES AS CULTURES OF PATIENCE

It wasn't easy to live lives of patient ferment. As best they could, the early Christians individually followed Jesus patiently. Where, we may wonder, did they learn the habitus of patient living? Most probably it was in Christian communities. There, together with others, individual believers were formed in the disciplines that gave a distinctive character to a new culture that was visible to others and that, in their view, offered hope for the world.

The vision for this new culture, as we have seen, came in significant measure from Jesus's Sermon on the Mount, to which the early Christians paid great attention. Intriguingly, it also came from poetic passages in the Hebrew Scriptures. In the 240s, Origen, theologian and catechist, pointed to one of these in a letter to his friend Julius Africanus. Origen asked:

> For who of all believers does not know the words in Isaiah? "And in the last days the mountain of the Lord shall be manifest, and the house of the Lord on the top of the mountains, and it shall be exalted above the hills, and all nations shall come unto it. And many people shall go and say, 'Come ye, and let us go up to the mountain of the Lord, unto the house of the God of Jacob; and He will teach us his way, and we will walk in it.' For out of Zion shall go forth a law and the word of the Lord from Jerusalem. And he shall judge among the nations, and shall rebuke many peoples; they shall beat their swords into

ploughshares, and their spears into pruning-hooks. Nation shall not lift up
sword against nation, neither shall they learn war any more."[1]

According to Origen, this text (Isa. 2:2–4; Mic. 4:1–4) is one that all believers
knew. How did they learn it? Was it a regular component in the catechesis
that formed catechumens as they prepared for baptism? Origen could speak
for the catechists of Alexandria in Egypt and of Caesarea and Jerusalem in
Palestine, where he taught, and possibly also for the leaders in Nicomedia,
where he wrote his letter to Julius. But Christian catechists and writers in
other parts of the ancient world also gave prominence to the "swords into
plowshares" text.[2]

    According to Gerhard Lohfink, this is the prophetic passage the early Chris-
tian writers cited more often than any other.[3] Writers used the passage in many
ways.[4] For example, Justin Martyr, in his *Dialogue with Trypho*, used it to
describe the new culture that was being formed in Christian communities. To
be sure, Isaiah's prophecy had not been fulfilled on a grand scale; the world
was full of injustice and war. But it was being fulfilled in the life of Christian
communities. From the Law, gentile as well as Jewish Christians learned true
worship and were taught by "the word which went forth from Jerusalem by
means of the apostles of Jesus." As a result, they and their communities were
being transformed: "We who were filled with war, and mutual slaughter, and
every wickedness, have each through the whole earth changed our warlike
weapons—our swords into ploughshares, and our spears into implements of
tillage—and we cultivate piety, righteousness, philanthropy, faith, and hope,
which we have from the Father Himself through Him who was crucified."[5] The
word of Jesus had changed the cultivating of these followers of Jesus—their
culture—in ways both comprehensive and intertwining. The Isaiah prophecy
gave imaginative expression to what they had learned from Jesus. Communities found it possible to live a habitus that embodied God's purposes in the
present; further, this habitus enabled their members to face the future with
both patience and a peculiar exuberance.

    1. Origen, *Ep. to Julius Africanus* 15, trans. F. Crombie, ANF 4:392.
    2. Justin, *1 Apol.* 39.1–3; *Dial.* 110.3; Hippolytus, *Haer.* 6.11; Irenaeus, *Haer.* 4.34.4; Ter-
tullian, *Adv. Jud.* 3; *Marc.* 3.21; 4.1; Cyprian, *Hab. virg.* 11; *Ad Quir.* 2.18; 3.10; Origen, *Cels.*
5.33; also see *Did. apost.* 6.5; Firmilian, in Cyprian, *Ep.* 75.1. Fourth-century citations include
Eusebius, *Praise of Constantine* 6.3–7; *Preparation for the Gospel* 1.4.2–5; Athanasius, *On the
Incarnation* 52; Cyril of Alexandria, *Comm. on Isaiah* 2.4; Jerome, *Comm. on Micah* 2.4.1–7.
    3. Gerhard Lohfink, "'Schwerter zu Pflugscharen': Die Rezeption von Jes 2.1–5 par Mi 4.1–5
in der Alten Kirche und im Neuen Testament," *Theologische Quartalschrift* 166 (1986): 184–209.
    4. Robert L. Wilken, "In novissimis diebus," *JECS* 1 (1993): 1–9.
    5. Justin, *Dial.* 110.3, trans. A. C. Coxe, ANF 1:254.

Apologetics Written and Lived

Early Christian apologetic writings had a distinctive, incarnational character. The churches, like society as a whole, were made up primarily of uneducated people; so it may seem surprising that the early Christian writers were motivated to produce *apologies*, reasoned statements that defended their lifestyle and convictions. From the time of Aristides of Athens in the early second century to the cosmopolitan Lactantius two centuries later, Christians wrote apologies. Scholars have often minimized the importance of these apologetic writings. They have observed that the early Christians themselves were modest about the extent to which their writing reached outsiders. Tertullian, for example, referred to "our writings, to which no one comes for guidance unless he is already a Christian."[6] A century later Lactantius reflected back over the Christian writings of the first three centuries AD and reported that none of them had interested the pagan literary public. In Lactantius's view, most of the Christian writers were not "wholly eloquent," and even the one who was undeniably eloquent—the rhetorician Cyprian—was philosophically lightweight.[7]

Recently Simon Price has pointed out how hit or miss the apologists' range of subjects was. He gives a long list of topics that apologists failed to treat properly: "There is little on the Bible, little on Christology, nothing about the Holy Spirit or the emerging doctrine of the Trinity; little on the Redemption (only Judgment); nothing about the Church, its ministry, sacraments, and other practices."[8] And Michael Green, assessing the apologetic writings for their evangelistic success, has concluded that there is "no example of an outsider being converted to Christianity by reading an Apologetic writing."[9] To critics ancient and modern, the apologists appear to have been unsuccessful.

Nevertheless the ancient Christians kept writing apologies. Why? In part, no doubt, because they hoped that some influential pagans would read their writing. And in the years after 180, a few scattered pagans may have begun to do this, as the Christian presence in society grew and the Christian arguments became more sophisticated.[10] When the apologists dedicated their works to emperors, imperial magistrates, and philosophers who were "reckoned to be teachers of

---

6. Tertullian, *Test.* 1, trans. S. Thelwall, *ANF* 3:175.
7. Lactantius, *Inst.* 5.1.22–28, trans. A. C. Coxe, *ANF* 7:136.
8. Simon Price, "Latin Christian Apologetics: Minucius Felix, Tertullian, and Cyprian," in *Apologetics in the Roman Empire: Pagans, Jews, and Christians*, ed. Mark Edwards, Martin Goodman, Simon Price, and Christopher Rowland (Oxford: Oxford University Press, 1999), 123.
9. Michael Green, *Evangelism in the Early Church* (London: Hodder & Stoughton, 1970), 233.
10. Harry Y. Gamble, *Books and Readers in the Early Church* (New Haven: Yale University Press, 1995), 112–13.

how to live well," they were no doubt expressing their hope that their writings would reach a wider circle of non-Christian readers.[11] Further, the apologists wrote to convince their readers of the innocence of the Christian communities' behavior. In fact, behavior figured largely in the apologists' writings because the Christians' clandestine lifestyle was subject to rumor, vilification, and attack. But more generally, the apologists wrote extensively on behavior because of their Christian conviction that the way people live expresses what they really believe.

Writing about Habitus

Reading apologetic writings written today would not lead one to this conclusion.[12] Contemporary apologetics is an intellectual discipline involving rational combat, intellectual jujitsu. The early Christian apologists, in contrast, talked about habitus as well as ideas; their discourse had to do with how people live as well as what they think. In their writings the apologists bore testimony to the changes that Christian conversion had brought about in their lives. In the mid-second century, Justin began his *First Apology* by stating his aim: "It is for us, therefore, to offer to all the opportunity of inspecting our life and teachings."[13] For Justin the life is as important as the teachings; indeed, the teachings are incomprehensible without the lived reflexes that exegete them.[14] Significantly, a century later the great intellectual Origen agreed: at the beginning of his apology *Contra Celsum*, he states that Christ "makes his defense in the lives of his genuine disciples, for their lives cry out the real facts."[15]

In the 170s the apologist Athenagoras, in his *Plea* to Marcus Aurelius and other emperors, wrote about the way Christians were habituated to live. "For we have been taught not to strike back at someone who beats us nor to go to court with those who rob and plunder us. Not only that: we have even been taught to turn our head and offer the other side when men ill use us and strike us on the jaw and to give also our cloak should they snatch our tunic." Later in the apology Athenagoras underscored this patient habitus: when the Christians are struck, they bless.[16]

11. Lactantius, *Inst.* 1.8, trans. Anthony Bowen and Peter Garnsey, TTH 40 (Liverpool: Liverpool University Press, 2003), 58; Justin, *1 Apol.* 1–2; Tertullian, *Apol.* 1.1.

12. Alan Kreider, "Ressourcement and Mission," *Anglican Theological Review* 96, no. 2 (2014): 253–54.

13. Justin, *1 Apol.* 3, trans. E. R. Hardy, LCC 1 (1953): 243.

14. Justin, *1 Apol.* 16.8.

15. Origen, *Cels.*, preface 2, trans. H. Chadwick, *Origen: Contra Celsum* (Cambridge: Cambridge University Press, 1965), 4.

16. Athenagoras, *Leg.* 1.3; 34.3, trans. W. Schoedel, *Athenagoras: Legatio* (Oxford: Clarendon, 1972), 5, 83.

Tertullian was in the same tradition. His *Apology* is saturated with descriptions of habitus; indeed, Tertullian designed the *Apology* so it would climax in chapter 39 with his presentation of the Christian community's common life. Clearly the early Christians thought their way of life was important, for lifestyle is not only a product of belief; it is a display of what people truly believe. Patristic scholar Everett Ferguson is unusual in his alertness to this: "The earliest Apologists make the description of the Christian life the main point in their exposition of Christianity. . . . [Even in the later Apologists] the argument from Christian living still holds a prominent place."[17] The early Christians sensed that their habitus was their most authentic way of communicating their message to outsiders, and they believed that some outsiders would respond to it as good news.

Writing for Internal Consumption

But weren't the apologists "writing chiefly for internal consumption"?[18] Probably. But that in no way diminishes their importance. The apologists knew that the insiders—the members of the Christian community and the catechumens who were being formed for membership—needed what they were writing. Indeed, the primary function of their apologetic writings was to contribute to the community's mission by building up the Christians and by strengthening their common life. Even if the outsiders didn't read the apologies, they would read the lives of the insiders! And they would read the Christians and their communities![19] As a result, when Christians lived a distinctive vision, they were challenging outsiders to investigate the Christian faith more deeply.

The apologists thus served the internal readership in several ways:

- They enabled Christians to sense that their faith was deeply rooted in their life experience.
- They built up the Christians' sense of self-respect, by conveying to them that although they were a minority movement, widely disdained and

17. Everett Ferguson, *Early Christians Speak: Faith and Life in the First Three Centuries*, rev. ed. (Abilene, TX: ACU Press, 1987), 201. See also Gustave Bardy, *La conversion au christianisme durant les premiers siècles* (Paris: Aubier, 1949), 149.

18. Ramsay MacMullen, *Christianizing the Roman Empire (A.D. 100–400)* (New Haven: Yale University Press, 1984), 21.

19. See, e.g., Galen's response to the Christians in his *Summary of Plato's Republic* 3, in *Religions of Rome*, vol. 2, *A Sourcebook*, compiled by Mary Beard, John North, and Simon Price (Cambridge: Cambridge University Press, 1998), 338: "Thus we now *see* the people called Christians."

occasionally persecuted, and although many of them were poor, their scholars could make a case for Christianity in conversation with recognized philosophers.

- They provided Christians with arguments they could use when engaging in conversations with their pagan neighbors.
- They enabled the church's intellectuals to engage in dialogue with the philosophical schools, to find common ground with them, and to be wise when they incorporated philosophical thinking into Christian doctrine.[20]
- They guided the gentile Christians as they reflected on their pagan past, sifting their inherited beliefs and practices so that they could disentangle themselves from what was destructive while finding new ways to express old things that they, as disciples of Christ, could continue to value.[21]

The apologists were indispensable participants in the patient ferment of the Christian mission, above all by fostering the distinctive lifestyle of Christians who would intrigue people, bless them, and attract them to faith.[22]

Inculturation—Christians Permeate Culture

But were the Christians of the early centuries distinctive? Their leaders kept telling them that they ought to be distinctive. Cyprian, in one of his catechetical precepts, stated baldly that "the believer ought not to live like the Gentile."[23] And certainly some of the Christians' neighbors viewed them as comprehensive misfits. From one of his contacts, Tertullian heard that the Christians were "unprofitable in business," which sparked one of his rants.

> We are not Brahmans, naked sages of India, forest-dwellers, exiles from life. We remember that we owe gratitude to God, the Lord, the creator. We reject no fruit of His labours. . . . So, not without your forum, not without your meat-market, not without your baths, shops, factories, your inns and market-days, and the rest of the life of buying and selling, we live with you—in this world [*in hoc saeculo*]. We sail ships, we as well as you, and along with you; we serve in the army [*militamus*],

20. Peter Lampe, *From Paul to Valentinus: Christians in Rome in the First Two Centuries* (Minneapolis: Fortress, 2003), 283–84.

21. Kwame Bediako, *Theology and Identity: The Impact of Culture upon Christian Thought in the Second Century and Modern Africa* (Oxford: Regnum Books, 1992), 32.

22. Robert Wilken, *The Christians as the Romans Saw Them* (New Haven: Yale University Press, 1984), 198: "The reason Christianity succeeded in making its way within the Roman world was due less to what Christians believed than to the way they lived."

23. Cyprian, *Ad Quir.* 3.34, trans. E. Wallis, *ANF* 5:544.

go to the country, to market with you. Our arts and yours work together; our labour is openly at your service. How we can seem unprofitable to your business, when we live with you and our living depends on you, I do not know.[24]

The Christians, says Tertullian, are everywhere. Almost everywhere, that is. Maybe most of them do not join the pagans in celebrating the uninhibited seasonal festivities of the *Liberalia*; maybe they do not buy incense. And of course Christians may do some things in their own way; they are temperate— we do "not use [God's] gifts to excess."[25] But the Christians are in society, sharing life with their neighbors. Tertullian gives hints that Christians have a distinctive style—by using the Latin verb *militare* he may mean that the Christians serve in the army without warring or killing (*bellare*).[26] Tertullian affirms society, but he also gives hints of conditionality.

In Clement of Alexandria, the same combination of affirmation and conditionality is evident. "Till the ground, we say, if you are a husbandman; but recognize God in your husbandry. Sail the sea, you who love sea-faring; but ever call upon the heavenly pilot. Were you a soldier on campaign when the knowledge of God laid hold of you? Then listen to the commander who signals righteousness."[27]

As Tertullian and Clement negotiated the relationship between solidarity with the wider culture and critique of it, they were engaging in what missiologists call *inculturation*. Inculturation is rooted in the recognition that Christianity, like every religion, is embedded in cultures. As Christian thinkers, missiologists affirm that Christianity can bring liberation to every culture; that is, it can enable the culture's best self to flourish as its people find Christ in their midst, living, teaching, and finding goodness in their culture. However, missiologists also affirm that religions, including Christianity, can be prisoners of culture—defying Christ and his way and succumbing to the gravitational pulls that in every culture lead to injustice, violence, and oppression. So, as Scottish missiologist Andrew Walls argues, when Christianity enters every culture, inculturation is inevitable. In every setting, including the cultures of the ancient Greco-Roman world, two principles are simultaneously at work:[28]

---

24. Tertullian, *Apol.* 42.1, trans. T. R. Glover, LCL 250 (1931), 191.

25. Tertullian, *Apol.* 42.2, 5–7 (Glover, 191–93).

26. Henri F. Secrétan, "Le Christianisme des premiers siècles et le service militaire," *Revue de Théologie et de Philosophie* 2 (1914): 345–65; Jean-Michel Hornus, *It Is Not Lawful for Me to Fight: Early Christian Attitudes toward War, Violence, and the State*, trans. Alan Kreider and Oliver Coburn (Scottdale, PA: Herald Press, 1980), 158–59, 174–75; Alan Kreider, "Military Service in the Church Orders," *Journal of Religious Ethics* 31, no. 3 (2003): 423–25.

27. Clement of Alexandria, *Protr.* 10, trans. G. W. Butterworth, LCL 60 (1919), 219.

28. Andrew F. Walls, *The Missionary Movement in Christian History: Studies in the Transmission of Faith* (Maryknoll, NY: Orbis Books, 1996), 6–9; also Robert Schreiter, "Inculturation of Faith or Identification with Culture," in *Christianity and Cultures: A Mutual Enrichment*,

The indigenizing principle: Christianity enters a culture and finds new expressions there, discovering understandings and customs that embody the way of Christ. Christians celebrate the culture and are at home in it; they are *residents* in it.

The pilgrim principle: Christianity enters a culture and finds ways in which the culture contradicts the way and teachings of Christ. So Christianity critiques the culture, and seeks to embody alternatives that challenge the culture and invite it toward a life in which injustice, violence and oppression are overcome. In the culture Christians are not fully at home; they are *resident aliens (paroikoi)* in it.

In the ancient world, when Christians were at their best, they sensed a dynamic interplay between indigenizing and being pilgrim, between affirmation and critique. They lived in existential tension between being at home and being strangers. Christians living in Carthage or Caesarea experienced two things: gratitude for the beauties in their local cultures and also discomfort with the distortions in their cultures to which the gospel had sensitized them. As a result, out of their love for their cultures, the Christians attempted to embody alternatives that pointed the way forward for the healing of their cultures. Both as individual believers and also as believing communities, they lived lives that contained a *yes* and a *no*. With both they aimed to make a positive contribution to the common good.

The passages from Tertullian and Clement that we have just read are good examples of Christians thinking in an inculturational way. But there is a classic text in which an early Christian most explicitly wrestles with the tugs and pulls of inculturation—the anonymous second-century Epistle to Diognetus.

For Christians are no different from other people in terms of their country, language, or customs. Nowhere do they inhabit cities of their own, use a strange dialect, or live life out of the ordinary. . . . They inhabit both Greek and barbarian cities, according to the lot assigned to each. And they show forth the character of their own citizenship [*politeias*] in a marvelous and admittedly paradoxical way by following local customs in what they wear and what they eat and in the rest of their lives. They live in their respective countries, *but* only as resident aliens [*paroikoi*]; they participate in all things as citizens, *and* they endure all things as foreigners. . . . They marry like everyone else and have children, *but* they do not expose them once they are born. They share their meals *but* not their sexual partners. They are obedient to the laws that have been made, *and* by their own lives they supersede the laws. . . . They are impoverished *and* make

---

ed. Norbert Greinacher and Norbert Mette (Maryknoll, NY: Orbis), 22, who speaks of "identification" with culture and "transformation" of culture.

many rich. . . . To put the matter simply, what the soul is in the body, this is what Christians are in the world.[29]

The nameless writer of this letter identifies the Christians with their neighbors. Christians are ordinary: they live in the same *insulae*, wear the same kinds of clothing, speak with the same idioms and accents as other people, and eat the local foods. But Christians are also extraordinary. They know the tension between their two citizenships that expresses itself in a commitment to the local culture that is clear but conditional. Christians are "cafeteria Carthaginians." They are people of both *and* (*kai*) and *but* (*alla*). They do some things that their neighbors do, *and* at times they do local things with greater intensity and energy than their non-Christian neighbors. *But* the Christians are also inconvenient: they view some local behaviors—that most people view as normal—to be dehumanizing and destructive. These behaviors are contrary to the Christians' own habituated values, and Christians simply cannot do them and be true to themselves. So they will marry like everyone else and have children *but* they will not expose unwanted infants on the local landfill. They will share food *but* they will not share sexual partners.

As a result, the Christians are hybrid people. They are *paroikoi*, resident aliens, living locally and participating in society, but not as full citizens.[30] They believe that their presence is for the benefit of the entire society. As the writer ambitiously puts it, "What the soul is in the body, this is what Christians are in the world." The neighbors, at times for good reason, are not always impressed by the believers. The writer of the Epistle to Diognetus knows that at times people persecute the Christians even when the Christians "make many rich." But the Christians don't live as they do out of an evangelistic calculus. They live as they do because this is who they are.

Distinctive Communities

The Christians' lifestyle embodies their habitus, the reflexes that reveal the inner character that resulted from their conversion. And their character manifests the distinctiveness of their theology. As we saw in chapter 2, the early Christians developed a theology of patience rooted in their understanding of God's character and the life and teaching of Jesus Christ. Their theology led them to espouse ways of doing things that were patient. These were distinctive,

29. *Diogn.* 5.1–6, 10; 6.1 (my emphases), trans. B. D. Ehrman, LCL 25 (2003), 139–41.
30. Pierre de Labriolle, "Paroecia," *Bulletin du Cange (Archivum Latinitatis Medii Aevi)* 3 (1927): 196–207.

challenging conventional values and resulted in a distinctive habitus that had to be taught and modeled in many areas of life. This habitus, they believed, attracted people to faith in Christ and to membership in the Christian communities. What were these patient Christian communities like, and how were they formed?

Distinctive Communities (1)—Patience in Business

The early Christians tried to find ways to express patience in their business dealings. Justin, who points to this in his *First Apology*, does not give details about how it worked. In chapter 16 he begins by recalling Jesus's teaching in the Sermon on the Mount on "being longsuffering (patient) and servants to all": when someone smites you on one cheek, you turn the other cheek; if compelled to go one mile, you go two miles; do not be angry. Justin sees missional reasons for this behavior: "Let your good works shine before men, that they as they see may wonder at your Father who is in heaven." Justin goes on:

> For we ought not to quarrel; he has not wished us to imitate the wicked, but rather by our patience and meekness to draw all men from shame and evil desires. This we can show in the case of many who were once on your side but have turned from the ways of violence and tyranny, overcome by observing the consistent lives of their neighbors, or noting the strange patience of their injured acquaintances, or experiencing the way they did business with them.[31]

How did this work out in the murky area of business in which Christians were attempting to be faithful to Jesus? What did patience mean for Christians who were business people? It probably had many meanings that varied with the person and place, whether carried on by men or by women who also "participated fully in business activities."[32] Perhaps patience meant that Christians would not press creditors for payment. Or perhaps it meant that Christians would be willing to speak the unadorned truth about a product they were selling. At times it may have meant that Christians refused to retaliate when another business person treated them unethically. Or, as Tertullian reports, it may have meant that when Christians borrowed money from pagans, they would not follow the customary practice of giving guarantees under oaths (which were forbidden to Christians) or be entangled with written

31. Justin, *1 Apol.* 16.3–4 (Hardy, 252).
32. Jane F. Gardner, *Women in Roman Law and Society* (Bloomington: Indiana University Press, 1986), 233–37.

contracts that were the equivalents of oaths.[33] Very likely patience meant that Christians would refuse to engage in litigation in the lawcourts, which they saw as a repudiation of their commitment to "act according to the teachings of godly patience."[34] In Alexandria, according to Clement, patience meant that when a Christian businessman gave a quote on something he was selling, he quoted only one price and spoke "plainly and honestly." Consolingly, Clement noted that if this meant that the Christian lost on a transaction, he would benefit spiritually: "he will at least gain in truth, and be the richer by an upright disposition."[35] Justin, in contrast, put the benefits of patience in terms of the church's growth. He saw that when non-Christians experienced patience in practice they were disarmed. In fact, some pagans were so attracted by the patient behavior of Christian business people that they "turned from the ways of violence and tyranny" and became believers.[36]

Distinctive Communities (2)—Sexual Discipline

The Christians' life was not solitary. The worship and common life of local Christian communities shaped the believers and gave them distinctive habitual approaches to issues that faced everyone in society. The Christians' habitus thus offered new options to society. For example, many contemporaries noted that the Christians were committed to sexual purity, and they admired this. Justin prioritized it. In his *First Apology* he begins his presentation of the sayings of Jesus as they applied to the Christians' life by discussing sexual continence (*sōphrosynē*). He underscores the urgent importance of this by citing, in his summary of teachings from the Sermon on the Mount, Jesus's command to his disciples to cut out the roving eye that misleads into incontinence (Matt. 5:29). He points to Christians in Rome "and in every nation" who have repudiated adulterous glances, avoided second marriages, and committed themselves to lifelong continence. Justin maintains that the Christians' sexual discipline attracted to the faith an "uncounted multitude of those who have turned away from incontinence."[37]

The North African apologist Minucius Felix agreed that the Christians' chaste lives spoke to a need in contemporary culture, encouraging people to investigate Christianity. Of course he knew that rumors of orgiastic behavior were circulating; people "throw the mud of infamous aspersions upon our

33. Tertullian, *Idol.* 23.
34. Tertullian, *Scap.* 2, trans. R. Arbesmann, FC 10 (1950), 153.
35. Clement of Alexandria, *Paed.* 3.11.78, trans. S. P. Wood, FC 23 (1954), 259.
36. Justin, *1 Apol.* 16.4 (Hardy, 252).
37. Justin, *1 Apol.* 15, esp. 15.7 (Hardy, 250).

boasted purity."[38] Athenagoras also knew this; he reported that his community in Athens carefully monitored the kiss of peace in their eucharistic services lest it should give a hint of credibility to the rumors—no believer was to "kiss twice because it was pleasurable."[39] The *Apostolic Tradition*, a church order in large measure written in the third century, indicates the importance that the early Christians accorded to sexual discipline by questions that teachers addressed to potential candidates for the catechumenate. What were the candidates' marital commitments? What was their sexual behavior? In the church, at least, there was not to be sexual scandal![40]

But the Christians were not concerned simply to avoid scandal. They believed that sexual purity was crucially important in forming Christian character and in shaping viable communities. Further, the Christians believed that sexual purity was a means of attracting outsiders. Minucius Felix's famous statement that "beauty of life encourages . . . strangers to join the ranks" had to do with the Christians' reputation for sexual discipline, which he saw as having implications for the church's growth.[41] Looking on from a distance, the philosopher Galen was of course not ready to become a Christian, but he was deeply impressed by the Christians' sexual behavior. Their "restraint in cohabitation" compelled him to take their faith seriously as a movement of philosophical substance.[42]

Distinctive Communities (3)—Men, Women, and Children

Nothing did more to make the Christian communities distinctive than their sheer heterogeneity. Not only were women and men together; so also were children and old people. In the late second century, the pagan Celsus criticized Christians for attracting "women and little children." Over a century later, the Christian philosopher Lactantius reported that pagans criticized Christians for having in their midst "our old women, whom they despise and . . . our children, too."[43] Unlike most associations and mysteries, the churches were

---

38. Minucius Felix, *Oct.* 31.1, trans. G. H. Rendall, LCL 250 (1931), 409. Rumors with some basis: see Irenaeus, *Haer.* 1.25.3; 2.31.2; Clement of Alexandria, *Strom.* 3.2.10; Justin, *1 Apol.* 26; Epiphanius, *Pan.* 26.4–5.
39. Athenagoras, *Leg.* 32.5 (Schoedel, 81).
40. *Trad. ap.* 15.6–7.
41. Minucius Felix, *Oct.* 31.7 (Rendall, 413).
42. Galen, *Summary of Plato's Republic* 3, in Beard, North, and Price, *Sourcebook*, 338. See also Athenagoras, *Leg.* 33.4.
43. Origen, *Cels.* 3.55 (Chadwick, 166); Lactantius, *Inst.* 5.19.14 (Bowen and Garnsey, 321). See also Tatian, *Or. Graec.* 32, trans. M. Whittaker (Oxford: Clarendon, 1982), 59: "Thus we wish all to hear, even if they are old women or youngsters, and in general every age enjoys respect with us."

communities which wanted women and actively recruited them. And children too: the Christians raised children from their infancy and shaped their habitus and thinking as Christians. In AD 165 in Rome, when the prefect Rusticus interrogated the philosopher Justin and his students, several of the students responded by expressing their indebtedness to their parents. "I listened gladly to the teaching of Justin," said Evelpistus, "but I also received my faith from my parents [in Cappadocia]." Another student, Paeon, similarly said that he received his faith from his parents. And a third, Hierax, simply said, "I have long been a Christian and ever shall be."[44] To be sure, their Christian faith could be deepened and refined, which was Justin's work, but it was rooted in the lives of families and local churches, whose task it was to "discipline their children in the reverential fear of God."[45] It is possible that these children, who had learned the Christian faith and habitus from their parents, were essential ingredients in the ferment that went on inside households, and they may have played a role in attracting non-Christians who shared life with them day in and day out.[46]

In light of the presence of children, it is surprising to note how little the early Christian sources tell us about the roles of children in Christian communities.[47] In lists of community members we find children as categories but never as named individuals.[48] The *Didascalia apostolorum*, which ordered the life of sizable communities in third-century Syria, devotes considerable attention to children, for whose training in crafts and "the word of the Lord" the bishop took responsibility. It also prescribes the places where the "young," the "children," and the "young girls" should sit or stand—on one side, or with their fathers or mothers. But the *Didascalia* tells us virtually nothing about the children's role in the church's worship or in its practical ministries.[49] In some places the children's presence in worship services was the result of their baptism at an early age. In places where child baptism occasionally took place but was not the norm, children may have been present as a result of an "infant dedication," which did not authorize their participation in the Eucharist.[50]

---

44. *Acts of Justin* 4, Recension B, trans. and ed. Herbert A. Musurillo, *The Acts of the Christian Martyrs* (Oxford: Clarendon, 1972), 50–51.

45. Pol. *Phil.* 4.2, trans. B. D. Ehrman, LCL 24 (2003), 339; *Did.* 4.9.

46. Margaret Y. MacDonald, "Was Celsus Right? The Role of Women in the Expansion of Early Christianity," in *Early Christian Families in Context: An Interdisciplinary Dialogue*, ed. David L. Balch and Carolyn Osiek (Grand Rapids: Eerdmans, 2003), 157–84, here 174.

47. Horn and Martens, *"Let the Little Children Come,"* 113.

48. E.g., Clement of Alexandria, *Quis div.* 34, trans. G. W. Butterworth, LCL 60 (1919), 343.

49. *Did. apost.* 4.11; 2.57.8.

50. David F. Wright, "Infant Dedication in the Early Church," in *Baptism, the New Testament and the Church: Historical and Contemporary Studies in Honour of R. E. O. White*, ed.

The roles of women are somewhat clearer. Women were not the titular leaders, but everyone knew that they were essential if the church was to live its vision of catholicity. To be true to itself, Christianity had to have two genders! How unlike the mystery cult of Mithras that appealed to soldiers. Critics made fun of the Christians, of course; and the believers responded by delighting in the presence of "our old women." Writers such as Lactantius emphasized that the women were there because they wanted to be. Christianity was voluntary and uncompelled; women and men were both in the church because "there is free will in it."[51]

The women were evidently also essential to enabling the Christians to live the vision that made them so widely attractive—their commitment to care for poor people. To be sure, all the Christians were to participate in caring for the poor. According to the *Apostolic Tradition*, only those candidates—male as well as female—who "honored the widows . . . and visited those who are sick" were admitted to baptism.[52] Tertullian's happy married couple shared together in the tasks of visiting the sick and attending the needy.[53] However, already in the second century pagans reported that it was especially women who were involved in caring for prisoners.[54]

The churches couldn't function without women. By the early fourth century a church order noted that it was especially a woman's task to "concern herself with the poor, her neighbours."[55] In order to do this, women didn't have to be literate, and it is likely that over 90 percent of the Christians were illiterate. But like all Christians, the women could memorize texts. Isaiah's "swords into plowshares" passage, for example, could give them a vision of the way to live in the new world that God had promised and that they were helping bring to reality.[56] Women who visited their neighbors and influenced their husbands were probably the church's most effective evangelists.

How did women and men participate in the common life of the communities? Various texts indicate that the common life was intense. Unlike most pagan associations, the Christian churches met often, at the very least once a week; Justin reports that his Roman congregation met much more frequently

Stanley E. Porter and Anthony R. Cross, JSNTSup 171 (Sheffield: Sheffield Academic Press, 1999), 362–64.

51. Lactantius, *Inst.* 5.19.11, 14 (Bowen and Garnsey, 320–21).
52. *Trad. ap.* 20.1 (BJP, 104).
53. Tertullian, *Ux.* 2.8.8.
54. Lucian, *Peregr.* 12–13.
55. *Canons of Hippolytus* (17), trans. Carol Bebawi, ed. Paul F. Bradshaw, Alcuin/GROW Liturgical Study 2 (Bramcote, UK: Grove Books, 1987), 19.
56. Origen, *Cels.* 3.55.

than that—"we are constantly together."[57] When the believers gathered for daily prayer or catechesis, for practical aid or fellowship, they met as "sisters" and "brothers" in a fictive family. Even into the third century, their meetings, although structured, seem to have been characterized by emotional intensity and unpredictability; in North Africa, women who were rarely the titular leaders nevertheless ecstatically prophesied and offered psalms, visions, and prayers.[58] It appears that when women and men experienced God in affective worship, they were enabled to act with courage and passionate discipline. This was necessary for all Christians, who often lived in precarious situations they could not control. But it was especially necessary for Christian women. Women who were slaves found it excruciatingly difficult to cope with the demands of pagan masters for sexual liaisons; and women in mixed marriages with pagans were no doubt grieved and repelled when their husbands demanded to abort or expose unwanted offspring. So it would not be surprising if Christian women felt liberated—both sexually and as people who rejected killing—when their husbands became believers.[59] At last they could live the church's teachings with the support of their husbands!

In the third century a process was under way that was transforming Christian community life, making it more like the patriarchal Greco-Roman society. The size of many Christian communities was growing, and the character of their worship was changing, not least their practice of the Eucharist. In many places, what was originally a real meal coupled with an act of thanksgiving was coming to be a ritual meal with token food.[60] Clergy, always men, presided at the gatherings, and opportunities for believers (including women) to exercise spiritual gifts withered. Facing pressures that constricted their participation in worship, Christian women appealed to the example of the intrepid Thecla, the apostle and disciple of Paul whose exploits were recorded in the novelistic *Acts of Paul and Thecla*.[61] In light of Thecla's precedent, they argued, surely it was right for Christian women to teach and baptize! But Tertullian, alluding to 1 Timothy 2:12, was adamant. "How could we

57. Justin, *1 Apol.* 67.1 (Hardy, 287).

58. Tertullian, *An.* 9.4; *Marc.* 5.8.4; Cecil M. Robeck Jr., *Prophecy in Carthage: Perpetua, Tertullian, and Cyprian* (Cleveland: Pilgrim Press, 1992), 128–34.

59. Rodney Stark, *The Rise of Christianity: A Sociologist Reconsiders History* (Princeton: Princeton University Press, 1996), 104.

60. Andrew McGowan, "Rethinking Agape and Eucharist in Early North African Christianity," *SL* 34 (2004): 133–46.

61. The literature on Thecla is immense; e.g., see Kate Cooper, *The Virgin and the Bride: Idealized Womanhood in Late Antiquity* (Cambridge, MA: Harvard University Press, 1996), 50–56, 64–66; Stephen J. Davis, *The Cult of St Thecla: A Tradition of Women's Piety in Late Antiquity* (Oxford: Oxford University Press, 2001).

believe that Paul should give a female power to teach and to baptize, when he did not allow a woman even to learn by her own right?"[62] Tertullian agreed that spiritually gifted women could prophesy during worship, but only if they were on the fringes of the gatherings; and it was necessary for male leaders to vet their prophetic messages.[63] Fifty years after Tertullian, Bishop Cyprian stated this as a principle for all catechumens in Carthage to learn: "That a woman ought to be silent in church."[64] At about the same time the Syrian *Didascalia apostolorum* ordered women to sit by themselves in worship, in the west end of the room farthest removed from the bishops and presbyters in the east, with the laymen in between.[65] When worshiping, women and men were in the same room, but the women's location reminded them of their inferiority.

Of course the ministries of women continued. As we shall see in chapter 8, well into the fourth century the widows continued to play an important role in the Syrian Christian communities. But they did this from their base at home, where they prayed and weaved wool under the authority of the bishops and presbyters.[66] As to the widows' earlier roles of visitation and outreach, the clergy increasingly entrusted this to women in the order of deaconesses, who seem to have been more amenable to clerical control.[67] Increasingly leadership within the church was patriarchal, and the married Christian women sensed this. Church leaders attempted to confine the women to their own homes under the authority of their husbands. Of course this was easier said than done. In the late fourth century, Bishop Ambrose, offended by behavior that at times may have had similar motivation to that of earlier Christian women, ordered women in Milan to stay at home and not run about in the streets; in Antioch and Constantinople, Bishop John Chrysostom gave similar instructions.[68] By the late fourth century, when women were still in the churches they were unequivocally under the authority of men. At least they were supposed to be in the churches. Their evangelistic verve and compassionate caregiving, so much a part of the life of the earlier Christians, had been stifled.

62. Tertullian, *Bapt.* 17, trans. S. Thelwall, ANF 3:677. In *Virg.* 9, trans. S. Thelwall, ANF 4:33, Tertullian not only forbade women to speak in church but also to teach, baptize, or preside at the Eucharist; they must not claim for themselves "any manly function" or any "sacerdotal office."

63. Tertullian, *An.* 9.4.

64. Cyprian, *Ad Quir.* 3.46, trans. E. Wallis, ANF 5:46.

65. *Did. apost.* 2.57.5.

66. *Did. apost.* 3.7.8.

67. *Did. apost.* 3.12.

68. Ambrose, *Comm. on Luke* 2.21; John Chrysostom, *Homily 61 on John* 160; *Homily on the Incomprehensibility of God* 11.39–40.

Distinctive Communities (4)—Manifestations of Divine Power

Most of the believers we have encountered were not powerful people. Few of them had sociocultural power. In the course of the third century, wealthier people began to join the churches, including some *decurions*—urban aristocrats, people of the equestrian order—and the wealth of the churches was growing and at times was considerable.[69] But the churches continued to mirror the profile of the entire society, which meant that most of their members remained people of varying degrees of poverty. The Christians also found themselves involved in struggles with a systemic web of forces that they saw as evil—social, spiritual, economic, religious, political. At times these forces persecuted them and attempted to humiliate, intimidate, and crush them.

Nevertheless, during the early centuries the Christians gave the impression of being confidently powerful. Why? In part because they believed that the struggles they were involved in were above all spiritual. They saw themselves as fighting not primarily against humans or institutions but against spiritual forces that were hostile to them and that impeded human flourishing. They saw their enemies as demons, personified spiritual forces that had considerable but limited power. In contrast to the pagans who understood the demons to be lower-ranking, intermediate spiritual beings that could be either benevolent or workers of mischief or evil, the Christians from an early stage viewed the demons as invariably bad.[70] The demons did have power—their role in engineering the crucifixion of Jesus was evidence of this. But the believers confessed that on the cross Jesus had exposed the true nature of the demonic powers and vanquished them. And not only that—he also, through the Holy Spirit, had unleashed unimaginable spiritual power for good in the world. The Christians claimed that they had access to this power. When the Christians encountered what they viewed as demonic forces, they believed they could defeat these forces through prayers for exorcism and healing.

Prayer for Exorcism

How did these prayers work in practice? The catechetical homilies of Origen give us a fascinating example. In the 240s Origen, the greatest theologian of early Christianity, went to Jerusalem to do a brief stint as a catechist. He spoke in daily sessions to catechumens, preparing them for baptism by

69. Wolfgang Wischmeyer, *Von Golgatha zum Ponte Molle: Studien zur Sozialgeschichte der Kirche im dritten Jahrhundert*, Forschungen zur Kirchen- und Dogmengeschichte 49 (Göttingen: Vandenhoeck & Ruprecht, 1992), 171–75.

70. Ramsay MacMullen, *Paganism in the Roman Empire* (New Haven: Yale University Press, 1981), 79–82; Everett Ferguson, *Demonology of the Early Christian World*, Symposium Series 12 (New York: Edwin Mellen, 1984), 108–17.

teaching them about the book of 1 Samuel. A scribe was there to record Origen's words. As we enter the scene, Origen is in full flow, speaking about the call of Hannah (1 Sam. 2).

> That is why the Scripture has taught us to reject terrestrial joys, perishable and decaying, to exult in eternal joys in the Lord, as Hannah rightly spoke, "My heart has exulted in the Lord." And at the very moment when these words were spoken, one of those attending was filled with an impure spirit and cried out. This provoked a rushing together of the people. . . . For when Hannah said, "My heart exults in the Lord" the hostile spirit was not able to bear our exultation in the Lord, but he wanted to change it to introduce in its place sadness and to prevent us from saying, "My spirit has rejoiced in the Lord." But we, not allowing ourselves to stop, said on the contrary more and more, "My spirit has rejoiced in the Lord," for the very reason that we see impure spirits tormented, for things like this lead many people to be converted to God, many to reform themselves, many to come to faith. God doesn't do anything without reason, and he doesn't permit anything to happen for naught. There are in fact lots of people who do not believe in the Word and who do not receive the delivery of the teaching, but when the demon seizes them, then they become converted.[71]

As this account makes clear, Origen was not taken aback by this turn of events. He had evidently experienced similar things previously.[72] Elsewhere he describes the approach that he takes to this kind of situation: he combats the demonic power by "the incantation of Scripture and by a constant repetition of the divine discourse."[73] So in Jerusalem, Origen—confident that the angels of God were protecting him and his catechumens—concentrated on driving away the evil spirit by a repetitive incantation of Hannah's exuberant praise. Then, when the demon-oppressed person had been freed from bondage, Origen turned to his catechumens and integrated what had just happened into his teaching, interpreting it for them. Origen concedes that week in and

---

71. Origen, *Hom. Sam.* 1.10, trans. and ed. Pierre Nautin and Marie-Thérèse Nautin, *Origène: Homélies sur Samuel*, SC 328 (Paris: Cerf, 1986), 133.

72. Parallel happenings are recorded among African independent churches: "Sometimes services are interrupted by evil spirits. In the midst of prayer or during singing and dancing, someone will cry out in a loud voice and fall to the ground in an act of spirit possession. . . . Prophets immediately surround the affected person. . . . They lay hands on the afflicted." Dana L. Robert and M. L. Daneel, "Worship among Apostles and Zionists in Southern Africa, Zimbabwe," in *Christian Worship Worldwide: Expanding Horizons, Deepening Practices*, ed. Charles Farhadian (Grand Rapids: Eerdmans, 2007), 59.

73. Origen, *Hom. Jos.* 20.1, trans. B. J. Bruce, FC 105 (2002), 176. In *Cels.* 8.58 (Chadwick, 497), Origen talks about the power of "the formula 'in the name of Jesus.'" When this "is pronounced by true believers, it has healed not a few people from diseases and demonic possessions and other distresses."

week out his lectures could be uneventful and that his catechumens could be unresponsive to his teaching. But when this kind of thing happened—when an encounter took place between God's power and demonic power and someone fell to the floor and people prayed—*then* people were converted to God. They believed, and they changed their way of living.

What are we to make of this story? We know Origen as a peerless theologian, but we rarely think of him as an exorcist. We would like to know what was going on. On this occasion (which scholars have rarely discussed), did Origen get overexcited and overstate things?[74] Was exorcism really as important as Origen says here? Was it something that often led to conversion? Some scholars have comforted themselves with a word that Origen uses four times in his *Contra Celsum*: "trace" (*ichnos*).[75] "*Traces* of that Holy Spirit who appeared in the form of a dove are still preserved among Christians."[76] "Traces" sounds distant, superseded, indistinct, and unimportant. By talking about "traces," Origen may have wanted to convey that in his view the divine irruptions of power were rarer and less potent than they had been in apostolic times. But we must not allow "traces" to minimize what Origen and his students experienced. This dramatic event in Jerusalem was a trace. In *Contra Celsum* Origen says that as a result of these traces "many have come to Christianity as it were in spite of themselves." He adds: "We have known many instances like this."[77]

Origen was not unique in testifying to instances such as this. Other early writers in disparate parts of the empire had experienced what Origen had— that people became Christians and churches grew in size through successful, prayerful combat with demonic forces. In late second-century Gaul, Irenaeus commented that Christians "in Jesus' name . . . drive out devils, so that those who have been thus cleansed from evil spirits frequently both believe and join themselves to the Church."[78] Soon thereafter in North Africa, Tertullian reported that the capitulation of demons in response to exorcistic prayer

74. For brief discussions of this incident, see Joseph T. Lienhard, "Origen as Homilist," in *Preaching in the Patristic Age: Studies in Honor of Walter J. Burghardt, S.J.*, ed. David G. Hunter (New York: Paulist Press, 1989), 46; P. Nautin and M.-T. Nautin, *Origène: Homélies sur Samuel*, 67; Ramsay MacMullen, *Christianity and Paganism in the Fourth to Eighth Centuries* (New Haven: Yale University Press, 1997), 9.

75. See, e.g., Gary B. Ferngren, *Medicine and Health Care in Early Christianity* (Baltimore: Johns Hopkins University Press, 2009), 69.

76. Origen, *Cels.* 1.46 (Chadwick, 42; PG 11:745); see also 1.2; 2.8; 7.8. For other examples, see *Passion of Perpetua* 1.5; Ambrosiaster, *Quaestiones Veteris et Novi Testamenti* 114.22; Bardy, *Conversion au christianisme*, 159n.

77. Origen, *Cels.* 1.46 (Chadwick, 42); see also 2.8 (Chadwick, 72): "If our word may be trusted, we also have seen [the traces]."

78. Irenaeus, *Haer.* 2.32.4, trans. A. Roberts, *ANF* 1:409.

"regularly makes Christians."[79] In the Western imperial capital of Trier, the early fourth-century theologian Lactantius reported that people, engaged in a struggle with a demonic power that is oppressing them, discovered that the divine power "which they have experienced" is stronger than the evil power. As a result, outsiders became believers in considerable numbers: these things "bring a great many people to God, in wonderful fashion."[80]

It was because of compassion that Christians prayed against the demons. Christians saw the demons as God's opponents who comprehensively spoiled and destroyed human life. They were convinced that many people were living in fear, sensing that they were in bondage to demons. "For many years Satan had bound us and held us captive," preaches Origen. But, he says, Jesus came to set us free! And people were captive not simply to generalized demons but to specific ills that manifested demonic power. For example, people were captive to "greed, which is a more subtle worship of idols"; for such people "the word and proclamation" of Christ brings release.[81] Justin provided a list of four specific addictions by which, in his view, the demons especially enslaved people: sexual compulsions, the magic arts, the desire to increase wealth and property, and hatred and violence.[82] But when humans set out to "attack the demons," Christ acted to free those who were enslaved. As we shall see in chapter 6, by the third century the church had well-developed processes of catechesis and baptism to liberate people for a life that is free in Christ. Exorcisms were integral to these processes.

PRAYER FOR HEALING

Prayer to God against the demons was not only exorcistic; it was not simply designed to free people from specific addictions. It also dealt with the healing of illnesses. In many early texts that deal with prayer, healing was a close neighbor to exorcism: "expelling demons, effecting cures, seeking revelations."[83] In a world in which illness lurked around every corner and life expectancy was short, health was bound to be a preoccupying concern; it was for good reason that the concern to make the sick well was central to ancient religions.[84] As Gary Ferngren has emphasized, Christians not only turned to exorcistic, nonscientific approaches to healing; they also accepted

---

79. Tertullian, *Apol.* 23.18 (Glover, 131).
80. Lactantius, *Inst.* 5.22.24 (Bowen and Garnsey, 329); also Minucius Felix, *Oct.* 27.5; Origen, *Cels.* 7.47.
81. Origen, *Hom. Jos.* 1.7 (Bruce, 35).
82. Justin, *1 Apol.* 14.2–3, trans. E. R. Hardy, LCC 1 (1953): 249–50.
83. Tertullian, *Spect.* 29, trans. T. R. Glover, LCL 250 (1931), 295.
84. MacMullen, *Paganism*, 49.

the practice of empirical Greek medicine.[85] For example, Origen urged that a Christian should "use medical means to heal his body." If the Christian wants to be distinctive, superior to "the multitude" of pagans, he should pray to the supreme God while he seeks the ministrations of ordinary doctors.[86] We have seen how Cyprian, in the midst of the great plague of 251, did not urge the Christians to pray exorcistic prayers and certainly not to pray from a safe distance for people who were desperately ill. No, Cyprian urged them to nurse sick people and touch them. He reminded them that they could act in this mortally dangerous way because their faith in Christ, which gave them hope for everlasting life, had healed their fear of death.[87]

Nevertheless, prayers for exorcism and healing recur in early Christianity. According to Clement of Alexandria, when the Christians gathered for worship, they engaged in the combat of prayer. As a ragtag "army without weapons" made up of "God-fearing old men . . . God-beloved orphans . . . widows armed with gentleness . . . [and] men adorned with love," they asked God for the subduing of "sickness at its height . . . [which would be] put to flight by the laying on of hands"; also for the shattering of "the violence of demons [which is] reduced to impotence by confident commands."[88] Very probably they stood as they prayed, with raised hands as "orants." The Christians' hands-raised prayers to God synergized with their hands-on efforts to combat both illness and demonic possession. The Christians became known to their contemporaries as healers and exorcists.

Anyone could exorcise, Origen observed. Exorcists did not need elaborate training; instead, the simplest Christian could master the prayers, adjurations, and formulas that were necessary to expel a demon from someone's soul and body.[89] Tertullian also saw "adjuring a demon" as something that any Christian could do; but a husband could do this with greater confidence if he was living in the right conditions, such as not having sex with his wife![90] By the middle of the third century, the churches appointed specific people to be exorcists. In Rome in the 250s there were lots of these, and in time they came to be a minor clerical order whose members played a part in baptismal preparation and responded to cases of suspected demonic possession.[91]

85. Ferngren, *Medicine and Health Care*, 13.
86. Origen, *Cels.* 8.60 (Chadwick, 498).
87. Cyprian, *Mort.* 20.
88. Clement of Alexandria, *Quis div.* 34 (Butterworth, 343). See also Tertullian, *Or.* 29.
89. Origen, *Cels.* 7.4.
90. Tertullian, *Exh. cast.* 10, trans. S. Thelwall, ANF 4:56.
91. Eusebius, *Hist. eccl.* 6.43.11; it is impossible to know how many exorcists there were, because the exorcists were lumped together with others: "fifty-two exorcists, readers and

Similarly, the early Christians believed that anyone could pray to God for the healing of people who were ill.[92] As Irenaeus indicated, these prayers were "frequently" efficacious.[93] The experience of communities indicated that certain people had "the gift of healing."[94] The *Apostolic Tradition* devotes a short chapter to this. It specifies that a church should not ordain someone who claims to have "received a grace of healing by a revelation." Instead, "events will show whether he is telling the truth."[95] The *Apostolic Tradition* was written to regulate the internal life of Christian communities. It simply assumes, matter-of-factly, that at times sick people were healed when believers prayed for them, and it observes that "events" indicate that sick people were more likely to recover when certain people—those with the spiritual gift of healing—prayed for them. Healing was a normal part of the church's life, and the gifts of the "healers" were revealed by the facts—by the people in their midst who had been sick and now were well.[96]

Christians did not pretend that they suffered less pain and had fewer misfortunes than others. Cyprian noted that his people experienced "hardships of flesh and torments of body." Like others they struggled with "burning fevers, torments of wounds, the death of dear ones." Cyprian did not tell Christians that they could quickly escape these trials by potent prayer. Instead, he reminded them of their commitment to patience. "Nothing else distinguishes the unjust and just more than this, that in adversities the unjust man complains and blasphemes because of impatience while the just man is proved by patience."[97] Nevertheless, Christians did pray, and their contemporaries sensed that they had unusual healing resources—which they expressed in their catacomb art that depicted Christ healing the paralytic, the woman with the issue of blood, and the blind person.[98]

Exorcisms and Healings in the Church's Growth

Exorcisms and healings were significant in the life of the early Christians, but how significant were they in the church's growth? Ancient writers, we have

door-keepers." It is significant that the church in Rome had a minor order of exorcists but no order (minor or major) of evangelists.

92. Justin, *Dial.* 39; Irenaeus, *Haer.* 2.31.2.

93. Irenaeus, *Haer.* 2.32.4, trans. A. Roberts, *ANF* 1:409.

94. R. J. S. Barrett-Lennard, *Christian Healing after the New Testament: Some Approaches to Illness in the Second, Third, and Fourth Centuries* (Lanham, MD: University Press of America, 1994), 57.

95. *Trad. ap.* 14 (Arabic) (BJP, 80).

96. Barrett-Lennard, *Christian Healing*, 252.

97. Cyprian, *Pat.* 17–18, trans. G. E. Conway, FC 36 (1958), 280.

98. Lee M. Jefferson, *Christ the Miracle Worker in Early Christian Art* (Minneapolis: Fortress, 2014), chaps. 3–4.

seen, more often mention exorcism than anything else as a cause of conversion to Christianity. Eminent modern historians have agreed with the ancients. Ramsay MacMullen has been the most insistent of these. In his view, exorcism was "the chief instrument of conversion," primarily because it provided "probative demonstrations" of the kind of "exceptional force" that alone could account for the people's otherwise inexplicable embrace of Christianity.[99] Not all historians have agreed that exorcism and healing were this important,[100] but I am inclined to do so. My approach, however, differs from MacMullen's.

In the competitive religious market of the ancient Roman Empire, a new religion could succeed only if it "worked."[101] People would join it only if it contributed something to their experience that made a difference in their lives, that rescued them from things that trapped them, and that brought them to greater wholeness. People lived in a world that they believed was saturated with spiritual powers, in which they felt frustrated, diminished, and trapped. At times these people sensed they were formed by conventions (a habitus) that dictated behaviors that imprisoned them. They were unhappy.

This is where exorcisms fit in. They were actions of humans, involving prayer and ritual, through which they believed that God acted to set people free. What exorcisms brought to them depended on the kind of bondage that they experienced. Was it an addiction to greed? Was it a preoccupation with sex or occult practices? Was it a sense of oppression by a particular spiritual power? Was it an inability to praise God? Was it an estrangement from an enemy that was impossible to overcome? Was it a physical or mental illness?[102]

Whatever the need, exorcisms were primarily personal; they addressed the concerns of individuals and their communities. To be sure, there are stories of public exorcisms, such as the account in Acts of John of the events in Ephesus in which John's exorcistic prayer effected the splitting of the statue of Artemis and the destruction of half of her temple, which led "the assembled Ephesians to cry out . . . We are converted."[103] But there are few such ac-

99. MacMullen, *Christianizing the Roman Empire*, 27. See also MacMullen, "Two Types of Conversion to Early Christianity," *VC* 37 (1983): 180–82; Ferguson, *Demonology*, 127, 129; Peter Brown, *The World of Late Antiquity* (London: Thames & Hudson, 1971), 55; Green, *Evangelism in the Early Church*, 123.

100. Robin Lane Fox, *Pagans and Christians* (San Francisco: Harper & Row, 1986), 329–30; Ferngren, *Medicine and Health Care*, 51.

101. For possible parallels in contemporary Africa, see Philip Jenkins, *The New Faces of Christianity: Believing the Bible in the Global South* (New York: Oxford University Press, 2006), 96.

102. For these examples, see Origen, *Hom. Luc.* 32.2; *Hom. Jos.* 1.7; also Justin, *1 Apol.* 14.2–3; Tertullian, *Or.* 29.

103. Acts of John 42–43, in *New Testament Apocrypha*, ed. E. Hennecke, W. Schneemelcher, and R. McL. Wilson (Louisville: Westminster John Knox, 1992), 2:188.

counts, and they reek of legend.[104] The better-attested exorcisms that were part of the life of the early Christians were not public exorcisms that forced entire populaces to convert by smashing statues and destroying buildings; instead, they were personal exorcisms. Their aim was to restore wholeness to people who had been torn apart; it was to integrate them inwardly and socially so that henceforth they would be able to live in freedom. Like most common activities of the pre-Constantinian Christians, exorcisms happened in domestic settings and involved individuals and small groups rather than crowds. Like Origen's exorcism, these domestic exorcisms at times may have been noisy (Origen and others were probably shouting out Hannah's phrase, mantra-like), and Origen saw it as involving "impure spirits tormented."[105] But there was no physical force here; Origen—and no doubt many other exorcists—were committed to nonviolence. At times, as in catechetical courses, exorcisms were scheduled, a planned part of the curriculum; but as in Origen's incident, they also took place spontaneously. When they did happen, they brought a sense of eventfulness, of the divine presence breaking into the experience of God's worshiping people. These were the *magnalia*, the miraculous works of God, that Christians saw as expressions of God's fidelity to them.[106] Unlike pagan healings in shrines of Asclepius, which could be very expensive, these were free.[107] And the experience of them kept Christians coming back to communities in which they said that they experienced the reality of God—a God who empowered them, as people of little power, to live with expectancy in difficult circumstances. Rumors that God was present in Christian gatherings may also have attracted outsiders to investigate Christianity. They told others what the Christians were experiencing, and the churches grew.[108]

104. MacMullen, *Christianizing the Roman Empire*, 25–27, provides two examples: the destruction of the Artemis cult in Ephesus (Acts of John 42–43); and the early fourth-century miracle in response to the martyrdom of Apphianus in Caesarea in Palestine, which led all the adults and children of the town to confess the God of the Christians (Eusebius, *Martyrs of Palestine* 4.14–15).

105. For noisy, violent imagery regarding exorcisms, see Cyprian, *Ep.* 69.15.2, trans. G. W. Clarke, ACW 47 (89), 44: "The human voice combined with the power of God scourges and scorches and torments the devil"; also Cyprian, *Don.* 5.

106. Tertullian, *Ux.* 2.7.

107. Tertullian, *Apol.* 37.9; Wolfgang Reinbold, *Propaganda und Mission im ältesten Christentum: Eine Untersuchung zu den Modalitäten der Ausbreitung der frühen Kirche,* FRLANT 188 (Göttingen: Vandenhoek & Ruprecht, 2000), 322.

108. Glossolalia was not part of the story that the early Christian writers told about the church's life and growth, according to Everett Ferguson, *Early Christians Speak* (Abilene, TX: ACU Press, 2002), 2:112–14; cf. hints in Tertullian, *Pat.* 12.10; *An.* 9.3; Cecil M. Robeck, *Prophecy in Carthage: Perpetua, Tertullian, and Cyprian* (Cleveland: Pilgrim Press, 1992), 98, 130.

Distinctive Communities (5)—Care for Poor People

Care for poor people was another area in which the Christian communities had habits and approaches that posed questions for contemporaries.
Outsiders looked at this and were impressed. In their world there were many
poor people. First-century Roman society was sharply vertical; according to a
recent study, 65 percent of the imperial population lived close to or below the
subsistence level.[109] From early on the Christian churches had a sprinkling of
richer members, and the number of these was growing. By the mid-third century Origen observed that wealthier people, especially women, were entering
the churches.[110] But the majority of the Christian communities continued to
struggle with realities of job insecurity, poor harvests, illnesses, and famines.
Tertullian notes that it was the Christian communities' response to the poor
people among them that inspired outsiders to comment, "Look, how they
love each other."[111]

This care for the poor resulted from a fundamental commitment the Christians made in baptism.[112] Some new members responded to these commitments by engaging in downward mobility; for example, Cyprian simplified his
clothing, diet, and lifestyle as he prepared for baptism.[113] At regular intervals
most members, according to their ability, brought donations for the church's
common funds that the community's leaders could put at the disposal of
needy members. Some congregations also had replenishable stocks of food
and clothing for their members.[114] According to 2 Clement 16.4, giving was
expected not only of the more prosperous members but of all believers; and
this giving could be modestly redistributive.[115] Responses to the church's

109. Walter C. Scheidel and Steven J. Friesen, "The Size of the Economy and the Distribution of Income," *JRS* 99 (2009): 85. For an even starker estimate of first-century Christians,
see Justin J. Meggitt's influential *Paul, Poverty and Survival* (Edinburgh: T&T Clark, 1998).

110. Origen, *Cels.* 3.9.

111. Tertullian, *Apol.* 39.7 (Glover, 177).

112. In *1 Apol.* 61.7, Justin makes explicit the baptizand's commitment to care for the
orphans and widows; also *Trad. ap.* 20.1, in which only those who honor the widows and visit
the sick can proceed to baptism.

113. Pontius, *Vit. Cypr.* 2, 6; cf. Tertullian, *Cult. fem.* 2.11.3, trans. R. Arbesmann, FC 40
[1959], 145, where a pagan says: "Since she became a Christian, she walks in poorer garb."

114. Tertullian, *Apol.* 39.11; *Gesta apud Zenophilum* 3, in *Optatus: Against the Donatists*,
trans. and ed. Mark Edwards, TTH 27 (Liverpool: Liverpool University Press, 1997), 154.

115. David J. Downs, "Redemptive Almsgiving and Economic Stratification in 2 Clement,"
JECS 19, no. 4 (2011): 493–517. According to Peter Lampe, second-century Rome shows an
"intensive exchange" between poor and wealthier Christians: "The social positions of those
who become Christians change. The position of some is raised slightly, . . . [due to] a limited
material equalization between the social levels" (*From Paul to Valentinus: Christians in Rome
in the First Two Centuries* [Minneapolis: Fortress, 2003], 140).

expectations of giving varied. In some communities there were no doubt freeloaders, people who "feigned to be Christians on account of their need of the necessities of life."[116] And in Rome and Syria there were wealthier Christians who skipped worship services, irritated by leaders who they felt were pressuring them to contribute according to their considerable means to the church's poor members.[117]

Providing for poor believers was a central emphasis of the Christian communities. Cyprian expressed this crisply in one of his precepts: "that every person ought to have care rather of his own people, and especially of believers."[118] But from an early date the Christians also provided for needy outsiders. In chapter 3 we saw that during the mid-third-century outbreak of the plague, the Carthaginian Christians—urged on by their bishop Cyprian—provided food and nursing not only for the household of faith but for non-Christians as well.[119]

The tradition of serving outsiders continued into the fourth century, when it led to a notable conversion in the Egyptian city of Thebes. Early in Constantine's reign, gangs of troops carrying out forced military conscription abducted peasants in upper Egypt to serve in the Roman legions and shipped them down the Nile. A vessel carrying these unwilling recruits docked in the city of Thebes, where the military authorities clapped them in prison to prevent them from escaping before being transported farther. Christians in Thebes heard about the prisoners' distress and responded by bringing them the food and drink that were unavailable in prison. Our account does not tell us who it was that brought the help, but very probably it was women who took the lead in practical ministries.[120] One of the prisoners, Pachomius, asked a local person who the people were who were bringing them help. It was the Christians, he was told, who "were merciful to everyone, including strangers." Pachomius pressed further, asking what a Christian was. His informant replied: "They are people who bear the name of Christ, the only begotten Son of God, and they do good to everyone, putting their hope in Him who made heaven and earth and us people." At this, according to the account, Pachomius's heart was "set on fire." In the fear of God he prayed and committed himself henceforth to serve God; and, in the tradition of the Christians who had helped him, he promised to "love all people and be their servant according

116. Origen, *Cels.* 1.67 (Chadwick, 62); Lucian, *Peregr.* 11–12.

117. Herm. *Sim.* 9.20.2; *Did. apost.* 2.56.4.

118. Cyprian, *Ad Quir.* 3.75, trans. E. Wallis, *ANF* 5:552.

119. Pontius, *Vit. Cypr.* 10.

120. For a parallel incident from the second century (fictional, to be sure, but probably growing out of actual experience), see Lucian, *Peregr.* 12, trans. J. Stevenson, *A New Eusebius*, rev. ed. (London: SPCK, 1987), 129: "From the break of day you could see aged women lingering about the prison."

to God's command." The military authorities soon herded Pachomius and the other conscripts back on board the ship, which continued down the Nile, but before long they released him. Upon being discharged, Pachomius made his way to a church, where, after a period as a catechumen, he was baptized.[121] The compassionate generosity of the Christians in Thebes responded to the needs of people who were not their members, which led to the conversion of Pachomius, who became the founder of the conventual monastic tradition. This kind of ministry must have affected other people as well. According to Henry Chadwick, "The practical application of charity was probably the most potent single cause of Christian success."[122]

Distinctive Communities (6)—Patience That Prohibits Taking Life

The Christians' commitment to a stance that comprehensively ruled out killing must have impacted their prospects of missional success. According to Origen, refusing to participate in "the taking of human life in any form at all" was a basic Christian commitment; it was a product of the Christians' patience, their refusal to retaliate, and their understanding of the way and teaching of Jesus. On this matter other writers—Tertullian, Athenagoras, Minucius Felix, and Lactantius—agreed with Origen.[123]

The prohibition on taking life had far-reaching consequences. One of these had to do with gladiatorial games. According to Tertullian, this prohibition was hard to implement. Evidently some baptized Christians were addicted to watching as the blood of animals and humans flowed freely. This outraged Tertullian. Didn't believers see how profoundly the ethos of the games impacted their habitus?[124] And what of prospective Christians? It is doubtful that the Christians' repudiation of the most popular form of mass entertainment enhanced their missional prospects! Other consequences of patience were experienced by families who said no to abortions or to putting unwanted infants to death by exposure.[125] And of course the prohibition on taking life had an effect on Christians in the Roman legions. There was a debate between Christians

121. *First Greek Life of Pachomius* 4–5, trans. Armand Veilleux, *Pachomian Koinonia*, vol. 1, *The Life of Saint Pachomius and His Disciples* (Kalamazoo, MI: Cistercian Publications, 1980), 300. I have twice replaced "men" with "people."

122. Henry Chadwick, *The Early Church* (Harmondsworth, Middlesex: Penguin Books, 1967), 55–56.

123. See Origen, *Hom. Num.* 19.5.1; Athenagoras, *Leg.* 35.6; Tertullian, *Apol.* 37.7; *Spect.* 2; also Lactantius, *Inst.* 6.20; Minucius Felix, *Oct.* 30.

124. Tertullian, *Spect.* 2–3, 12, 25; Theophilus, *Autol.* 3.15.

125. Athenagoras, *Leg.* 35.6; Minucius Felix, *Oct.* 30.5–6. See the many patristic passages cited in Ronald J. Sider, ed., *The Early Church on Killing: A Comprehensive Sourcebook on War, Abortion, and Capital Punishment* (Grand Rapids: Baker Academic, 2012); also Erkki

who were conservatively committed to Christ's "inspired legislation," who ruled out all participation in the military,[126] and the small but growing number of more progressive Christians who justified warring for the empire. In between the two were the writers of the *Apostolic Tradition*, who forbade a catechumen or baptized believer from entering the legions, but permitted him, if he were attracted to the faith while in the legions, to stay there on one condition: "Let him not kill."[127] This must have limited Christianity's attractiveness to some people. On the other hand, Justin Martyr viewed the question from a larger missional perspective. He pointed out that when people converted to Christianity, they renounced the demons whose "slaves and servants" they had been; as a result, their approach to enemies was transformed. "We who hated and killed one another and would not associate with men of different tribes because of [their different] customs, now after the manifestation of Christ live together and pray for our enemies and try to persuade those who unjustly hate us." Justin asserted that the church's growth was a product of the Christians' distinctive approach to enemies. Why do Christians love and pray for and persuade their enemies? So the enemies will become brothers: "so that they [our enemies], living according to the fair commands of Christ, may share with us the good hope of receiving the same things [that we will] from God, the master of all."[128]

Distinctive Communities (7)—Patience That Does Not Compel

The Roman Empire's religious scene was kaleidoscopically varied and proud to be "infinitely tolerant."[129] It also was an environment in which the Christians, by virtue of their nonconformity, at times found themselves in lethal trouble. The Christians' response across the first three centuries was consistent. Christian writers prior to Lactantius in the early fourth century did not use the language of patience to justify religious freedom. But their approach to mission throughout was a patient one. Their experience inclined

---

Koskenniemi, *The Exposure of Infants among Jews and Christians in Antiquity*, Social World of Biblical Antiquity 2/4 (Sheffield: Sheffield Phoenix, 2009), 88–110.

126. In *Cels.* 8.68 (Chadwick, 504), Origen gives the pagan Celsus's reading of classical Christian behavior: "If everyone were to do the same as you, there would be nothing to prevent him from being abandoned, alone and deserted, while earthly things would come into the power of the most lawless and savage barbarians." For arguments presented by more accommodationist Christians in the legions, see Tertullian, *Idol.* 19. Commenting on the debate are Kreider, "Military Service," 415–42; and George Kalantzis, *Caesar and the Lamb: Early Christian Attitudes on War and Military Service* (Eugene, OR: Cascade Books, 2012), 119.

127. *Trad. ap.* 16.9–11 (Sahidic) (BJP, 88–90).

128. Justin, *1 Apol.* 14.3 (Hardy, 249–50).

129. MacMullen, *Christianizing the Roman Empire*, 16.

them in this direction. They had come to the Christian faith because they themselves had been moved by the embodied qualities of Christians and their communities, and because Christian ideas made sense of the way the Christians lived. They had become Christians, against the compelling powers of convention and the law, because of what they had seen and experienced. They knew that they had not been forced to believe; instead, defying force in order to believe, they had come to Christianity as "an assertion of true liberty."[130]

To people like these, Christian writings made sense. Clement of Alexandria wrote: "For God does not compel, since force is hateful to God, but He provides for those who seek."[131] Irenaeus wrote: God works "by means of persuasion. . . . [God] does not use violent means to obtain what he desires."[132] The Epistle to Diognetus states: "Compulsion is not God's way of working."[133] Tertullian added that obligatory worship is false worship: "No one, not even a man, will wish to receive reluctant worship."[134] The question was not whether a religion was legal but whether it was true. The Christians measured a religion's truth not primarily by intellectual criteria but by its affects on people. How did a religion affect its adherents' lives? How did it impact other people whose lives it touched? Early in Constantine's reign the Christian philosopher Lactantius challenged the Christians' critics to evaluate a religion by how it affected ordinary people, simple people, "our old women . . . [and] our children too." He invited debate based on the experience of actual people.

There is no need for violence and brutality; worship cannot be forced; it is something to be achieved by talk rather than blows, so that there is free will in it. They must unsheathe the sharpness of their wits; if the reasoning is sound, let them argue it! We are ready to listen if they would tell; if they keep silent, we simply cannot believe them, just as we do not yield when they use violence. . . . Let them copy us, and so bring out the reason in it all; we use no guile ourselves, though they complain we do; instead, we teach, we show, we demonstrate. No one is detained by us against his will—anyone without devotion and faith is

130. Minucius Felix, *Oct.* 38.1 (Glover, 431). For interpretive frameworks on the early Christians' views regarding coercion and liberty, see Everett Ferguson, "Voices of Religious Liberty in the Early Church," *Restoration Quarterly* 19 (1976): 13–22; Peter Garnsey, "Religious Toleration in Classical Antiquity," in *Persecution and Toleration*, ed. W. J. Sheils, Studies in Church History 21 (Oxford: Blackwell, 1984), 1–27.

131. Clement of Alexandria, *Quis div.* 10 (Butterworth, 289).

132. Irenaeus, *Haer.* 5.1.1, trans. A. Roberts, *ANF* 1:527.

133. *Diogn.* 7.4, trans. E. R. Fairweather, *Early Christian Fathers*, ed. C. C. Richardson, LCC 1 (1953), 219.

134. Tertullian, *Apol.* 24.6 (Glover, 133).

no use to God; but when truth detains, no one departs. . . . Religion must be defended not by killing but by dying, not by violence but by patience.[135]

Lactantius believed that the church's growth would depend not on pressure but on proof—on the believers' lives, which demonstrated across time whether their beliefs have authenticity. Some people of course would leave the Christian communities, and the churches would allow them to do so for the same reason that they opposed religious compulsion. Patience is the true defender of religion.

Final Judgment—the Christians' Warning

To be sure, the early believers did not force or compel. They refused to sanction the use of compulsion for the defense of religion.[136] But didn't the Christians' message contain threats? And when the Christians refused to seek vengeance, wasn't this at times because they believed that the vengeful work was God's business? These are reasonable questions. In the middle of the second century the author of the Epistle to Diognetus wrote that God in sending Christ "willed to save man by persuasion, not by compulsion, for compulsion is not God's way of working." But he added a proviso. Someday there will be a reckoning: God will send Christ "as our Judge, and who shall stand when he appears?"[137] A century later Cyprian coupled the Christians' call to live without retaliation to their confidence that God will be judge: "That when a wrong is received, patience is to be maintained, and that vengeance is to be left to God."[138] Repeatedly the Christian writers stated their trust in the God who is at work reticently and inexorably; but they added their confidence that one day, in the fullness of time, God can "avenge the unjust sufferings of his servants."[139] For many Christians the prospect of eventual, inexorable judgment was an essential component of their patience; as oppressed people, they saw judgment for their oppressors as the operation of God's justice, and they looked forward to the vindication that God would bring about in the fullness of time.[140]

135. Lactantius, *Inst.* 5.19.11–12, 22 (Bowen and Garnsey, 320–21).
136. Passages such as that written by Justin in *1 Apol.* 16.14 (Hardy, 252–53) show that at times Christian writers could see the attractions of compulsion: "So we ask that you too should punish those who do not live in accordance with [Christ's] teachings, but merely say that they are Christians."
137. *Diogn.* 7.3–4 (Fairweather, 219).
138. Cyprian, *Ad Quir.* 3.106 (Wallis, 555).
139. Lactantius, *Inst.* 5.20.9 (Bowen and Garnsey, 324).
140. Cyprian, *Demetr.* 17, trans. R. J. Deferrari, FC 36 (1958), 182: "Our certainty of the vengeance which is to come makes us patient."

The certainty of judgment was also an argument that Christians used to appeal to potential converts. The day of resurrection and judgment is coming when God will try all people; he will judge not only what people think or profess but also how they behave. The invitation followed: repent now and save yourselves from condemnation! In the mid-second century Justin Martyr contended that God in judgment will send "into eternal fire" those who are found not living by the teachings of Jesus.[141] Justin was unique in linking punishment specifically to the way people lived Jesus's teachings,[142] but most Christian writers agreed that God will judge people on the way they live. And the consequences will be everlasting; according to Justin, some people will be "punished for endless ages . . . with the evil demons." In his treatise *To Demetrianus* Cyprian restated this prospect: "An ever burning Gehenna and a devouring punishment of lively flames will consume the condemned, and there will be no means whereby the torments can at any time have respite and end."[143]

Cyprian and Justin were courageous men, martyrs-to-be, whose lives had the ring of authenticity. From them, sentences like these may have come across as compassionate warnings to people whom they were trying to save from avoidable suffering. But from others, words like these may have seemed to exert psychological force, to twist arms to move people toward the Christian community. At times this may have been a primary motive in people's conversion. Of course, in public Christians did not preach judgment, or anything else for that matter. But in private they at times spelled out fiery consequences. That is how some pagans experienced the Christians. Around AD 200 Caecilius charged that the Christians "threaten the whole world with destruction by fire, as though the eternal order of nature established by divine laws could be upset."[144] But people didn't hear this message in a vacuum. People who entered into conversation with Christians had generally been sufficiently attracted by believers' love for each other to have that as a background as they investigated Christianity. They may have sensed that because the Christians genuinely believed that a fiery fate awaited unbelievers, their warnings expressed their loving concern.

The threat was there, and it troubled some early Christians. It made Tertullian squirm, but he consoled himself; because "the fear of eternal punishment" drove people "to be better men," it was "silly—but useful"![145] Origen

---

141. Justin, *1 Apol.* 16; 28; 52; see also *1 Apol.* 17; 21; 44.

142. The Matthean Jesus foresees punishment for those who do not live his teachings (Matt. 7:15–27).

143. Cyprian, *Demetr.* 24 (Deferrari, 189).

144. Minucius Felix, *Oct.* 11 (Rendall, 341).

145. Tertullian, *Apol.* 49.2 (Glover, 219).

wrestled with this at greater length than Tertullian, and he too concluded that the threats were a justifiable means to an end. In Origen's experience, the threats were primarily useful in persuading "the more simple-minded" people and helped to bring them to "moral improvement." Without "fear and the suggestion of punishment," people would lack "the capacity for any other means of conversion and repentance from many evils."[146]

The Christians' Habitus and the Church

The habitus of the early Christians knitted together distinctive behavioral acts, borne in their bodies, that revealed their fundamental values. On the basis of what we have seen so far in this book, components of the habitus included:

- *Meeting frequently*: The Christian community is the believers' primary community.

- *Standing in prayer, arms raised*: Christians are confident that they are in touch with the powerful God who can defeat the powers that hold people captive.

- *Praising and thanking God*: God, who raised Jesus from the dead, is at work; Christians can be patient, believing that in him all things are possible, that no action on their part is urgent. Patience grows out of praising the God who holds all things securely.

- *Making the sign of the cross*: Christians recall Christ's saving work and appropriate his protective presence.

- *Eating together* (at eucharistic and other meals): Christians share the table as a new family.

- *Giving the kiss of peace*: Christians bond together in love, as equals.

- *Memorizing texts* (the Sermon on the Mount, Isaiah 2:2–4, and many others): Christians inwardly appropriate resources that encourage them and point to new possibilities.

- *Visiting the poor, the sick, and prisoners*: Christians declare that people have dignity and that deeds matter.

- *Exercising hospitality*: Christians receive and feed visitors.

- *Putting money in the collection box*: Christians voluntarily contribute to the common fund, enacting and embodying the belief that poor people matter and that sharing is a fundamental value.

146. Origen, *Cels.* 3.7–9; 5.16 (Chadwick, 180–81, 277).

- *Replenishing the stocks of food and clothing*: Christians care for each other.
- *Feeding needy people*: Christians care for outsiders and enemies.
- *Discerning carefully*: Christians decide what in culture to say yes to and what to say no to.
- *Being truthful*: Christians do not swear oaths.
- *Maintaining sexual purity*: Christians are faithful to marriage partners, and do not look lustfully on others.
- *Observing disciplines that limit impatient behavior*: Christians do not retaliate, do not abort or expose infants, do not kill, do not watch blood sports.
- *Being willing to lose out* (in business, law, and verbal arguments): Christians exercise patience, and do not litigate or coerce.
- *Allowing people to leave the church*: Christians do not compel belief.
- *Facing death without fear*: Christians can live riskily and experimentally.

This list of the Christians' habitus—the practices and being of their corporal identity—is partial. But it shows the reflexes of the Christians and indicates the character of their assemblies. According to Origen, the churches were "another sort of country, created by the Logos of God."[147] As gatherings of "people who have been helped," the churches were "evidences of Jesus' divinity."[148] Tertullian saw the church as a "city set on a mountain [that is] to shine in the midst of darkness and stand out among those who are sunk down. . . . It is our good works that make us to be the lights of the world." And, according to Tertullian, the Christians must attempt not only to be good but also to be visible to the watching world: "It is not enough for Christian modesty merely to be so, but to seem so, too."[149]

Reversions to Old Habitus (1)—"Bad Christians"

When things were working properly, being good and being visible were the Christians' primary means of attracting outsiders. What Minucius Felix said around 200 was true throughout the third century: "As for the daily increase in our numbers, that is no proof of error, but evidence of merit; for beauty of life encourages its followers to persevere, and strangers to join the ranks."[150]

147. Origen, *Cels.* 8.75 (Chadwick, 510).
148. Origen, *Cels.* 3.33 (Chadwick, 150).
149. Tertullian, *Cult. fem.* 2.13.1–3 (Arbesmann, 147–48).
150. Minucius Felix, *Oct.* 31.7 (Rendall, 411–13).

But things did not always work properly. From an early date hypocrisy was a major challenge. In light of the Christians' vision of witness that I have just stated, this was inevitable. From the New Testament onward, some believers expressed strong commitments and failed to be faithful to them. According to the first surviving Christian sermon, misleadingly known as the *Second Epistle of Clement*, this was already a problem in the middle of the second century. According to "Clement," when the Christians talked about loving your enemies, their neighbors had been interested. But when they found that the Christians didn't do what they said, they dismissed Christianity as "a myth and a delusion." From Clement's perspective, Christians had to embody the message if the churches were to grow.[151]

By the time of Origen in the middle of the following century, the theme of hypocrisy had become even more urgent. The churches had spread to many cities, and their memberships had increased significantly. The growth led to problems. In the 240s in Caesarea in Palestine, as Origen prepared catechumens for baptism he struggled against the unfaithful behavior of the faithful—baptized people whom Origen called "bad Christians."[152] Origen had a long memory. He recalled the early years of the third century when Christians had lived faithfully and when catechumens had prepared for baptism amid martyrs and confessors. But now there were lots of Christians, and they had become soft. "If we judge the matters in truth and by numbers, if we judge the matters by intention and not from the spectacle of many gathered, we are not now faithful."[153] The Christians' public behavior belied their convictions: they "agitate the forum with lawsuits and weary [their] neighbors with altercations."[154] Their participation in the church was also unsatisfactory: they skipped worship services, and when they attended, it was to "spend time . . . for gossip, not for the word of God."[155] Their habitus, instead of being distinctively Christian, had reverted to conventional patterns: "They are completely disgusting in their actions and habit of life, wrapped up with vices and not wholly 'putting away the old self with its actions.'"[156] Venting his frustration about people who had skipped his catechetical sessions, Origen fulminated against "Christians" who were politely respectful to the churchmen but whose lifestyles paid no attention to their teaching: "[The people] come to church and bow their head to the priests, exhibit courtesy,

151. See 2 Clem. 13.3, trans. C. C. Richardson, LCC 1 (1953), 198.
152. Origen, *Hom. Ezech.* 6.8.4, trans. T. P. Scheck, ACW 62 (2010), 95.
153. Origen, *Hom. Jer.* 4.3.2, trans. J. C. Smith, FC 97 (1998), 34.
154. Origen, *Hom. Exod.* 1.5, trans. R. E. Heine, FC 71 (1982), 234.
155. Origen, *Hom. Jos.* 1.7, trans. B. J. Bruce, FC 105 (2002), 35.
156. Origen, *Hom. Jos.* 10.1 (Bruce, 110).

honor the servants of God, even bring something for the decoration of the altar or church—yet they exhibit no inclination to also improve their habits, correct impulses, lay aside faults, cultivate purity, soften the violence of wrath, restrain avarice, curb greed."[157]

Could these people heed the Christian call to change? Origen despaired: the people "do not wish to correct themselves but persist in these things until extreme old age." In response, Origen implored his hearers to confront those who were absent from his catechetical sessions so that they might be saved: "'As long as it is day' let us do what is good and work at correcting ourselves so that by our actions and way of life and even habits, we may deserve to be ennobled and become worthy to receive 'the spirit of adoption' so that, preferably, we may be considered among the sons of God."[158] Origen was up against it. Because of the "multitudes" of those who by the 240s had become Christians, the bad behavior of Christians on the ground was testing his theology of Christian witness—"that men may see your good works and praise your Father who is in heaven."[159] Vigorous preaching and intensive catechizing was Origen's contribution to the church's response to a problem that would not go away. By the early fifth century the problem had become so acute that some theologians updated the church's theology of witness so that they no longer emphasized the Christians' exemplary behavior.[160]

Reversions to Old Habitus (2)—Questionable Inculturation

When Christians were true to their calling, inculturation indigenized wholesomely. But indigenization could get out of control, losing contact with the Christians' pilgrim calling, as in the story of Gregory of Pontus. In the 230s Gregory, a brilliant young man from a Christian family from backward Neocaesarea in Pontus (northern Asia Minor), went to sophisticated Berytus (Beirut) in Syria to study law. Caesarea, where Origen was teaching, was near Berytus. When Gregory traveled to Caesarea, he fell under the influence of Origen, who converted him to the study of theology and to Christian discipleship. Origen dazzled Gregory with his learning and eloquence; but, according to Gregory, it was Origen's behavior that was decisive in transforming his life: "Not . . . in mere words only did this teacher go over the truths concerning

---

157. Origen, *Hom. Jos.* 10.3 (Bruce, 112).
158. Origen, *Hom. Jos.* 10.3 (Bruce, 113).
159. Origen, *Hom. Lev.* 5.7.2, trans. G. W. Barkley, FC 83 (1990), 102. In the 240s Origen often uses "multitudes" to describe the large number of people coming to the faith, as in *Cels.* 2.63; 3.18, 21; 6.2, 14.
160. See, e.g., Augustine, *Serm.* 223A.

the virtues with us; but he incited us much more to the practice of virtue, and stimulated us by the deeds he did more than by the doctrines he taught."[161]

In 238 Gregory returned to his homeland in remote Pontus as a missionary bishop. Almost a century and a half later, Gregory of Nyssa wrote a *Life of Gregory*, which recounts adventures of the earlier namesake.[162] The *Life* gives pride of place to Gregory's combat with demons. When Gregory arrived back in Pontus, his ministry began with a power contest with the warden of a local pagan temple. Gregory's prayers led to the miraculous relocation of a huge boulder, and the warden was converted. Thereafter, according to the *Life*, Gregory effected many miracles, both healings and nature miracles. For example, in 251 when the great plague broke out, the people found safety when they were physically close to the praying Gregory. "The one means of salvation" was not, as in Cyprian's Carthage, the Christian community caring for the sick; instead it was being in the praying presence of bishop Gregory: "through having the great Gregory in the house, . . . [by prayer he repelled] the disease that fell upon it."[163] Throughout the *Life*, it is Gregory's preaching backed up by his miracle working that brings people to conversion: "Vision coincided with hearing and the tokens of divine power illumined it through both." Gregory put to work what he had observed in Caesarea; he arranged for catechesis to be given to the converts: "He [Gregory] taught servants to be dutiful to their masters; people with power, to care benevolently for their subjects; the poor person, that the sole wealth was virtue, which everyone could possess according to his ability; the one proud of his wealth was in turn admonished to be steward, not lord, of his possessions."[164]

In 251 when the persecution under Decius began, thirteen years had elapsed after Gregory's return to Neocaesarea, and many local people, despite Gregory's miracles, were still pagans. The Decian persecution tore the Christian community apart. The believers in Pontus were under great pressure, and like Gregory many of them left the city. Pagans moved to possess the Christians' properties. The Christians' protection came about through Gregory's prayers. Together with the converted temple warden (who was by now a deacon), Gregory went to a nearby hilltop and prayed for the defeat of the persecuting powers and the protection of the believers. Gregory's prayers and his

161. Gregory Thaumaturgus, *Orat. paneg.* 9, trans. S. D. F. Salmond, *ANF* 6:31.

162. For an overview of Gregory and his lifework, see Henri Crouzel, "Gregor I (Gregor der Wundertäter)," in *RAC* 12 (1983): 779–93.

163. Gregory of Nyssa, *Life of St. Gregory Thaumaturgus* 102–3 (957B–C), trans. in *Paganism and Christianity, 100–425 C.E.: A Sourcebook,* ed. R. MacMullen and E. N. Lane (Minneapolis: Fortress, 1992), 214.

164. Gregory of Nyssa, *Life of Gregory* 47 (924A), trans. M. Slusser, FC 98 (1998), 62.

miracle-working were both remarkably successful. They led not only to the repulsion of the persecutors but also to "the sudden transformation of the whole people."[165] Or almost the whole people: Gregory of Nyssa informs us that when Gregory first returned to Pontus, there were seventeen Christians, and thirty years later when he died, there were seventeen pagans.[166]

The rapid Christianization of Pontus came at a price. If the hagiographer Gregory of Nyssa is to be trusted, the Christianization was rooted in Bishop Gregory of Pontus himself, who used wonderworking to impact the bodies of the healed people and thereby change their faith. And Gregory, who had studied with Origen, knew the importance of an embodied witness. But this was a slow method, and Gregory was in a hurry. It would take decades to implement a catechesis that would be deliberate enough to change the habitus of the baptismal candidates. Further, Gregory may have lacked catechists. If the *Life* records the contents of his catechesis accurately ("servants to be dutiful to their masters," etc.), Gregory didn't attempt to change much in the dominant values of Pontus society, and he required little in the way of the formation of a patient habitus.

Intriguingly, Gregory did employ another form of patience. In contrast to Cyprian and Origen, for whom conversion was ethically demanding and lasted several years, Gregory attempted to reeducate his Pontus neighbors by a process of indigenization that would last for generations. Gregory calculated that lots of people would become Christian if they could continue to engage in practices that were familiar to them as pagans. He was acutely aware that the Decian persecution had fractured his Christian community. And so, to cope with the persecution's aftermath, Gregory decided to adopt a novel approach; in order to knit the entire local populace together as Christians, he would bless the anniversaries of local martyrs and make these occasions for *refrigeria*. *Refrigeria*—time out of mind, these banquets in cemeteries on the graves of the departed had been a way that local people had enjoyed remembering their ancestors. And also celebrating their lives with drinking and cavorting.[167] So Gregory Christianized the *refrigeria*, muting the church's objections to them, and accepting the price of a little cavorting.

165. Gregory of Nyssa, *Life of Gregory* 85 (948A), 98 (956A) (Slusser, 75, 84).

166. Gregory of Nyssa, *Life of Gregory* 98 (953D) (Slusser, 84).

167. For descriptions of the *refrigeria*, see Ramsay MacMullen, *The Second Church: Popular Christianity, A.D. 200–400*, SBL Writings from the Greco-Roman World Supplement Series 1 (Atlanta: Society of Biblical Literature, 2009), 24–25, 77–80; Hugh Lindsay, "Eating with the Dead: The Roman Funerary Banquet," in *Meals in a Social Context: Aspects of the Communal Meal in the Hellenistic and Roman World*, ed. Inge Nielsen and Hanne Sigismund Nielsen (Aarhus: Aarhus University Press, 2001), 67–80.

In re-educating his whole generation to a new life at one time . . . [Gregory] allowed his subjects to cavort a little in the yoke of faith through merriment. Since he understood that in bodily rejoicing the immaturity and lack of discipline of the multitude remained stuck in the error of idolatry, in order that first of all the main thing might then be achieved in them, namely, to look to God instead of to vain religious practices, he let them rejoice at the memories of the holy martyrs, and experience good emotions, and exult, so that when with the passage of time their life had been naturally transformed to what is more noble [and] more and more strict, their faith would be directed to that end.[168]

In the latter half of the third century, church leaders in other parts of the Christian world were similarly making their peace, *pro tempore*, with funereal banquets.[169] In so doing they were addressing a deep concern, shared by people in many cultures, to give proper honor to the departed. And they were bringing into the church's life a form of feasting, drinking, and dancing that local peoples had practiced for generations. The churchmen's blessing may at times have been diffident, but from Gregory's time through the fourth century some Christian leaders used the *refrigeria* to enable the churches to be more indigenizing and less pilgrim, and by this means to reach people who had been daunted by more demanding forms of early Christianity.[170]

Conclusion

Origen and Gregory, both in the mid-third century, help us see ways the church was growing. Ferment was bubbling and taking many forms—healing and inculturation as well as the patient formation of habitus. In many places Christianity was moving up the social scale. It still included the poorer people who had predominated from the outset, but now it increasingly incorporated wealthier people. In the 240s in Caesarea, Origen noted that "a multitude of people" was coming to faith, "even rich men and persons in positions of honor, and ladies of refinement and high birth." Some of these, he speculated sourly, had "become leaders of the Christian teaching for the sake of a little prestige."[171] These people—often no doubt from the order of the *decurions*, the urban aristocrats—were finding churches to be places where their lives were transformed, even as they brought their learning and cultural confidence to provide leadership as bishops and presbyters. For the comfortably off converts,

168. Gregory of Nyssa, *Life of Gregory* 95–96 (953B–C) (Slusser, 83).
169. *Did. apost.* 6.22.2; MacMullen, *Second Church*, 77.
170. See, e.g., Augustine, *Ep.* 29, to Alypius.
171. Origen, *Cels.* 3.9 (Chadwick, 134).

becoming a Christian was not a step upward in society. Although according to Origen the new converts found advantage—"a little prestige"—in the Christian subculture that they had entered, they also found "disgrace" in "the rest of society" (which in most places was over 90 percent of the populace). But the Christian presence was now large enough for the wider society to notice.

How did the Christians appear to the rest? Origen, as a pastoral homilist, acknowledged that the Christian communities were full of "bad Christians." He urged them to repent, for their own salvation as well as for the sake of the Christian witness in the world.[172] But Origen, as an apologist, was able to maintain the traditional Christian stance—that the Christian witness in the world was rooted in people whose lives Christ had transformed. As Origen stated in his *Contra Celsum*, the churches, living by Christ's teaching, when "compared with the assemblies of the people where they live," stand out "as lights in the world." This, he claimed, was evident to everybody. All people could see that "even the less satisfactory members of the Church and those who are far inferior when compared with the better members are far superior to the assemblies of the people."[173]

Whether or not this was the case, the church in the Roman Empire was growing. This growth was not because "evangelism was the prerogative and duty of every church member."[174] Rather, it was primarily because the Christians and their churches lived by a habitus that attracted others. The Christians' focus was not on "saving" people or recruiting them; it was on living faithfully—in the belief that when people's lives are rehabituated in the way of Jesus, others will want to join them. This happened gradually, one person at a time, largely through face-to-face encounters and not least from parents to children. As Justin's student said to the persecuting prefect in Rome: "I received this good faith from my parents."[175]

Wolfgang Reinbold has developed a model for the church's growth that I find credible.

If the Christians raise their children as Christians and the Christian man in the course of a generation also can convince only *one* of his pagan neighbors, and the Christian woman can convince only *one* of her pagan friends lastingly of the truth of their faith, he and she have done more (!) than we must presuppose in order to be able to explain the growth of the church in the first three centuries.[176]

172. Origen, *Hom. Ezech.* 6.8.5 (Scheck, 95).
173. Origen, *Cels.* 3.29 (Chadwick, 147).
174. Green, *Evangelism in the Early Church*, 274.
175. *Acts of Justin* 4, Recension B (Musurillo, 51).
176. Reinbold, *Propaganda und Mission*, 351.

Not all Christians would have done precisely this. Some would have done much more: their relational gifts and contagious faith would have led a number of their neighbors and friends to find life and healing in the Christian community. Some Christians must have done less. Some children no doubt responded positively to their parents and faith communities; others didn't. And the sources indicate people who had been members of a Christian community who for some reason dropped out.[177] But the Christians' numbers nevertheless were on an upward trajectory—not spectacularly but by patient ferment. This, the Christians believed, was God's work and not theirs. So they did not engage in frantic action to save those who were not baptized; instead they entrusted the outsiders to God. The church, patiently, also entrusted itself to God, who would bring people into "the community of saints participating in truth" by the arduous means of catechesis and baptism.[178] In chapter 6 we will examine these routes into the church.

177. E.g., Pontius, *Vit. Cypr.* 16.
178. Hippolytus, *Comm. on Daniel* 18.6, trans. T. C. Schmidt, *Hippolytus of Rome: Commentary on Daniel* (North Charleston, SC: Create Space, 2010).

PART 3

FORMING THE HABITUS

— 6 —

CATECHESIS AND BAPTISM

By the late third century a movement that in the first century had been statistically insignificant had become a substantial religious minority with millions of adherents. Why did these people join the church? Why did they defy the disincentives? In previous chapters I have argued that Christianity grew by attraction. Outsiders became Christian because, for example, they observed the patient way Christians did business with them. We have observed some pagans who found their own rituals unsatisfactory and were willing to consider alternative approaches that Christians embodied. We have seen outsiders expressing amazement at the confident behavior of Christian women and wondering at the source of their power. We have seen outsiders who heard rumors of the *magnalia* (events of spiritual power) that occurred in Christian gatherings. We have watched as outsiders observed that Christians had distinctive ways of living—burying their poor, refusing to expose unwanted infants, not swearing oaths. Non-Christians observed Christians and scrutinized them; they were aware of the Christians' character and behavior. According to Tertullian, they said, "Look . . . how they love one another . . . and how they are ready to die for each other."[1]

But, we may wonder, why did the Christians behave as they did? What motivated them to live in ways that were interesting enough to cause outsiders to say "Look!"? Athenagoras, a late second-century philosopher in

1. Tertullian, *Apol.* 39.7, trans. T. R. Glover, LCL 250 (1931), 177.

Athens, when responding to queries about Christian behavior, said, "We have been taught," and he referred his readers to what "our teaching [*logoi*] says." "Teaching" was important and could have real impact; according to Athenagoras, it "has made itself heard with a loud cry."[2] In this teaching, "reasoned discourse" was essential. But according to Athenagoras, the witness of the local Christians was rooted less in words than in the habits of people, who in reflexive behavior "do not rehearse words but show forth good deeds" that people could see.[3] The behavior that performed these good deeds was shaped by intentional formation. The believers knew that their practices were not acquired genetically or absorbed from the pagan society. As Tertullian put it around AD 200, "Christians are made, not born."[4]

So how were Christians made? By a process of formation that, as time progressed, was increasingly self-conscious. It was rooted in the habitus of the communities—their reflexive behavior. It was embodied knowledge rooted in predispositions that guided the Christians' common life and expressed themselves in practices. These predispositions shaped worship practices that became essential, formative parts of the communities' habitus. These predispositions also expressed themselves in concentrated form in the initiation processes culminating in baptism that formed the candidates for communal membership.

Christians maintained that if they were attractive, it was not because they were born that way. It was because they had been reborn—changed, converted—to be attractive. Outsiders could see the results of the formation but not the formation itself, which happened privately, secretly, out of the public eye.

In this chapter and the next, I will contend that the Christians' habitus was formed patiently, unhurriedly, through careful catechesis as well as through the communities' reflexive behavior, and that it was renewed in the regular worship of the Christian assemblies. By the late second century many Christian communities had decided that outsiders—non-Christians—could not be admitted to their worship services.[5] The Christians determined that it was not appropriate for outsiders to be admitted to the power-filled center of the their worship—prayer and the Eucharist. As the second century progressed,

2. Athenagoras, *Leg.* 11.2–3, trans. W. Schoedel, *Athenagoras: Legatio* (Oxford: Clarendon, 1972), 22–25.

3. Athenagoras, *Leg.* 11.4 (Schoedel, 25).

4. Tertullian, *Apol.* 18.4 (Glover, 91). See also Tertullian, *An.* 1, "A man becomes a Christian; he is not born one," trans. S. Thelwall, *ANF* 3:176; or Jerome, nearly two hundred years later: "For we are not born Christians, but become Christians by being born again" (*Against Vigilantius* 7, trans. H. W. Fremantle, *NPNF*[2] 6:420).

5. Cf. Paul F. Bradshaw, *Reconstructing Early Christian Worship* (Collegeville, MN: Liturgical Press, 2010), 23. For evidence from about AD 200 of the Christians' "secret" assemblies, see Minucius Felix, *Oct.* 8.3; 9.4; and Tertullian, *Nat.* 1.7.

there were enough experiences of persecution to persuade the Christians in Athens that if "lying informers" were allowed into their services, the result might be "our slaughter."[6] So the growth of the Christian communities, which was a result of their visibly interesting behavior, was rooted in the parts of their life that were invisible, inaccessible to outsiders. Pagans could observe Christians who were economically compassionate and say "Look." Pagans could not, however, observe a Christian worship service and say "Look." And yet I contend that it was the Christians' invisible activities that enabled their visible lifestyle to be attractive. These invisible activities were the sine qua non of the growth of the churches in the Roman Empire. It was not Christian worship that attracted outsiders; it was Christians who attracted them, and outsiders found the Christians attractive because of their Christian habitus, which catechesis and worship had formed.

Of course, in the first three centuries the Christians experienced huge changes. Primary among these was a growth in numbers: in the century before Constantine, some Christian congregations became sizable, with hundreds of members. At first it was not so. The late second-century *Martyrdom of Andrew* tells of a congregation in Greece (the Peloponessus) that met in a bedroom.[7] Around 200, Tertullian, in Carthage, was concerned that members of his house church would "worship too vociferously," bothering the inhabitants of neighboring apartments in what was evidently a large apartment building.[8] Tertullian was still in the small house church period. But half a century later things were very different, at least for some Christians. For example, in Caesarea Maritima in Syria, Origen catechized in a large domestic church that seems to have taken over most of an apartment building. While Origen taught in the main meeting room about the book of Exodus, others were "in the furthest corners of the Lord's house," playing truant and telling profane stories.[9] Unlike Tertullian, Origen wasn't concerned about spiritually overheated members who would bother the neighbors; he was concerned about tepid members of a church grown big and impersonal who would lose out by not hearing his teaching.

---

6. Athenagoras, *Leg.* 1.3 (Schoedel, 5). For the ongoing problem of informers, see evidence from early fourth-century Spain in the Canons of Elvira 73, in Samuel Laeuchli, *Power and Sexuality: The Emergence of Canon Law at the Synod of Elvira* (Philadelphia: Temple University Press, 1972), 134.

7. Michael Philip Penn, *Kissing Christians: Ritual and Community in the Late Ancient Church*, Divinations: Rereading Late Ancient Religion (Philadelphia: University of Pennsylvania Press, 2005), 100.

8. Tertullian, *Or.* 17, trans. and ed. A. Stewart-Sykes, *Tertullian, Cyprian, Origen: On the Lord's Prayer* (Crestwood, NY: St. Vladimir's Seminary Press, 2004), 53.

9. Origen, *Hom. Exod.* 12.2, trans. R. E. Heine, FC 71 (1982), 369.

Other changes were equally far reaching. The service times had changed. Typically the earlier churches held their primary meetings in the evenings, but by the first half of the third century most had their main services in the morning. The churches had moved from being a meal society to being a worship assembly, and their primary meeting had moved from dinner to breakfast. Another change had to do with the food that was served in the liturgies. The full meals that had characterized early Christian services were being replaced by symbolic tokens of bread and wine in a cultic meal. And the words that were spoken were changing in character: from spontaneous utterances spoken by many after the evening meals to monological addresses given by clergy to morning congregations worshiping in larger assemblies.[10]

These changes were real, but there were significant continuities as well. Some of these had to do with ethos. For example, throughout the early Christian centuries horizontal relationships among the believers of differing economic and social groups were extremely important, an expression of the Christian gospel and a prerequisite for authentic worship. Another continuity was the domesticity of the church's life. During the early centuries Christians met and worshiped in private buildings, not public ones; they met in houses, not in basilicas or temples.[11] And a further continuity: the worship of the Christians was secret, closed to outsiders. Christian worship was for Christians, not for curious connoisseurs of cult or even for tentative inquirers.

Extending through the early centuries are practices fundamental to the church's life, even as the churches grew and evolved. In this chapter we will deal with two of them—catechesis and baptism. In each case we will observe how these practices formed the Christians to be participants in a common life whose habitus was attractive.

The Practices in the Conversion of Cyprian

The story of one of early Christianity's prominent recruits, Cyprian, can help us understand how the Christians' practices worked.[12] Thascius Cyprian, a

10. Andrew McGowan, "Food, Ritual, and Power," in *Late Ancient Christianity*, ed. Virginia Burrus, A People's History of Christianity 2 (Minneapolis: Fortress, 2005), chap. 6. For further discussion of these changes, see chap. 7 below.

11. Edward Adams has emphasized that early Christian meeting places were varied and complex, not just houses; see Adams, *The Earliest Christian Meeting Places: Almost Exclusively Houses?*, LNTS 450 (London: Bloomsbury T&T Clark, 2013), 10.

12. The sources for Cyprian's conversion are his letter/treatise *To Donatus* and Pontius's *Life of Cyprian*. Accounts of his conversion are found in Michael M. Sage, *Cyprian* (Cambridge, MA: Philadelphia Patristic Foundation, 1975), 128–35; Allen Brent, *Cyprian and Roman Carthage* (Cambridge: Cambridge University Press, 2010), 25–29.

prominent North African aristocrat, became a believer in the mid-240s. He was from Carthage and was wealthy and urbane, at home in the world of rhetoric—as he put it, "in courts of justice, in the public assembly, in political debate, [in which] a copious eloquence may be the glory of a voluble ambition."[13] Cyprian knew the attractions of this world: its splendid banquets, its clothing that glittered with gold and purple, and its eminence that drew crowds of clients.

Although Cyprian took part in this worldly habitus and responded to its luxury and excess with habitual assent, he was not happy and he knew it. Soon after his conversion, he wrote a letter to his friend Donatus that reveals the inner turmoil that had gripped him. According to Cyprian, his own cultural habitus was "deeply and radically engrained" within him. And Cyprian had many questions. Was the habitus, he wondered, innate or acquired? Was it possible to escape his habitus so he could live with the habitus of the Christians? Could he be liberated from a world that he found both seductive and oppressive? Could someone who "has been used to liberal banquets and sumptuous feasts . . . learn thrift"? Could he be content with "ordinary and simple clothing" or find happiness without the buzz of fawning supplicants?[14]

At some point Cyprian met someone he thought could help him—Caecilianus, a Christian presbyter whose life seemed to Cyprian to be as free as his own was constricted. Caecilianus addressed Cyprian's concerns, led him to acknowledge "the true divinity," and introduced him to the Christian community. When Cyprian chose to enter the outer vestibule of the church's life—the catechumenate—Caecilianus was his sponsor, "the friend and comrade of his soul."[15]

It's not clear how long Cyprian's period as a catechumen lasted, and we don't know precisely what he studied. Pontius's *Life of Cyprian* reports that Cyprian, possibly along with other catechumens, "loved the poor"; one imagines that in Carthage catechumens regularly participated in the church's care of widows, the sick, and strangers. According to Pontius, at this time Cyprian gave a substantial portion of his inherited estates for their relief. Further, Pontius reports that Cyprian imitated Christians whose lives he admired.[16]

As Cyprian observed the community's habitus and learned the Christians' reflexes and habits, he experienced inner turbulence. As Cyprian tells the story to Donatus, he did not struggle to believe what the Christians believed. Rather, he struggled to live in keeping with the Christians' habitus. Cyprian felt himself "held in bonds by the innumerable errors of [his] previous life." Was it, he wondered, really possible for him to escape these? Was someone

---

13. Cyprian, *Don.* 2, trans. E. Wallis, *ANF* 5:275.
14. Cyprian, *Don.* 3–4 (Wallis, 276).
15. Pontius, *Vit. Cypr.* 4, trans. E. Wallis, *ANF* 5:268.
16. Pontius, *Vit. Cypr.* 2.3.6 (Wallis, 268–69).

like him—privileged, influential, habituated to comfort—"capable of being born again"?[17] Was it conceivable that he could enter into an alternative habitus—the habitus of the Christian church—with a lifestyle different from the one he found oppressive? Could he live a lifestyle of simplicity, sufficiency, fearlessness, and mutuality? Despairing of this, Cyprian reports that at times he "indulged [his] sins," possibly by engaging in recidivistic binges.[18] But guided by Caecilianus, "the parent of his new life," Cyprian took the decisive step: he submitted to Christian baptism. As Cyprian tells the story, it was baptism that made the difference—it was a watershed and a catharsis.

> By the help of the water of new birth, the stain of former years had been washed away, and a light from above, serene and pure, had been infused into my rec-onciled heart,—after that, by the agency of the Spirit breathed from heaven, a second birth had restored me to a new man;—then, in a wondrous manner, doubtful things at once began to assure themselves to me . . . what before had seemed difficult began to suggest a means of accomplishment, what had been thought impossible, to be capable of being achieved.[19]

Washed, reborn, illumined, and "animated by the Spirit of holiness," Cyprian was moved to his core. It was a deeply emotional experience, mediated by ritual practice, that empowered him to be re-formed as a Christian. As a result of his baptism, Cyprian was at last able to do what had seemed impossible, to embrace the countercultural habitus of the Christian church.[20] Shortly after his baptism, Cyprian submitted himself to ordination as a presbyter and then bishop. Before long, in his treatise To Quirinus 3, he assembled materials for use in forming this habitus in a new generation of catechumens. In Cyprian's view he was doing these things as a free man. In contrast to his experience as a pagan, Cyprian's life as a member of the baptismal community was filled with "liberty and power."[21] Of course, no conversion is all-encompassing; the changes brought about by the powerful practices of catechesis and baptism didn't alter Cyprian entirely, nor should they have done so. Cyprian remained a rhetor, an educated African aristocrat. This ongoing inculturation into the deep values of his native society was in many ways beneficial, and it helped

---

17. Cyprian, *Don.* 3–4 (Wallis, 275–76).

18. Cyprian, *Don.* 4 (Wallis, 276).

19. Cyprian, *Don.* 4 (Wallis, 276).

20. Elisabeth Fink-Dendorfer, *Conversio: Motive und Motivierung zur Bekehrung in der Alten Kirche*, Regensburger Studien zur Theologie 33 (Frankfurt-am-Main: Peter Lang, 1986), 40–43; cf. Maurice F. Wiles, "The Theological Legacy of St. Cyprian," *Journal of Ecclesiastical History* 14, no. 2 (1963): 140–41.

21. Cyprian, *Don.* 5.

him provide leadership for the church in dangerous times. But the continuities also had questionable dimensions that, for example, determined that the administrative shape Cyprian gave the church would be indelibly Roman.[22]

At this point Cyprian and his hagiographer stop short. Their accounts are precious—personal, detailed, and emotionally revealing—but incomplete.[23] They do not describe other aspects of African Christianity that must have shaped Cyprian—the kiss of peace with which the Christian community received him after his baptism; the community's homilies and prayers; and the Eucharist. To get a fuller account of the practices that initiated converts into the Christian communities and habituated them to their habitus, we must turn to other sources.

Didache—Training for Christian Community

We start with the Didache, one of the most revealing of these sources and in the view of some scholars also one of the earliest.[24] The Didache makes sense when it is seen as a "training" or "instruction" that a community, probably in Palestine, used to incorporate new members.[25] The text is short enough to be easily memorized by potential members, who learned what the text meant by apprenticing themselves to community members, who were examples, craftsmen of the Christian way. The aim, according to Thomas O'Loughlin, was irreversibly to "alter the habits of perception and standards of judgment of novices coming out of a pagan life style."[26]

What kind of training program did that require? How did the ordinary community members who apparently served as the trainers do this apprenticing? For one thing, they focused the novices' attention on central predispositions that pervaded the community's common life. The Didache establishes two of these. One of them, which it sets forth at the outset, is that life requires radical choice. To make this point, the Didache uses the classical image of "two ways," going back to Deuteronomy (30:19–20), the Psalms, and the

22. Brent, *Cyprian*, 28, 75, 286–87.
23. Jean Molager comments that *To Donatus* is the first Christian autobiographical conversion story that does not contain romance. See Molager, ed., *Cyprien de Carthage: À Donat; et La vertu de patience*, SC 291 (Paris: Cerf, 1982), 22.
24. All quotations from the Didache come from the translation of C. C. Richardson, in *Early Christian Fathers*, LCC 1 (1953), 171–79.
25. Aaron Milavec, ed., *Didache: Text, Translation, Analysis, and Commentary* (Collegeville, MN: Liturgical Press, 2003); Thomas O'Loughlin, *The Didache: A Window on the Earliest Christians* (Grand Rapids: Baker Academic, 2010), 35.
26. Thomas O'Loughlin, "The Missionary Strategy of the *Didache*," *Transformation: An International Journal of Holistic Mission Studies* 28, no. 2 (2011): 84n.

Prophets, the way of life and the way of death.[27] The lives of all—members as well as apprentices—are shaped by their choice between the two ways in all aspects of daily life. The second predisposition that recurs throughout the Didache is making the commandments of Jesus the heart of one's way of life. The Didache's countercultural habitus grows out of a mingling of these predispositions—to live the way of life means to live the teachings of Jesus!

Further, the Didache gives weight to this mingling by insisting that these themes must be embodied and practiced. For example, the Didache begins its treatment of the two ways by citing "bless those who curse you, and pray for your enemies," and goes on to present other ways that the Christian habitus differs from "the way the heathen act."[28] Why was blessing and loving the enemy so prominent? Possibly because when people joined the community, they encountered acute hostility.[29] The community's experience was also essential in shaping the Didache's approach to poverty. Some members had received aid from the community; they must also be willing to give. "Do not hesitate to give and do not give with a bad grace. . . . Do not turn your back on the needy, but share everything with your brother and call nothing your own. For if you have what is eternal in common, how much more should you have what is transient!"[30] The community's habitus involved hospitality, physical work, daily gatherings with other members, and twice-weekly communal fasts. The community's common life was intense, which led the Didache to emphasize "reconciling those who are at strife"; the Didache forbade members who were alienated from their fellow believers to take part in the community's meals—real meals with nourishing food that were eucharistic—until they were reconciled.[31]

The habitus of the Didache's community was what they did, and the Didache is insistent on the importance of practice. One example is the way it required members to respond to itinerant prophets who came to the community. The members were to welcome the prophets and to receive their teaching, but not without caution; they were to differentiate true prophets from false ones. The true prophets were not those who said inspiring things; they were those who "behave like the Lord." The Didache notes, "It is by their conduct that the false prophet and the [true] prophet can be distinguished." In a community whose members were taught to obey the teachings of Jesus and "hate all hypocrisy," a faithful lifestyle was the indicator of Christian authority: "Every prophet

27. Did. 1.1–2 (Richardson, 171).
28. Did. 1.3–5 (Richardson, 171).
29. Aaron Milavec, The Didache: Faith, Hope, and Life of the Earliest Christian Communities, 50–70 C.E. (New York: Newman, 2003), 113–14.
30. Did. 4.5–8 (Richardson, 173).
31. Did. 4.3; 14.1–2; 15.3.

who teaches the truth but fails to practice what he preaches is a false prophet."[32] An emphasis on practice also permeated the baptismal rite by which outsiders joined the community. The community's members who instructed taught the candidates "all these points"—the community's habitus—and the candidates learned the habitus primarily by living it. Then, when the candidates were deemed to be ready for baptism, the baptizer and other community members joined them for several days of fasting. The baptism took place, if possible, in running water.[33] Only those who had developed the reflexes of the community's way of life and then were baptized could be admitted to its eucharistic meals.[34] Thus trained and fed, the community's members shared in the life of the community. The Didachist did not discuss how the life of the community impacted the world or attracted new members, possibly because such discussion seemed unnecessary; the habitus of the community was attracting as many people to its life as the community's catechetical formation could cope with.

Aristides—the Earliest Apology

The attractive habitus of the Christians also is central to the *Apology* of Aristides.[35] Writing in the mid-second century to the emperor Antoninus Pius, probably from Athens, Aristides invites the emperor to consider the Christians, whose exemplary practices he contrasts to those of the empire's pagan inhabitants. He attributes the Christians' practices to the teachings of Jesus: "They have the commandments of the Lord Jesus Christ himself engraven on their hearts, and these they observe."[36] As a result, their common life had distinctive characteristics: they were sexually disciplined, truthful, and financially reliable (they "do not deny a deposit"), and they loved their neighbors. More surprisingly, they loved their enemies: "They comfort such as wrong them, and make friends of them; they labour to do good to their enemies."[37] They loved each other, cared for the widow and the orphan, and had a remarkable practice of economic sharing especially with reference to burials.

> When one of their poor passes away from the world, and any of them sees him, then he provides for his burial according to his ability; and if they hear that

32. *Did*. 11.8–10 (Richardson, 177).
33. *Did*. 7.1–3 (Richardson, 174).
34. *Did*. 9.5.
35. All quotations from Aristides's *Apology* come from J. Stevenson, *A New Eusebius,* rev. W. H. C. Frend (London: SPCK, 1987), 52–55.
36. Aristides, *Apol*. 15.3 (Stevenson, 53).
37. Aristides, *Apol*. 15.5 (Stevenson, 53).

any of their number is imprisoned or oppressed for the name of their Messiah, all of them provide for his needs, and if it is possible that he may be delivered, they deliver him. And if there is among them a man that is poor and needy, and they have not an abundance of necessaries, they fast two or three days that they may supply the needy with their necessary food. (15.8–9)

The community's habitus dealt in distinctive ways with perennial problems of truthfulness, sexual fidelity, provision, protection, and burial. And according to Aristides, the heart of their habitus was worship. The community engaged in daily praise—they observed morning prayers and had prayers throughout the day; at mealtime they gave "thanksgiving" (*eucharist*) over their food and drink. Aristides especially emphasizes the intensity and centrality of intercessory prayer in their lives: "I have no doubt that the world stands by reason of the intercession of Christians."[38]

But how did the community form people so that someone from the "world" could hear about the community? Aristides commends the Christians' writing, which reveals "a new people, and there is something divine mingled with it," but he does not mention the practices of baptism or evangelism. The Christians communicated their faith intramurally to members of their households (servants or children), persuading them to become Christians.[39] But, according to Aristides, among outsiders the Christians were reticent; they didn't proclaim their good deeds "in the ears of the multitude." Rather, "they take care that no one shall perceive them, and hide their gift." Was this because their "conduct" was so attractive—from it "flows forth the beauty that is in the world"[40]—that it would lead to a growth so rapid that it would outrun the capacity of the community to form new members and thus would inevitably lose its attractiveness?

Justin—from Addiction to Freedom

Justin's *First Apology*,[41] which he wrote in Rome about AD 150, spells out the Christian communities' habitus more fully than Aristides's *Apology* does. Justin was a "pneumatic teacher," a philosophical instructor who imparted "words of truth" to students in his rooms above the Myrtinian baths.[42] Many

38. Aristides, *Apol.* 16.6 (Stevenson, 53).

39. Aristides, *Apol.* 16.5, 15.6 (Stevenson, 54, 53).

40. Aristides, *Apol.* 16.1–2 (Stevenson, 54).

41. All quotations from Justin's *1 Apology* come from E. R. Hardy, trans., in *Early Christian Fathers*, ed. C. C. Richardson, LCC 1 (1953), 161–82.

42. *Acts of Justin* 3, Recension B; trans. and ed. Herbert A. Musurillo, *Acts of the Christian Martyrs* (Oxford: Clarendon, 1972), 49; Ulrich Neymeyr, *Die christlichen Lehrer im zweiten*

of the students were already Christians when they came to Justin. It is not certain whether Justin served Roman house churches as a formal catechist, although it is likely that he was well connected with the developing catechetical programs of the Christians in Rome. Justin also was a participant in a Roman house church and thus understood its habitus. Like Aristides, Justin saw the Christians' habitus as the heart of his apologetic. Anyone exploring the Christians' faith would need to consider their "life and teachings"; according to Justin, what they taught had a great deal to do with how they lived.[43]

Justin doesn't provide a lengthy exposition of the Roman Christians' predispositions and practices. But early in the *Apology* he presents the Christians' lifestyle as a kind of counter-habitus to the lifestyle of the empire's non-Christian inhabitants. Justin sees the Romans' life as a habitus of un-freedom, characterized by addictive practices in four primal areas: sexual ethics, marred by fornication; the occult, trapped by magical arts; wealth and possessions, distorted by competitive acquisitiveness; and violence and xenophobia, filled with hatred and murder toward people of different tribes and customs. Justin reports that Christians also struggled with these primal areas. All of them, Christians have discovered, are seductive and potent. And they are immensely hard to unlearn—not least because, in Justin's view, they are expressions of demonic power and manipulation. But Christians, Justin claims, have been liberated from the old habitus in order to enter into a new habitus, a new normality. Having been "persuaded,"[44] Christians have renounced their old habitus and entered an alternative, life-giving habitus in each of the four areas: in sex, continence; in place of magic, dedication to God; in wealth, "bringing what we have into a common fund and sharing with everyone in need"; in violence and xenophobia, "living together and praying for our enemies, and trying to persuade those who unjustly hate us." This new habitus, Justin contends, is rooted in the teachings of Christ, "whose word was the power of God."[45] Justin proceeds at length to spell out the teachings of Christ as they apply to sex, affection for all people (including enemies), wealth and sharing, patience and anger, and truth telling. The teachings of Christ transform the lives of members so that they build distinctive communities whose habitus—whose predispositions and practices—attracts outsiders (14, 16, 39). The teachings of Christ are at the heart of the Christians' counter-habitus, and they must

Jahrhundert: Ihre Lehrtätigkeit, ihr Selbstverständnis und ihre Geschichte, VCSup 4 (Leiden: Brill, 1989), 33.

43. Justin, *1 Apol.* 1.3 (Hardy, 243).
44. Justin, *1 Apol.* 14, 44, 55, 61.
45. Justin, *1 Apol.* 14.2–4 (Hardy, 249).

be embodied: "Those who are found not *living as he taught* should know that they are not really Christians, even if his teachings are on their lips."[46]

This is strong stuff, and it raises a question: how, in the communities about which Justin is writing, did people learn the teachings of Christ not just with their heads but with their bodies? How did Roman Christians become habituated so that they lived the way of Christ reflexively? It was one thing for Justin to say, "We have been taught and do teach these things truly";[47] it was another to develop a pedagogy that formed habitus in a situation in which habitus was a subject of contention. Was it possible for a community to develop the practices necessary to maintain its new life over against a pagan habitus that was well established and deeply seductive, respected by society's elite, informed by deep narratives, and made immediate by omnipresent visual arts? In such a situation, could the Christians physically renounce the old habitus and supplant it with a new habitus? And if so, how?

Justin's *Apology* gives us hints about the Roman Christians' approach to this. No doubt their approach didn't always work as well as Justin would have liked. For example, Hermas's writings, coming from Rome at a slightly earlier period than Justin's, reveal his anguish at Christians who in his view arrogate too much wealth for themselves and do not share with those in need.[48] Nevertheless, in Justin's *Apology* there is a cluster of practices that demonstrate an approach to Christian initiation that is congruent with habitus change.

- *Friends becoming companions*: Central to Justin's approach are Christians who are present in society, engaging in relationships with non-Christians in which significant issues of faith and lifestyle arise. The reason the friends of Christians are attracted to Christianity may well be the Christians' distinctive approach to life issues—for example, to the "patient" way the Christians operate their businesses.[49] According to Justin, the Christians' dialogical style is one of "persuasion" that invites further investigation. If the inquirers wish to proceed in investigation, some of their Christian friends may accompany them in their journey. The term that Justin uses for these friends is "we," which indicates his own involvement.[50]

- *Catechesis in preparation for baptism*: In the next step, the interested parties present themselves for baptism. Justin gives little information about this step. He does, however, report that unspecified catechists teach the

---

46. Justin, *1 Apol.* 16.8 (Hardy, 252).
47. Justin, *1 Apol.* 14.4 (Hardy, 250).
48. Herm. Vis. 3.9.1.
49. Justin, *1 Apol.* 16.4.
50. Justin, *1 Apol.* 61.2; 65.2.

candidates. Justin knows how varied the people are and is aware of the huge challenges—pastoral and catechetical—of re-forming their habitus. Some Christians are sophisticated; most are "uneducated and barbarous in speech." Justin writes, "Among us you can hear and learn these things from those who do not even know the letters of the alphabet."[51] Justin knew that although perhaps 90 percent of the Roman populace was illiterate, illiteracy did not impede Christian discipleship.[52] The Christian habitus was lived by extremely diverse people. What then did the catechists teach them? No doubt they taught topics that Justin deals with in his *Apology*, and certainly the teachings of Jesus run through it like a leitmotif. The candidates not only learn (and memorize?) the teachings; their faith and imagination is formed as they see how Christians embody Jesus's teachings in their habitus—in the daily life of the Christian communities and the Christians' life in the workaday world. The catechists remind the candidates of the commitment that all Christians make, and reaffirm in baptism, to wash themselves from anything that would keep them from caring for the poor, the orphan, and the widow (Isa. 1:16–20). By this point, some candidates may turn back. According to Hermas, "when they recall what the life of true purity involves, they change their minds and return to pursue their evil desires."[53] Nevertheless, other candidates proceed to baptism, provided they meet three criteria: they are acting freely and under no compulsion (they are "children of free choice and knowledge"); they are persuaded that the church's teachings are true; "and [they] promise that they can live accordingly."[54]

- *The baptismal rite*: Justin's account of this rite is low key. He informs us that the candidates, who have made these commitments, pray to God with fasting for the remission of their sins (for having lived lives shaped by a pagan habitus?). Meanwhile, he says, "we [sponsors and companions] pray and fast along with them." The baptism involves washing in the water, which the baptizands experience as illumination. Justin imparts little emotional coloration to the baptism.[55]

- *The post-baptismal incorporation in the assembly*: "We" then lead the newly baptized believers to something they have not previously

51. Justin, *1 Apol.* 60.11 (Hardy, 280).

52. Harry Y. Gamble, *Books and Readers in the Early Church* (New Haven: Yale University Press, 1995), 4–10; W. V. Harris, *Ancient Literacy* (Cambridge, MA: Harvard University Press, 1989), 328–31.

53. Herm. Vis. 3.7.3, trans. B. D. Ehrman, LCL 25 (2003), 211.

54. Justin, *1 Apol.* 61.2 (Hardy, 282).

55. Justin, *1 Apol.* 61.2 (Hardy, 282).

experienced—their new family ("those who are called brothers"). The
prayers they offer together are "earnest," asking God that the new brothers and sisters and the rest of the Christian family may be "keepers of
what is commanded" in a world that is dangerous for Christians. The
prayers end with the church's familial kiss, and their Eucharist ensues,
full of praise and glory and thanksgiving.[56] The Eucharist is private;
access to the meal is restricted. But the new believers are now a part
of this privileged circle. They are among those who are at home in the
church's habitus—who believe that what "we" teach is true, who have
received baptism, and who are committed to embodying the message
("who live as Christ handed down to us").[57] After the service they find
confirmation of what they probably knew earlier—that the Christians
"are constantly together" and engage in redistributive economic sharing.[58]

- *Sunday Eucharist*: On the eve of Sunday (Saturday evening) or on Sunday
  morning, the community gathers for its main weekly assembly, which,
  like other practices of the church, forms the community's habitus. For
  example, the *sermon* consciously aims at habitus formation. After
  the reading from the Gospels ("the memoirs of the apostles") and the
  Prophets, the president in a discourse urges the community to live what
  they have heard—to devote themselves to "the imitation of these noble
  things."[59] Thus, formation continues in the church's weekly gathering as
  believers apply Jesus's teachings to their lives. The president knows that
  the community must live the gospel if outsiders are to find the gospel
  credible. The *Eucharist* also reinforces the habitus. After the prayers,
  which Justin only mentions, the "uncommon" gifts are brought for the
  Eucharist, and the president sends up thanksgivings "to the best of his
  ability."[60] The elements of the symbolic meal are distributed to each
  person, and bread is left over for the deacons to take to members of the
  community who are absent—but linked together by the meal. Finally,
  the *offering* builds the habitus. Justin emphasizes that it, like adherence
  to Christianity in general, is uncoerced: "Those who prosper, and who
  so wish, contribute, each one as much as he chooses to." The offering
  is deposited with the community's president, who uses it for orphans,

---

56. Justin, *1 Apol.* 65.1–2 (Hardy, 285).
57. Justin, *1 Apol.* 66.1 (Hardy, 286).
58. Justin, *1 Apol.* 67.1, 6–7 (Hardy, 287); cf. Peter Lampe, *From Paul to Valentinus: Chris-*
tians in Rome in the First Two Centuries (Minneapolis: Fortress, 2003), 140: the Roman churches
provided a "limited material equalization between the social levels."
59. Justin, *1 Apol.* 67.3–4 (Hardy, 287).
60. Justin, *1 Apol.* 67.5 (Hardy, 287).

widows, sick people, prisoners, and travelers who are staying with the church. As Justin repeatedly emphasizes, caring for the needy is a central value in the church's *habitus*, and it is the president's job—as the one responsible for the maintenance of a community freed from the bondage to competitive materialism—to make sure that the community takes this seriously. By doing so, the president is the "protector of all those in need."[61]

The *Apostolic Tradition*—a General Model?

During the first two centuries there was considerable variety in the liturgical practices of the early Christian communities.[62] Even within Rome, the practices of Justin's house church may have been different from the practices of Christians in house churches only a brief walk away. And practices of communities in other parts of the world—in Syria or Egypt or North Africa—may have been very different from those in Rome. Nevertheless, by the late second century Christian communities in many places were coming to a new self-confidence. By AD 180–200 Christians were becoming stronger numerically and leaving more records—archaeological, artistic, and literary. The connections between the Christians in various parts of the world were also intensifying; there was a growing tendency of Christians to influence each other and to develop similar approaches to common problems. Something like this may well have happened in the areas of catechesis and mission.

A text that embodies this maturing process is the famous *Apostolic Tradition*.[63] Most scholars used to attribute this to Hippolytus, a third-century Roman priest/bishop, and they maintained that the document records the practice of the Roman church. Although some still do this, the work of Paul Bradshaw and his colleagues at the University of Notre Dame has persuaded me that the *Apostolic Tradition* is not the product of one author or group of authors and is not the record of the church of one place.[64] Instead, it is "living literature" that writers pasted together in communities in North Africa and Rome, and possibly in Egypt as well. The process of assembling the *Apostolic*

61. Justin, *1 Apol.* 67.7 (Hardy, 287).

62. Paul F. Bradshaw, *The Search for the Origins of Christian Worship: Sources and Methods for the Study of Early Liturgy*, 2nd ed. (New York: Oxford University Press, 2002), 53.

63. The translation I use is by Paul F. Bradshaw, Maxwell E. Johnson, and L. Edward Phillips, *The Apostolic Tradition: A Commentary*, Hermeneia (Minneapolis: Fortress, 2002) (henceforth BJP).

64. Bradshaw, *Search for the Origins*, 80–83, 95–96. For a different approach that sees the *Apostolic Tradition* as a multilayered work, with third-century Roman origins, see Alistair Stewart-Sykes, trans. and ed., *Hippolytus: On the Apostolic Tradition* (Crestwood, NY: St. Vladimir's Seminary Press, 2001), 49–50.

Tradition as we now have it was gradual, incorporating materials written in Greek possibly across a century and a half, from the mid-second through early fourth centuries. As a result, we must be cautious in making precise claims about early Christian practices on the authority of the *Apostolic Tradition*. Nevertheless, because the *Apostolic Tradition* contains information that is detailed and illuminating, it makes good sense to take it seriously. Communities from west to east received this document, translated it into four languages, and revised it, at times considerably.[65] In the fourth century, new church orders were written in its tradition.[66] These give the *Apostolic Tradition* a distinctive authority among the documents of the early church. In a sense, we can think of the process by which the *Apostolic Tradition* was compiled and diffused as an exercise in patience. How fascinating it is as a source for the subject of this chapter—catechesis and baptism. In the paragraphs that follow, I will be exploring chapters 15–21 of the *Apostolic Tradition* in an attempt to see how people became Christians in the period between Justin Martyr and Constantine.[67]

The *Apostolic Tradition*'s model for becoming Christian can be schematized as follows:

1. Evangelism	First Scrutiny: Relationships & Jobs	2. Catechumenate	Second Scrutiny: Habitus & Character	3. Baptismal Preparation	Third Scrutiny: Exorcism	4. Baptism
Encountering Christians, finding a sponsor		Hearing the Word		Hearing the gospel		Singing a new song*
Years or months		Until "character" is formed		Weeks or months		For life

*The phrase "singing a new song" comes not from the *Apostolic Tradition* but from Origen, *Hom. Exod.* 5.5.

65. The BJP edition of the *Apostolic Tradition* gives English translations in four parallel columns of the Latin, Sahadic (Syriac), Arabic, and Ethiopic texts.

66. *Canons of Hippolytus*, from Egypt in the late 330s; *Apostolic Constitutions*, from Syria in the 380s; the *Testament of Our Lord*, contested origins (following G. Sperry-White, I prefer Asia Minor in the latter half of the 300s). For dates, see Bradshaw, *Search for the Origins*, 83–87; Sperry-White, *The Testamentum Domini: A Text for Students* (Bramcote, Notts: Grove Books, 1991), 6.

67. Paul F. Bradshaw proposes that the "core rite" underlying chaps. 15–20 of the *Apostolic Tradition* comes from the late second century. See his "The Profession of Faith in Early Christian Baptism," *Evangelical Quarterly* 78, no. 2 (2006): 110; also BJP, 124.

Stage 1. Evangelism—"Encountering Christians, Finding a Sponsor"

Unlike many churches today, the third-century churches described by the *Apostolic Tradition* did not try to grow by making people feel welcome and included. Civic paganism did that. In contrast, the churches were hard to enter. They didn't grow because of their cultural accessibility; they grew because they required commitment to an unpopular God who didn't require people to perform cultic acts correctly but instead equipped them to live in a way that was richly unconventional.

The churches chose this approach for good reasons. The first was theological: they believed that the God whom they worshiped revealed himself in Jesus of Nazareth, an embodied human who at ultimate cost demonstrated the way to live, and that Jesus's way was saving and life giving for individual humans and their communities. It was vital for the Christians to live in his way, unusual though it was, because they thought that it was true. The second reason was evangelistic: the churches' primary witness was a product not of what Christians said but of how they lived. It was rooted in the assumption that the lives of Christians and their communities provided embodied evidence of the truth of their words. How could the Christians undercut this approach to mission? By admitting new people too quickly whose behavior compromised the Christians' distinctive attractiveness.

What happened was this. Non-Christians and Christians worked together and lived near each other. They became friends. Non-Christians were at times attracted by the Christians and interested in exploring Christianity further. The Christians could not take them to Sunday worship services—these were off limits to people until they had been catechized and baptized. But the Christians could invite their friends to go with them early on a weekday to meet the church's "teachers." Would the teachers admit them to a process of study and habituation—lasting for some time—that would eventually lead to their admission to the community? Would they admit them as catechumens en route to baptism?

The non-Christian applicants went with their friends/sponsors to meet the church's teachers. In this meeting, called the First Scrutiny, the teachers—at times clergy, at times laity—gave primary attention to the sponsors and asked them to "bear witness" about the candidates.[68] The sponsors had to answer questions, not about what the candidates believed or (as in conventional associations) about whether they could pay hefty initiation fees (the churches

68. *Trad. ap.* 15.1.

required none), but about how the candidates lived.[69] Why this concentration
on how they were living? There were two reasons.

The first reason was the candidates' *teachability*. The teachers wanted to
know that the candidates were living in such a way that they were able "to hear
the Word." Can they appropriate what the teachers are teaching? According to
the *Apostolic Tradition*, the church gave major attention to these questions. And
for good reason. The teachers, like the early Christians generally, believed that
the surest indication of what people thought was the way they lived, and they
were convinced that the candidates' behavior was the most reliable predictor of
whether they would be able to learn the Christians' habitus. The teachers, with
the candidate standing by, pressed the sponsor about the candidate's behavior
in light of the church's deep rejection of idolatry, adultery, and killing. Would
the way the candidate has been living enable him or her to "hear the Word"
(to master the church's teaching with their bodies as well as their brains)? For
example, actors who gave pagan theatrical performances—could they hear the
Word in a community which vigorously repudiated polytheism? Gladiators
who killed in the arena—could they hear the Word in a community that forbade the taking of life? Prostitutes—could they hear the Word in a community
that emphasized chastity and continence? The *Apostolic Tradition* specifies
that, in each case, these people needed to leave their professions if they were
to be accepted as potential Christians; their professional commitments made
it impossible for them to comprehend the Christians' teaching.[70]

In the case of certain other professions, however, it was somewhat different.
The *Apostolic Tradition* asserts that their practitioners would be capable of
hearing the Word on one condition—if they took socially costly steps necessary to modify their behavior. Painters, for example, could be accepted as
catechumens if they refrained from depicting pagan themes.[71] As for soldiers,
the *Apostolic Tradition* assesses them, like the members of other professions,
by their capacity to hear the Word: did their external professional commitments—the tasks and milieux and religious commitments of their jobs—enable
them to receive the Christian good news in churches that emphasized patience
and in which reconciliation with the alienated brother was a precondition
for prayer?[72] The *Apostolic Tradition*'s assumption is clear. Inner and outer
are inextricable; if you live in a certain way in everyday life, you cannot hear,

69. Compare H. A. Drake, "Models of Christian Expansion," in *The Spread of Christianity
in the First Four Centuries: Essays in Explanation*, ed. W. V. Harris (Leiden: Brill, 2005), 5: "the
relatively low criterion for admission to Christianity."

70. *Trad. ap.* 16.4; 7.12.

71. *Trad. ap.* 16.3.

72. *Trad. ap.* 16.10–11. See also Cyprian, *Dom. or.* 23.

comprehend, or live the gospel that the Christian community is seeking to embody as well as teach. The church will not baptize people in hopes that they will change thereafter.

The church's *witness* was the second reason that the teachers carefully examined the candidates in the First Scrutiny. As a catechumen, would the candidate's behavior represent the church well or let the church down? Christians are to "be competitors . . . among the nations [*gentes*]" by their exemplary behavior; if they behave conventionally, the pagans will conclude that there is nothing in Christianity worth investigating.[73] So if a potential candidate is married to a husband (who may be pagan), let her be admitted as a catechumen, provided she is willing to be taught "to be content with her husband."[74] Her admission is conditional on receiving teaching; as we have seen, the church was open to having women members, chaste and sexually disciplined, who were married to pagan men. However, the church categorically refused to admit to the catechumenate other candidates whose occupations contradicted the church's teaching. For example, in the case of men who were makers of idols or gladiators whose profession involved killing, the teacher's verdict was crisp: "Let them cease or be cast out."[75]

But for the sake of the church's witness, other candidates whose jobs were at least in part acceptable could be admitted on the condition that they gave up their unacceptable behavior. For example, in some places soldiers had been attracted to the Christian communities that rejected all forms of killing, including killing in warfare. So the teachers responded to a soldier by saying, "Let him not kill a man. If he is ordered, let him not go to the task nor let him swear." If the soldier was unwilling to submit to this limitation of his professional behavior, the verdict was "Let him be cast out."[76] Four times in chapters 15 and 16 of the *Apostolic Tradition*, the teachers accept applicants on the condition that they receive teaching; three times they accept applicants on the condition that they give up unacceptable behavior; and ten times the teachers respond by categorically refusing applicants. In one case, the teachers are astonishingly flexible: when a man teaching young children (whose lessons involve pagan stories) has no other trade, the teachers determine that "he should be forgiven." Church leaders of a later age might have said, "Let's admit them as they do their current jobs and eventually, when they have 'heard the word,' they will think their way into a new life." The church of the *Apostolic Tradition* says in effect, "No, our approach is the opposite.

73. *Trad. ap.* 29A (BJP, 152).
74. *Trad. ap.* 15.6 (BJP, 82).
75. *Trad. ap.* 15.7; 16.3 (BJP, 83, 88).
76. *Trad. ap.* 16.10–11 (BJP, 90).

We believe that people *live their way into a new kind of thinking*. If we admit them as they engage in idolatry, immorality, and killing, they will be unable to 'hear the word,' and they will change the church, fatally compromising its distinctiveness, which is the basis of our witness."[77]

Stage 2. The Catechumenate—"Hearing the Word"

Despite these hurdles, the church's teachers admitted many people to the catechumenate. In this process the candidates' Christian friends were essential. The sponsors were important not only as go-betweens, bridgefolk in the initial meeting with the teachers, but also as supporters of the catechumens throughout the catechumenate, which could last three years or more. Earlier in this chapter we met Caecilianus, whom Cyprian called "the friend and comrade of his soul."[78] For Cyprian, an apprentice-Christian who was learning the craft, Caecilianus served as a kind of master Christian. Sponsors such as Caecilianus accompanied the candidates during their catechumenate, in which they experienced huge changes.

The phrase that summarizes the catechumenate is "hearing the Word."[79] This came in many forms. To be sure, the catechumens received a great deal of verbal input. But the catechists also challenged them to change by example and experience. The catechumens were engaged in the adventure of exploring a community whose values were different from the dominant society. They had new stories to learn, new slogans to memorize, and new ways to behave. At first they no doubt found some of these uncomfortable. The candidates could not cope with this cluster of newness on their own. Many early Christians recognized this. Clement of Alexandria, writing around AD 200, observed:

> Now it is perhaps impossible all at once to cut away passions that have grown with us, but with God's power, human supplication, the help of brethren, sincere repentance and constant practice success is achieved. It is therefore an absolute necessity that you who are haughty and powerful and rich should appoint for yourself some man of God as trainer and pilot. Let there be at all events one whom you respect, one whom you fear, one whom you accustom yourself to listen to when he is outspoken and severe, though all the while at your service.[80]

---

77. One other category of persons whom the teachers did not admit to the catechumenate were those "who have a demon"; they were not to hear the word of instruction until they had been cleansed (*Trad. ap.* 15.8). This paragraph owes much to James K. A. Smith, *Imagining the Kingdom: How Worship Works* (Grand Rapids: Baker Academic, 2013), 79–80; also to Richard Rohr, *Simplicity: The Art of Living* (New York: Crossroad, 1991), 59.

78. Pontius, *Vit. Cypr.* 4 (Wallis, 268).

79. *Trad. ap.* 15.1; 17.1.

80. Clement of Alexandria, *Quis div.* 40–41, trans. G. W. Butterworth, LCL 60 (1919), 355.

Sponsors like Clement knew that when the time came at the end of the catechumenate for the church leaders to choose the catechumens who would be baptized, they—the accompanying "trainers and pilots," not the candidates—will face the Second Scrutiny. In this examination the sponsor gives account to the church's leaders for the candidate's progress during the catechumenate. Above all, the sponsor has to affirm that the candidate has changed: not only the candidate's thinking (that was the easy part), but also the candidate's behavior, character, and reflexes—in short, the candidate's habitus. The Second Scrutiny revolved around the sponsor's assessment of the candidate's "character" (*tropos*). Has the candidate's "character" changed so that it reflects the virtues and practices of the church?[81] If so, the church will baptize them as Christians. But it wasn't the candidate who answered these questions; it was their sponsor, their accompanying advocate.

In addition to providing the sponsors, the church provided resources that formed the catechumens' character. One was *liminality*. This was symbolized by a room in the building where the church met—"the place where one is instructed."[82] When the newly appointed catechumens entered this room, they were doing something risqué and potentially dangerous; they were leaving their old world with its respectability, assumptions, and commitments and were reconnoitering, from a distance, the new world on the other side of baptism. The theologian Origen likened the catechumens' experience to the Israelites' crossing the Red Sea; in this, they had left their bondage in Egypt but had not yet crossed the Jordan.[83] Like the Israelites, the catechumens were in the wilderness, a place of unlearning and learning, of testing and deciding. In this liminal place, the catechumens had to choose—did they want to go back to their old life, or did they want to take the risk of being immersed in a new life?

A second resource, appropriate for this period of "hearing the Word," was *instruction* (*catechesis*). According to the *Apostolic Tradition*, the people, both the baptized faithful and the catechumens, often gathered in the same place before they went to work to receive instruction from catechists (lay and clergy).[84] Frustratingly, the *Apostolic Tradition* gives only hints about the curriculum of their teaching. The catechists proclaim "things that are profitable for everyone" and raise topics that the catechumens do not expect ("things you do not think about"). Further, they address issues having to do

81. *Trad. ap.* 17.2 (BJP, 96).
82. *Trad. ap.* 41.2 (BJP, 194).
83. Origen, *Hom. Jos.* 4.1. Origen could be flexible in his analogies; in another sermon (*Hom. Exod.* 5.5) he likens baptism to the crossing of the Red Sea (cf. 1 Cor. 10:1–2).
84. *Trad. ap.* 19.1.

with everyday life—things "that are proper for you to do in your home."[85] The *Apostolic Tradition* is somewhat more explicit in its description of the teachers' style, which must have been authoritative and inspirational. The catechumens sense "in [their] heart that God is the one whom [they] hear speaking," and they receive the teaching as a gift from the Holy Spirit. This strengthens their faith.[86] But the *Apostolic Tradition* makes clear that the catechumens are not allowed to forget that they are still in the wilderness. The catechetical sessions end with events that emphasize the catechumens' liminality: with prayers in which the catechumens pray separately from the faithful, and with the kiss of peace, which excludes the catechumens because their kiss "is not yet holy."[87] Finally, just before the catechumens depart, the teacher lays hands on them and dismisses them.[88] The catechumens leave with the sense that, having prayed in the church, they have been empowered to "escape the evil of the day."[89]

A third resource is *practices*. During the catechumenate the candidates learned about the Christian faith by verbal teaching and, perhaps more importantly, by doing things. Actions that involve the body activate kinesthetic learning; they build up bodily habits and form reflexes that express the community's values. As we saw at the end of the previous chapter, the Christians' habitus was made up of many bodily actions. The *Apostolic Tradition* concentrates on four of these. The first of these, the sign of the cross, it mentions repeatedly. It indicates that signing with the cross is a breastplate against the devil, and it instructs the candidates how to make the sign on their forehead and eyes.[90] A second practice that it mentions is caring for the poor. Honoring the widows and visiting the sick were practices that expressed the community's primary concerns, and catechumens were expected to engage in these.[91] A third practice, in which the catechists were to teach and encourage the catechumens, is prayer. Christians were to pray at home according to a well-developed schedule, but—the *Apostolic Tradition* instructs the catechumens—if they are in another place where a visibly Christian action could cause trouble, they should pray to God discreetly, in their hearts.[92]

---

85. *Trad. ap.* 41.3 (BJP, 194).
86. *Trad. ap.* 41.2 (BJP, 194).
87. *Trad. ap.* 18.3 (BJP, 100).
88. *Trad. ap.* 19.1. BJP, 102 notes that *Apostolic Tradition* is the only text prior to the late fourth-century *Apostolic Constitutions* (8.6.1–9.11) that reports a liturgical rite of the laying on of hands and the dismissal of the catechumens.
89. *Trad. ap.* 41.2 (BJP, 194).
90. *Trad. ap.* 41.14; 42.1, 4.
91. *Trad. ap.* 20.1.
92. *Trad. ap.* 41.5; 42.1.

A practice that the *Apostolic Tradition* does not mention is Sunday morning eucharistic services. In Caesarea in Palestine, Origen's Sunday homilies constitute part of the church's instruction of its catechumens; these make it explicit that catechumens are present in the service of the word.[93] However, the *Apostolic Tradition* does talk about the Lord's Supper (*cena dominica*) meals. In the community of the *Apostolic Tradition*, were these non-eucharistic *agapē* services? Or were they eucharistic, the community's primary weekly worship services?[94] They took place in the evenings. In them lamps were lit, food was eaten together, and the bishop engaged in postmeal teaching in response to the people's questions—strong practices that a newcomer would need to learn. And once again, at this meal service the catechumens' position was liminal. The *Apostolic Tradition* instructs them to stand (not sit) and to receive not ordinary bread but bread that had been exorcised.[95] Despite their liminal status in many activities, it is likely that the catechumens participated more intensely and frequently in practices in the Christian community than they had done as participants in pagan rites.

A fourth resource is the *diverse Christian community*. Candidates came from differing backgrounds—Jewish and pagan, Greek and Roman. They also were of both sexes and a range of social classes. Most were poor and some were slaves, but a few were comfortably well-off. Some of the candidates were illiterate; the *Apostolic Tradition* specifies a form of teaching "if [the candidate] can read."[96] Somehow the church's teaching was meant to reach all of these, for all were important in the Christian church. The teachers conveyed to the candidates that, although they valued education (Origen in Caesarea made no bones about this fact), refined learning was not the point; the catechesis was not designed to produce sophisticated thought but "character" and "virtuous living." The church's growth was the product, not of the Christians' persuasive powers, but of their convincing lifestyle.[97]

Entering the Christian community was a challenge for the catechumens. As they explored becoming Christians, the candidates generally did not move geographically—their catechists expected them to stay in the place where they were known and accountable.[98] Nevertheless, even when they stayed in one

93. Origen, *Hom. Luc.* 21.4; 22.5; 32.2.

94. "Recent research would recognize the existence of quite a wide range of forms of Christian sacred meals in the first two or three centuries before the classic eucharistic shape emerged as preeminent" (BJP, 160).

95. *Trad. ap.* 27.1; 28.5.

96. *Trad. ap.* 41.2 (BJP, 194).

97. *Trad. ap.* 17.2; 20.1.

98. Upper Egypt has a record of catechumens being sent by their churches to other churches for catechesis. Especially, some catechumens were sent "for edification" to a senior leader, Papa

location, they experienced transition from one world to another, from one habitus to another, from one cluster of narratives, rituals, priorities, and reflexes to another cluster that at significant points was markedly different. According to the *Apostolic Tradition*, the church assessed the candidates' habitus shift in its Second Scrutiny. How had the catechumens progressed during their period of hearing the Word? The church's leaders, facing the sponsors of those who were "chosen to prepare for baptism," asked the sponsors about the candidates' progress in developing Christian character. "[Their] way of life should be examined. [Have they] lived virtuously while they were being catechized? Have they honored the widows, visited the sick, fulfilled all good works? If those who have brought them bear witness that they have done so, let them hear the gospel."[99]

The leaders did not ask about the candidates' orthodoxy, about their mastery of doctrine, about their memorization of biblical passages, about their piety or prayer life. They did not ask about the many areas of distinctive Christian habitus that catechumens were attempting to master. They did not ask about the candidates' opinions and attitudes—for example, what they thought about poor people. They did, however, want to know how the candidates treated poor people. Actions said it all. Pontius in his *Life of Cyprian* was correct; in his brief treatment of Cyprian's experience during his time as a catechumen, he gives prominent attention to one thing—"the poor, whom as a catechumen [Cyprian] had loved."[100] The church leaders, screening people for baptism, wanted to know about the candidates' habitus. Were the candidates rewired so that spontaneously, reflexively, they were living like Christians—with their treatment of the widows and sick as the church's iconic, self-defining practice? If so, the *Apostolic Tradition* declares, "Let them hear the gospel."[101] They will enter stage 3, the period of final preparation culminating in stage 4, their baptism.

The Content of Catechesis (1)—General Topics

During the period of hearing the Word that prepared them for the Second Scrutiny, what had the catechumens heard? What had the church leaders wanted to impart to them? Irritatingly, the *Apostolic Tradition* doesn't tell us. It leaves us with a big gap. In the fourth century this gap doesn't exist; Cyril, Ambrose, John Chrysostom, and Augustine all left texts that document their

---

Sotas of Oxyrhynchus, who evidently excelled at catechesis. See AnneMarie Luijendijk, *Greetings in the Lord: Early Christians and the Oxyrhynchus Papyri*, HTS 60 (Cambridge, MA: Harvard University Press, 2008), 83, 86, 111.

99. *Trad. ap.* 20.1–2 Arabic (BJP 104).
100. Pontius, *Vit. Cypr.* 6 (Wallis, 269).
101. *Trad. ap.* 20.2 (BJP, 104).

catechetical priorities in Jerusalem, Milan, Antioch, and Hippo. For the pre-Constantinian period I have tried to fill the gap by collating scattered writings from the third century. These do not report systematically the catechetical approaches in any one place. But the composite is illuminating. I present it under nine headings.

Transforming the habitus. Irenaeus insisted that the church's overarching goal was "renewing [people] from their old habits into the newness of Christ."[102] Tertullian agreed, commenting that God had given free will to people so that they might "constantly encounter good by spontaneous observance of it, and evil by its spontaneous avoidance."[103] But the spontaneity of habitus did not just happen; it needed to be formed, not least in the area of idolatry.

Avoiding idolatry. Idolatry, according to Tertullian, is suffocating; it sucks people down to Hades. "The fear of [idolatry is] our leading fear; any 'necessity' whatever is too trifling compared to such a peril." So the church's law, peculiar to Christians, is avoiding idolatry in its many permutations in society; and the church's teaching, "inculcated on such as are entering it," prepares the catechumens to be alert to idolatry and, at all costs, to renounce it.[104]

Learning the master narrative. The catechists knew that people are profoundly formed by the stories they tell; therefore, many catechists made it a priority to present to the catechumens the Bible's narrative, which would replace the pagan stories as their primary fund of memory. From the fourth and fifth centuries there are reports of this from the pilgrim Egeria, who heard Cyril's catechetical homilies in Jerusalem. Augustine also presented a narrative-based catechesis that he offers to the catechist Deogratias.[105] This vision already animated people in the pre-Constantinian period. In late second-century Lyons, Irenaeus sketched an extensive survey of salvation history that he prepared for catechetical purposes.[106] And as we shall see shortly, in Caesarea Origen based his homilies on the Old Testament books that he treated both narratively and allegorically. For Origen, the story had to be learned before it could be *understood*.

Learning the teaching of Jesus. Many catechists saw that instructing the catechumens in the teaching of Jesus was central to their catechesis. In

102. Irenaeus, *Haer.* 3.17.1, trans. A. C. Coxe, *ANF* 1:444.

103. Tertullian, *Marc.* 2.6, trans. P. Holmes, *ANF* 3:302.

104. Tertullian, *Idol.* 24, trans. S. Thelwall, *ANF* 3:75–76.

105. Egeria, *Travels* 46.2–4, trans. and ed. John Wilkinson, *Egeria's Travels to the Holy Land*, rev. ed. (Warminster, England: Aris & Phillips, 1981), 144; Augustine, *First Catechetical Instruction* 1–2; Jean Daniélou, "L'histoire du salut dans la catéchèse," *La Maison-Dieu* 30 (1952): 19–20.

106. Everett Ferguson, "Irenaeus' *Proof of the Apostolic Preaching* and Early Catechetical Tradition," StPatr 18, no. 3 (1989): 119–40.

Athens in the 170s, Athenagoras reports what the Christians there have been taught. He begins his *Plea regarding Christians* by loosely quoting Jesus's words from the Sermon on the Mount/Plain: "For we have been taught not to strike back at someone who beats us nor to go to court with those who rob and plunder us." In chapter 11 he proceeds to go "through our teaching in detail" and once again begins by quoting Jesus's words: "What then are the teachings on which we are brought up? 'I say to you, love your enemies, bless them who curse you, pray for them who persecute you, that you may be sons of your Father in heaven who makes his sun rise upon the evil and the good.'" Jesus's teachings explain why ordinary Christians—"common men, artisans, and old women"—"do not rehearse words but show forth good deeds."[107]

Memorizing biblical passages. Origen, writing in the 240s to his friend Julius Africanus, makes a passing comment: "For who of all believers does not know the words in Isaiah? 'And in the last days the mountain of the Lord shall be manifest . . . and they shall beat their swords into ploughshares,'" and so on.[108] The vast majority of Christians were illiterate, but Origen knew that they often had astonishing memories, and so Christian teachers used their teaching to fill the people's memories with significant biblical texts such as this poetic, visionary passage from Isaiah. Tertullian also recognized the power of memorization. In his treatise *On Patience*, he urges his readers to respond nonviolently to attacks. Tertullian assumes that it will not be easy for them to live the life of Christian patience and that their newly learned habitus will come under strain. When this happens, Tertullian tells his African Christian readers that they can draw on biblical passages they have memorized. "If one tries to provoke you to a fight, there is at hand the admonition of the Lord: 'If someone strikes you,' he says, 'on the right cheek, turn to him the other also.' . . . If a spiteful tongue bursts out in cursing or wrangling, recall the saying: 'When men reproach you, rejoice.'"[109]

Catechists and pastors often dictated these memory passages to their people, and at times—as in the game of "telephone"—the passages no doubt changed somewhat. This was true even when Christians could read. A recent study of Perpetua's use of the Bible, for example, has concluded that her "knowledge

---

107. Athenagoras, *Leg.* 1.4; 11.1–4, 4–5, 22–25; Theophilus, *Autol.* 3.14. For other examples, see Everett Ferguson, "Love of Enemies and Nonretaliation in the Second Century," in *The Contentious Triangle: Church, State and University*, ed. Rodney L. Peterson and Calvin A. Pater (Kirksville, MO: Thomas Jefferson University Press, 1999), 92: "There is ample evidence . . . that the teachings of Jesus on love for enemies and nonretaliation were central to early Christian moral catechesis."

108. Origen, *Letter to Julius Africanus* 15, trans. F. Crombie, ANF 4:392.

109. Tertullian, *Pat.* 8.2–3, trans. R. Arbesmann, FC 40 (1959), 207.

was not the knowledge of a reader of these texts, but rather that of a listener."[110] She could have said, like later North Africans who were being interrogated, "I have [the Scriptures] but they are in my heart."[111]

Imitating role models. The catechumens were conscious that they were apprentices, and they learned to be Christians by watching believers whom they admired. They often had initially approached the church because of a Christian whose behavior or attitudes had especially appealed to them. These relationships often continued between the catechumens and the people who now were their sponsors. Throughout Cyprian's period as a catechumen, Caecilianus continued as "the friend and comrade of his soul." When Cyprian was baptized, Caecilianus was there as "the parent of his new life." Eventually, when Cyprian was martyred, he commended his wife and children to Caecilianus's care. It is not surprising that Cyprian, who "always imitated those who were better than others," was deeply shaped by Caecilianus.[112] Imitation of this sort must have continued in many places where the master-apprentice relationship was a normal part of the catechetical process.

Fostering a culture of peace. In early third-century Alexandria, the philosopher Clement saw catechesis as a time when believers are trained in distinctive values. He observed that the Athenians and Spartans have the famous legal systems of Solon and Lycurgus. But when one joins God's people, one has a different country (heaven) and a different lawgiver (God). Clement cited a cluster of laws that are characteristic of God's country, the first two of which are "thou shalt not kill; thou shalt not commit adultery."[113] Throughout his writings, Clement described these nonkilling, nonadulterous people as people of peace who are formed in catechesis. God has created humans to be peaceable: "man is an instrument made for peace."[114] But humans have been stunted by sin. The catechumenate is a time to "cut out sins like parasitic growths."[115] In the course of their catechesis, God's people "are educated not for war but for peace."[116] Clement comments: "We do not

110. Walter Ameling, "*Femina Liberaliter Instituta*—Some Thoughts on a Martyr's Liberal Education," in *Perpetua's Passions: Multidisciplinary Approaches to the "Passio Perpetuae et Felicitatis,"* ed. Jan N. Bremmer and Marco Formisano (Oxford: Oxford University Press, 2012), 98–99.

111. *Acts of the Abitinian Martyrs* 12, in *Donatist Martyr Stories: The Church in Conflict in Roman North Africa*, trans. and ed. Maureen A. Tilley, TTH 24 (Liverpool: Liverpool University Press, 1996), 37.

112. Pontius, *Vit. Cypr.* 3–4 (Wallis, 268–69).

113. Clement of Alexandria, *Protr.* 10, trans. G. W. Butterworth, LCL 60 (1919), 233.

114. Clement of Alexandria, *Paed.* 2.4.42, trans. S. P. Wood, FC 23 (1954), 131.

115. Clement of Alexandria, *Strom.* 2.96.1–2, trans. J. Ferguson, FC 85 (1991), 221.

116. Clement of Alexandria, *Paed.* 1.12.99 (Wood, 87).

train our women like Amazons to manliness in war; since we wish the men even to be peaceable."[117] In their catechesis Christians become "a peaceful people," "soldiers of peace" in God's "bloodless army" who wear "the armor of peace." Marshaled by God in "the ranks of peace," they "stand in array against the evil one."[118] The peaceableness of the Christians' culture is expressed by telltale things, such as the signet rings Christians buy in the markets to authenticate documents. What images should there be on these rings? According to Clement, the rings may have an intaglio of "a fish or ship in full sail . . . or a ship's anchor" but not of "a sword or bow, for we cultivate peace."[119]

Kinesthetics. Catechumens learned to be Christian by learning to do habitually what the Christians did, not least with their bodies. At the end of chapter 5 we saw that the habitus of the Christians included reflexive actions such as standing when praying, replenishing stocks of food and clothing, and receiving visitors hospitably. The habitus also included bodily practices that the Christians exercised many times a day in the course of their lives—especially making the sign of the cross. As Tertullian put it, "We make the sign of the cross on our foreheads at every turn, at our going in or coming out of the house . . . and in all ordinary actions of daily life."[120] The pagans saw Christians do this, mocked it, and could view it as suspicious activity. But Christians believed that it had the protective power of a spiritual breastplate. The apprentice Christians needed to learn how to make the sign of the cross, when to make it, when to be seen making it, and when to do it invisibly. The *Apostolic Tradition*, in a passage clearly directed to catechumens, urges them to make a practice of signing their foreheads and eyes with the cross, imitating those who are more experienced at this than they are.[121]

Practical issues. Catechists taught their charges about situations that they would confront. How should they behave in a public bath? Teachers quoting the *Didascalia apostolorum* could inform them.[122] As to clothing, how should

---

117. Clement of Alexandria, *Strom.* 4.8, trans. W. Wilson, ANF 2:420.

118. Clement of Alexandria, *Paed.* 2.2.32 (Wood, 121); *Protr.* 11 (Butterworth, 247).

119. Clement of Alexandria, *Paed.* 3.3.59 (Wood, 246); Paul Corby Finney, "Images on Finger Rings and Early Christian Art," in *Studies on Art and Archaeology in Honor of Ernst Kitzinger on His Seventy-Fifth Birthday*, ed. William Tronzo and Irving Lavin, Dumbarton Oaks Papers (Washington, DC: Dumbarton Oaks Research Library and Collection, 1987), 181–86.

120. Tertullian, *Cor.* 3.4, trans. E. A. Quain, FC 40 (1959), 237.

121. *Trad. ap.* 42.1, 4.

122. *Did. apost.* 1.8.26–1.9.4. Alistair Stewart-Sykes (in *The Didascalia apostolorum: An English Version with Introduction and Annotation* [Turnhout: Brepols, 2009], 115n) sees 1.8.26 as having a catechetical origin.

an aristocrat such as Cyprian subdue his dress "to a fitting mean"?[123] Cyprian needed to learn that! In preparation for a possible persecution, what should the catechists teach "those who are young in faith and catechumens" about how to respond under interrogation?[124]

The Content of Catechesis (2)—Cyprian's *To Quirinus* 3

Another way to fill the *Apostolic Tradition*'s tantalizing gap (which provides a catechetical structure but no content) is to turn to Bishop Cyprian's *To Quirinus* 3.[125] We are fortunate that this text has survived; it provides an account of the topics that Cyprian recommended for teaching to catechumens in Carthage. Cyprian wrote it in tense times. In the late 240s, just before the outbreak of the Decian persecution, a certain Quirinus, who may have been a catechist in the church there, approached the recently appointed bishop, Cyprian, for help with curriculum writing.[126] Quirinus asked for a list of "heads," pithy statements that would summarize "the religious teaching of our school [*religiosam sectae nostrae disciplinam*]." These would provide an overall picture of the Christian faith, giving a summary of "heavenly precepts" so that Quirinus's mind "might have a wholesome and large compendium nourishing its memory."[127] Cyprian, who had been a Christian for only a few years, produced the text known as *To Quirinus*, Book Three.[128] It contains 120 statements (for example, "That the sick are to be visited" [109]), for each of which Cyprian provides biblical passages cited in full. Some of these statements are supported by a single passage, others by several passages, and the most copious by thirty-six biblical passages. Cyprian cites passages from Genesis to Revelation, with New Testament texts outnumbering those from the Old Testament and the book of Matthew cited most often.[129] Cyprian passed these passages on to Quirinus in a document

---

123. Pontius, *Vit. Cypr.* 6 (Wallis, 269).

124. *Did. apost.* 5.6.4 (Stewart-Sykes, 204).

125. The Latin text of *Ad Qurinum* 3 is in *Sancti Cypriani Episcopi Opera*, ed. R. Weber, CCL 3 (Turnhout: Brepols, 1976), 73–179. I use the translation of Ernest Wallis, ANF 5:528–57.

126. Johannes Quasten, ed., *Patrology*, vol. 2, *The Ante-Nicene Literature after Irenaeus* (Westminster, MD: Christian Classics, 1950), 363.

127. Cyprian, *Ad Quir.* 3, preface (CCL 3:73; Wallis, 528).

128. Somewhat earlier, Cyprian wrote two books of texts with biblical excerpts for Quirinus. These were more personally directed, designed for "forming the first lineaments of your faith" (*Ad Quir.* 1, preface), and they deal with more restricted topics: *Ad Quir.* 1 (in 24 heads) on the church's relation to Israel; *Ad Quir.* 2 (in 30 heads) on Christology. Although *Ad Quir.* 3 was written later, it has been packaged together with the other two books as *Ad Quirinum* (*Testimonium libri III*).

129. In *Ad Quir.* 3, Cyprian cites texts from the Old Testament 183 times (×), the New Testament 254×, and the "Apocrypha" 36×. He cites Matthew 58× (28× from the Sermon on the Mount), the Psalms (50×), 1 Corinthians (36×), Proverbs (26×), Luke (22×), John (22×), Romans (21×), and so forth in diminishing numbers.

that he hoped would be easy to read and useful pedagogically—a tool to enable his catechumens to memorize the precepts and the biblical texts and to repeat them frequently (*frequenter iterantur*).[130]

Is *To Quirinus* 3 a catechetical text? And is it worth our attention today? Most scholars have ignored *To Quirinus* 3 and at times have implied that it is one of the dullest pieces in patristic literature. It is, after all, only a list; in the words of one unenthusiastic scholar, it "enumerates, without much order, a great number of moral precepts."[131] An authoritative recent survey of the catechetical literature of the early Christians ignores *To Quirinus* 3 altogether.[132] Clearly, *To Quirinus* 3 is not a work of argued theology. It is utilitarian, not elegant. But scholars are now seeing its importance as a catechetical writing, and one of them, Everett Ferguson, claims that "it represents the teaching given [by the North African church] on the eve of the Decian persecution."[133] It provides a revealing insight into Cyprian's pastoral priorities for his churches and also demonstrates his formidable biblical competence. Cyprian may have been a recent convert, but *To Quirinus* 3 shows that his struggle with the challenges of the Christian faith had led him to immerse himself in the Bible. As we saw earlier, what especially troubled Cyprian in his struggle to become a Christian was his addiction to an elite lifestyle. Significantly, in *To Quirinus* 3 he addresses this issue immediately, in precept 1: "Of the benefits of good works and mercy." The thirty-six texts that Cyprian cites in support of this primary precept are some of the most potent in biblical literature, beginning with Isaiah 58:7 ("Break your bread to the hungry, and bring the houseless poor into your dwelling") and going on to Jesus's statement in Matthew 25:37 ("Inasmuch as you did it not to one of the least of these, you did it not unto me."). Cyprian wants his hard-won understandings of the Bible and life, summarized in his precepts, to be equally useful to the Carthaginian Christians. He wants them to "labour with deeds, not with words."[134]

130. Cyprian, *Ad Quir.* 3, preface (CCL 3:73; Wallis, 528).

131. R. Weber, "Introduction," in CCL 3:liii. Cyprian's authorship has been challenged by Charles A. Bobertz, "An Analysis of *Vita Cypriani* 3.6–10 and the Attribution of *Ad Quirinum* to Cyprian of Carthage," *VC* 46 (1992): 112–28. It has been accepted by Everett Ferguson, "Catechesis and Initiation," in *The Origins of Christendom in the West*, ed. Alan Kreider (Edinburgh: T&T Clark, 2001), 239; Alistair Stewart-Sykes, "Catechumenate and Contra-Culture: The Social Process of Catechumenate in Third-Century Africa and Its Development," *St. Vladimir's Theological Quarterly* 47, nos. 3–4 (2003): 299–300; and Andy Alexis-Baker, "*Ad Quirinum* Book Three and Cyprian's Catechumenate," *JECS* 17, no. 3 (2009): 362.

132. Marcel Metzger, Wolfram Drews, and Heinzgerd Brakmann, "Katechumenat," *RAC* 20 (2005): 514–15. An older study by Michel Dujarier (*A History of the Catechumenate: The First Six Centuries*, trans. Edward J. Haasl [New York: Sadlier, 1979]) also ignores *Ad Quir.* 3.

133. Ferguson, "Catechesis and Initiation," 239.

134. Cyprian, *Ad Quir.* 3.96 (Wallis, 554).

Like any catechist who cares intensely that his hearers will live their faith as well as think about it, Cyprian needed to teach in a way that ordinary Carthaginians who became Christians, primarily poor people, could understand what he was saying and remember it.[135] That is why he offers them both precepts and biblical texts. The precepts are conceptually, grammatically, and verbally simple, and the biblical passages that he supplies reinforce and amplify them. For example, Cyprian buttresses precept 8 ("That anger must be overcome, lest it constrain us to sin") with texts from Jesus, Paul, and Proverbs, beginning with "Better is a patient man than a strong man; for he who restrains his anger is better than he who takes a city" (Prov. 16:32). Cyprian knows that the vast majority of the Carthaginians—perhaps 85 to 90 percent—are illiterate.[136] He also realizes that most of them come from pagan backgrounds in which religious texts are not important.[137] And undoubtedly he knows from experience that ordinary Carthaginians have astonishing memories. As a result, he is determined to mobilize those memories so that the biblical texts will live for all believers, literates as well as illiterates, enabling them to cherish the texts inwardly and put them to work outwardly. Like other North African Christians—such as Tertullian fifty years before him and the Abitinian martyrs fifty years after him—Cyprian wants Christians, when under pressure, to respond by using biblical passages—"I have them in my heart."[138]

How did this memorization work? Mary Carruthers, who has worked on memorization in antiquity, emphasizes the importance of the order and location of materials so that they can engage the receptor's "locational memory."[139] In light of her work, Andy Alexis-Baker's careful studies have shown that *To Quirinus* 3's opening section (precepts 1–23) has "a coherent and distinct pattern" in which Cyprian presents two of his cardinal concerns—that the believers engage in economic sharing and that they live nonviolently.[140] In later parts of the treatise, Alexis-Baker has found thematic clusters of precepts dealing with specific biblical books and with topics of particular

135. Minucius Felix, "Most of us are poor," *Oct.* 36.2, trans. G. H. Rendall, LCL 250 (1931), 425; Walter C. Scheidel and Steven J. Friesen, "The Size of the Economy and the Distribution of Income," *JRS* 99 (2009): 90: "Subsistence-level households must have formed a solid majority even in urban settings."

136. Gamble, *Books and Readers*, 4, 10.

137. Robin Lane Fox, "Literacy and Power in Early Christianity," in *Literacy and Power in the Ancient World*, ed. Alan K. Bowman and Greg Woolf (Cambridge: Cambridge University Press, 1994), 126–27.

138. Tertullian, *Pat.* 8.2; also see *Acts of the Abitinian Martyrs* 12, in Tilley, *Donatist Martyr Stories*, 37.

139. Mary Carruthers, *The Craft of Thought: Meditation, Rhetoric, and the Making of Images, 400–1200* (Cambridge: Cambridge University Press, 1998), 11–12.

140. Alexis-Baker, "*Ad Quirinum* Book Three," 362.

use to catechumens in their final preparations for baptism.[141] But otherwise
To Quirinus 3 seems to lack Carruthers's "locational-inventory structures,"
and the word *random* keeps coming to mind.[142] If the catechumens remem-
bered Cyprian's precepts, how then did they appropriate them? It must have
been that the biblical passages that he suggests called his precepts to mind
and amplified them. Cyprian's 120 precepts represented for him a coherent
ensemble of teaching that Quirinus and other catechists could use, and the
biblical passages that Cyprian added to them provided not only validation
of the precepts but also an earthiness and color that made them come to
life. We can hear the catechist intoning precept 26: "That it is of small account to be baptized and to receive the eucharist unless you profit both in
deeds and works."[143] Then, when the people have heard the supporting Bible
texts, we can hear them repeating, "Shine as lights in the world" (Phil. 2:15).
Perhaps the hearers more readily appropriated the biblical texts than they
did Cyprian's precepts!

To Quirinus 3 registered in the minds and lives of the catechumens because
it addressed their concerns. Their world was full of stress; there was conflict,
poverty, and at times persecution. Forty-eight of Cyprian's 120 precepts deal
with matters of belief, which Cyprian expresses in language that laypeople can
understand; for example, "That nothing must be preferred to the love of God
and of Christ";[144] and "That no one should be made sad by death, since in . . .
dying [is] peace and the certainty of resurrection."[145] As in his other writings,
Cyprian sees the devil at work in the world, but he also sees God's greater
power.[146] And although God is at work, God is not in a hurry: as Cyprian
asserts in precept 35, "God is patient to the end that [humans] may repent of
our sins and be reformed."[147] In the fullness of time God will act "suddenly"
to bring an end to the world, to right all wrongs and to effect judgment for
all.[148] In the meantime, Cyprian tells the catechumens, "our faith concerning
those things which are promised ought to be patient." Cyprian underlines
this by citing Romans 8:24–25: "We are saved by hope."[149] The catechumens
learn that hope-filled Christians engage in "strong conflict" against the devil
using two means: engaging in urgent prayer ("stand bravely [in prayer], that

---

141. Ibid., 376–77.
142. Ferguson, "Catechesis and Initiation," 241.
143. Cyprian, *Ad Quir.* 3.26 (Wallis, 542).
144. Cyprian, *Ad Quir.* 3.18 (Wallis, 539).
145. Cyprian, *Ad Quir.* 3.58 (Wallis, 548).
146. Cyprian, *Ad Quir.* 3.80.
147. Cyprian, *Ad Quir.* 3.35 (Wallis, 544).
148. Cyprian, *Ad Quir.* 3.89, 99 (Wallis, 553, 554).
149. Cyprian, *Ad Quir.* 3.45 (Wallis, 546).

we may conquer") and—Cyprian's signature theme—following Christ as the example of living.[150] Praying and following Christ shape the catechumens in their dealings both with outsiders (pagans) and with fellow Christians.

As to outsiders, Cyprian teaches the catechumens that they should behave differently from their associates and family members who follow other authorities. In precept 34 he is blunt: "That the believer ought not to live like the Gentile." Of course, Christian catechumens associated with pagans on many levels. Cyprian instructs those who are the pagans' slaves to "serve their carnal masters better."[151] Catechumens may also have been married to pagans. Cyprian reminds them that Christians are not to marry pagans,[152] but clearly many of them, especially women, had done so, either after their conversion or before. So like all Christian women, the catechumens married to pagan men should remain with their husbands, but if for some reason they must "depart," they are to remain unmarried.[153]

Catechumens who were business people interacted with pagans continually. Cyprian urges them to behave distinctively: they are not to charge interest, and they are to pay their workers' wages promptly.[154] If their pagan business contacts urge them to swear oaths to verify weights or prices, they are not to do so. Cyprian reminds them of Jesus's words: "I say unto you, swear not at all."[155] To be sure, catechumens are not to be in conflict with other believers about matters of business, but at times that happens. When it does, the believers are not to take the matter before gentile judges.[156] Of course, pagans and Christians are neighbors who lived in close proximity to each other. Whatever the circumstances, catechumens are to remember precept 49: "That even our enemies must be loved." To emphasize God's impartial love for all people, including the enemy, Cyprian cites a phrase of Jesus that he often quoted: "Your Father who is in heaven makes his sun to rise on the good and the evil" (Matt. 5:45).[157]

So in *To Quirinus* 3 Cyprian taught the catechumens how to respond to outsiders. He presented the apprentice believers with precepts that formed a web of responses to tangible and at times tense life situations. Following Pierre Bourdieu, I have called this *habitus*, a way of life—rooted in a host of biblical passages and especially in the teachings of Jesus—that over time, with

---

150. Cyprian, *Ad Quir.* 3.117, 39 (Wallis, 546, 556).
151. Cyprian, *Ad Quir.* 3.72 (Wallis, 552).
152. Cyprian, *Ad Quir.* 3.62.
153. Cyprian, *Ad Quir.* 3.90.
154. Cyprian, *Ad Quir.* 3.48, 81.
155. Cyprian, *Ad Quir.* 3.12 (Wallis, 536).
156. Cyprian, *Ad Quir.* 3.44.
157. Cyprian, *Ad Quir.* 3.49 (Wallis, 546).

practice, becomes embodied and habitual.[158] The catechumens' task was to learn to live this way of life. For them, the catechumenate was the window of time in which they trained and practiced the reflexes of body and mind that enabled this lifestyle to become second nature. Cyprian was convinced that as the catechumens were formed in Christ's way of responding to outsiders and fellow Christians, they would find that they were free. He called this habitus "the Lord's yoke," which was "easy" because it was rooted in Christ's call and teaching.[159]

But how were the catechumens to deal with fellow believers? What were components of reflexive practice, of habitus, that characterized life within healthy Christian communities? In chapter 5 we noticed that the habitus of the early Christians consisted in part of reflexive bodily gestures—for example, standing in prayer, making the sign of the cross, exchanging the kiss of peace. In *To Quirinus* 3 Cyprian prescribes only one gesture—that believers should stand when a bishop or presbyter enters the room.[160] Here his concentration is on broader themes that, he emphasizes, must be expressed in bodily action that he calls *factis*—deeds. Catechumens must learn to "labour not with words, but with *factis*." To underscore the importance of deeds, Cyprian gives the catechumens Matthew 7:24–27: Jesus's story about people who hear his teachings and do not do them, and whose houses, built on the sand, fall down.[161]

Cyprian introduced the catechumens to the lived habitus of the Christian community. According to him, Christians have distinctive ways of dealing with each other. A first principle, to which Cyprian returns in several precepts, is that the Christians have a primary commitment to other believers. Precept 75: "That every person ought to have care rather of his own people, and especially of believers." Catechumens were to learn how to "support one another," how to "bear one another's burdens."[162] Entry into this family—"[the believer's] own people"—was precious; it was costly, effected by baptism. But Cyprian emphasizes that, unlike pagan associations, life within the Christian communities was financially free, "without price."[163] Those who entered this family

158. For a mature statement of Pierre Bourdieu's understanding of habitus, see his *Pascalian Meditations*, trans. Richard Nice (Stanford, CA: Stanford University Press, 2000), 130–46. For further discussion of habitus, see chap. 3 above.

159. Cyprian, *Ad Quir.* 3.119 (Wallis, 556).

160. Cyprian, *Ad Quir.* 3.85. In house-based churches, in which there had at times been tension between wealthy home owners and the emerging episcopacy, the habitus that Cyprian prescribes gives precedence to the clergy. Cyprian cites one biblical text for this practice: Lev. 19:32.

161. Cyprian, *Ad Quir.* 3.96, also 3.26; CCL 3:168–69, 121.

162. Cyprian, *Ad Quir.* 3.9 (Wallis, 535).

163. Cyprian, *Ad Quir.* 3.100 (Wallis, 554).

were to live distinctively; "the believer ought not to live like the Gentile."[164] Instead, they were to be formed into people who have been given "an example of living [*exemplum vivendi*] in Christ."[165] According to the biblical texts that Cyprian uses to illustrate this precept, the Christian community, like Jesus, is to embody nonretaliation, self-emptying, and service to others.[166]

According to Cyprian, this communal lifestyle is sustained by worship. Catechumens learn that baptism constitutes the community and is essential for salvation. According to precept 25, until they have been "baptized and born again," catechumens cannot attain to the kingdom of God. In precept 97 Cyprian urges them not to procrastinate but to "hasten to faith and attainment."[167] The Eucharist likewise is to "be received with fear and honour."[168] But both baptism and the Eucharist, if they are to be efficacious in the life of the believer, must be expressed in "deeds and works."[169] Cyprian underscores this with Matthew 5:16: "Let your light shine before men."[170] Worship shapes character.

How does this distinctive Christian lifestyle express itself? Cyprian begins with a subject that was centrally important to him—economics. As Alexis-Baker has emphasized, Cyprian's first precepts urge the catechumens to be involved in economic sharing.[171] According to precept 1, richer catechumens (such as Cyprian himself) discover the "benefit of good works and mercy." But precept 2 emphasizes that it is important for all believers, even those of "smallness of power," to participate in assistance for the poor that was *mutual* aid. Precept 9 underscores that "Christians ought to sustain each other," which Cyprian supports with Galatians 6:2: "Bear one another's burdens." And precept 109 urges catechumens to visit the sick. Catechumens will enter a community in which believers give economic aid to needy fellow Christians, not primarily to poor people in the surrounding culture. Alexis-Baker points out that Cyprian, having discussed economic sharing, immediately moves on to another contentious issue—violence. In the first twenty-three of his precepts, Cyprian intersperses

---

164. Cyprian, *Ad Quir.* 3.34 (Wallis, 544).

165. Cyprian, *Ad Quir.* 3.39 (Wallis, 545); CCL 3:131.

166. *Ad Quir* 3.38; by being *nonretaliating* (1 Pet. 2:21–23: "For Christ suffered for us, leaving you an example, that ye may follow his steps, . . . who, when he was reviled, reviled not again"); by *self-emptying* (Phil. 2:7: "emptied himself, taking the form of a servant"); by *serving*, washing the feet of others (John 13:14–15: "For I have given you an example, that you also should do as I have done to you").

167. Cyprian, in *Ad Quir.* 3.97, uses the same text, Sirach 5:7, that Augustine used to urge catechumens to enroll for baptism (e.g., *Serm.* 82.14).

168. Cyprian, *Ad Quir.* 3.94 (Wallis, 554).

169. Cyprian, *Ad Quir.* 3.96 (Wallis, 554).

170. Cyprian, *Ad Quir.* 3.26 (Wallis, 542).

171. Alexis-Baker, "*Ad Quirinum* Book Three," 363–66, 369–70.

nonviolence with economics and devotes no fewer than fourteen precepts to a nonviolent lifestyle.[172] Catechumens are to be nonviolent in their attitudes, words, and physical bearing; they are to be humble, to accept oppression, to overcome anger, to refuse to curse and slander, to accept martyrdom, and to forgive others.[173] In five of his precepts, Cyprian specifically enjoins Christians to live with *patientia*.[174] Cyprian sums up the Christians' nonviolent distinctiveness by recalling the biblical command not to return evil for evil.[175] This approach differed from respected pagan teaching; it required a rehabituating on the part of the catechumens that was no doubt painful at times.

Speech, lifestyle, and families—these are additional areas of the Christians' distinctive habitus that Cyprian presents to the catechumens. They are to learn to speak humbly, nonjudgmentally, not noisily or boastfully, and certainly not foolishly and offensively. They are not to lie and not to demean or flatter others.[176] Their dress is to be simple. Female catechumens, like other Christian women, are not to dress in a worldly manner, and male catechumens must not wear tufts of hair on their heads or pluck their beards. Unlike Cyprian in his pre-Christian days, catechumens are to eat simply and not seek "the lust of possessing, and money."[177] Families and households are to be guided by particular disciplines. In passages reminiscent of the New Testament household codes, Cyprian urges Christian children to obey their parents and Christian parents not to be harsh with their children. Servants are to submit to frequent correction, and Christian masters are to be gentle.[178] People who are marginal in society are to be protected. Cyprian cites seven biblical passages to emphasize the community's protection of widows and orphans.[179] But his precept that widows "that are approved" officially are to be honored may be less than enthusiastic.[180] And Cyprian warned that the sin of fornication is grave, by implication for men as well as women.[181]

Why would people join this community? As noted, in *To Quirinus* 3 Cyprian devotes 120 precepts to introducing the catechumens to the range of the church's life, both intramural and extramural. But he doesn't include a single precept urging catechumens to engage in mission. Why not? Why didn't it

---

172. Ibid., 366–68, 371–73.
173. Cyprian, *Ad Quir.* 3.5, 6, 8, 12, 14, 16, 22.
174. Cyprian, *Ad Quir.* 3.8, 35, 45, 106.
175. Cyprian, *Ad Quir.* 3.5–6, 8, 13, 16, 22, 23.
176. Cyprian, *Ad Quir.* 3.5, 21, 40–41, 104, 107, 115.
177. Cyprian, *Ad Quir.* 3.36, 83–84, 60, 61.
178. Cyprian, *Ad Quir.* 3.70–73.
179. Cyprian, *Ad Quir.* 3.74 (two texts), 113 (five texts).
180. Cyprian, *Ad Quir.* 3.74, 113.
181. Cyprian, *Ad Quir.* 3.63.

occur to Cyprian to add a 121st precept: "That we must present the gospel to the Gentiles, persuading them of its truth"? Wasn't Cyprian interested in mission? I believe that he was and that his precepts in *To Quirinus* 3 are evidence of this. Indeed, in my view *To Quirinus* 3 was his attempt to equip the Christians of Carthage to participate in mission as he understood it.

How is *To Quirinus* 3 a work on mission? Consider the situation. Cyprian wrote it at a time when people, despite formidable disincentives, were becoming Christians. He wrote it to assist a catechist who was preparing catechumens, candidates for baptism. He sensed that the church was growing because it interested the non-Christians; as he put it, repeating a North African commonplace, "We do not preach great things; we live them."[182] A church that grew because of the intriguing wholeness of its life—Cyprian sensed that God was at work in this, unspectacularly, patiently. The church would continue to grow if the people lived in ways that interested and attracted outsiders.

Cyprian's *To Quirinus* 3 is an attempt to help catechists such as Quirinus form people so their lives bear testimony to their Lord. Cyprian senses that the people are subject to gravitational pulls that will make them want to engage in Christian worship without allowing their habitus to be reformed to involve reflexive discipleship of Jesus. Further, he senses that Christians will want to talk a lot about their faith—"labour with words," he puts it—but not live their faith.[183] And to this Cyprian says no. He knows that the liturgy by itself is not the point; the words are not the point. In precept 103 he says, "We must abstain from much speaking." And, as he puts it in precept 52, it is fundamentally erroneous to require faith: "The liberty of believing and not believing is placed in free choice." Instead, the way forward is to profit from the Eucharist by living distinctively, "both in deeds and works," and it is to "labor . . . with deeds"![184] In *To Quirinus* 3, Cyprian teaches the catechumens the many dimensions of a lived response to the gospel, of an embodied habitus in which following Jesus has come to be reflexive. Habitually, Christians will share economically and care for the poor and the sick, widows and orphans; habitually, they will engage in business with truthfulness, without usury, and without pursuing profit to the extent of going before pagan judges; habitually, they will be a community of contentment and sexual restraint; habitually, they will behave with the multifaceted nonviolence of patience.[185] And through this, "God is patient" and will bring people to repent of their sins and become

---

182. Cyprian, *Pat.* 3; Minucius Felix, *Oct.* 38.6.
183. Cyprian, *Ad Quir.* 3.96 (Wallis, 554).
184. Cyprian, *Ad Quir.* 3.26, 96.
185. Cyprian, *Ad Quir.* 3.106 (Wallis, 555).

catechumens so they can discover what it means, practically, experientially, to "be reformed."[186]

One wonders how Quirinus received *To Quirinus* 3. Did he in fact use Cyprian's precepts in his catechesis? If so, what pedagogical techniques did he use? Did he alter their order, heighten the emphasis on certain precepts, and deemphasize other precepts—or did he omit some precepts altogether? How did he balance the teaching of precepts and the biblical passages that support them? Did Quirinus turn to Cyprian for counsel as he taught? How successful was Quirinus in getting his catechumens to memorize the precepts and biblical passages? How did he flesh out the precepts and texts in fuller explanations and exhortations?

However we might speculate about these questions, it is clear that *To Quirinus* 3 was influential. In the *Acts of Montanus and Lucius*, written in Carthage shortly after Cyprian's death in 258, half of the biblical citations occur in *To Quirinus* 3.[187] More broadly, Cyprian's treatise had a considerable influence on later Christian writers, including Lactantius, Jerome, Pelagius, Augustine, and Quodvultdeus.[188] The more serious question is this: as the church in North Africa grew in numbers and wealth, did *To Quirinus* 3 help Christians develop the extraordinary habitus of communities faithfully following Christ?[189]

The Content of Catechesis (3)—Origen's Catechetical Homilies

Another source for third-century catechesis—better known than Cyprian's *To Quirinus* 3—is the homilies of Origen. In the early 230s Origen, the transcendently gifted philosopher-teacher from Alexandria, had fallen out with his bishop, Demetrios. As a result, he moved to Palestine, where he had earlier spoken to great acclaim, and Bishop Theoctistus of Caesarea promptly ordained him as a presbyter and gave him an assignment in teaching and preaching. This assignment required Origen to develop new pedagogical skills. In Alexandria he had primarily taught small groups of people who were literate and philosophically inclined; in Caesarea he faced the task of catechizing "the multitudes" of those who were coming to faith—people with a vast range of literacy and intellectual gifts.[190] Origen worked hard at this task. For some

186. Cyprian, *Ad Quir.* 3.35 (Wallis, 544).

187. Alexis-Baker, "*Ad Quirinum* Book Three," 375n.

188. Quasten, *Patrology*, 2:363; R. de Simone, "The Baptismal and Christological Catechesis of Quodvultdeus," *Augustinianum* 25 (1985): 266.

189. Cyprian, *Ad Quir.* 3.39; cf. Cyprian, *Laps.* 11–12.

190. John McGuckin, "The Life of Origen (ca. 186–255)," in *The Westminster Handbook to Origen*, ed. John McGuckin, Westminster Handbooks to Christian Theology (Louisville: Westminster John Knox, 2004), 17; Origen, *Cels.* 7.59.

years he gave daily catechetical homilies to catechumens en route to baptism, and he gave weekly homilies in the church's eucharistic services, in which some catechumens were present. Of his homilies, 279 have survived, and they give a sense of the content and approach of Origen's catechesis.[191]

In Caesarea, as in the *Apostolic Tradition*, when people were interested in joining the church, they were examined by specially appointed Christians who performed a First Scrutiny of their "lives and conduct." If the examiners decided that the applicants had "devoted themselves sufficiently to the desire to live a good life" and seemed unlikely to "indulge in trickery," they admitted the applicants to the catechumenate.[192] Associating themselves with those who were already catechumens represented a decisive step for new arrivals; Origen likens it to crossing the Red Sea and entering the wilderness, where they would "submit to the precepts of the Church . . . [and] hear the Law of God."[193] All sorts and conditions of people were there—adolescent boys, slaves, and "common folk," not just the "more intelligent" whom Origen had taught in Alexandria.[194] Origen was committed to teach them all and lead them to the baptism that would be their gate to the promised land.

The catechumenate in Caesarea seems to have had two stages.[195] Stage 1 began with instruction on morals. Regardless of the candidate's background, Origen began with basic things that he called the "milk" of behavior—"the correction of morals, the amendment of discipline, and the first elements of religious life and simple faith."[196] The catechumens needed to discover what it meant to "submit to the precepts of the Church."[197] Origen did not provide much detail about what this entailed, but in a response to the pagan philosopher Celsus he provided an interesting example.

Celsus, writing in the 180s, had censured the Christians for trading in "old stuff," for repeating in "vulgar terms" teaching that philosophers such as Plato had elegantly stated long ago. As evidence, Celsus pointed to the Christians' "precept" that "you must not resist a man who insults you. . . . If someone

---

191. Henri Crouzel, *Origen*, trans. A. S. Worrall (Edinburgh: T&T Clark, 1989), 43.

192. Origen, *Cels.* 3.51, trans. H. Chadwick, *Origen: Contra Celsum* (Cambridge: Cambridge University Press, 1965), 163.

193. Origen, *Hom. Jos.* 4.1, trans. B. J. Bruce, FC 105 (2002), 52.

194. Origen, *Cels.* 3.54; 7.46 (Chadwick, 165, 434).

195. The structure of the catechumenate in Caesarea is somewhat hazy. Neither its content nor its duration is as clear-cut as Pierre Nautin thought (*Origène: Sa vie et son oeuvre*, Christianisme Antique 1 [Paris: Beauchesne, 1977], 395). It was not a three-year package of biblical exposition, for it contained more than biblical catechesis, and its duration appears to have been variable. As in the *Apostolic Tradition*, it appears to have had two stages.

196. Origen, *Hom. Judic.* [*Judges*] 5.6, trans. E. A. D. Lauro, FC 119 (2009), 82.

197. Origen, *Hom. Jos.* 4.1 (Bruce, 51).

strikes you on one cheek, yet you should offer the other one as well."[198] In reply, Origen didn't dispute that this was something the Christians taught or that this Christian teaching resembles what Plato had taught. Instead, he shifted the subject of the conversation—to cooking. The philosophers, he conceded, cooked wholesome food, but in a spicy and sophisticated way that appealed only to a few—a tiny minority of "rich and luxurious people" who made up the "supposed better classes." Christians, in contrast, cooked wholesome food simply, in such a way that it benefited the health of "innumerable people" who were brought up "in farm houses and poverty." Unlike the philosophers, Christians cooked "for the multitude" and prepared "the same very wholesome quality of food by means of a literary style which gets across to the multitude of men."[199] Origen argued that Jesus and Plato both had spoken about nonretaliation, but Jesus spoke simply and comprehensibly in such a way as to move masses of dissimilar people—the kinds of people who make up the church. And, Origen added, life matters more than style: "The idea about being long-suffering is not corrupted by the poor literary style."[200] In Origen's experience, nonviolence was a part of the "milk"—morals, discipline, and precepts—that the catechists taught at the outset of stage 1.[201] But Origen did not say how they trained the candidates to live this nonviolence, reflexively, as habitus.

Stage 1 also involved the "milk" of biblical narrative. Daily, probably before going to work in the morning, the catechumens gathered to hear homilies in which Origen introduced them to the Old Testament Pentateuch and prophets.[202] After someone read a biblical passage, Origen spoke about it lengthily—his extemporaneous discourses (recorded by a stenographer) average about an hour in length. He spoke simply, aware that many of his hearers were unlearned and illiterate, but he alluded to deeper meanings that he invited his hearers to explore with him. When he didn't understand the meaning of a passage, he was candid; and when he found something that he disagreed with, he shared his struggle with the catechumens. The church in Caesarea seems to have asked catechumens to begin their Bible study with Genesis,[203] but beyond that it did

198. Origen, *Cels.* 7.58 (Chadwick, 443).

199. Origen, *Cels.* 7.59–60 (Chadwick, 444–45).

200. Origen, *Cels.* 7.61 (Chadwick, 446).

201. In his homilies Origen spoke vastly less than Cyprian did about poverty; when he addressed it, he always spiritualized the issue. See Adele Monaci Castagno, "Origen the Scholar and Pastor," in *Preacher and Audience: Studies in Early Christian and Byzantine Homiletics*, ed. Mary B. Cunningham and Pauline Allen (Leiden: Brill, 1998), 79–80.

202. Origen, *Hom. Jos.* 4.1.

203. With evident debt to Origen, a church in Oxyrhynchus in upper Egypt referred to stage 1 (beginning) catechumens as "catechumens in Genesis" or "catechumens in the beginning

not have an orderly scheme of covering the Old Testament narrative. There may have been a rolling sequence of readings. The bishops (of Caesarea and Jerusalem) kept close tabs on Origen's teaching and made suggestions about what he should teach. On one occasion Origen reported that he was dealing with a topic they had requested that he talk about.[204]

Origen did not deal sequentially with the Old Testament books; when he concluded his homilies on Jeremiah, he jumped back to Numbers.[205] When he homilized about the Old Testament, he also did not hesitate to cite New Testament passages. For example, as he spoke about Leviticus, he referred to Paul's dictum "the letter kills" (2 Cor. 3:6), which in his view could apply to passages in the Gospel accounts as well as in Leviticus. He referred to Jesus's saying, "Let the one who does not have a sword sell his tunic and buy a sword" (Luke 22:36) and commented, "Behold, this is the letter of the gospel, but 'it kills.'" He added that there is hope "if you take it spiritually."[206] So Origen was constantly pointing his catechumens forward—not just toward more "milk" but toward a new stage in which, by exercising their "senses," they would have a deep "understanding of the word of God."[207]

After some time, candidates entered stage 2. This happened when, in a Second Scrutiny, those who scrutinized them determined that they were doing "all in their power to live better lives."[208] At this point, catechists began to give the candidates solid food as they prepared themselves for baptism.[209] Origen asked for the catechumens' prayers, that they may "labor together with me, so that in these obscure and hidden passages the Lord may deign to make known to us the light of truth."[210] In addition to the daily homilies, candidates now could attend the "services of the word" in the Sunday eucharistic services, in which they heard homilies based on the Gospels.[211] Origen's homilies on Luke's Gospel survive; in them he appealed specifically to the catechumens not to shrink back, not to be afraid, but to follow Jesus.[212] He urged them

---

of the gospel" (Luijendijk, *Greetings in the Lord*, 86, 118). It is unclear how newly admitted catechumens were able to concentrate on Genesis when the pool of catechumens whom they had just joined were at other stages of their training.

204. Origen, *Hom. Ezech.* 13.1.1–2.

205. Origen, *Hom. Jer.* 12.3.1.

206. Origen, *Hom. Lev.* 7.5.5, trans. G. W. Barkley, FC 83 (1990), 146–47.

207. Origen, *Hom. Gen.* 14.4, trans. R. E. Heine, FC 71 (1982), 201.

208. Origen, *Cels.* 3.59 (Chadwick, 163). In Oxyrhynchus, stage 2 catechumens were called "catechumens in the congregation" (Luijendijk, *Greetings in the Lord*, 115, 118).

209. Origen may also have had smaller catechetical groups for "the few," in which he developed "the rational piety . . . of more intelligent people" (*Cels.* 7.46 [Chadwick, 434]).

210. Origen, *Hom. Jos.* 20.4 (Bruce, 180).

211. Origen, *Hom. Luc.* 7.7; 22.6; 32.6.

212. Origen, *Hom. Luc.* 7.8.

to prepare for baptism by "spending time in good living."[213] Like John the Baptist, he urged them—"men, women, catechumens"—not to be a "brood of vipers" but to leave behind their old "habits and customs."[214]

What specifically did Origen have in mind? He said that he wanted his hearers to "improve their habits, correct impulses, lay aside faults, cultivate purity, soften the violence of wrath, restrain avarice, curb greed."[215] But when did he talk about these in practical ways or indicate how he and other catechists were attempting to re-form the catechumens' behavior? In his homilies he rarely did so. In the weekday homilies that the catechumens continued to attend, Origen attempted to inspire his hearers to listen to the teachings of Jesus that equipped them for battle, especially against spiritual enemies.[216] He also urged his catechumens, in light of Jesus's teachings, to think through whether they would swear oaths.[217] He urged them to develop the habitus of prayer using memorized scripture; if the catechumens "patiently persevere[d]" in memorizing key biblical passages, evil powers would be "driven away by the incantation of Scripture and by a constant repetition of the divine discourse."[218]

Origen struggled with his catechumens. He was aware that some of them absented themselves from the morning catechetical sessions.[219] Others came and misbehaved, not mutually investigating the texts and comparing them.[220] Origen's way of carrying himself—his charisma—had inspired Gregory of Pontus and changed his life, but it was less compelling to some people in Caesarea who misbehaved.[221] This worried Origen. Their behavior, he reminded them, was crucial, for behavior was the basis on which outsiders—Greeks, philosophers, and "common folk"—would make their decisions for or against Jesus. They must ask themselves whether their lives opened doors for Jesus or whether they caused people to judge him negatively and to turn away from Christianity.[222]

At some point, the catechumens presented themselves for baptism. In Caesarea, as in the *Apostolic Tradition*, there was no clearly defined time at which

213. Origen, *Hom. Luc.* 21.5, 7, trans. J. T. Lienhard, FC 94 (1996), 90–91.

214. Origen, *Hom. Luc.* 22.5–6, 8 (Lienhard, 94–95).

215. Origen, *Hom. Jos.* 10.3 (Bruce, 112).

216. Origen, *Hom. Lev.* 5.5.5.

217. Origen, *Hom. Jer.* 5.12.1.

218. Origen, *Hom. Jos.* 20.1 (Bruce, 176). In the exorcism that he performed in Jerusalem, Origen used this means of praying by scriptural incantation, as in *Hom. Sam.* 1.10 (see discussion in chap. 5 above).

219. Origen, *Hom. Gen.* 10.3.

220. Origen, *Hom. Exod.* 12.2.

221. Gregory Thaumaturgus, *Orat. paneg.* 9; Robert L. Wilken, "Alexandria: A School of Training in Virtue," in *Schools of Thought in the Christian Tradition*, ed. Patrick Henry (Philadelphia: Fortress, 1984), 24–25.

222. Origen, *Hom. Jer.* 14.8, trans. J. C. Smith, FC 97 (1998), 143.

the catechumenate would end. It depended on the individual. Origen was concerned that some people were attempting to be baptized "without caution and careful consideration."[223] Other people troubled him by dallying.[224] He was concerned about all who didn't "attempt to correct or alter their habits."[225] He held out for them a longing for the "great feast" that is ahead of them.[226] Conventions of the time permitted him to speak about baptism and the Eucharist only in vague terms: "those venerable and magnificent sacraments, which are known to those who are permitted to know these things."[227] But when candidates convinced the church leaders that their habitus had been renewed, that they had left behind their former "habits" and "customs," then was the right time for them to be baptized. In baptism people left the wilderness and "the Jordan [was] parted," at which point they "enter[ed] the land of promise."[228] Then, Origen promised them, Jesus would receive them and become for them "the leader of a new way."[229] In his apologetic mode, Origen informed his readers that the Christians' method of initiation converts people, "not merely one or two but a very large number of people," improves them, and disposes them to "goodness."[230] Origen was vague about how this happened, but he was categorical about its results.

Two Questions about the Catechumenate

Before moving on to stage 3 of the *Apostolic Tradition*'s model for becoming a Christian, we must address two remaining questions about the catechumenate. First, why weren't converts baptized immediately upon "conversion"? The catechetical agendas of Cyprian and Origen are elaborate and slow moving. In contrast, the approach of the New Testament Christians had been simple and swift. In Acts 8:38 the Ethiopian eunuch was baptized immediately upon confessing Jesus to be the fulfillment of Old Testament prophecy; and in Acts 10:47, when the apostle Peter saw the centurion Cornelius and his household filled with the Holy Spirit, he asked, "Can anyone withhold the water for baptizing these people who have received the Holy Spirit just as we have?" Nobody investigated these people's lifestyles before they were baptized, and nobody taught them the Bible's story or provided moral or theological

---

223. Origen, *Hom. Luc.* 21.4 (Lienhard, 90).
224. Origen, *Hom. Jos.* 9.9.
225. Origen, *Hom. Jos.* 10.3 (Bruce, 112).
226. Origen, *Hom. Gen.* 14.4 (Heine, 201–2).
227. Origen, *Hom. Jos.* 4.1 (Bruce, 53).
228. In *Hom. Exod.* 5.5, Origen likens baptism itself (rather than just entering the catechumenate) to the crossing of the Red Sea (cf. 1 Cor. 10:1–2).
229. Origen, *Hom. Jos.* 4.1 (Bruce, 53).
230. Origen, *Cels.* 4.53 (Chadwick, 228).

catechesis. The nascent Christians evidently assumed that the candidates, as Jews or God-fearers, knew these things already. As Gerhard Lohfink puts it, "Judaism was the catechumenate of the primitive Church."[231] What people didn't know they could learn after baptism.

By the second century things were changing. It was not that the Christians forgot the New Testament precedents. People continued to appeal to them.[232] But in many places the Christians' connections with Judaism were loosening. Increasingly the prospective Christians were ordinary pagans, not Jews or pagans with connections to Jews. These pagans could experience the power of healings and exorcisms; they could be moved by the Christians' exemplary lives and the love of God that they embodied. But the Christian leaders decided that none of these, by themselves, made for conversion. The candidates' narratives, theological understandings, and moral reflexes were still pagan.

In the second century—at varying times from place to place—Christians decided to slow conversion down by insisting that their converts embody change that reflected the teaching and character of Jesus. They insisted on this in part because of what the Jesus whom they worshiped had said, but also because they discovered that embodied change was essential to Christians' witness. If people talked like Christians but behaved like pagans, pagans would not become Christians, and the church would not remain Christian. So the Christian leaders gradually developed the approaches to conversion that we are studying in this chapter. Conversion, they were convinced, is multidimensional. From their perspective, conversion was not just an experience of divine power; it was not just a feeling; it was not just a change of thinking. Conversion was a process that can involve all of these but must involve two other things: the embodied reformation of the convert (habitus change) brought about through catechesis and a bodily ritual (baptism) in which the candidate declares that Jesus is Lord, identifies primarily with the Christian family ("I am a Christian"), and commits himself or herself to living in the Christian way.[233] In the second to fourth centuries, Christians incorporated this understanding of conversion in their programs of formation that shaped

---

231. Gerhard Lohfink, *Does God Need the Church? Toward a Theology of the People of God*, trans. Linda M. Maloney (Collegeville, MN: Liturgical Press, 1999), 268.

232. Examples are Pontius, *Vit. Cypr.* 3 (Wallis, 268), which reflects on the Ethiopian eunuch and compares those from a Jewish background with those "coming from the ignorant heathens." A century and a half later, North African Christians appealed to the eunuch in urging Augustine to jettison the slow change of the catechumenate; he should teach the rule of faith to candidates and baptize them immediately. Augustine was not impressed (Augustine, *Faith and Works* 1.1; 9.14).

233. From the vantage point of the early Christians, it would therefore have been impossible to speak of Constantine's experience of 312 as "conversion."

the candidates into authentic Christians. The process was not a hurried one; it called on both groups within the Christian community—believers and catechumens—to exercise the hopeful patience that the church taught in catechesis.

The second question about the catechumate is, how long did the catechumenate actually take? The early texts that deal with catechesis did not give a time. But the *Apostolic Tradition did* give a time: "Let the catechumens hear the Word for three years."[234] This was not a rigid specification of a three-year catechumenate.[235] If the candidate was "earnest and perseveres well in the work," it could take less than three years. If the candidate was unreceptive, it could take more. "The time is not judged, but the character [*tropos*] only is that which shall be judged."[236] So how long did the catechumenate last? As long as it took for the candidates' character to be formed, for their habitus to be changed, for them to experience what Orthodox theologian Vigen Guroian calls "deep ontological repair."[237] It was a process that exemplified patience: the catechists did not manipulate people or hurry them along, and the catechumens were content to collaborate actively, over an indeterminate period of time, in a process they could not control.[238]

Given the magnitude of the issues with which catechists and students were struggling, three years wasn't a long period of time.[239] The issues of teaching and character formation that the catechists and catechumens dealt with must have taken considerable time simply to talk about. It would take far more time for them to be lived—to become habitual, second nature, embodied in the habitus of the apprentices becoming Christians. Like Cyprian, when catechumens confronted changes that challenged their deeply engrained reflexes, they probably experienced moments when they felt they couldn't change one more thing! Some of them might have had fits of recidivism, like Cyprian "indulging his sins," possibly binging on an extravagant meal![240]

234. *Trad. ap.* 17.1 (BJP, 96).
235. Cf. P. Nautin, *Origène*, 395, 401.
236. *Trad. ap.* 17.2 (BJP, 96).
237. Vigen Guroian, *The Melody of Faith: Theology in an Orthodox Key* (Grand Rapids: Eerdmans, 2010), 50.
238. Robin Lane Fox, *Pagans and Christians* (San Francisco: Harper & Row, 1986), 317: "People felt that they were exploring a deep mystery, step by step."
239. Maxwell E. Johnson (*The Rites of Christian Initiation*, rev. ed. [Collegeville, MN: Liturgical Press, 2007], 118–19) provides examples from the Canons of Elvira of relatively lengthy catechesis (two, three, or five years) but expresses caution about the idea that "the pre-Nicene Church knew a general catechumenate of three years' duration." I agree that there was no general three-year catechumenate. However, the catechists faced a huge challenge in forming the catechumens' habitus and changing their character, so in my view it would not be out of the question for some candidates to have a three-year (or longer) catechumenate.
240. Cyprian, *Don.* 4 (Wallis, 269).

The catechumens, when they sensed that the sessions were challenging them too deeply, were tempted to stay home.[241] Some no doubt wanted to turn back.[242] So the catechists and sponsors were very important. Similar to sponsors in twelve-step movements today, they shepherded the candidates through the ups and downs of habitus change. For good reason, one contemporary theologian calls the catechumenal group "a recovery group."[243] Another, drawing on the military discipline of changing human reflexes, calls it "boot camp."[244] In the late fourth century, John Chrysostom called the catechumenate a "wrestling school."[245] Struggle along with others in a disciplined group was necessary if the church was to grow in such a way that the individual candidates' habitus changed so the world could see embodied evidence of the gospel's power.

Stage 3. Baptismal Preparation—"Hearing the Gospel"

We have devoted numerous pages to the catechumenate, stage 2 of the *Apostolic Tradition*'s four-stage journey toward membership in the church. We have observed how unhurried the process was, and how rigorous. We can understand the pagan jibe: "If everyone wanted to become a Christian, the Christians probably will not want them."[246] But the Christians did want them, and the candidates in large number persevered. After church leaders examined the candidates' character in the Second Scrutiny, they admitted them to stage 3 to receive final preparation for baptism.[247] In the years of their catechumenate they had "heard the Word"; now, in the weeks before their baptism, they would "hear the gospel." This involved teaching, repeated exorcisms, and baptismal preparations.

241. *Trad. ap.* 41.2–3 makes it clear that the catechumens had to "choose" to go to the sessions and not to stay home or be late.

242. Cf. Shepherd of Hermas's earlier references to people attracted to baptism: "When they recall what the life of true purity involves, they change their minds and return to pursue their evil desires" (Vision 3.7.3 [Ehrman, 211]).

243. Lee Camp, *Mere Discipleship: Radical Christianity in a Rebellious World* (Grand Rapids: Brazos, 2003), 114.

244. Philip Kenneson, "Gathering: Worship, Imagination, and Formation," in *The Blackwell Companion to Christian Ethics*, ed. Stanley Hauerwas and Samuel Wells (Malden, MA: Blackwell, 2004), 58.

245. John Chrysostom, *Baptismal Instructions* 9.29, trans. P. W. Harkins, ACW 31 (1963), 141. Origen likened catechumens to "athletes," those enrolled "in the contest of religion," "fighting," "battling" (*Hom. Jer.* 27.3.7 [Smith, 255]).

246. Origen, *Cels.* 3.9 (Chadwick, 133).

247. In some places, after admission to stage 3 ("hearing the gospel"), the candidates were no longer "catechumens"; depending on location, they were now "chosen ones" (*electi*, in Rome), "seekers together" (*competentes*, in North Africa), or "illuminands" (*phōtizomenoi*, in the East).

Hearing the gospel. What did that phrase mean? An article by liturgical scholar Paul Bradshaw has stimulated thinking on this. Bradshaw proposes three possibilities.[248] First, hearing the gospel could have meant at long last hearing the teachings and words of Jesus, "which were considered too sacred . . . to be read to any but the baptized and those who were about to be baptized." Second, hearing the gospel could have meant being allowed to be present in the services when the New Testament Gospels were read. Or third, hearing the gospel could have meant listening to an exposition of the central doctrines of the Christians, which the church leaders presented late in the catechumenate because they earlier had given the most attention to encouraging the catechumens to behave attractively.

Notwithstanding Bradshaw's authority, the first of these seems unlikely. "Hearing the gospel" could not have meant that catechumens were now for the first time hearing the teachings and words of Jesus, because the sources show that these were at the heart of early Christian catechesis as well as conversation.[249] To be sure, as I have noted repeatedly, the catechists emphasized that Christians' behavior was the key to Christian witness, and they attempted to build communities that were attractively different from their pagan surroundings. But this did not mean that they limited "Jesus's own words" to the baptized. Indeed, the catechists were convinced that the teachings of Jesus, more than anything else, enabled and inspired the catechumens to change their behavior.

The catechists knew that the teachings of Jesus were never just ethical but were deeply rooted in affirmations about God's character and work that were good news. For example, in *To Quirinus* 3.49 Cyprian tells the North African catechumens "that even our enemies are to be loved." This was ethics. But to substantiate this Cyprian gave the catechumens a supportive memory text, Matthew 5:44–45, which says that if they love their enemies, they will be "children of your Father in heaven" who participate in God's all-embracing love that sends rain on the just and the unjust. This was gospel. For Cyprian, ethics were rooted in gospel!

For the catechists, there was no shying away from the teaching of Jesus. That came in the late fourth century, when catechists such as Bishop Ambrose

248. Paul F. Bradshaw, "The Gospel and the Catechumenate in the Third Century," *JTS* 2/49, no. 1 (1998): 143–52, esp. 150–52. Reprinted in his *Reconstructing Early Christian Worship* (Collegeville, MN: Liturgical Press, 2010), chap. 4.

249. See, e.g., 2 Clem. 13.4, trans. C. C. Richardson, LCC 1 (1953), 198: "When the heathen hear God's oracles on our lips, they marvel at their beauty and greatness. . . . When, for instance, they hear from us that God says, '. . . Love your enemies and those who hate you,' . . . they are amazed at such surpassing goodness."

of Milan based their ethical catechesis not on the precepts of Jesus but on the Old Testament—"the lives of the patriarchs [and] the precepts of the Proverbs."[250] Ambrose's sermons on behavior are based not on Jesus and New Testament figures but on Abraham, Joseph, Isaac, and Jacob.[251] Ambrose took this approach because he was acutely aware that in his era it was the Arian heretics who appealed to Christ as a model.[252] No such concerns hindered the pre-Nicene Christians from making the teachings of Jesus central.

The second of Bradshaw's proposals is possible. According to some local traditions, the liturgical reading of the Gospel could have been strictly hedged. As a result, in some places, shortly before their baptism the candidates were allowed to be in the congregation when the Gospel was read. In Caesarea in Syria, for example, Luke's Gospel was read every Sunday just before Origen preached to a congregation that included advanced catechumens but not, conceivably, the more junior catechumens.[253]

The third proposed meaning of hearing the gospel is the most likely. In the third century many local communities had their own "rules of faith," which stated economically their common belief. In North Africa, Tertullian reported that in baptism "we make profession of the Christian faith in the words of its rule."[254] Other communities would have had similar rules of faith. The period prior to baptism was the time when the church's leaders and catechists presented this rule to the candidates, who no doubt memorized it. They presented it in a way that they chose and controlled. It is likely that leaders did not want their members to engage in freewheeling discussion of doctrine with outsiders. This may explain why the roughly contemporaneous bishop in the Syrian *Didascalia* was offended when the widows supported by his church talked freely with interested outsiders. No matter how interested the outsiders were, the widows had no business talking with them about "the incarnation and suffering of Christ . . . [and] the redemption of his passion." The widows were not theologians; more seriously, they were getting things out of order: first the inquirers must experience a rehabituation of

250. Ambrose, *The Mysteries* 1.1, trans. R. J. Deferrari, FC 44 (1963), 5. In the earlier Latin tradition, cf. Tertullian, *Pat.* 3.11; in the Greek tradition, cf. Clement, *Strom.* 7.12.80: "The Christian is filled with joy, uttering and doing the precepts of the Lord" (trans. H. Chadwick and J. E. L. Oulton, LCC 2 [1954]: 144).

251. Ferguson, "Catechesis and Initiation," 248–52.

252. Robert L. Wilken, *Remembering the Christian Past* (Grand Rapids: Eerdmans, 1995), 127.

253. Origen, *Hom. Luc.* 7.7; 22.6; 32.6; Charles Whitaker, "Baptism," in *Essays on Hippolytus*, ed. Paul Bradshaw, Grove Liturgical Study 15 (Bramcote, Notts: Grove Books, 1978), 53; Joseph T. Lienhard, ed., *Origen: Homilies on Luke; Fragments on Luke*, FC 94 (Washington, DC: Catholic University of America Press, 1996), xix.

254. Tertullian, *Spect.* 4, trans. S. Thelwall, ANF 3:81.

behavior, and only then were they ready to be taught doctrine. If outsiders were really interested, the widows must refer them to the leaders who will make them catechumens, guide them as they change their behavior, and teach them properly![255]

But in North Africa, according to Tertullian, the bishops did allow candidates to discuss theology—at the right time. The right time was the weeks prior to baptism. In earlier stages of the catechesis, the candidates had concentrated on behavior and the reformation of habitus. Now, however, even "the simple . . . who always constitute the majority of believers" could explore theological complexities. As an example, Tertullian mentions a session in which the candidates discussed the nature of God. The community's polemic, as well as its rule of faith, had drawn the people away from a plurality of gods to the one true God. But now, in catechesis, the people discovered that the Christian God is an "economy" (*oikonomia*), the Three in One. This "startled" them and, Tertullian implies, led to vigorous interchange.[256] One wonders how often this kind of conversation happened. At any rate, already in the third century, doctrine played an important role in the final stages of pre-baptismal catechesis. In the fourth century, when in many places a concern for distinctive Christian behavior evaporated, doctrinal precision became the catechists' overwhelming concern.

As the candidates moved toward baptism, the catechists receded and exorcists took their place. Daily, according to the *Apostolic Tradition*, exorcists laid their hands on the candidates. "It was as important for Christians to name what they turned away from as to name what they turned toward."[257] When the day of baptism approached, the bishop himself exorcised each candidate so that he knew that each one was holy, good, and undefiled. This was the Third Scrutiny, and it was decisive. If the bishop discovered that certain candidates were "not good" (not clean or not living rightly), those people were not to be baptized because they did not really "hear the Word faithfully"—the catechesis had not taken hold, and their behavior had not been transformed.[258] The other candidates, those who were "pure," could proceed to be baptized. Throughout the weeks of hearing the gospel, the exorcisms at times may have been routine, but they were significant. In the minds of the participants, the weeks preceding baptism were a time of ongoing liberation and cleansing in

255. *Did. apost.* 3.5.5; 3.6.1; 3.5.3 (Stewart-Sykes, 184–85).
256. Tertullian, *Against Praxeas* 3.1, trans. P. Holmes, *ANF* 3:598–99.
257. Margaret R. Miles, *Carnal Knowing: Female Nakedness and Religious Meaning in the Christian West* (Boston: Beacon Press, 1989), 44.
258. *Trad. ap.* 20.3–4; Henry Ansgar Kelly, *The Devil at Baptism: Ritual, Theology, and Drama* (Ithaca, NY: Cornell University Press, 1985), 86–87.

which Christ triumphed over the "stranger" in the life of the candidate and "detoxified" the dominant culture.[259]

Stage 4. Baptism—"Singing a New Song"

On the day preceding their baptism the candidates, having fasted, gather together under the direction of the bishop. At his command they pray and kneel down, and for a final time he exorcises them, breathing into their faces and signing them with the cross. Then they spend the night in vigil, listening to readings and exhortations (*Trad. ap.* 20.8–9). The climax of the event comes at cockcrow on Sunday morning. The candidates gather near flowing water, often no doubt outdoors in the sea or a river.[260] The water is blessed. And then, as the *Apostolic Tradition* calmly puts it, "let them strip naked." Vulnerable, "divested of the distinguishing marks on which the hierarchy of ancient society depended," the candidates go down into the water.[261] Each one renounces Satan and is anointed with the oil of exorcism. Then, giving answers to three creedal questions, each one is baptized three times in the name of the Father, the Son, and the Holy Spirit.[262] They die to their old selves, and they arise as Christians who are newly alive. They are anointed with the oil of thanksgiving, put on their garments, and enter into the church. There for the first time they experience the loving solidarity of their new family. They pray with all the people, no doubt raising their hands. They

259. *Trad. ap.* 20.4 (BJP, 104); Georg Kretschmar, "Das christliche Leben und die Mission in der frühen Kirche," in *Kirchengeschichte als Missionsgeschichte*, vol. 1, *Die alte Kirche*, ed. Heinzgünter Frohnes und Uwe W. Knorr (Munich: Chr. Kaiser, 1974), 104; William H. Willimon, *Peculiar Speech: Preaching to the Baptized* (Grand Rapids: Eerdmans, 1992), 59.

260. Cf. Tertullian, *Bapt.* 4.

261. Peter Brown, *The Body and Society: Men, Women and Sexual Renunciation in Early Christianity* (London: Faber & Faber, 1989), 49. Ancient approaches to questions of women's modesty in naked baptism include the following three: women themselves performing the rite (repeatedly prohibited); dressed woman deacons going into the water with naked female baptizands; women undressing to receive pre-baptismal anointing from women deacons but donning a light undergarment for the baptism performed by men. See Paul F. Bradshaw, "Women and Baptism in the *Didascalia Apostolorum*," *JECS*, 20, no. 4 (2012): 641–45.

262. *Trad. ap.* 21.3, 12–18. The order of baptism is significant: small children first, including those who are not "able to speak for themselves" (for whom parents or another family member will speak); then grown men; and finally grown women (*Trad. ap.* 21.4–5). In the *Apostolic Tradition* we do not yet have a community that routinely baptizes newborn infants. On the baptism of the "little ones" (including some who could not answer the baptismal interrogatories for themselves), see David F. Wright, "At What Ages Were People Baptized in the Early Centuries?," StPatr 30 (1997): 389–94; Everett Ferguson, *Baptism in the Early Church: History, Theology, and Liturgy in the First Five Centuries* (Grand Rapids: Eerdmans, 2009), 366–79. Cf. Anthony N. S. Lane, "Did the Apostolic Church Baptise Babies? A Seismological Approach," *Tyndale Bulletin* 55, no. 1 (2004): 109–30.

exchange the kiss of peace. And then for the first time they take part in the Eucharist, in which they receive milk and honey as well as bread and wine. They have entered the promised land and, as Origen so expressively put it, they are prepared to "sing a new song!"[263]

It is not hard to imagine the emotional impact of these experiences. Margaret Miles has written about the way the baptismal practices "realize—make real—in a person's body the strong experiences that, together with the religious community's interpretation of that experience, produced a countercultural religious self."[264] The experience of baptism and the Eucharist could be overwhelming. According to Eusebius, the emperor Constantine, when "initiated by rebirth," was "awestruck at the manifestation of the divinely inspired power."[265]

As we have seen in this chapter, for most new believers (if not for Constantine) baptism and the Eucharist came at the culmination of a lengthy process of catechesis. Over a period of preparation that often lasted several years, the catechumens had encountered visions of new life and bodily actions that enticed them and stretched them into ways of behaving that at times they found uncomfortable. They wondered: could they become the kind of persons in thought and reflex that they were catechized to be? Could they embody the Christians' habitus? As they struggled with these questions, and as their thinking and behavior gradually changed, the catechumens learned patience. But catechesis could only bring the candidates so far.

Therefore, when the church leaders thought that the candidates were ready, they admitted the candidates to baptism. After years of patience, baptism was a breakthrough. Its ritual, expressing risk and death, enacted the cost of the decision: possible persecution as a result of joining an illegal *superstitio*; loss of respectability and kudos in the eyes of peers; broken relationship with family members. But the ritual also did something—it expressed the work of God and enacted it. Cyprian testifies to this: "By the help of the water of new birth" he has experienced forgiveness of all his sins and reconciliation with God; "by the agency of the Spirit breathed from above" he has become "a new man." Intriguingly, Cyprian relates this to catechesis. It is baptism that now enables him to live the vision that he has received from his catechists. That vision will remain enticing and challenging, but it will no longer be an unreachable ideal. At last Cyprian can live the habitus of a Christian, simply, contentedly. "What before had seemed difficult [to me] began to suggest a means of accomplishment, what [I had] thought impossible [is] capable of

263. Origen, *Hom. Exod.* 5.5 (Heine, 284).
264. Miles, *Carnal Knowing*, 24.
265. Eusebius, *Vit. Const.* 4.62.4, trans. A. Cameron and S. Hall, *Eusebius: Life of Constantine* (Oxford: Oxford University Press, 1999), 178.

being achieved."[266] Later Christians also emphasized the greatness of baptism. Writing in the 440s, Pope Leo I called it "the principal and greatest sacrament."[267]

As the early church grew, catechesis and baptism opened the way to worship. The sermon, the prayers, the kiss of peace, and the Eucharist—these like catechesis and baptism formed the character of the Christians, aligning them with God's purposes and habituating them to the surprising ways of Christ's church. Without worship the patient ferment of God's mission was unthinkable. We will turn our attention to it in the coming chapter.

266. Cyprian, *Don.* 4–5 (Wallis, 276). For Cyprian's theology of baptism, see Ferguson, *Baptism in the Early Church*, 357–61.

267. Leo I, *Ep.* 16, to Sicilian bishops; in Thomas M. Finn, *Early Christian Baptism and the Catechumenate: Italy, North Africa, and Egypt*, Message of the Fathers of the Church 6 (Collegeville, MN: Liturgical Press, 1992), 82.

7

WORSHIP

Why did the early Christian church grow? As we have seen in previous chapters, it grew because Christians behaved in ways that were distinctive and suggested novel approaches to thorny problems. It grew because the patience Christians exhibited was counterintuitively creative. But it was not easy to prepare people in the Greco-Roman world to live in this way. Christians in various parts of the empire developed programs of catechesis to ready candidates for membership. Their distinctive, embodied character attracted new people to the faith. Christian catechetical approaches were unrivaled in the ancient world and powerfully shaped the church's witness.

But the ongoing energizing center of Christian communal life was not catechesis but worship. Christians claimed that week by week they encountered God in worship—from the heart (affective) as well as from the head (mental).[1] Further, their worship was from the body. Their encounter of God in worship involved bodily gestures and rites that became habitual, repetitive, reflexive ways of being. These physical patterns became their habitus, "a handed-down way of being."[2] They bore their habitus in their bodies, not only when they were in worship services, and not only when they were with other Christians, but as they lived their daily lives at work and with their

1. Tertullian, *Apol.* 30.4, trans. T. R. Glover, LCL 250 (1931), 151.
2. James K. A. Smith, *Imagining the Kingdom: How Worship Works* (Grand Rapids: Baker Academic, 2013), 81, 182.

neighbors. In their worship services Christians believed they encountered God, who was active, sovereign, and unpredictable. God, known to them through Jesus Christ—whose words and ways were often surprising—was unconventional and was making them unconventional. Christ's sayings functioned not only as material to teach in their worship but also as organizing principles that guided their acts and gestures in worship. Especially Matthew 5:23–24 was formative: "[If you] remember that your brother has something against you, leave your gift there before the altar and go; first be reconciled to your brother" (RSV). Christians claimed that through their worship services God changed them and strengthened them to cope with precarious realities and daunting problems of daily living.

Meals/Eucharists

At the heart of early Christian worship was table fellowship. Throughout the first three centuries Christian communities gathered once a week for a meal. Across time these communities moved from an early model, which Tertullian called "our small feasts," to a later model, which Origen called a "great feast."[3] I call these models the "evening banquet" and the "morning service." Both kinds of meals involved remembering Jesus as the communities ate bread and drank from the cup. Both were private: they took place in buildings that were often domestic and from which outsiders could be excluded. Both were accompanied by reading, teaching, and prayers. Each had a distinctive habitus that needed to be shaped and that formed the character of the worshipers. However, as we shall see, there were also significant differences between these two models.

Evening Banquet

Greco-Roman culture valued banquets, which customarily had two parts: an evening meal (Greek *deipnon*, Latin *cena*) was followed by a time of entertainment (*symposion, symposium*), at which people gave speeches, conversed, and drank.[4] This two-part meal took place in domestic settings, lasted several

---

3. Tertullian, *Apol.* 39.14 (Glover, 14); and Origen, *Hom. Gen.* 14.4, trans. R. E. Heine, FC 71 (1982), 201.

4. Blake Leyerle, "Meal Customs in the Greco-Roman World," in *Passover and Easter: Origin and History to Modern Times*, ed. Paul F. Bradshaw and Lawrence A. Hoffman (Notre Dame, IN: University of Notre Dame Press, 1999), 29–61. For comment, see Gerard Rouwhorst, "The Roots of the Early Christian Eucharist: Jewish Blessings or Hellenistic Symposia?," in *Jewish and Christian Liturgy and Worship: New Insights into Its History and Interaction*, ed. Albert

hours, and enabled face-to-face encounters. The earliest description we have of Christian worship is the meal described in 1 Corinthians 11 in which all shared an evening meal. The meal was followed by the symposium in chapter 14, to which "each one" could contribute (1 Cor. 14:26).

The Pauline model—an evening meal providing real sustenance and also in remembering Jesus; a multivoiced symposium in which all could pray and contribute; face-to-face relationships in a domestic setting—was still present 150 years later in Tertullian's community in Carthage.[5] This durability is not surprising. The two-part meal was deeply embedded in the culture of late antiquity, and Christians persisted in using it because they found that it was conducive to their common life. As time passed the Christian communities Christianized the banquet and developed a habitus that made it distinctive. According to Tertullian, Christians at some point gave it a new name—*agapē*—that expressed its character as love.[6]

The first part, the meal, commences with an opening prayer. Tertullian emphasizes the modest quantities of food and drink that the participants consumed. This is to make sure that there will be leftover food for the needy— "with God there is greater consideration for those of lower degree"—and that participants will be able to rouse themselves for their midnight prayers. The modest consumption of food and drink is also in keeping with Christian simplicity, discipline, and prayer. Tertullian, typical of the early Christians, is reticent to talk publicly about the cultic dimension of the meal; in this account he does not refer to the bread and wine.[7]

Tertullian gets more explicit when he discusses the second part, the after-dinner symposium. The banqueters wash their hands, and lights are lit. Then each one (*quisque*) takes part in a time of free worship—singing, speaking, drawing from their own hearts as well as possibly from the Scriptures. This may be the time when community members utter testimonies and prophesies;

Gerhards and Clemens Leonhard (Leiden: Brill, 2007), 295–307, esp. 303, 305. Rouwhorst points out that the evening meal/symposium was known to Jews as well as Greeks, and further, that the Christian communities never simply copied the models they inherited: instead, they appropriated and transformed them.

5. Tertullian, *Apol.* 39.16. I assume that the first part of chap. 39, in which Tertullian describes the "proceedings with which the Christian association occupies itself" (39.1–13), describes not special prayer services but rather the *symposium* part of the same "small feasts" that he describes in 39.14–21 (Glover, 173–83). See also Paul F. Bradshaw and Maxwell E. Johnson, *The Eucharistic Liturgies: Their Evolution and Interpretation* (Collegeville, MN: Liturgical Press, 2012), 30–31.

6. For Tertullian and other Christians in the first two centuries, the word *agapē* referred to a eucharistic meal (cf. Jude 12); the word *eucharist* meant the consecrated bread, not the entire meal/rite. Andrew McGowan, "Rethinking Agape and Eucharist in Early North African Christianity," *SL* 34 (2004): 169–71.

7. Tertullian, *Apol.* 39.16–18 (Glover, 181).

it is likely when they memorize Scriptures and learn and repeat the "precepts" that these inform their unusual behavior.[8] Christians need to learn the habitus of the symposium—its niceties but also its underlying values: empowering the less educated and unconfident, cherishing the more powerful and yet restraining them, and making all participants sensitive to the divine presence and the dynamics of the community. A time of prayer, in which the believers stand up and "mass their forces to surround [God]," ends the symposium, but not until the believers have sealed the prayer by exchanging the "kiss of peace."[9] The worshipers-banqueters then go home, having "dined not so much on dinner as on discipline."[10]

Who attends this meal? Clearly the baptized members of the community are there. It is likely, although we cannot be sure, that catechumens and children of members are present.[11] The participants meet with other people, unrelated to them, who are *Christiani* and *Christianae*, brothers and sisters in the new Christian family. Given the general demographic profile of Carthaginian Christians, some participants in the banquet are poor; in their hunger they are attracted to a religious gathering that provided real food. Many people are present who in the wider society are powerless, of no account, and who will never have enough money or influence to be at a non-Christian banquet. Here, in the Christian banquet, they have worth. Not only can they eat; they also can speak. In the symposium they discover that they have gifts; they have voices and worthwhile things to contribute. This experience forms them: "Christianity made the least-expected groups articulate."[12] Standing alongside the other believers, they learn to pray, and watching the other believers, they learn to live the lifestyle shaped by the community's precepts.

All participants have to learn the habitus of the Christian banquet. The poor, who have never been at a banquet, need to learn the politesse and discipline of a meal. The richer members, who may have frequented an association's banquets, need to learn the values of a community that does not seat people by rank but values the poor as equals. And all—poorer and richer—need to learn to share life and worship with people different from themselves. All participants eat the same food; further, they receive the same Eucharist.[13]

8. Tertullian, *Apol.* 39.3 (Glover, 175).
9. Tertullian, *Apol.* 39.3–4, 17–18 (Glover, 175, 181); Tertullian, *Or.* 18.
10. Tertullian, *Apol.* 39.19 (Glover, 181).
11. Catechumens could still have been present at this time, excluded from the eucharistic action and limited to the liturgy of the Word only when churches discontinued the full meal and moved to the morning-service model. See Paul F. Bradshaw, "The Reception of Communion in Early Christianity," *SL* 37 (2007): 167.
12. Robin Lane Fox, *Pagans and Christians* (San Francisco: Harper & Row, 1986), 330.
13. Cf. Gregory of Nazianzus, *Oration* 40.27.

Are inquisitive pagans at the meal? In Paul's Corinth, "outsiders or unbeliev-ers" are present (1 Cor. 14:23), and the Didache tells us that they are present at the community's meals, although they are not allowed to eat or drink the eucharistic bread and wine.[14] As persecution heightened, it is likely that well before Tertullian's time the Christians excluded outsiders from their eucha-ristic meals.[15] Pagans of this period assumed that Christian gatherings were secret, impenetrable to outsiders. Nevertheless, they were interested in what the Christians did in their "secret and nocturnal rites." Outsiders were especially intrigued by the Christians' eating: "Their form of feasting is notorious; it is in everyone's mouth."[16] The result was a luxuriant profusion of rumors—rumors about colorful Christian misbehavior at the closed meetings and also about outbreaks of the numinous.[17] Christians did not worry that absence of the pagans from their services constituted a lost opportunity. Their worship was not evangelistic; it was not "seeker sensitive." Their intent in worshiping was to glorify God rather than to attract outsiders. And since they believed that authentic worship formed the worshipers, they believed that in the course of time the behavior of those so formed would attract outsiders. From a Christian perspective, the outsiders' criticism or curiosity was preferable to their indif-ference. If at times outsiders were willing to approach Christians to undergo catechesis so they could see for themselves, that was the desirable bonus!

Morning Service

In the second century some Christian communities began to hold their main weekly meetings on Sunday morning rather than Saturday evening. Around AD 112 provincial governor Pliny reported from Bithynia (in the north of modern Turkey) that Christian groups he encountered assembled in the morning before daylight; in response to imperial pressure against as-sociations (which the emperors saw as centers of subversion), they had ceased to meet in the evenings.[18] In Rome in midcentury, Justin Martyr's reports about his church do not mention evening meetings. Whatever other domestic churches in Rome may have done, Justin's church evidently held its weekly assemblies in the morning.[19] The tradition of the Sunday morning service thus

14. Did. 9.5.
15. Tertullian (*Nat.* 1.7, trans. P. Holmes, *ANF* 3:115) refers to Christian assemblies as "our secret congregations"; cf. Bradshaw, "Reception of Communion," *SL* 37 (2007): 167.
16. Minucius Felix, *Oct.* 9.3, 6, trans. G. H. Rendall, LCL 250 (1931), 337–39.
17. Tertullian, *Apol.* 7.8–13; *Ux.* 2.7.
18. Pliny the Younger, *Ep.* 10.96.
19. Paul F. Bradshaw, *Eucharistic Origins* (Oxford: Oxford University Press, 2004), 68–69, 72–73.

originates early, but it does not quickly replace the evening banquet. As we have seen, the banquet was the accepted pattern around AD 200 in Tertullian's Carthage; fifty years later it was still common in Cyprian's Carthage, although larger congregations had adopted the morning service.[20] As Cyprian reported, numbers had grown, so that "when we dine we cannot call all the people together to share in our meal."[21] Christians in some places continued to meet in the evenings as a minority practice, often denounced by councils and bishops, but the morning service, in which the food was "tokenized," gradually became the norm.[22]

The morning service was in the tradition of the evening banquet, but it expressed itself in a somewhat different form, which has become classical—the *ordo* of Western liturgical tradition.[23] It had several elements:

- *Order of service*: The Word now preceded the sacrament. Whereas in the evening banquet the meal (including the bread and wine) had come before the Word (in the symposium), in the morning service the Word (readings and sermon) came before the meal (the reception of the consecrated elements).
- *Quantity of food*: The quantity was now slight. The evening banquet's meal was replaced by a symbolic meal with "normative tokenization" of bread, wine, and water.[24]
- *Quantity of words*: The words that ordinary worshipers spoke decreased, and the words that the leaders—the clergy—spoke increased. The sermons grew longer, and the style of worship became monological rather than communal.

In chapters 65–67 of his *First Apology*, Justin Martyr provides two accounts of the morning service. One of these is a baptismal service and the other evidently a normal weekly service. In order to sense the formative power of the morning service—the way it shaped the habitus of the believers—we will draw from both accounts to reconstruct the service as Justin described it.[25] It

20. McGowan, "Rethinking Agape and Eucharist," 133–46.

21. Cyprian, *Ep.* 63.16.1, trans. G. W. Clarke, *The Letters of St. Cyprian of Carthage*, ACW 46 (New York: Newman, 1986), 3:107.

22. Andrew McGowan, "Food, Ritual, and Power," in *Late Ancient Christianity*, ed. Virginia Burrus, A People's History of Christianity 2 (Minneapolis: Fortress, 2005), 156; Synod of Laodicea, Canon 28, in C. J. Hefele, *Histoire des Conciles* (Paris: Letouzey & Ané, 1909), vol. 1, part 2:1015; Socrates, *Hist. eccl.* 5.22.

23. Gordon W. Lathrop, *Holy Things: A Liturgical Theology* (Minneapolis: Fortress, 1993).

24. McGowan, "Food, Ritual, and Power," 156.

25. We prefer to use the account in Justin, *1 Apol.* 65–67, rather than from *Trad. ap.* 21.25–38.

had an order that will be familiar to Christians in the liturgical traditions; it has worn well across the centuries. But from the beginning this service had local particularities. Justin's community was no doubt shaped by meeting in his dwelling above a bathhouse in a crowded section of Rome,[26] and in the post-Constantinian period some habitus-shaping practices of the early forms of the morning service would disappear. What were the actions in this service?

GATHERING

On the day called Sunday the believers gather in a place, often a house. Almost certainly they meet in the early morning. It is inconvenient for them to get up in time to be there. Everyone is aware of time pressure: the readings last "as long as time permits," for Sunday is not a holiday and members have to go to work.[27] The domestic setting is typical for pre-Constantinian believers. The property is privately owned, inconspicuous, and flexible. Within a large tenement building (*insula*) it can at times be expanded by incorporating a neighboring apartment.[28] Or the church can move its meetings to a larger property—to a workshop or to a larger apartment that may have a suite of rooms in which the community can do what Justin's church viewed as normal: accommodate guests or store the financial and material contributions of the believers.[29] In short, the house is a "community center,"[30] but it is also a home. When members go there, they find a faith family who are "constantly together"; they meet with "those who are called brethren."[31] They are aware that admission is restricted to their fellow family members; and they know that, whatever their wealth or social status, they will be known and at home there.

The community's worship takes place in an environment that is familial and equalizing, with practical programs of sharing.[32] The worship takes

---

26. Harlow Gregory Snyder, "'Above the Baths of Myrtinus': Justin Martyr's 'School' in the City of Rome," *HTR* 100, no. 3 (2007): 349, 359–60.

27. Justin, *1 Apol.* 67.3; cf. Origen, *Hom. Luc.* 38.6; and Paul F. Bradshaw, *Eucharistic Origins* (New York: Oxford University Press, 2004), 69.

28. Edward Adams, *The Earliest Christian Meeting Places: Almost Exclusively Houses?*, LNTS 450 (London: Bloomsbury T&T Clark, 2013), 8–9.

29. Justin, *1 Apol.* 67.1. In early fourth-century North Africa, large and well-equipped churches met in buildings they called "houses." See *Acts of the Abitinian Martyrs* 2, in *Donatist Martyr Stories: The Church in Conflict in Roman North Africa*, trans. and ed. Maureen A. Tilley, TTH 24 (Liverpool: Liverpool University Press, 1996), 29; *Gesta apud Zenophilum* 3, in *Optatus: Against the Donatists*, trans. and ed. Mark Edwards, TTH 27 (Liverpool: Liverpool University Press, 1997), 153.

30. Richard Krautheimer, *Rome, Profile of a City, 312–1308* (Princeton: Princeton University Press, 1980), 33.

31. Justin, *1 Apol.* 65.1; 67.1, trans. E. R. Hardy, LCC 1 (1953): 285, 287.

32. As in Justin, *1 Apol.* 67.6–7.

place in a "utopian space,"[33] a place where things are as they ought to be. Like the evening banquet, the morning service is an act of worship, but it has become sparer, more efficient, more formal. The worshipers do not gather around tables; in many places they sit in rows, looking at the backs of other believers' heads, which can lead to a habitus of anonymity and inequality.[34]

READING AND TEACHING

According to Justin, the community's weekly worship begins with the reading of "the memoirs of the apostles or the writings of the prophets." Justin does not indicate who chooses the Scriptures or whether the reading is from a Gospel or from the Old Testament or both.[35] A reader takes up the Scripture, reading clearly, so that the people can hear, and efficiently, so as not to take too long. The people, many of whom are illiterate, probably listen closely and attempt to memorize passages of the Scriptures. The "president" of the community then gives a talk (*dia logou*) in which he applies the passages that have just been read to the lives of the believers; he "urges and invites us to the imitation of these noble things." According to Justin, in the *dia logou* the president exposits the Scriptures so that the believers will imitate them, allowing the Bible to shape their habitus and behavior. This is crucially important because of the community's regulation that "only those who live as Christ handed down to us" can take part in the "food we call Eucharist."[36] Justin does not tell his readers whether, as happens with later homilists, the people can interrupt the talk with questions, making the *dia logou* dialogic.[37] At this point—the end of the service of the Word—in the third century, catechumens will leave the assembly. Justin does not record whether this happens in his church.[38]

---

33. Michel de Certeau, *The Practice of Everyday Life*, trans. Steven F. Rendall (Berkeley: University of California Press, 1984), 16. I owe this reference to Tex Sample, *Hard Living People & Mainstream Christians* (Nashville: Abingdon Press, 1993), 70.

34. On this, cf. *Did. apost.* 2.57.2–5.

35. Justin, *1 Apol.* 67.3 (Hardy, 287; Munier, 122). The readings from the "Prophets" may have included Moses, seen as author of the Pentateuch: Gerard A. M. Rouwhorst, "The Reading of Scripture in Early Christian Liturgy," in *What Athens Has to Do with Jerusalem: Essays on Classical, Jewish, and Early Christian Art and Archaeology in Honor of Gideon Foerster*, ed. Leonard V. Rutgers (Leuven: Peeters, 2002), 326.

36. Justin, *1 Apol.* 66.1 (Hardy, 286).

37. For examples of interruptions in Origen's homilies, see *Hom. Jer.* 1.7; 1.8; 5.13. For interruptions of Augustine's sermons, see F. Van der Meer, *Augustine the Bishop: The Life and Work of a Father of the Church*, trans. Brian Battershaw and G. R. Lamb (London: Sheed & Ward, 1961), 427–28.

38. Bradshaw, "Reception of Communion," 167.

Prayers and the Kiss

After the reading and teaching, the entire assembly stands up and offers prayers. No doubt many worshipers raise their hands as orants. According to Justin, they pray mightily/vigorously (*eutonos*) and communally (*koinas*). For the community this is evidently a time of passionate spiritual engagement, in which the worshipers pray for believers in many places and for themselves. At the end of the prayers, Justin writes, "We greet each other with a kiss."[39] Of course, given the pressures of time, the prayers and the kiss, like the readings, cannot be too lengthy.

The Lord's Supper

Immediately after the kiss, bread and wine and water are brought, and the president "sends up prayers and thanksgivings." He does not use a fixed, written eucharistic prayer. According to Justin he prays according "to the best of his ability." The president may use customary outlines or "conventions," but he is improvising.[40] As he prays in his own idiom, he articulates the people's common praise and consecrates the food that "is the flesh and blood of that incarnate Jesus."[41] The worshipers respond with enthusiasm: they "sing out their assent saying the 'Amen.'"[42] The deacons serve small portions of the consecrated food and drink to everyone present and afterward take it to absent members of the community. The meal spreads outward, forming the character of the worshipers and playing an essential part in the life of their community, which is committed to care for orphans, widows, prisoners, and sojourners.[43]

39. Justin, *1 Apol*. 65.1–2 (Hardy, 285–86); cf. C. Munier, *Saint Justin Apologie pour les Chrétiens* (Fribourg: Éditions Universitaires, 1995), 129.

40. The only known written eucharistic prayer from the first three centuries (*Trad. ap.* 4) may have been a later interpolation, and in any case *Trad. ap.* 9.3–4 clarifies that it should not be a model, but that each president should pray according to his ability (BJP, 37, 44, 70). On the early Christian practice of improvised eucharistic prayer, see Allen Bouley, *From Freedom to Formula: The Evolution of the Eucharistic Prayer from Oral Improvisation to Written Texts*, Studies in Christian Antiquity 21 (Washington, DC: Catholic University of America Press, 1981), 90; R. P. C. Hanson, "The Liberty of the Bishop to Improvise Prayer," in his *Studies in Christian Antiquity* (Edinburgh: T&T Clark, 1985), 113–16; Achim Budde, "Improvisation im Eucharistiegebet," *Jahrbuch für Antike und Christentum* 44 (2001): 127–41.

41. Justin, *1 Apol*. 66.2 (Hardy, 286).

42. Justin, *1 Apol*. 67.5, trans. Everett Ferguson, *Early Christians Speak: Faith and Life in the First Three Centuries*, rev. ed. (Abilene, TX: Abilene Christian University Press, 1987), 81; and in Munier, *Saint Justin Apologie*, 122. Most translators either ignore *epeuphēmei* altogether or render it in pallid, emotionally neutral ways; in contrast, Ferguson faces into the term's meaning as "assent with a shout of applause," thereby taking the risk of making early Christian eucharistic worship seem enthusiastic.

43. Justin, *1 Apol*. 67.6; Cyprian, *Pat*. 14, trans. L. J. Swift, *The Early Fathers on War and Military Service* (Wilmington, DE: Michael Glazier, 1983), 48: "After the reception of the Eucharist the hand is not to be stained with the sword and bloodshed."

The habitus of the worshipers in the morning service differed in many ways from that of worshipers in the evening banquet, but there were continuities.[44] The members entered into an alternative world, a utopian space, where things were different from the outside world. There was a new family, sensitivity to economic needs, and an equalizing tendency. There was encounter with the Bible and teaching by leaders with whom there could be interaction. There were opportunities to stand and pray as well as to greet brothers and sisters in peace and be reconciled. And there was the ritual meal, now with token elements, which enabled a sacramental encounter with the living Lord. Indeed, as congregations grew and connections with other believers became less intense, this sense of connection with the divine through the eucharistic elements became more intense. Perhaps this helps explain why, by the middle of the third century, many churches saw it necessary to be organized and efficient in excluding outsiders from the assembly. The deacons, bouncers at the door, were necessary not only to guard a place in which there is *mana*—localized, supernatural power—but also to protect an interloper from the "tremors and convulsions" that could come from eating unworthily.[45]

Let us look in greater detail at the sermon, the prayers, and the peace greeting.

Sermon

The Christians of the early centuries gave surprisingly little attention to the sermon. In the book of Acts it is of course otherwise. There the classical action of the main actors in the story, Peter and Paul, is the public oration. The apostles address gatherings of strangers. They also speak more conversationally in domestic settings to people they know. But after the two apostles were executed, public orations largely disappeared, no doubt because of persecution. "We have no historical text which refers to formal, open-air sermons outside a church after the Apostolic age."[46] The churches grew, steadily but inexorably, almost completely without missionary preaching.[47]

---

44. Some churches in which the Sunday service had come to be standard continued to practice solemn evening meals in the earlier Christian tradition; at times, as in *Trad. ap.* 25–28, the line between Eucharist and *agapē* could have been blurred. See BJP, 144–45; Alistair Stewart-Sykes, trans. and ed., *Hippolytus: On the Apostolic Tradition* (Crestwood, NY: St. Vladimir's Seminary Press, 2001), 140–43.

45. For several illustrations of the power, see Cyprian, *Laps.* 26, trans. R. J. Deferrari, FC 36 (1958), 79–80; for the deacons, see *Did. apost.* 2.57.6–7.

46. Lane Fox, *Pagans and Christians*, 284.

47. See Michael Green, *Evangelism in the Early Church* (London: Hodder & Stoughton, 1970), 197.

"Preaching"—inspirational, exhortative, instructional speech—of course took place in the life of the pre-Christendom church. The words for preaching—*homiliae, sermones, exhortationes, dia logou*—all occur in the life of Christians who met in private settings. As we saw in chapter 6, speeches were vehicles of catechesis, and here we note that they also were present in the congregations' worship services. Not surprisingly the forms of speech changed across time. It is notable that Christians didn't write treatises about the sermon. They didn't reflect about its theology and practice, or discuss its contributions to their life. Nor did they take the trouble to preserve sermons; except for Origen, only a few sermon texts have survived from the first three centuries. One wonders why this should be so. For example, Bishop Cyprian of Carthage was a gifted rhetorician who repeatedly addressed his congregations; his legacy includes eighty-one letters but for some reason not one sermon text.

Nevertheless, as we shall see, sermons were important in early Christianity. They not only contributed to the life of the Christians and their communities; they also contributed to the churches' numerical growth—not by addressing groups of outsiders in a missionary way (that would have been dangerous) but by forming the believers so that they embodied a message that pagans could find credible.

As we have seen, in the first two centuries when believers met regularly for worship, they typically met at table, at the evening banquet. During the second part of the banquet, the symposium, participants interactively brought diverse gifts—and among these were prophetic speeches. In the early second century, in one of the churches in Rome, the prophet/community leader Hermas showed what prophetic speech could be like. Hermas's church had many poor and powerless members, and he had an intense concern that they should "practice justice" (*dikaiosynē*).[48] His gift of prophetic perception was pricked by believers in his community who "only believed" and whose lifestyles were "embroiled" in enterprise. These believers were mixed up with "business deals, wealth, [and] friendships with outsiders," but what Hermas the seer "saw" in the church was not businessmen but vineyards—good vineyards that, untended, had become "barren due to thorns and many kinds of weeds" so that they could "understand nothing at all."[49] Hermas was given words to share what he saw with the brothers and sisters in his church's symposium. When Hermas spoke, there may have been a frisson of excitement in the gathering. He recorded some of his messages in his book *The Shepherd*, which

---

48. Herm. Mand. 8.9–10, trans. Carolyn Osiek, *Shepherd of Hermas: A Commentary*, Hermeneia (Minneapolis: Fortress, 1999), 128.
49. Herm. Mand. 10.1.4 (Osiek, 135).

traveled widely as an early Christian best seller. In the papyrus documents from Oxyrhynchus in upper Egypt, fragments of Hermas occur as often as fragments of the Gospel of John![50]

Hermas knew that he wasn't the only one who received visions. So in *The Shepherd* he indicates how the congregations should recognize the true visionary. Ethics and habitus are basic: "You can tell the one who has the spirit of God by the way of life." The authentic prophet is unassertive, "makes [himself] poorer than everyone else," and does not "live in luxurious habits."[51] But when "the angel of the prophetic spirit that rests upon that person fills the person," then the prophet "speaks to the whole crowd as the Lord wishes."[52] According to Hermas, prophetic perception and exhortation were a normal part of the evening worship services of the Roman Christians, not the vocation of only one prophet.

The source of visions in Hermas's Roman church was the Spirit, rarely the Scriptures.[53] But in the century that followed, as the canon began to take shape, that changed. Tertullian reports in his *Apology* that the Scriptures had come to be central to the Carthaginian Christians' after-dinner worship. At table, according to Tertullian, the Christians after the prayers "read the books of God," which seems to have led to comment by various participants; further, the teaching was deepened as the participants inhabited the "precepts" (by which Tertullian often means Jesus's sayings). Then followed the "exhortations." These may have been admonitory speeches, possibly unplanned words spoken by various people who urged the community to take the words seriously and to apply them to their lives. The "rebuke" and "divine censure" that Tertullian mentions may have told the people the consequences of thinking the teachings but not living them.[54] In another of his writings, *On the Soul*, Tertullian speaks of "talks" (*adlocutiones*)—evidently plural and given by participants—which followed the reading of Scriptures and the singing of Psalms. Meanwhile, while the community was worshiping, a "sister" received revelations, which she shared with the community's leaders after the

50. AnneMarie Luijendijk, *Greetings in the Lord: Early Christians and the Oxyrhynchus Papyri*, HTS 60 (Cambridge, MA: Harvard University Press, 2008), 20–21. For Hermas's wide popularity, see Peter Lampe, *From Paul to Valentinus: Christians in Rome in the First Two Centuries* (Minneapolis: Fortress, 2003), 236.

51. Herm. Mand. 11.7–9, 12 (Osiek, 139–40).

52. Herm. Mand. 11.9 (Osiek, 139).

53. Alistair Stewart-Sykes, "Hermas the Prophet and Hippolytus the Preacher: The Roman Homily and Its Social Context," in *Preacher and Audience: Studies in Early Christian and Byzantine Homiletics*, ed. Mary B. Cunningham and Pauline Allen (Leiden: Brill, 1998), 41–42.

54. Tertullian, *Apol.* 39.3–4 (Glover, 175).

worshipers left.[55] One would like to know how Spirit and Word interacted to empower the people and direct their action. If only we knew as much about Tertullian's exhortations as we do about Hermas's visions.

With Justin Martyr in mid-second-century Rome we enter a community that has moved its worship from the evening banquet to the morning service, from Saturday evening to early Sunday morning.[56] According to Justin, the Scriptures occupy a central place in the worship: "The memoirs of the apostles or the writings of the prophets are read as long as time permits."[57] The move to the morning has forced everyone to get up an hour or more earlier than usual, so Justin probably experienced what Basil of Caesarea reported two centuries later: "Many artisans, employed in manual labours and who earn just enough at their daily work to provide for their own nourishment, are surrounding me and obliging me to be brief."[58] To people worshiping God before going to work, the "president" of the assembly speaks in a manner that is practical and to the point. He revisits the Scriptures that have been read and "in a discourse [*dia logou*] urges and invites us to the imitation of these beautiful things."[59]

In Justin's community it is not enough for the Scriptures simply to be read and to influence the ideas of the people; the Scriptures must also impact the way the believers treat each other and behave toward outsiders. The president's discourse must enable the people to be imitators of Jesus; it must form the believers so their habitus—their reflexive behavior—comes to resemble their Master's. As Justin's community understands things, there are good reasons for the sense of urgency here.[60] All the believers—the president and the people—know that, as Justin puts it earlier in his *Apology*, they are truly Christians only if they live as Christ taught; they also know that only those "who live as Christ handed down to us" can take part in the Eucharist.[61] Without habitus change one is not a Christian. The presbyter speaks, probably extempore, without notes. He looks at the people and admonishes them. As he applies

55. Tertullian, *An.* 9.4, trans. S. Thelwall, ANF 3:188; PL 2:660.

56. Bradshaw (*Eucharistic Origins*, 68–69) notices that Justin's account does not explicitly state that the Sunday service took place in the morning, but he comments that it may have been a morning service to which a Eucharist was attached—which I think is probable.

57. Justin, *1 Apol.* 67.3 (Hardy, 287).

58. Mary B. Cunningham, "Preaching and the Community," in *Church and People in Byzantium*, ed. Rosemary Morris (Birmingham: University of Birmingham, 1990), 33.

59. Justin, *1 Apol.* 67.4 (Hardy, 287).

60. They must live by what Maxwell E. Johnson has called the "law of acting" (*lex agendi*); see his *Praying and Believing in Early Christianity: The Interplay between Christian Worship and Doctrine* (Collegeville, MN: Liturgical Press, 2013), 97–98.

61. Justin, *1 Apol.* 16.8; 66.1 (Hardy, 252, 286).

the biblical texts to the situations that he knows about—in their daily lives and in the community that they form together—something is happening that is momentous, essential to the welfare and witness of the church.

Justin's model of the role of preaching in the morning service is a strong one: *Bible reading precedes preaching, which applies the Bible to the lives of people, who allow it to shape their daily lives and work.* Did Justin's community actually follow the model? And did other communities follow it?[62] If only there were more surviving sermons to enable us to test this! There are several sermon texts that clearly don't fit Justin's model: Melito's *On the Pascha*, whose "extravagant rhetorical forms" were hardly appropriate to speak to the practical issues that a typical congregation faced; and the anonymous *On the Dice Players*, which, although colorful, addresses only one issue.[63]

However, one writing, the Second Letter of Clement to the Corinthians, indicates that Justin's model was found in other communities. Despite its title, this is clearly not a letter. Instead, it is similar to the sermon that Justin describes in his *Apology*.[64] It is an address to a community, whom the author calls "brothers" or "brothers and sisters."[65] It is presented after the reading of passages of Scripture. And it exhorts the listeners to apply the Scriptures to their life situations. In all these ways the model in 2 Clement is similar to Justin's model. But it differs in one significant way: it was not extemporaneous but written—"I am *reading* you an exhortation." Most unusually for his time, the preacher wanted this sermon to survive.[66] Opinions differ widely as to where the preacher preached 2 Clement,[67] but most experts agree on the timing—it was written at about the time of Justin, the mid-second century. And how illuminating it is about the life and worship of second-century Christians.

---

62. Alistair Stewart-Sykes, *From Prophecy to Preaching: A Search for the Origins of the Christian Homily*, VCSup 59 (Boston: Brill, 2001), 242–43; Paul F. Bradshaw, *The Search for the Origins of Christian Worship: Sources and Methods for the Study of Early Liturgy*, 2nd ed. (New York: Oxford University Press, 2002), 98–100, 139.

63. Stuart G. Hall, ed., *Melito of Sardis: On Pascha and Fragments* (Oxford: Clarendon, 1979), xix; Scott T. Carroll, "An Early Church Sermon against Gambling (*CPL* 60)," *Second Century* 8 (1991): 83–95.

64. Alistair Stewart-Sykes has argued that 2 Clement is not a sermon but a "prebaptismal exhortation" (*From Prophecy to Preaching*, 176–87). In contrast, I view it as a sermon, for reasons that I cite and because the preacher engages with issues that the entire community is facing, not just catechumens.

65. See 2 Clem. 1.1; 4.4; 5.1; 10.1; 19.1.

66. See 2 Clem. 19.1, trans. C. C. Richardson, LCC 1 (1953), 201.

67. On the place of origin of 2 Clement, Stewart-Sykes proposes Corinth (*From Prophecy to Preaching*, 185n); Robert Grant is confident of Rome (*The Apostolic Fathers* [New York: Thomas Nelson, 1965], 2:109); C. C. Richardson suggests Egypt (LCC 1:186); P. F. Beatrice says Syria or possibly Egypt (*Encylopedia of the Early Church*, ed. A. Di Berardino [New York: Oxford University Press, 1992], 1:181).

After a reader has read passages from Isaiah 54 and Matthew 9, the preacher briefly reflects on these. He reminds the congregation that when they had been perishing—"on the brink of destruction"—God had saved them through Christ's suffering. "Such mercy" has transformed their lives, and the believers must respond by acknowledging Christ.[68] But how, the preacher asks, should the believers acknowledge him? Quoting Jesus (Matt. 7:21), he urges them not merely to say "Lord, Lord" but instead to acknowledge him by "doing the things he says, not disobeying his commands." He says to his congregation, including himself: "We should acknowledge [Christ] by what we do, by loving one another. . . . [We should be] sympathetic with one another and not be attached to money."[69] He is aware that there are tensions in the congregation. Some of these are apparently intergenerational; there are stresses between the younger Christians and their seniors, and some of these stresses have to do with economic sharing.[70] At times these stresses express themselves in a lack of love. This is tragic, for it seriously impairs the church's witness.[71] According to the preacher, when the Christians explain their faith to pagan neighbors, they talk about the teachings of Christ, and the pagans respond by being "astonished at their beauty and greatness." But, he warns, when the neighbors note that "our actions do not match our words, they turn from astonishment to blasphemy" and dismiss Christianity as "some kind of myth and error."[72]

> When they hear from us that God has said, "It is no great accomplishment for you to love those who love you; it is great if you love your enemies and those who hate you." And when they hear these things, they are astonished by their extraordinary goodness. But then when they see that we fail to love not only those who hate us, but even those who love us, they ridicule us and the name is blasphemed.[73]

The way forward for their witness, according to the preacher, is not to stop talking about Jesus's teachings about enemy love—that thought did not occur to him! Instead, the way forward is to repent of hypocrisy so that they once again will live the teachings of Jesus and as a result can speak about them with integrity. When their common life has areas in which love is lacking, they must repent of these and repair them. For the preacher's

68. See 2 Clem. 2.7; 3.1–3, trans. B. D. Ehrman, LCL 24 (2003), 169.
69. See 2 Clem. 3.4; 4.2–4 (Ehrman, 169, 171).
70. See 2 Clem. 19.2; 20.1.
71. See 2 Clem. 9.6.
72. See 2 Clem. 13.2–3 (Ehrman, 185).
73. See 2 Clem. 13.4 (Ehrman, 185–87).

congregation this will involve restoring their practices of mutual aid, in which all members express love for each other.[74] And, the preacher adds, the people must come together for worship more frequently. Worship is the generative core of their life; in it they "help one another and bring those who are weak back to what is good." They do these things by exhorting each other—they "turn one another around and admonish one another." The presbyters admonish the people as well, and their admonitions are indispensable in helping the members keep their vision, so that "when we return home we should remember the commandments of the Lord and not be dragged away by worldly desires."[75] Worship—including the mutual admonitions of the members and sermons of their leaders—is essential to keep the Christians' life and witness on course.

In the century after the preacher of 2 Clement, thousands of sermons were given, but few survive. The sermons of this period were extemporaneous (designed for the occasion) and ephemeral. But in the 230s and 240s sermons began to survive. In Caesarea, when Origen rose to the challenge of giving sermons to catechumens and a local congregation, stenographers were present to transcribe his sermons, thanks to a wealthy supporter.[76] Unlike earlier preachers, Origen could speak with the sense that his audience would include posterity as well as the people who faced him as he spoke. He gave a large number of sermons, approximately three hundred of which are extant, including thirty-nine on the Gospel of Luke, which he gave to early morning gatherings of his congregation in Caesarea.[77] When he told them of his aim, Origen was humble: "We should rise at daybreak and pray to God that we might be able to eat at least the crumbs that fall from his table."[78]

Origen's Sunday sermons were short, lasting between six and fifteen minutes, vastly shorter than his weekday catecheses. Each sermon began with a reading of a passage from Luke's Gospel, in consecutive order; on one occasion there also was a reading from a New Testament epistle.[79] Origen commented on these passages to his audience, which included various groups—"catechumens

---

74. See 2 Clem. 16.4; David J. Downs, "Redemptive Almsgiving and Economic Stratification in 2 Clement," *JECS* 19, no. 4 (2011): 511.

75. See 2 Clem. 17.2–3 (Ehrman, 193).

76. Eusebius, *Hist. eccl.* 6.36.1.

77. According to Henri Crouzel (*Origen*, trans. A. S. Worrall [Edinburgh: T&T Clark, 1989], 30), Origen may have written out his *Homilies on Luke* before delivering them, unlike his weekday homilies, which he extemporized and which stenographers transcribed. However, in Origen's Lukan homilies I find many spontaneous touches (e.g., *Hom. Luc.* 11.5; 12.2) and therefore suspect that stenographers transcribed these as well.

78. Origen, *Hom. Luc.* 38.6, trans. J. T. Lienhard, FC 94 (1996), 158.

79. Origen, *Hom. Luc.* 12.2.

and faithful . . . women, men and children."[80] At times he spoke to these as distinct groups. In Homily 22, for example, he addresses catechumens, expositing Luke 3. He appeals to the catechumens, no doubt in the final stages of preparation, to approach their baptism seriously. A candidate must show "fruits worthy of repentance." He must not "remain in his original state" but must "leave behind his habits and his customs."[81]

What might this mean for Origen's hearers? In Luke 3, John the Baptist gives pointed instruction to his hearers who want to be baptized; he requires the tax collectors, soldiers, and people who have two coats to change their habitus.[82] In comparison to the Baptist, Origen is not specific. He urges his audience to "possess peace and patience and goodness," but he jumps over the verses (Luke 3:12–14) in which John challenges his hearers to change their lives. As to children, Origen addresses them, speaking about Jesus's obedience to his parents (Luke 2:49–51): "Children, we should learn to be subject to our parents." But he has nothing specific to say to the children; instead, he urges all his hearers, as children, to be subject to the father whom God has chosen for them—the bishop or the presbyter—even though he may be "a lesser man put in charge of better men."[83] The same is true when Origen, basing his teaching on Luke 2:33–38, addresses women: "Women, look on Anna's testimony and imitate it." But Origen's message is really to all believers—they must avoid the spiritual dangers of second marriages.[84]

Of course, Origen in his Sunday sermons shows his delight in the Bible and his unrivaled learning. He expresses a passionate spirituality; he loves Jesus and longs for his hearers to "gaze on Jesus. For, when you look to him, your faces will be shining from the light of his gaze."[85] Origen also shows pastoral concern. He senses that some of his hearers' lives are not worthy of their baptism, and in his view this will get them into trouble both in this world and the next. Origen asserts that it is important not only to state principles but to "follow them up with an application."[86] Whatever happens—whether "rivers swell" or "persecution rages"—his hearers will be secure when they live their faith, building their "house out of the various solid stones of God's commandments."[87] When he says these things,

80. Origen, *Hom. Luc.* 32.6 (Lienhard, 133).
81. Origen, *Hom. Luc.* 22.5, 8 (Lienhard, 94–95).
82. Origen, *Hom. Luc.* 22.1, 4–6 (Lienhard, 92–94).
83. Origen, *Hom. Luc.* 20.5 (Lienhard, 86).
84. Origen, *Hom. Luc.* 17.10 (Lienhard, 74).
85. Origen, *Hom. Luc.* 32.6 (Lienhard, 133).
86. Origen, *Hom. Luc.* 1.5 (Lienhard, 8).
87. Origen, *Hom. Luc.* 26.5 (Lienhard, 111).

Origen stands in the tradition of his predecessors Justin and the preacher of 2 Clement.

Origen states his concern for application, but in his Sunday homilies on Luke he rarely applies the message. Instead, he seems disengaged from local reality. Origen rarely points to specific teachings of Jesus that his hearers must "imitate" in their situations. No doubt this is in part because of the passages in Luke that Origen preaches about. For example, Origen's thirty-nine sermons on the Gospel of Luke proceed consecutively until Homily 33, which ends with Luke 4:27. Between that and Homily 34, which begins with Luke 10:25, there is a yawning gap of no less than six chapters. In the gap are Jesus's "Sermon on the Plain" (including the Beatitudes and love of enemies teachings of Luke 6), Jesus's dealings with women (Luke 7 and 8), and Jesus's missional sending of twelve disciples and seventy disciples (Luke 9 and 10). The final five homilies (35–39) are scattered out across the final fourteen chapters of the Gospel and skip over Jesus's teachings (in Luke 12) about wealth. These texts in the gaps deal pointedly with habitus, the formation of reflexive, distinctive Christian behavior. If Origen's homilies seem semidetached from reality, perhaps it's because he skipped these passages. His homilies also do not deal with the Lukan Passion Narrative. Why these gaps? Was it because his sermons on these texts have disappeared, like many of his other sermons? Was it because the Caesarea community had a lopsided lectionary? Or was it because the bishops, who at times directed Origen's choice of topics for his weekday catechesis, for some reason steered him away from these passages?[88] We cannot know, but we observe: in the form in which they survive, Origen's Sunday sermons come across as generic; they do not address a specific congregation in its struggles to embody the faith but are impersonal and applicationless. Origen's sermons have become "scholasticized."[89]

However, in the 250s the earlier tradition of Justin Martyr and 2 Clement still lived on, and in many churches was probably normal. An example of the tradition in practice is the sermon that Bishop Cyprian gave to his congregation in Carthage during the virulent outbreak of plague early in that decade.[90] We know of this sermon not because Cyprian's text has survived—he may have extemporized the sermon on the spot—but because Cyprian's biographer, Pontius, took notes. In chapter 3 I discussed this sermon at length, and here I want briefly to underscore two central points.

---

88. Origen, *Hom. Ezech.* 13.1.1.
89. Stewart-Sykes, *From Prophecy to Preaching*, 269.
90. Cyprian's biographer, Pontius, tells the story in his *Vit. Cypr.* 9 (trans. M. M. Müller and R. J. Deferrari, FC 15 [1952], 13–14).

First, Cyprian, in the face of this overwhelming crisis, speaks to the people from the Bible—"from Holy Writ." Pontius doesn't tell us what the text of Cyprian's sermon was, but his notes indicate that it was one of Cyprian's core texts, Matthew 5:44–48. Drawing on this, Cyprian says that it is crucially important that Christians treat desperately ill people by providing practical help. The crisis requires "a proper observance of charity." This involves entering the houses of sick people, touching them, feeding them bread and giving them water, and loving them even when they are outside the Christian community, even when Christians view them as persecutors and enemies. Quoting Jesus, Cyprian tells his people that when they are doing this, they are doing more than the pagans, who love only their own friends and family. Why should believers do this? Why risk infection? Because God is generous and acts generously, and God wants his children to imitate him. According to Pontius, Cyprian paraphrases Matthew 5:45: God "continually makes his sun rise and imparts sudden rain to nourish the seeds, showing all these kindnesses not merely to his own friends."[91]

Second, according to Cyprian, the purpose of the biblical texts that he quotes is not to change the thinking of believers but their lives. "Should not one who professes to be a son of God imitate the example of his Father? It is proper for us to correspond to our birth, and it does not become those who are clearly reborn in God to be degenerate, but, as a son, the descendant of a good father should rather prove the imitation of his goodness."[92] Cyprian the preacher ponders the text and exposits it, reminding the people that this is a treasure they share together. The preacher then applies it to the situation of the people so that they will live it, so it will change their lives and prepare them to risk their lives. Through this the people grow in a habitus that is no doubt already familiar to them but is different from that of other people—a habitus that imitates God by loving their enemies. As Pontius puts it, the hearers in response to Cyprian's sermon "accomplished what is good for all, not merely for those of the household of faith."[93]

In Carthage, Cyprian was doing what Justin in Rome had called for: after the reading of the Bible, he "urges and invites [the people] to the imitation of these beautiful things."[94] Cyprian applied the Bible to the lives of the believers, and they, in response, were encouraged to live in a distinctive way that communicated the Christian message to outsiders. When this happened, the sermon was important to the growth of the church.

---

91. Pontius, *Vit. Cypr.* 9 (Müller and Deferrari, 14). For other texts in which Cyprian cites Matt. 5:45, see, *Pat.* 5; *Ad Quir.* 3.49; *Zel. liv.* 15.
92. Pontius, *Vit. Cypr.* 9 (Müller and Deferrari, 14).
93. Pontius, *Vit. Cypr.* 10 (Müller and Deferrari, 15), citing Gal. 6:10.
94. Justin, *1 Apol.* 67.4 (Hardy, 287).

Common Prayers

The early Christian writers gave exceptional attention to prayer, vastly more than to the sermon. Three early writers—Tertullian, Cyprian, and Origen—wrote treatises on prayer.[95] Their purpose was to guide the believers about the practicalities of corporate prayer. What posture should the praying believers have? What gestures should they use? How should they tend relationships with each other so they could pray efficaciously? What concerns was it right for them to pray about? What words should they use, and how precise should these be? What range of emotions could they allow themselves? As they addressed these questions, the writers also addressed theological questions about the efficacy, power, and necessity of prayer. They wrote with a strong sense of the numinous experienced in common prayer. Christians needed this experience. Prayer enabled them not only to cope with the dangers of day-to-day living but also to do joyfully the risky things that enabled the church to grow—to travel to new places, to touch plague victims, to see enemies as potential brothers. Christians' lives depended on their prayer, and they believed that the well-being of the empire, indeed of the world, did as well. As second-century apologist Aristides put it, "The world stands by reason of the intercession of Christians."[96]

Stance and Gesture

According to Justin and the *Apostolic Tradition*, the newly baptized believer was introduced to the worshiping community at the time of prayer.[97] This was not accidental, for the prayer time was a power center of early Christian worship. In the people's prayers the new believer found some things that were familiar. She encountered a familiar habitus—men and women who, like pagans, prayed standing, with eyes open and hands raised, outstretched in the position of the orant, the praying person.[98] In pagan iconography, the orant connoted family loyalty, or the soul of a deceased person. In their nascent art, the Christians adopted the orant—typically a female—as the most common

95. Tertullian, *On Prayer* (*De oratione*); Cyprian, *On the Lord's Prayer* (*De dominica oratione*); Origen, *On Prayer* (*De oratione*). In contrast, no early Christian treatise on the Eucharist has survived.

96. Aristides, *Apol.* 16, trans. J. Rendel Harris, Texts and Studies 1 (Cambridge: Cambridge University Press, 1891), 50.

97. Justin, *1 Apol.* 65.1; see also *Trad. ap.* 21.25.

98. Graydon F. Snyder, *Ante Pacem: Archaeological Evidence of Church Life before Constantine* (Macon, GA: Mercer University Press, 1985), 19–20; Robin Margaret Jensen, *Understanding Early Christian Art* (London: Routledge, 2000), 32–37.

depiction of the Christian. They could do this confidently, because the stance of the orant was the stance of the Christian at prayer—in private as well as in the Christian assembly. Origen wrote in his treatise on prayer:

> While there are many ways of bodily deportment [in prayer], there can be no doubt that the position of extending one's hands and elevating the eyes is to be preferred above all others; for the position taken by the body is thus symbolic of the qualities proper to the soul in the acts of praying. This we say should be, except under particular circumstances, the normal position taken. Circumstances can permit us to pray with propriety while sitting—for example because of some serious foot ailment.[99]

So the orant stance was familiar to the new Christian. But much would strike her as new. Christians ascribed new meaning to the stance. The open eyes looked up into heaven. The outspread hands indicated innocence but also mimed the cross and manifested the Christian's "readiness for any torture."[100] Further, Christians—in a manner unparalleled among pagans—prayed together. Their place of worship was a place of corporate prayer, with many people praying, standing near each other, standing (they believed) "before the face of God."[101] The clergy apparently did not dominate these prayers, and many believers—including the least educated—felt free to contribute. Rarely were the corporate prayers of the Christians of the first three centuries characterized by silent listening. Instead, the Christians often offered spoken prayers of thankfulness. In Justin's Rome they praised God "for our creation and all the means of health, for the variety of creatures and the changes of the seasons."[102] In addition, the believers spoke prayers of petition and intercession. These could be fervent. In some communities, as people prayed they groaned and cried out.[103] In North Africa people prayed simultaneously.[104] Praying believers could also use physical gestures. According to Clement, in Alexandria the high fever of a sick person was "put to flight by the laying on of hands." The prayers could take on an exorcistic tone, with "confident commands" shattering the "violence of demons."[105]

99. Origen, *Or.* 31.2, trans. J. J. O'Meara, ACW 19 (1954), 131.
100. Tertullian, *Apol.* 30.7 (Glover, 153). See also Tertullian, *Or.* 14; Minucius Felix, *Oct.* 29.6.
101. Origen, *Or.* 11.4; Cyprian, *Dom. or.* 4, trans. and ed. A. Stewart-Sykes, *Tertullian, Cyprian, Origen: On the Lord's Prayer* (Crestwood, NY: St. Vladimir's Seminary Press, 2004), 67.
102. Justin, *1 Apol.* 13.2 (Hardy, 249).
103. Justin, *1 Apol.* 65.1; Cyprian, *Dom. or.* 4.
104. *Passion of Perpetua* 7.1.
105. Clement of Alexandria, *Quis div.* 34, trans. G. W. Butterworth, LCL 60 (1919), 343.

Repeated Phrases

In North Africa participants in congregational prayers seem to have repeated certain formulas: "O God, have mercy. To you be thanks. . . . I cannot thank you enough." "I pray, O Christ. Praise to you."[106] In a setting of corporate, unprogrammed prayer, worshipers may have imported phrases from "appointed prayers," texts they used in their homes.[107] At times they may have spontaneously brought into common worship fragments of the Lord's Prayer, "the proper and normal prayer," which they prayed several times a day at home: "With frequently repeated prayers do we entreat and beg that the day of his kingdom may come."[108] There is no explicit record of the Lord's Prayer being used in eucharistic services until the late fourth century.[109] But there could have been unrecorded uses of the Lord's Prayer in earlier eucharists. And it is conceivable that believers recited the entire Lord's Prayer in the congregational prayers. Tertullian may well have designed his treatise *On Prayer*—which exposits the Lord's Prayer—as one of the final instructions of catechumens prior to their baptism; Cyprian may have intended his *On the Lord's Prayer* for the same audience.[110] In this treatise, Cyprian observes that the Lord's Prayer is a corporate prayer that addresses *Our* Father; it was not given for someone who prays "individually and alone." According to Cyprian, Christians use the Lord's Prayer properly as a means of drawing the people's intercessions to a conclusion: "How much more effectively should we obtain what we ask in the name of Christ if we ask it using his own prayer."[111]

Meeting Specific Needs

Origen in Caesarea saw it as natural that believers, rich and poor, would stand so close together in prayer that they would overhear each other; and because of what they heard, they could engage in acts of mutual aid, meeting each other's needs. Origen refused to dismiss these overhearings as coincidental. When the Christians gather to pray, he says in his treatise *Prayer*, angels are present and "act together with us." A doctor "is standing by one who is sick and is praying for health; . . . it is manifest that he would be moved to

---

106. *Acts of the Abitinian Martyrs* 6, 12 (Tilley, 32, 37). These phrases, uttered when Christians were experiencing persecution and torture, may well have been habitual expressions in the church's common prayer.

107. Origen, *Cels.* 6.41, trans. H. Chadwick (1965), 356.

108. Tertullian, *Or.* 10, trans. A. Stewart-Sykes, *Lord's Prayer*, 10; Cyprian, *Mort.* 18, trans. E. Wallis, *ANF* 5:473.

109. Kenneth W. Stevenson, *The Lord's Prayer: A Text in Tradition* (London: SCM, 2004), 47.

110. Stewart-Sykes, *Lord's Prayer*, 23–24.

111. Cyprian, *Dom. or.* 3, 8 (Stewart-Sykes, *Lord's Prayer*, 66, 69).

heal the one who prays." A wealthy person "hears the prayer of a poor person who lifts up an appeal to God on account of his necessity. It is obvious that he will fulfill the prayer of the poor person."[112]

How different the Christians' praying was from that of the pagans. For pagans, verbal precision was of the essence. If prayers were to be efficacious, those offering them had to use exact formulae without any omission or deviation. A monitor listened for quality control, to ensure that the praying was faultless. In contrast, according to Tertullian, "without a monitor [*sine monitore*] we pray from the heart."[113] In the early centuries Christian common prayer was improvisatory, not scripted; it was prayer without paper. It was prayer not just for the professional religionists, and not just for the literate, but for all, depending on their need and their spiritual gift. According to Adalbert Hamman, Christian prayer was "existential prayer."[114] It was gutsy and practical, passionate and immediate. It grew out of the struggles and concerns of the people who prayed, many of whom had little control over their lives. If at times it was noisy, that was unsurprising. The Christians' practical praying reflected the character of the Christian God who cares less about cultic precision than about meeting the needs of people who worship him, righting their wrongs and healing their suffering when they cry out to him. According to Tertullian, prayer was at the heart of Christian worship because it gave power to powerless people. In response to God's command, prayer was the Christians' "rich and greater sacrifice [*opimam et maiorem hostiam*]."[115]

Coping with Stress

Why did people come to worship services week after week? Many came because they couldn't live—couldn't survive—without prayer. Christians were of varied social backgrounds. The more prosperous faced discrimination as Christians; they also faced the rejection that their nonconformist approaches to their professions sometimes entailed. Many other Christians were poor, many were illiterate, and most were nonelite people who, according to a recent study, "faced powerful social stressors."[116] These stressors recur in early Christian accounts of prayer. A famous prayer from late first-century Rome

112. Origen, *Or.* 11.4–5 (Stewart-Sykes, *Lord's Prayer*, 136). See also Origen, *Or.* 31.5.
113. Tertullian, *Apol.* 30.4 (Glover, 151).
114. Adalbert-G. Hamman, *La prière*, vol. 2, *Les trois premiers siècles* (Tournai: Desclée, 1963), 109.
115. Tertullian, *Apol.* 30.5 (Glover, 152–53).
116. Jerry Toner, *Popular Culture in Ancient Rome* (Cambridge: Polity Press, 2009), 74.

(1 Clement 59.4) refers to the following kinds of stress: sickness, weakness, hunger, imprisonment, despair, and "falling" (apostasy?). A century later in Carthage, Tertullian listed the Christians in need who pray: people who are dying, weak people, ill people, people possessed by demons, prisoners and those who are in bonds, people threatened by robbers, poor people who need support and rich people who need to be ruled, the persecuted, and the apostates.[117] In Alexandria, Clement mentioned travelers whose "sinking ship rises, steered by the prayers of saints alone," and city dwellers threatened by "the attack of robbers [which] is made harmless, being stripped of its weapon by pious prayers."[118] Prayer had to do with life, with sufferings known and feared, and Christians "speak to a God who is present and who hears them."[119]

The prayers of the people not only undergirded their lives; they broadened their horizons. Christian prayers spanned the Mediterranean world. Justin informs us that at a baptismal service in Rome the congregation offered common prayers not only for their own members and the one who was newly baptized but also for "all others everywhere."[120] At about the same time in Smyrna in Asia Minor, just before he was executed by burning, Bishop Polycarp prayed night and day "for the churches throughout the world, as was his custom."[121] In many places Christians also prayed for their enemies and the emperors. Tertullian asked regarding Jesus's command to pray for enemies, "Who are more the enemies and persecutors of Christians, than those against whose majesty we are accused of treason"—that is, the emperors?[122]

Disorderly Prayers

Because the stakes were high, common prayers could get overheated and disorderly. As Jacob Taubes puts it in describing the early Pauline communities, "You must imagine prayer as something other than singing in the Christian church; instead there is screaming, groaning, and the heavens are stormy when people pray."[123] Around AD 200 Tertullian recognized that even in their evening banquet services still common in Carthage, the Christian habitus of

---

117. Tertullian, *Or.* 29.
118. Clement of Alexandria, *Quis div.* 34 (Butterworth, 343).
119. Origen, *Or.* 8.2 (Stewart-Sykes, *Lord's Prayer,* 130). See also Origen, *Or.* 12.1.
120. Justin, *1 Apol.* 65.1 (Hardy, 285).
121. Mart. Pol. 5.1, trans. B. D. Ehrman, LCL 24 (2003), 373.
122. Tertullian, *Apol.* 31.2 (Glover, 155).
123. Jacob Taubes, *The Political Theology of Paul,* trans. Diana Hollander (Stanford, CA: Stanford University Press, 2004), 73. See also Henry Chadwick and Peter Brown, "Prayer," in *Late Antiquity: A Guide to the Postclassical World,* ed. G. W. Bowersock, Peter Brown, and Oleg Grabar (Cambridge, MA: Harvard University Press, 1999), 650: "Among Christians, as among other groups, the gestures of prayer were expected to be melodramatic and noisy."

erect, open-eyed, hand-raised prayer could get distorted by demonstrative physicality: our hands, he said, should "not be raised very high in the air, but only slightly and to a proper position."[124] Fifty years later, in the larger-scale morning service model that had become the new norm in the city, Cyprian fretted that believers were still tossing about their prayer "at random with uncouth voices" and praying with "turbulent loquaciousness." These things shouldn't happen. When believers gather for common prayers with a priest, they ought to be "mindful of modesty and discipline." God "is not to be admonished by shouts."[125] Origen was concerned that the Christians should not be "like a pagan who babbles. . . . The babbler is one who speaks much."[126] As the Christian assemblies grew in size and sophistication, their leaders gave increasing attention to discipline and decorum.

Patience

Tertullian voiced another concern—the believers' experience that the God to whom they passionately prayed did not always answer immediately. The church, he wrote, is like the little ship in Matthew 8:24 in which Jesus's disciples are being tossed about by waves (persecutions and temptations), and the Master does not respond: "In his *patience* [he] is as it were asleep." Tertullian urged believers to be patient. At the right time, in response to the prayers of the people, the Master would awaken, "calm the world and restore tranquility to his own."[127]

Spiritual Combat

Answers to prayers were at times slow in coming. The people persisted in the common prayers of the church because they believed that these made a difference in their lives. In the Greco-Roman world, even literate, more prosperous Christians were in many ways powerless and vulnerable. The perils of pandemics and childbirth affected everybody, rich and poor alike. But prayer helped people cope. For all Christians, according to Tertullian, "prayer is a wall of faith, our arms and weapons that protect us on every side against our enemy" (the devil). And, he exulted, "we never go forward unarmed."[128]

124. Tertullian, *Or.* 17, trans. E. J. Daly, FC 40 (1959), 172.
125. Cyprian, *Dom. or.* 4, trans. R. J. Deferrari, FC 36 (1958), 129–30.
126. Origen, *Or.* 21.1–2 (O'Meara, 71).
127. Tertullian, *Bapt.* 12, trans. Ernest Evans, *Tertullian's Homily on Baptism* (London: SPCK, 1964), 29.
128. Tertullian, *Or.* 29, trans. Everett Ferguson, *Inheriting Wisdom* (Peabody, MA: Hendrickson, 2004), 251.

Prayer as spiritual combat was also a central theme for Clement of Alexandria. Christians are "an army without weapons, without war, without bloodshed, without anger." How countercultural the soldiers of this army are—"an army of God-fearing old men, of God-beloved orphans, of widows armed with gentleness, of men adorned with love." These make up a nonviolent army that contends with God. "This is the only good force," wrote Clement, "to force God and to seize life from God."[129] Or as Tertullian put it, as believers in Carthage pray together, they "mass [their] forces to surround God. . . . This violence that [they] do him pleases God."[130]

Some Christians placed an emphasis less on their struggle with God than on their prayerful combat with demonic forces—the principalities and powers. Origen was most articulate about this struggle. "For you who are redeemed by Christ," he challenged believers in Caesarea, "a physical sword has been removed from your hands." But this did not mean they were powerless. "In its place the 'sword of the Spirit' has been given and you must seize it."[131] Christians fight by means of "prayers and fasts, justice and piety, gentleness, chastity and all the virtues of self control." And the result? "One saint who prays is much more powerful than countless sinners who wage war."[132] So pray and live faithfully, Origen urged the Caesarean believers: "If you wish to prevail, lift up your hands and your deeds."[133] Along with faithful action, prayer was the Christians' means of being socially responsible.

The Power of Prayer

But the Christians were irresponsible! This was a commonplace that the pagan Celsus had stated eloquently fifty years earlier in his *True Word*. When the Christians refused to participate in the Roman legions, Celsus challenged them: "If everyone were to do the same as you, there would be nothing to prevent [the emperor] from being abandoned, alone and deserted, while earthly things would come into the power of the most lawless and savage barbarians."[134]

Origen, responding fifty years later, could have pointed out defensively that in fact there were some Christians in the Roman legions.[135] But he was not in the mood to be defensive. Instead he countered that Christians contributed more to

---

129. Clement of Alexandria, *Quis div.* 34, 21 (Butterworth, 343, 315).
130. Tertullian, *Apol.* 39.2 (Glover; 175).
131. Origen, *Hom. Num.* 20.4.3, trans. T. P. Scheck (Downers Grove, IL: IVP Academic, 2009), 131.
132. Origen, *Hom. Num.* 25.2.2; 25.4.1 (Scheck, 154).
133. Origen, *Hom. Exod.* 11.4, trans. R. E. Heine, FC 71 (1982), 359.
134. Origen, *Cels.* 8.68 (Chadwick, 504).
135. See, e.g., Tertullian, *Idol.* 19; Tertullian, *Cor.* 11.

the peace and security of the Roman Empire than the Roman legionaries "who go out into the lines and kill all the enemy troops that they can." Christians were more effective at bringing peace and security because they took up the "whole armor of God" (Eph. 6:11). While others fought, Christians prayed. By their prayers the believers "destroy all demons which stir up wars, violate oaths, and disturb the peace." By praying and performing ascetic practices the Christians were "cooperating in the tasks of the community." No, they would not fight for the emperor; but the Christians were a "special army of piety through [their] intercessions to God." Spiritual warfare leads to the destruction of "everything which is . . . hostile to those who act rightly."[136]

Prayer, Origen was convinced, actually makes a difference. In the early Christian tradition, Origen viewed prayer as a resource of unimaginable power. Intercessions are more powerful than armies, so Christians contribute most to the common good by their prayers.[137] Indeed, it was the early Christians' practice of prayer that empowered them and gave them buoyancy. Because they believed that God answers prayers, they could take risks, live lives that were eventful and imprudent, and be faithful to a *superstitio* that could get them into hot water. There was power here, and outsiders got a whiff of it and wanted in.[138] Scholars have noted in bewilderment that the early Christians did not spend a lot of time praying for the conversion of outsiders.[139] Instead, energized by the power of God that they experienced in worship, many of them lived interesting lives. And the rumors got out. Christian worship was a place of empowerment. "Who," Origen asked, "on hearing these things, will not be summoned to the army of God? Who will not be inspired to fight for the church against the enemies of the truth?"[140] The outsiders wanted access to the power center of prayer.

Fencing the Prayers

The third-century community in Syria that produced the *Didascalia apostolorum* was open to receiving outsiders who would repent and say "I believe."

136. Origen, *Cels.* 8.73 (Chadwick, 509).
137. For examples of others who believed similarly, see Aristides, *Apol.* 16.6; Hippolytus, *Comm. Dan.* 3.24.7.
138. See, e.g., *Passion of Perpetua* 9.1.
139. Yves Congar, "Souci du salut des païens et conscience missionaire dans le Christianisme postapostolique et préconstantinien," in *Kyriakon: Festschrift Johannes Quasten,* ed. Patrick Granfield and Josef A. Jungmann (Münster: Aschendorff, 1970), 4–6. To the examples that Congar cites (1 Clem. 59.4; Ignatius, *To the Ephesians* 10.1; Aristides, *Apol.* 17.2; Justin, *Dial.* 108; *Did. apost.* 2.56; Cyprian, *Dom. or.* 17), I add the following: Clement of Alexandria, *Strom.* 7.7.41; 7.12.80; *Did. apost.* 5.16.3; Justin, *Dial.* 35.8; Pol. *Phil.* 12.3; Cyprian, *Demetr.* 20; Pontius, *Vit. Cypr.* 9; *Const.* 8.10.16.
140. Origen, *Hom. Num.* 25.4.3 (Scheck, 157).

It would admit them a certain distance—to the congregation to hear the homilies. But it would not admit them to "communicate in prayer," at least not quickly. First they had to participate in the catechumenate: they had to hear the Word, submit themselves, and leave the service after the homily and before the common prayer. When "they [saw] that they [did] not *communicate* with the church," and when this wore on them, *then* they would truly submit themselves. They would "repent of their former deeds and seek reception into the church *for prayer*." It was prayer that the outsiders wanted, and prayer that the church so carefully protected.[141]

Why was this community so concerned to fence in its prayer? Because its leaders recognized how important prayer was for their lives and witness, and they knew that if the relationships in the community were broken, their prayers could be frustrated and even nullified. Of course, tensions would arise between members who got angry with each other. These had to be reconciled immediately, for lasting anger begets sin. The *Didascalia* points to a liturgical statement of Jesus that the community took with great seriousness: "If you are making your offering upon the altar and there recall that your brother is angry with you, leave your offering before the altar and go first to be reconciled with your brother. Then go to make your offering" (Matt. 5:23–24).[142] The community's offering to God was its "prayer and Eucharist." But, the *Didascalia* warns, "if you continue in anger with your brother, or he with you," these will be stymied, stifled; "your prayer shall not be heard, nor shall your Eucharist be accepted." Even if believers pray often—three times in an hour—their prayer shall be unfruitful, for "God will not listen to you on account of your hostility towards your brother." So the *Didascalia* urges its community's members to go and make peace with their brothers and sisters. "Forgive your neighbour and your prayer will be heard and the offering which you make shall be acceptable to the Lord."[143] To facilitate the reconciliation, the *Didascalia* establishes a conflict resolution process led by the bishop.[144] What if a flood of new people suddenly came to the *Didascalia*'s community, attracted by powerful prayer? The results could be dire. If the newcomers, who had not submitted to the formational process of catechesis, brought into

---

141. *Did. apost.* 2.39.6, trans. and ed. Alistair Stewart-Sykes, *The Didascalia apostolorum: An English Version*, Studia Traditionis Theologiae 1 (Turnhout: Brepols, 2009), 162, with emphasis added. Similarly, in Pontus in the mid-third century, Bishop Gregory stated his policy of admitting penitents and catechumens to "the Scriptures and doctrine" but excluding them from "the privilege of prayer" (Gregory, *Canonical Epistle* 11, trans. S. D. F. Salmond, *ANF* 6:20).

142. *Did. apost.* 2.53.2–3 (Stewart-Sykes, 172).

143. *Did. apost.* 2.53.4–5, 9 (Stewart-Sykes, 172–73).

144. *Did. apost.* 2.54.1–2.56.4. For a discussion of this, see chap. 8 below. Also see Alan Kreider, "Peacemaking in Worship in the Syrian Church Orders," *SL* 34, no. 2 (2004): 177–90.

the church the anger-producing, resentment-cherishing habitus of the wider society, the effects on the community's prayer and worship would be devastating. At war with each other, the community's members would be unable to pray freely. They would be powerless against the pressures of the society that surrounded it. They knew that if a community whose strength is prayer is unable to pray, the community will atrophy!

Jesus's Law of Prayer

It was not only the Syrian community of the *Didascalia apostolorum* that ascribed binding authority to Jesus's liturgical saying found in Matthew 5:23–24. Other communities also recognized that right relationships are a condition for authentic worship. Cyprian, in his famous treatise *On Unity*, gives this a name—Jesus's "law of prayer." This rule prescribes that a member who comes to worship angry cannot pray until he is reconciled with his brother; only then can he offer his gifts to God.[145] In his treatise *On the Lord's Prayer*, Cyprian repeats this "clear rule." "God does not accept the sacrifice of one who is in dispute, and sends him back from the altar, ordering him first to be reconciled to his brother, so that he may pacify God by praying as a peacemaker. The *greater sacrifice to God* is our peace and brotherly agreement, as a people unified in the unity of the Father and the Son and the Holy Spirit."[146]

Tertullian agrees. According to his treatise *On Prayer*, the church's most important instruction about prayer is simple: reconciliation is a precondition for prayer. Before beginning to pray, Christians must resolve any "offense or discord" they have with other believers. Tertullian cites the familiar passage Matthew 5:23–24: "We should not go up to the altar of God before resolving whatever there might be of offence or discord contracted with the brothers." He equates anger toward a brother with homicide. "How can one approach the peace of God without peace?"[147] With differing nuances Tertullian and Cyprian said the same thing: for Tertullian the Christians' prayer was their "rich and better sacrifice" (*opimam et maiorem hostiam*); for Cyprian the Christians' reconciled brotherly agreement was their "greater sacrifice to God" (*sacrificium Deo maius*).[148] For both writers, prayer was central to Christian worship. It was the offering of people whose life "in the peace of God" was expressed by the peace that they enjoyed with each other. This peace was monitored and enabled by the church leaders, who hedged the peace by restricting access to

---

145. Cyprian, *Unit. eccl.* 13 (Wallis, FC 36, 108).
146. Cyprian, *Dom. or.* 23 (Stewart-Sykes, *Lord's Prayer*, 82–83, with emphasis added).
147. Tertullian, *Or.* 11 (Stewart-Sykes, *Lord's Prayer*, 49–50).
148. Tertullian, *Apol.* 30.5 (Glover, 153); Cyprian, *Dom. or.* 23 (Stewart-Sykes, *Lord's Prayer*, 83).

prayer. And the peace was expressed bodily by a rite—the kiss of peace with which the brothers and sisters greeted each other in every eucharistic service.

Kiss of Peace

After the believers have concluded the prayers, according to Tertullian "they shall give the kiss of peace." Tertullian is the inventor of the term "the kiss of peace."[149] According to him, the kiss looks backward. As "the seal of prayer" it validates the prayer that precedes it. How, he asked, "can prayer be complete when it is divorced from the holy kiss? . . . What sort of sacrifice is that from which one departs without making peace?"[150] Tertullian here represented the evening banquet tradition, in which free worship including prayers ends the evening that began with the Lord's Supper at table. But for Justin, Cyprian, and others in the morning service tradition that gradually replaced the evening banquet, the exchange of the kiss also looks forward. It prepares the people for the Eucharist that immediately followed the prayers. When Tertullian wrote, peacemaking in worship already had a considerable history. From a very early date, both the author of the Didache and Hermas saw reconciliation as a precondition for the community to celebrate the Lord's Supper; and in the mid-second century, in the early stages of the morning service tradition, Justin Martyr reported that in his Roman house church "we greet each other with a kiss" after the common prayers, evidently as a means of preparing relationships for the Eucharist that followed immediately.[151]

In the morning service tradition, the peace greeting occupied a sensitive, crucial position between these central actions of early Christian worship, the prayers and the Lord's Supper. The kiss of peace formed a ritual bridge between them that had its own significance. At the heart of Christian worship was a community whose habitus both celebrated and made peace.

Inculturating the Kiss

The kiss is a fascinating example of inculturation. The Christians adopted a practice of the wider culture and gave it a meaning that was distinctive and

149. Tertullian, *Or.* 18. For studies of the kiss of peace, see Michael Philip Penn, *Kissing Christians: Ritual and Community in the Late Ancient Church* (Philadelphia: University of Pennsylvania Press, 2005); L. Edward Phillips, *The Ritual Kiss in Early Christian Worship*, Alcuin/GROW Joint Liturgical Studies 36 (Cambridge: Grove Books, 1996); Eleanor Kreider, "Let the Faithful Greet Each Other: The Kiss of Peace," *Conrad Grebel Review* 5 (1987): 29–49.
150. Tertullian, *Or.* 18 (Stewart-Sykes, *Lord's Prayer*, 54).
151. *Did.* 14.2; 15.3; Herm. Vis. 3.9.10; Justin, *1 Apol.* 65.2 (Hardy, 286).

potent. In Greco-Roman society the kiss was important, but people were squeamish about discussing it; there is very little pagan literature on kissing.[152] Of course, the family was the primary nexus of relationships in which people kissed. Parents and children kissed each other, as did married couples. At times, friends kissed each other.[153] But the kiss was bounded; it was an expression of affection and love within acceptable limits, and by and large these were private. Beyond those limits, in public life, the kiss was demonstrative and utilitarian; it was "a symbol of social stratification and status," a ritual of hierarchy.[154] The kiss of greeting had its place in court ceremonial; depending on rank, people kissed the hem of the emperor's robe, his knee, or his hand. Also there was kissing between established figures and inferior people, sycophants, men of ambition. "How did you come to be a judge? Whose hand did you kiss?" Rank was all-important, and only equals "kissed on the level."[155]

Into this world came the Christians, who were not reticent to mention the kiss. Already in the New Testament, writers admonish members of the fledgling Christian communities to greet one another by means of a kiss. In the first New Testament letter, Paul urges the Thessalonians—who were manifestly not all "equals"—to "greet all the brethren with a holy kiss" (1 Thess. 5:26). Three other letters close with the same phrase.[156] And 1 Peter 5:14 uses "the kiss of love." Often these phrases are surrounded by references to peace: "Agree with one another, live in peace; and the God of love and peace will be with you. Greet one another with a holy kiss" (2 Cor. 13:11–12). Scholars have speculated that the background to these "kissing Christians" is Jesus himself, whom a disciple greeted at a traumatic moment in a way that was evidently habitual—Judas's kiss (Matt. 26:49).[157]

Religious movements rarely emphasize the kiss. As William Klassen has noted wryly, "Ethical teachers are not noted for urging people to kiss."[158] And it raises the question: why did the leaders of the early churches see the kiss as important? Is it possible that Paul and other Christian leaders urged their people to exchange the kiss greeting because it was a practice that could sustain a Christlike habitus across time? But kissing in a religious setting was countercultural, and it made early Christians uncomfortable—like the

152. William Klassen, "The Sacred Kiss in the New Testament: An Example of Social Boundary Lines," *New Testament Studies* 39 (1993): 126.

153. Klaus Thraede, "Kuss," in *RAC* 22 (2007): 549.

154. Ibid., 551.

155. Ramsay MacMullen, *Corruption and the Decline of Rome* (New Haven: Yale University Press, 1988), 63, 127.

156. See Rom. 16:16; 1 Cor. 16:20; 2 Cor. 13:12.

157. Klassen, "Sacred Kiss," 128–29; Penn, *Kissing Christians*, 18–19.

158. Klassen, "Sacred Kiss," 130.

washing of feet does for many Christians today.[159] So they had to practice it, and they had to be *reminded* to practice it! Because they needed constant counterformation, they needed to make the kiss not just a part of baptismal or other special services but a part of the regular life of their congregations, a sine qua non of their worship.

Why was this practice so important? Because the kiss of peace (as it came to be called) in an embodied way defined their identity, and because it maintained their life as communities of peace.

- *Identity*: The Christians were a new family of brothers and sisters in Christ that members entered through baptism. The family was nongenetic, transnational, and catholic in every sense. In it, people who in the wider society were manifestly unequal—poor and less poor people, literates and illiterates, women and men—manifested their equality. In this bodily gesture people who did not belong together experienced "unity" in a new bounded society. By means of the kiss, family members, in the presence of God, developed a habitus that expressed their love for each other and enabled them to experience "radical intimacy."[160] In the kiss the members experienced embodied worship; with emotion and passion they knew the reality of what Pentecostal theologian Steven Land calls "orthopathy."[161] Their hearts were stirred not least because, in the perspective of the wider society, what they were doing together was improbable and reprehensible. Week by week, the kiss they exchanged convinced them that the new social reality was solid and satisfying, and it bonded them anew to each other.

- *Reconciliation*: Christians, this catholic (nonhomogeneous) group of people, had to learn to live together. This was not easy. They missed each other's cultural cues, and they offended each other. Together they were in the process of learning the cues of the new habitus they were developing, but this took time. They viewed their common life as a miracle, but they were on a journey in which miscues and misunderstandings were inevitable. So when they assembled for their weekly services in which they prayed and shared in the Lord's Supper, in the kiss of peace they celebrated their unity in Christ and asked forgiveness

---

159. Thomas O'Loughlin, "From a Damp Floor to a New Vision of Church: Footwashing as a Challenge to Liturgy and Discipleship," *Worship* 88, no. 2 (March 2014): 137–50.

160. L. Edward Phillips, "The Ritual Kiss in Early Christian Worship" (PhD diss., University of Notre Dame, 1992), 270.

161. Steven J. Land, *Pentecostal Spirituality: A Passion for the Kingdom* (Sheffield: Sheffield Academic Press, 1993), 13, 136.

for their sins that hurt each other. Cyprian, a bishop who knew about this practice, called it "the maintenance of peace." Quoting Jesus's seventh Beatitude, Cyprian noted that by definition the children of God are "makers of peace." They are "gentle of heart, guileless of tongue, harmonious of sentiment, sincerely attached to one another by the bond of a common mind."[162] But he knew that Christians were not always like that, that they had conflicts and disputes; and the consequences of this were frightening: "God does not accept the sacrifice of one who is in dispute." So God "sends him back from the altar, ordering him first to be reconciled to his brother, so that he may pacify God by praying as a peacemaker."[163] In every week's worship service, the kiss of peace was the practice in which the believers who were at peace blessed each other in the peace of Christ, and in which, when they recognized that they were not reconciled, they (under the supervision of the bishop) could experience God's peacemaking. Then, as reconciled siblings in God's family, they could eat together at the Lord's table.

What did the peace greeting look like in a typical weekly service? The sources give us a few hints. Around AD 200 in Tertullian's Carthage the prayers came at the end of the church's evening banquet worship. But in Rome fifty years before that, in the first description both of the morning service model and of the kiss in worship, Justin Martyr presents the kiss as the bridge between the prayers and the Eucharist. Evidently describing his house church in Rome, Justin recounts the arrival of a newly baptized believer among "those who are called brothers, where they are assembled." With the new brother in their midst, the congregation "earnestly" offered common prayers for their range of concerns, including their new brother. When they finished the prayers, they "greet[ed] each other with a kiss" and then celebrated the Lord's Supper.[164] The *Apostolic Tradition*, sometime thereafter, supplies additional details.[165] On weekdays, after the morning teaching sessions attended by both believers and catechumens, the kiss was exchanged, but only by the faithful—men greeting men, and women greeting women. The catechumens prayed separately and did not give the peace: "Their kiss is not yet holy."[166]

162. Cyprian, *Unit. eccl.* 24, trans. Maurice Bévenot (Oxford: Clarendon, 1971), 97.
163. Cyprian, *Dom. or.* 23 (Stewart-Sykes, *Lord's Prayer*, 83). For a parallel passage, see Tertullian, *Or.* 11.
164. Justin, *1 Apol.* 65.2 (Hardy, 286).
165. BJP, 124 states that the *Apostolic Tradition*'s "core material may well go back to the mid-second century."
166. *Trad. ap.* 18.2–4 (BJP, 100).

Their kiss became holy when they were baptized and the bishop kissed them. Then they were brought into the congregation to "pray together with all the people." After this, the *Apostolic Tradition* says, "Let them offer the peace with the mouth." The Eucharist then ensued.[167]

Neither of these accounts tells us how the leaders or congregation behaved, or how the new believers experienced their prayerful and kissful incorporation in the body. From less systematic documents we get hints about the tone of the assemblies and the behavior of the prayers. Tertullian emphasizes that the kiss after the prayer was "an activity in which all participate." "All" would include a considerable variety of people, including an evidently prosperous woman whose pagan husband's outrage would not be mollified by the thought that the Christian brothers whom she was kissing were members of her new family.[168] Michael Philip Penn sees the kiss as a "tool for creating group unity" in the church.[169] It did this by being an embodied practice that bonded the group emotionally. In 250 the exiled Cyprian communicated this bonding in a letter to confessors in Carthage who had refused to burn incense to the gods: "There is nothing which could give me greater pleasure or more noble delight than at this moment to be kissing those lips of yours which have confessed the Lord."[170] But, whatever good it did for the Christian community, the kiss could also cause trouble with the Christians' genetic families.[171]

The kiss of peace was no doubt a major cause of rumors alleging orgiastic behavior among Christians. At times some Christian groups evidently did behave outrageously.[172] Even leaders of groups that behaved relatively well were alert to inevitable dangers. Athenagoras referred to Christians in late second-century Athens who, at the time of the peace greeting, kiss "twice because it was pleasurable."[173] In the early third century, Clement complained of believers in Alexandria whose kissing was noisy. "There are some," he bewailed, "who make the assembly resound with nothing but their kisses." They should greet one another, he said, with "a mouth that is chaste and self-controlled."[174] Christian leaders such as Origen, who early in his life had been an impassioned kisser of martyrs, later was concerned that the kiss of peace must be chaste; like the *Apostolic Tradition* he seems to have limited the kiss

167. *Trad. ap.* 21.25–26 (BJP, 120).

168. Tertullian, *Or.* 18 (Stewart-Sykes, *Lord's Prayer*, 54); *Ux.* 2.4.

169. Penn, *Kissing Christians*, 45.

170. Cyprian, *Ep.* 6.1.1, trans. G. W. Clarke, ACW 43 (1984), 63.

171. Penn, *Kissing Christians*, 45.

172. Stephen Benko, "The Libertine Gnostic Sect of the Phibionites according to Epiphanius," VC 21 (1967): 103–19.

173. Athenagoras, *Leg.* 32.5, trans. W. R. Schoedel (Oxford: Clarendon, 1972), 81.

174. Clement, *Paed.* 3.11.81–82, trans. S. P. Wood, FC 23 (1954), 261.

to the same sex, thereby adding to the momentum that would steadily cut down the catholicity of the reconciling.[175] Nevertheless, the kiss was important. For every outsider who might be put off by rumors of Christian misbehavior, there were others who were amazed and attracted by rumors of Christians who in their worship kissed unequals. Christians were enacting a new world in which equality and reconciliation were possible.

Unity and Peace

For Tertullian, as for many early Christian leaders, the "primary instruction" was not how to handle the sexual overtones of kissing. It was rather how to prepare the believers, in a radically new way, to pray in unity and peace. This was urgently essential, because like many early Christian thinkers Tertullian was convinced that God would not hear the prayers of an angry Christian whose relationships were broken.[176] On this matter Cyprian was even more categorical than Tertullian.[177] We do not know how, in the worship services in Tertullian's and Cyprian's churches, the peace greeting began. In the churches of the Syrian *Didascalia* the beginning is clear. The bishops, recalling Matthew 5:23–24, were to initiate the peace: "Bishops, it is so that your prayers and oblations may be acceptable that, when you are standing at prayer in the church, a deacon calls out in a loud voice: 'Is there anyone who maintains anger with his neighbour?' And if persons who have a lawsuit or a quarrel between themselves are found you may persuade them and make peace between them."[178]

According to the *Didascalia* the believers then would go about, exchange greetings, and (if they were estranged from people) make peace. The kiss may have been a part of the greetings, but the *Didascalia* does not mention it. A century or so later in Jerusalem, Bishop Cyril, in his instructions on worship to the newly baptized, did mention the kiss—at the same place in the service, right after the deacon's invitation to reconciliation.[179] So in the same period in Asia Minor did Bishop Theodore of Mopsuestia, who found it hard to bring injured parties together at the time of the kiss because there were so many people in the assemblies.[180] In Syria, Jerusalem, and Asia Minor, as in

175. Eusebius, *Hist. eccl.* 6.3.4; Origen, *Comm. Rom.* 10.33; see also *Trad. ap.* 18.2.
176. Tertullian, *Or.* 11.
177. Cyprian, *Dom. or.* 23.
178. *Did. apost.* 2.54.1 (Stewart-Sykes, 173).
179. Cyril, *Mystagogic Catechesis* 5.3. On the authorship and dating of these catecheses, see Maxwell E. Johnson, "Christian Initiation in Fourth-Century Jerusalem and Recent Developments in the Study of the Sources," *Ecclesia Orans* 26 (2009): 143–61.
180. Theodore of Mopsuestia, *Mystagogic Catechesis* 4.34–41.

Tertullian's and Cyprian's North Africa, the church leaders recommended a physical gesture of peace as essential—both to enact reconciliation and to create a condition for a valid eucharistic service. So peace greetings took place, week after week. In many places they involved the kiss of peace, and they shaped the habitus of Christians.

Peace Spills Out

What effect did this practice have? In addition to reconciling the community's members and enabling their worship, the peace greeting spilled out into their lives. The Christians carried peace with them. According to Tertullian, when Christians visited a home, they said, "Peace to this house." How, he asks the believers, could you do this "unless you give peace to those who are in the house in return for that received?"[181] Christians visited confessors in prison and kissed their chains.[182] In Perpetua's North African community, the kiss of peace appears in dreams and visions.[183] The "peace" built a sense of transgeographical family. Communities in Egypt received strangers from other cities as "brothers," allowing them to take part in the Lord's Supper and no doubt sharing materially with them, when they came "in peace" with the recommendation of another church.[184] In martyrdoms—those of Perpetua and her companions, but also of Habib and Amuna and others—the kiss of peace figures prominently.[185]

The kiss of peace also shaped Christian witness. Believers, many of them poor, emerged from worship with the exhilarating knowledge that they had kissed unequals on the level. *I, a struggling stoneworker, have kissed a decurion!* Whatever others might say about them, the believers knew that they were people of worth, brothers and sisters in Christ. They knew this in their bodies. Outsiders would look at them and wonder what had happened to them in worship that gave them dignity and confidence. Of course, despite the reputation that Christians cultivated for loving their enemies, they did not always deal peaceably with each other.[186] Unreconciled conflict was bad wit-

181. Tertullian, *Or.* 26 (Stewart-Sykes, *Lord's Prayer*, 62).
182. Tertullian, *Ux.* 2.4.
183. *Passion of Perpetua* 10.13: in Perpetua's fourth vision, her trainer kissed her and said, "Peace be with you, daughter"; 12.6: in Saturus's vision, the elders rose and "gave the kiss of peace"; trans. Maureen A. Tilley, in *Religions of Late Antiquity in Practice*, ed. Richard Valantasis (Princeton: Princeton University Press, 2000), 393–94.
184. Luijendijk, *Greetings in the Lord*, 86, 88, 123.
185. *Passion of Perpetua* 21.7; *Martyrdom of Shamuna, Guria, and Habib* (ANF 8:700); Eusebius, *Hist. eccl.* 2.8.
186. See 2 Clem. 13.4.

ness. It caused the Christians, fearing that pagans would note their hypocrisy, to press the alienated brothers to be "reconciled in peace, so that in Christ's name we may celebrate peace with joy."[187] Everywhere in the morning service tradition the peace prepared Christians to participate in the Eucharist.

Conclusion

The growth of the church in the early centuries was a product of the church's worship. That this would be so is counterintuitive because for most of this period the church excluded nonbaptized people from their worship. But there is one early Christian text that documents their approach, crisply and completely. In the late 330s, somewhere in Egypt, an unknown writer compiled the *Canons of Hippolytus*, a church order that revised the *Apostolic Tradition*. Occasionally its compiler altered the text so that it reflected changing conditions, and at times the compiler had a kind of imaginative breakthrough that expressed the assumptions that undergirded the *Apostolic Tradition*'s practice. One of these breakthroughs came as the compiler finished the lengthy description of the baptismal candidates' journey. The candidates have traveled from exploring the faith, through scrutiny and catechesis, to the climax and culmination—baptism and the Eucharist. The newly baptized Christians stand, "born again like little children," and receive the milk and honey of the age to come. And the compiler exults:

> Thus [the baptized catechumens] have become *complete* Christians and have been fed with the body of Christ. They will strive in wisdom, so that their life may shine with virtue, not before each other only, but also before the Gentiles so that they may imitate them and become Christians and *see* that the progress of those who have been illuminated is high and better than the common behaviour of people.[188]

Worship and catechesis have formed the new Christians so they are *kāmil* (Arabic)—complete, accomplished, and whole.[189] Other people look at these fully developed Christians and can *see* that they behave uncommonly,

---

187. *Gesta apud Zenophilum* 9; in *Paganism and Christianity, 100–425 CE: A Sourcebook*, ed. Ramsay MacMullen and Eugene N. Lane (Minneapolis: Fortress, 1992), 253.

188. *The Canons of Hippolytus* (19), ed. Paul F. Bradshaw, trans. Carol Bebawi, Alcuin/GROW Liturgical Study 2 (Bramcote, UK: Grove Books, 1987), 24–25, with emphasis added. The parallel passage (*Trad. ap.* 21.38 [BJP 122]) is less expansive: "And when these things have been done, let each one hasten to do good work."

189. *Les Canons D'Hippolyte*, ed. René-Georges Coquin, Patrologia Orientalis 31, fascicle 2 (Paris: Firmin-Didot, 1966), 384–85.

attractively. As a result, new people are inquisitive and then come forward to become catechumens, and when they are fully formed they are baptized. They in turn, as new Christians who are nourished by worship, fascinate others by their distinctive witness. The process repeats itself, and the church grows.

8

"WISE DOVES" IN THE
DIDASCALIA APOSTOLORUM

It is time for us to become more patient—to slow down and narrow our focus. It's tempting to generalize broadly about the early Christians, especially because so little information about them has survived. We know nothing about most churches, and for many geographical areas we have only scattered bits of information. It is hard to be concrete.

However, occasionally a source such as *The Teaching of the Apostles* comes to our assistance. This document, generally known by its Latin name, the *Didascalia apostolorum*, provides a mass of information dense enough to give a good sense of what was going on in a particular region. The *Didascalia* shows us real people in action—deaconesses washing the feet of the sick, rich people skipping worship services because they will be asked to give to the poor, and laypeople being "like wise doves, at peace with one another, striving to fill the church."[1] Of course, even the *Didascalia* won't permit us to freeze-frame a community on a particular day or year. But although it is geographically limited, the *Didascalia* is chronologically expansive and gives us not a snapshot but a moving picture of a community across a period of time.

---

1. See *Did. apost.* 2.56.4, trans. and ed. Alistair Stewart-Sykes, *The Didascalia apostolorum: An English Version*, Studia Traditionis Theologiae 1 (Turnhout: Brepols, 2009), 174.

The *Didascalia* is a church order that comes from a cluster of communities in Syria in the third century whose members have "seen great light, Jesus Christ our Lord."[2] Like other church orders, it provides guidance for church leaders about ways to structure the life of Christian communities—their leadership, their liturgical life, and their approach to social and ethical problems. The *Didascalia* is a major piece of writing, which in its most recent English translation extends to over 160 pages. Its only complete surviving text is in Syriac, but most scholars think it was originally written in Greek.[3] It provides solid, specific, and "thick" information about its Christian communities. This is the most detailed source for the pre-Constantinian period from anywhere, East or West. And, for our purposes, the *Didascalia* is valuable because it provides a picture of Christian communities at a time when the church, not yet associated with power, was growing by attraction.

Forming Communities of Jews and Gentiles

Where were the *Didascalia*'s communities? In an area, probably in Syria, where Jews and gentiles were close neighbors. They "walked along the same streets, did their shopping at the common market-place, suffered from the same diseases, epidemics and wars, and therefore shared a lot of ideas and concepts about which they talked with each other."[4] Intriguingly, the *Didascalia* ushers us into a world in which Jews and gentiles were not only neighbors but also members together in the same communities of faith. In third-century Syria the categories that we assume about this period—"rabbinic Judaism" and "Christianity"—were not yet fixed.[5] The *Didascalia* addresses "you of the [Jewish] people who have come to belief in Jesus . . . and have seen great light, Jesus Christ Our Lord," and it immediately goes on to address "you who are of the gentiles. . . . When Jesus Christ our Lord and teacher appeared a light dawned upon you as you looked upon and put your trust in the promise of an everlasting Kingdom. You removed yourself far from the

2. *Did. apost.* 5.16.3 (Stewart-Sykes, 218).
3. Paul F. Bradshaw, *The Search for the Origins of Christian Worship: Sources and Methods for the Study of Early Liturgy*, 2nd ed. (New York: Oxford University Press, 2002), 79. Substantial fragments survive in a sixth-century Latin document.
4. Han J. W. Drijvers, "Syrian Christianity and Judaism," in *The Jews among Pagans and Christians*, ed. Judith Lieu, John North, and Tessa Rajak (London: Routledge, 1992), 128; quoted by Charlotte Elisheva Fonrobert, "The *Didascalia apostolorum*: A Mishnah for the Disciples of Jesus," *JECS* 9, no. 4 (2001): 488.
5. Fonrobert, "*Didascalia apostolorum*," 485, 508; Daniel Boyarin, *Dying for God: Martyrdom and the Making of Christianity and Judaism* (Stanford, CA: Stanford University Press, 1999), chaps. 1–2.

habitual conduct of former times . . . but have believed and been baptized in him."[6] In its style and tone, the *Didascalia*'s idiom is Jewish; as Charlotte Elisheva Fonrobert comments, it is "one of the voices of Judaism."[7] In that idiom it confesses Jesus to be the Messiah, and its communities' members are gentile as well as Jewish.[8]

When was this fascinating text written? Scholars used to date the *Didascalia* with some confidence in the 230s. But recently in a new edition Alistair Stewart-Sykes has challenged this. Stewart-Sykes argues that the *Didascalia* was not written at one time but, like other church orders, was a work of "living literature," pasted together from materials written across a century or more—possibly from the early third to early fourth centuries.[9] Not all scholars agree with Stewart-Sykes's approach or the dates he assigns to specific parts of the *Didascalia*.[10] But his approach is helpful—it enables us to read the *Didascalia*'s text modestly and to make sense of some of its unevennesses and inconsistencies. Alas, his approach is also frustrating, because as we read the lines (and between the lines), we observe communities in flux, with major changes taking place that we can't date precisely. As leadership styles, relationships between rich and poor, and the participation of women in outreach all change, uncertainties about the date of segments of the text keep us from dating these changes confidently. Our conclusions will have to be provisional.

But how interesting the *Didascalia* is. Its authors were evidently writing for a cluster of communities, of varying sizes, within easy communicating distance of each other. Some of them clearly were growing. To be sure, some communities were smaller than others. For example, the *Didascalia* provided instructions for communities that were too small to appoint from among their members a bishop who was aged at least fifty, and even who was "lettered"; other communities were big enough to assume the bishop's age and literacy.[11] Some communities had good-sized assemblies that were struggling with issues

---

6. *Did. apost.* 5.16.4–6 (Stewart-Sykes, 218).

7. Fonrobert, "*Didascalia apostolorum*," 487.

8. For other readings of the *Didascalia*, see Anders Ekenberg, "Evidence for Jewish Believers in 'Church Orders' and Liturgical Texts," in *Jewish Believers in Jesus: The Early Centuries*, ed. Oskar Skarsaune and Reidar Hvalvik (Peabody, MA: Hendrickson, 2007), 649–52; Robin Lane Fox, *Pagans and Christians* (San Francisco: Harper & Row, 1986), 557–60.

9. See Stewart-Sykes's introduction to his edition of the *Didascalia apostolorum*, with a summary of his argument on 54. For "living literature," see Bradshaw, *Search for the Origins*, 82–83.

10. See, e.g., the review by Paul F. Bradshaw in *Worship* 84, no. 5 (2010): 474–75.

11. *Did. apost.* 2.1.2 (Stewart-Sykes, 117–18). However, those who were "unlettered" were to be "persuasive and skillful with words, and of advanced years."

of crowding and space: "if there is no room," the church has to do different things than it will if "there is room."[12] In general the churches were apparently growing, at peace with their neighbors but aware that persecution hovered over them ("If we are called to martyrdom"). As the churches grew, despite potential danger, the *Didascalia* taught new believers in Jesus to "imitate his teaching and his patience."[13]

Coping with Growth

The *Didascalia*'s authors were not particularly concerned about mission. They assumed the churches were growing but didn't write much about growth. Significantly, they didn't urge the clergy or laity to evangelize. According to their understanding, spreading the message was God's work, and it was their calling to be "helpers for God."[14] But they wanted their communities to develop practices that expressed the gospel with integrity, both in their members' relationship to outsiders and especially in their behavior toward each other. And they were concerned for the communities to navigate through changes they were experiencing from the late second century onward as a result of the churches' growth. These changes had many dimensions:

- The communities' leaders, traditionally unpaid and bivocational, were less and less able to cope with the challenges facing them.
- A caste of professional clergy—bishops and deacons—had emerged, supported financially by the giving of nonclerical Christians (the laity).
- The clergy attempted to reduce the influence of Christians who had been central to the life of the church in the era of volunteerism—eminent laypeople, householders who had wealth and social clout, and also enthusiastic laypeople, notably women who spontaneously took the lead in the churches' missional outreach.
- As the number of members and converts increased, so also did sin and misbehavior in the communities.
- Increased misbehavior in turn led to the development of programs of catechesis and penance.[15]

12. *Did. apost.* 2.57.8 (Stewart-Sykes, 176).
13. *Did. apost.* 5.6.2; 5.7.24 (Stewart-Sykes, 204, 210).
14. *Did. apost.* 2.54.4 (Stewart-Sykes, 173).
15. This list of changes owes much to Georg Schöllgen, "From Monepiscopate to Monarchical Episcopate: The Emergence of a New Relationship between Bishop and Community in the Third Century," *The Jurist* 66 (2006): 114–28.

As these changes were under way, the *Didascalia* faced in two directions—toward the Jews and toward the gentiles. In their dealings with the Jews, the *Didascalia*'s authors were on home ground. They seem to have had easier access to the Jews than to the gentiles; they were evidently in frequent touch with Jewish acquaintances, friends, and family. But they were aware of many Jews who rejected Jesus as Messiah. These people, whom they called "the former people," were on the *Didascalia*'s social and intellectual horizon, and the authors referred to them with hope as those who yet will "come to believe in him."[16]

Freeing Jews from the "Secondary Legislation"

The *Didascalia*'s authors devoted most of their attention to other Jews—who may or may not have been members of the *Didascalia*'s communities. These people shared their commitment to Jesus as Messiah but continued to live by the entire Torah. The authors called these Jews "dear brothers," but they were concerned that their approach was burdensome and unsustainable.[17] To these people the *Didascalia*'s authors offered an alternative way to read the Hebrew Scriptures. They accepted the authority of the Law—the Ten Words of Exodus 20 preceding the golden-calf incident of Exodus 32. They called this "the Law" and contrasted it with the "secondary legislation" (*deuterōsis*)—the ceremonial, purity, and moral legislation that Moses gave to punish the people's infidelity. The Law as they defined it is indissoluble, but the secondary legislation is transitory because its provisions are intolerable—"chains" and "burdensome loads."[18] When Jesus came, he brought freedom; he "showed what is life-giving, and destroyed what avails nothing and abolished whatever does not give life," including the secondary legislation.[19] The *Didascalia*'s authors viewed the passages, from Exodus through Deuteronomy, in light of Jesus's invitation in Matthew 11:28: "Come to me, all who labor and are heavy-burdened, and I will give you rest." The Savior, the *Didascalia*'s authors argued, leads "us, who became his disciples from among the Hebrews, . . . away from our burdensome loads."[20] According to the *Didascalia*'s authors, this approach had transformed the lives of Jewish followers of Jesus in practical ways. For example, since the Messiah freed them from the secondary

16. *Did. apost.* 5.14.18; 5.16.4 (Stewart-Sykes, 216, 218).
17. *Did. apost.* 6.22.10 (Stewart-Sykes, 257).
18. *Did. apost.* 6.17.6 (Stewart-Sykes, 244).
19. *Did. apost.* 6.19.1 (Stewart-Sykes, 249).
20. *Did. apost.* 6.17.6 (Stewart-Sykes, 244).

legislation, women in menstrual flux no longer needed to absent themselves from prayer and the Eucharist in the churches. Further, the *Didascalia*'s authors observed that Jews who had repudiated the "secondary legislation" were able to live freely under Roman rule in a way that Jews who wanted to live under the entire Law could not. The authors appealed to these Jews directly. Since the Romans were ruling and the Jews were scattered among the gentiles, the Jews couldn't be obedient to the entire Torah: "You cannot stone the evildoer, nor execute adulterers, nor discharge the ministry of the sacrifices," and so on. But Jewish people who obeyed the Law and followed Christ could possess abundant blessings.[21] "[God] said in the Law 'You shall not kill', and so anyone who does kill is condemned in accordance with the Roman law and is so under the law. If you are conformed in what you do to the rule of the church and to the form of the Gospel you shall not be disappointed in putting your hope in the Lord."[22] The "you shall not kill" of Exodus 20:13 agrees with the Savior's law—the "simple law, pure and holy, in which the Saviour set his name"—which is "the rule of the church" that has left all killing behind.[23] In this reading of the Law, the *Didascalia* joined its understanding of ritual purity to its commitment to the sanctity of life characteristic of many early Christian communities.[24] Its authors knew that some Jewish people resonated with this approach.

Freeing Gentiles from "the Habitual Conduct of Former Error"

But the *Didascalia*'s authors didn't just appeal to Jews. They called all people, gentiles as well as Jews, to come to Jesus—to take his yoke upon them and find rest for their souls. As they pointed out, a yoke is designed to enable efficient lifting and to be shared between two equal parties. Within the *Didascalia*'s communities, because Jews and gentiles were yoked together in Christ, it became possible to carry out the Law—both the Decalogue and the teachings of the Messiah Jesus. The common obedience to the Law, they exulted, "governs and unites us in a single accord."[25] Further, gentile believers now joined with Jewish believers in prayer for "the people," so that many Jewish people might "find forgiveness . . . and return to the Lord Jesus Christ."[26]

21. *Did. apost.* 6.19.3 (Stewart-Sykes, 249).
22. *Did. apost.* 6.19.5 (Stewart-Sykes, 250).
23. *Did. apost.* 6.15.2 (Stewart-Sykes, 238).
24. Ronald J. Sider, ed., *The Early Church on Killing: A Comprehensive Sourcebook on War, Abortion, and Capital Punishment* (Grand Rapids: Baker Academic, 2012), 168–71.
25. *Did. apost.* 6.18.5 (Stewart-Sykes, 245).
26. *Did. apost.* 5.16.7 (Stewart-Sykes, 218).

The *Didascalia*'s approach to the Jews was rooted in debates with friends, but its approach to the gentiles was rooted in contact with people it knew less well in the surrounding society. The gentiles were omnipresent. They populated the bazaars, baths, and theaters, and they represented a culture that was seductive to both Jewish and gentile disciples of Jesus. The gospel was open to the gentiles: "And we do not even withhold life from the pagans when they repent, put away and reject their error."[27] But the route of these people to the life of the community was arduous. The church required them to abandon idolatrous worship and then submit themselves to a process of character formation so that they would no longer engage in "the habitual conduct of former error."[28]

The *Didascalia*'s authors noted that the number of gentiles was increasing in the Christian communities, but they did not urge Christians to tell potential members about the churches' intramural life. They didn't want pagans to know about Christians' failures—their conflicts and lawsuits, the occasions when their care of the poor broke down. And they didn't want to tell pagans about the Christian communities' worship. As the authors put it, "It is improper that what occurs or what is spoken in church should emerge and be revealed."[29] Nor did the authors discuss evangelistic methods or admonish believers to make a priority of converting the gentiles. Only once, exceptionally, did they urge members to seek the conversion of outsiders, "those who are wild."[30] In general the authors focused their attention on forming viable Christian communities, apparently in the belief that believers' lifestyle and virtues, as well as their mysterious common life, would attract pagan people to join the Christian communities.

Formation—Worship Shapes Habitus

How did this formation work? To get a sense of how the *Didascalia* attempted to form the character of its communities, let us attend a worship service of one of its communities. Although some of the *Didascalia*'s communities are evidently small, this one is substantial. Like most early Christian communities, it meets in a "house." At the east end sit the presbyters, surrounding the bishop's seat. Not far from the presbyters but separate from them are the laypeople—first the men and then the women. The young and the old, divided

---

27. *Did. apost.* 2.39.4 (Stewart-Sykes, 161).
28. *Did. apost.* 5.16.6 (Stewart-Sykes, 218).
29. *Did. apost.* 3.10.7 (Stewart-Sykes, 190).
30. *Did. apost.* 2.56.4 (Stewart-Sykes, 174).

by gender, have special places, and the children stand on one side. The bishop is responsible for the good ordering of the assembly, and the deacons are his agents for keeping order.[31]

In the community we are visiting, there are two deacons. One of these, the inside deacon, stands in front of the assembly to ensure that nobody sits in an inappropriate place or misbehaves. If anyone "is whispering or going to sleep or laughing or gesticulating," the deacon is to stop them.[32] The outside deacon stands in the doorway as a kind of bouncer, scanning everyone who comes to the services and making judgments about visitors who are not members of the community. If the visitor is a "daughter of the church" of good report in a nonheretical congregation, the deacon is to lead her to the place in the assembly that is appropriate for her. If the visitor is a presbyter, he is to sit with the presbyters; and if the visitor is a bishop, he is to sit with the bishop and be invited to address the people and possibly even pray over the cup in the Eucharist.[33]

But what if—while the service is under way and the bishop is speaking—a man or woman from this or another congregation arrives late, and what if this person "is honoured in the world"? The *Didascalia* makes it clear to the members that the bishop's teaching is of highest importance, so nothing should interrupt it—certainly not the late arrival of an eminent layperson. A brother should make a place for the rich person, and if there is no place for him, a brother who is "charitable and full of good will" and courtesy, should spontaneously get up, offer his seat, and stand nearby. The bishop should keep an eye on this, without slowing his teaching. But if he sees a young congregant who doesn't behave with the appropriate reflex and give his place, and therefore an elderly man or woman has to stand, the bishop is to shame the slacker, making the person stand at the back behind the others. And for good reason: in this way "those others may learn to give up their places to those who are more honourable."[34]

What if "a poor man or woman should arrive"? What if a poverty-stricken person comes, "whether from the same district or of another congregation, most especially if they are well on in years, and they have no place"? Then the bishop should do something exceptional: "you, bishop," the *Didascalia* orders, shall interrupt your sermon, and make a place for the poor people and give them your own chair. You "should act for them from your heart, even should you sit on the ground yourself."[35] The bishop—the community's

31. *Did. apost.* 2.57.3–6 (Stewart-Sykes, 175).
32. *Did. apost.* 2.57.10 (Stewart-Sykes, 176).
33. *Did. apost.* 2.58.1, 3 (Stewart-Sykes, 176).
34. *Did. apost.* 2.58.4–5 (Stewart-Sykes, 177).
35. *Did. apost.* 2.58.6 (Stewart-Sykes, 177).

leader—is to make a scene! By embodied example he is to teach behavior that demonstrates the community's convictions: that in the church all Christians are of worth; that the church has no special regard for wealthy or eminent people; and that the church honors poor people. In the assembly there shall be no "respect of persons" (or of worldly eminence).[36]

This account is an example of the community's leaders consciously shaping the assembly's habitus—its embodied order and behavior—which expresses its deep values. As we have seen in earlier chapters, habitus is reflexive behavior, learned over time by repeated bodily action. Every person has a habitus, as does every group. For the newcomers to replace their old habitus with a Christian habitus, they must be taught. And they must practice with their bodies. Although their habitus will change slowly, and at times awkwardly, it can change.[37] In the *Didascalia*'s community, changes with regard to respect of persons were taking place, making this kind of habitus training essential.

Bishops—Refusing to Be Respecters of Persons

So what was going on with "respect of persons"? The *Didascalia* hints that for some time changes had been taking place in the communities that had led to alterations in their leadership and functions.[38] The critical change in the *Didascalia*'s assemblies seems to have been a product of their low-key evangelism: their numbers were growing. The early Christian communities were relatively small; they met in a variety of domestic settings and were often hosted by the most prosperous person among them. These communities' leaders often were the owners of dwellings, and it was natural for members to accord respect of persons to their hosts and other eminent people. From the outset the churches had emphasized caring for the needy, and this involved many believers participating voluntarily. Evidently, evangelistic conversations with outsiders (Jews and gentiles) happened serendipitously, according to gift and opportunity; and when catechesis and baptismal preparations took place, they were casual and unsystematic. But late in the second century the

---

36. Georg Schöllgen, *Die Anfänge der Professionalisierung des Klerus und das kirchliche Amt in der syrischen Didaskalie*, Jahrbuch für Antike und Christentum, Ergänzungsband 26 (Münster: Aschendorff, 1998), 180–83. It is significant that, in the Syrian world of the *Didascalia*, the bishops' priority was not to court well-connected people but to curtail their power. The bishops seem to have assumed that the rich would stay and pay/give, and in due course the rich would themselves colonize the episcopacy. And, as the decurions became bishops throughout the third century, the *Didascalia*'s strategy seems to have been successful.

37. Pierre Bourdieu, *Pascalian Meditations*, trans. Richard Nice (Stanford, CA: Stanford University Press, 2000), 141–46, 161.

38. Schöllgen, *Die Anfänge der Professionalisierung des Klerus*, 3, 182–83.

church reached a tipping point. According to Georg Schöllgen, the church's numbers had grown to the point that their patterns of order and behavior were no longer working well and needed to be changed.[39]

The result is the kind of community whose habitus we see taking shape in the *Didascalia*. The *Didascalia*'s communities were led by bishops who were responsible for the welfare of the entire community. Increasingly, the bishops' authority was rooted not in their social eminence, education, or wealth but in their office and spiritual calling. Like the presbyters and deacons, the bishops were becoming a part of a clerical order that was visibly distinct from the laity. The bishops couldn't do everything; they delegated authority. But these leaders—called "fathers," "physicians," even "kings"—were responsible for the church's communal life, relief for the poor, and catechesis.[40]

According to the *Didascalia*, "the bishop should not be a respecter of persons, not one who stands in deference to the rich or who pleases them beyond what is right."[41] Many of "the rich," whom the *Didascalia* addresses directly, were unhappy with the bishops. They directed withering criticism at the bishops who, they alleged, didn't take proper care of the poor and even "despised" them.[42] When the bishops rebuffed their comments about discipline, the rich were irritated—wasn't it all right for them to whisper a word in the bishop's ear or put a contribution in their hand to protect someone from excommunication?[43] At times the rich stonewalled, expressing their disapprobation bodily by "distancing themselves" from the church. They evidently didn't want to be in worship services in which deacons pressured them to give money to an episcopally controlled central treasury.[44] To the rich, respect of persons seemed a sensible limitation on episcopal power.

The bishops responded by exercising the powers of their office. They were the teachers, able to distinguish "between the law and the secondary legislation."[45] They were the pastoral liturgists: in baptism, "through the imposition of the bishop's hand, the Lord bore witness to each of you, as his holy voice was heard saying, 'You are my son, this day I have begotten you.'"[46] They were the recipients of the people's donations so that they, collaborating with the deacons, could take on the burdens—food, clothing, and other

39. Schöllgen, "From Monepiscopate to Monarchical Episcopate," 115–16.
40. *Did. apost.* 2.33.1; 2.34.1; 2.41.3 (Stewart-Sykes, 155–56, 162).
41. *Did. apost.* 2.5.1 (Stewart-Sykes, 120–21).
42. *Did. apost.* 2.31.2 (Stewart-Sykes, 154).
43. *Did. apost.* 2.43.5.
44. *Did. apost.* 2.36.3–4 (Stewart-Sykes, 158–59).
45. *Did. apost.* 2.5.4 (Stewart-Sykes, 121).
46. *Did. apost.* 2.32.3 (Stewart-Sykes, 155).

necessities—of all the people.[47] Most crucially, they and not the rich members were the curators and promoters of the community's highest value—peace.

An Ecosystem of Peace

Peace is a theme that recurs repeatedly in the *Didascalia*.[48] In its authors' perspective, peace was at the core of the work of Jesus in the Gospels, where he urged his followers to imitate him in peacemaking.[49] The *Didascalia*'s authors were convinced that Jesus's peaceable way is salvific: "the way of peace is our Savior."[50] And they believed that Jesus called his church to reflect his work by living in right relationships and unanimity of spirit. To attain this they were convinced that the bishops must take the lead. They must "announce peace," embody peace, and "strive to make peace with all."[51] In all aspects of their ministry the bishops were to build and conserve the peace that is essential to the church's character; as the *Didascalia* puts it, they were to "shepherd the entire people in peace."[52] In its essence, according to the *Didascalia*'s authors, the church was an ecosystem of peace.[53]

The *Didascalia* gives attention to the practical dimensions of peacemaking because the ecosystem was under threat.[54] There were conflicts in the communities. Accusations and misunderstandings flew back and forth, at times not surprisingly about the misuse of money and status. No doubt some conflicts reflected the differences of culture and tradition that were inevitable in mixed communities of Jews and gentiles. The *Didascalia*'s authors took these conflicts seriously. They quoted Jesus in the Sermon on the Mount (Matt. 5:23–24): "If you are making your offering upon the altar and there recall that your brother is angry with you, leave your offering before the altar and go first to be reconciled with your brother. Then go to make your offering."[55] Resolving conflict, Jesus seemed to be saying, must precede

47. *Did. apost.* 2.25.8.
48. Especially in *Did. apost.* 2.19–21 and 2.44–58.
49. *Did. apost.* 2.24.4.
50. *Did. apost.* 2.21.5 (Stewart-Sykes, 139).
51. *Did. apost.* 2.54.3; 2.37.3 (Stewart-Sykes, 173, 159).
52. *Did. apost.* 2.19.3 (Stewart-Sykes, 137).
53. Wolfgang Wischmeyer refers to the *Didascalia*'s attempt to "realize the eschatological community of peace at least in the worship service" (*Von Golgatha zum Ponte Molle: Studien zur Sozialgeschichte der Kirche im dritten Jahrhundert*, Forschungen zur Kirchen- und Dogmengeschichte 49 [Göttingen: Vandenhoeck & Ruprecht, 1992], 145).
54. Alan Kreider, "Peacemaking in Worship in the Syrian Church Orders," *SL* 34, no. 2 (2004): 177–90.
55. *Did. apost.* 2.53.3 (Stewart-Sykes, 172).

worship. According to the *Didascalia*, prayer was the church's heartbeat; indeed, its authors claimed that some outsiders wanted to be admitted into the church specifically so they could pray with the believers, conscious of the special power that was palpable there.[56] The authors often coupled prayer with the Eucharist, in both of which the Christians believed they encountered God. And when peace was absent—when there was injustice among members or relationships were broken—in the view of the authors the church's worship was null and void.

> The offering to God which is ours is prayer and eucharist, but if you continue in anger with your brother, or he with you, your prayer shall not be heard, nor shall your eucharist be accepted. . . . A person should pray carefully at all times, but God does not hear those who bear anger and rebuke towards their brother. Even should you pray three times in an hour it shall avail you nothing.[57]

The consequence of broken relationships within the community was catastrophic—the atrophy of its worship.

Peacemaking Worship

To prevent this disaster, and to ensure that the church's "prayers and oblations may be acceptable," the *Didascalia*'s churches developed a rite. Every week in their Sunday liturgy, at the bishop's urging a deacon cried out, "Is there anyone who maintains anger with his neighbor?"[58] At this point the peace greeting may have taken place, when brothers and sisters mingled to exchange the kiss.[59] If the members had relationships that were seriously strained, the deacons, whom the bishop charged to find out about conflict and misbehavior, urged the aggrieved parties to approach the bishop. The bishop, who throughout his life proclaimed and announced peace, was now in a position to make peace. If the parties' grievances were not deep-seated, the bishop was able to settle the dispute on the spot. But if the people's conflicts were intractable, a process of hearings ensued in a kind of episcopal court whose hearings began the next Tuesday. The bishop listened to the accuser as well as the accused, and evaluated their "conduct and actions in the world." Then, if possible by the following Sunday, he pronounced a judgment that "brings

56. *Did. apost.* 2.39.6: People "seek reception into the church for prayer" (Stewart-Sykes, 162).
57. *Did. apost.* 2.53.4–5 (Stewart-Sykes, 172).
58. *Did. apost.* 2.54.1 (Stewart-Sykes, 173).
59. As in a parallel passage in the late fourth-century *Apostolic Constitutions* 2.57.17; see also Cyril of Jerusalem, *Mystagogic Catechesis* 5.3.

about peace" between them.[60] If more than a week was necessary, the bishop could be involved in hearings across time. At the culmination of protracted hearings, when the bishop finally pronounced judgment, he at times found it necessary to excommunicate one of the parties. But this was not meant to break relationships. The *Didascalia* gives details of a process in which the bishops accompanied the excommunicated members, called penitents, on their journey of reincorporation into the community. The *Didascalia*'s authors were convinced that these means were necessary to enable the church to conserve the "peace" that is the church's "beauty" and "proper form."[61]

How should we view this peacemaking process? Is it conflict resolution? To be sure. Is it also liturgical theology? Although this suggestion may seem far-fetched, the peacemaking process clearly is that too. The reconciliation begins and is completed in worship, and the *Didascalia*'s authors were convinced that if the community was not at peace, its worship would be worthless.

Peacemaking Evangelism

But imagine! Could this peacemaking process also be evangelistic? Could peacemaking help the church grow? The *Didascalia*'s authors contended that when the bishop made peace within his congregation, he was "a helper for God, that the number of those being saved may increase, for this is the will of the Lord God." It is God whose work it is to save people; God calls humans to help him by praying the Lord's Prayer ("Your will be done on earth as in heaven") and by making peace.[62] God's desire, the *Didascalia* claims, is that "all should believe and be saved. . . . It is his will that he should give life to all, and it is his pleasure that those who are saved should be numerous." But people who are contentious, layfolk as well as clergy, are of no help to God. Indeed, they reduce the people of God. Either they expel from the church the people they accuse, or they themselves leave the church, in both cases sinning against God by scattering God's flock.[63] But the calling of believers in Syria was to be "wise doves" who make peace and gather the "wild" outsiders into the church.

> For we, by the power of the Lord God, have been gathering from all nations and languages and have brought them to the church through much labour and

60. *Did. apost.* 2.45.3–2.50.1 (Stewart-Sykes, 167–69).
61. *Did. apost.* 2.43.4 (Stewart-Sykes, 165).
62. *Did. apost.* 2.54.4–2.56.1 (Stewart-Sykes, 173).
63. *Did. apost.* 2.55.2–2.56.3 (Stewart-Sykes, 173–74).

toil and danger every day that we might do the will of God and fill the house, that is the holy catholic church, with guests who rejoice and exult and praise and glorify God who called them to life. Thus you laypeople should be like wise doves, at peace with one another, striving to fill the church, converting and taming those who are wild, bringing them into her midst. And this is the great reward should you deliver them from fire and present them to the church, established and faithful.[64]

"Wise doves"—in the *Didascalia*'s world, profoundly shaped by Matthew's Gospel,[65] this expression may be an elision of two words in Jesus's missionary imperative: "Behold, I am sending you out . . . so be wise as serpents and innocent as doves" (Matt. 10:16–17). It is these people, peaceable and unthreatening, who attracted the outsiders to the Christian assemblies in which peace was made and peacemakers were formed. Who were these wise doves? Certainly all members were called to be like this. All Christians could live at peace with one another and find ways to share that life with outsiders, leading to friendships with them and introductions to the church's leaders and catechists. And intriguingly, according to the *Didascalia*, it seems to have been Christian women who played a central role in the church's growth.

Women in Witness—Wives and Deaconesses

Some women were wives, married to either Christian or pagan men. The *Didascalia*'s authors urged the wives not to offend their husbands but rather to "demonstrate religion through modesty and gentleness." In a manner similar to what we saw in chapter 4, the *Didascalia*'s wives were to behave in a way that "those who are of the heathen may be turned and grow into faith." Many believing men in the communities must have entered as a result of the patient witness of their wives. The *Didascalia* notes that the behavior of Christian wives might similarly affect the pagan women who were members of their households.[66]

Also important in the *Didascalia*'s communities were the deaconesses. These had an honored role in the community; they were "a type of the Holy Spirit." They were appointed by the bishop and were accounted as lesser clergy.[67]

---

64. *Did. apost.* 2.56.3–4 (Stewart-Sykes, 174).

65. The *Didascalia apostolorum* cites Matthew (84×), Mark (5×), Luke (19×), John (4×), and a few passages in the Pauline corpus: 1 Corinthians (2×), Ephesians (2×), 1 Timothy (9×), but none in Romans or Galatians.

66. *Did. apost.* 1.10.3 (Stewart-Sykes, 116).

67. *Did. apost.* 2.26.6 (Stewart-Sykes, 151). In addition, the bishop is a type of God, the deacon a type of Christ, the presbyters a type of the apostles, and the widows and orphans a type of the altar.

Their primary task was "the ministry of women." As women, the deaconesses could reach into places that were closed to Christian men, notably the houses of pagans. There they found believing women to whom they ministered; they cared for those who were sick and bathed those who were beginning to recover.[68] There they also found pagan women, whom they evidently invited to approach the church. When the time came for these new believers to be baptized, the deaconesses played an essential role. Since "it is not right that a woman should be seen by a man," in administering baptism the bishop could lay hands on their heads, but it was the deaconess that anointed their bodies with "the oil of anointing" and then went down into the water with them.[69] As the newly baptized women came out of the water, the deaconess received them and provided them with ongoing instruction "so that the mark of baptism may be kept intact in chastity and holiness."[70] According to the *Didascalia*, the deaconesses provided exemplary service. Thanks to them, the Christian community became known for sacrificial, hands-on care of its members, which was demonstrated in the houses of pagans, who were no doubt intrigued by what they saw the deaconesses doing.

Bridling the Widows

But in the *Didascalia*'s communities there was another recognized group of ministering women—the widows.[71] These women were problematic for the church's leaders. They were unmarried, aged over fifty, and sustained by the bishop out of the believers' donations to the church. The *Didascalia* referred to widows as the "altars of God," a term that Polycarp had already used in

68. *Did. apost.* 3.13.1 (Stewart-Sykes, 194).
69. The women baptizands were evidently fully clad when the bishop laid his hands on them. They took off their outer garments as the deaconesses anointed their bare bodies; and they put on linen undergarments for their baptismal immersion, performed by male clergy. See Paul F. Bradshaw, "Women and Baptism in the *Didascalia Apostolorum*," *JECS* 20, no. 4 (2012): 643.
70. *Did. apost.* 3.12.3 (Stewart-Sykes, 193).
71. The literature on the widows is immense. See Bonnie B. Thurston, *The Widows: A Women's Ministry in the Early Church* (Minneapolis: Fortress, 1989), especially chaps. 6–7; Charlotte Methuen, "Widows, Bishops and the Struggle for Authority in the *Didascalia apostolorum*," *Journal of Ecclesiastical History* 46 (1995): 197–213; C. Methuen, "'For Pagans Laugh to Hear Women Teach': Gender Stereotypes in the *Didascalia apostolorum*," in *Gender and Christian Religion*, ed. R. N. Swanson (Woodbridge, Suffolk: Boydell Press, 1998), 23–35; Michael Penn, "'Bold and Having No Shame': Ambiguous Widows, Controlling Clergy, and Early Syrian Communities," *Hugoye: Journal of Syriac Studies* 4, no. 2 (2001): 159–85; Jan N. Bremmer, "Pauper or Patroness: The Widow in the Early Christian Church," in *Between Poverty and the Pyre: Moments in the History of Widowhood*, ed. Jan N. Bremmer and L. P. Van den Bosch (London: Routledge, 1995), 31–57.

the second century.[72] In the *Didascalia*'s scheme of things, the calling of widows was simple—to sit at home, to spin wool for the benefit of the poor, and above all to pray for donors and the entire church.[73] But it was not always so simple, as is clear from the *Didascalia*'s frustrated comments.

In the *Didascalia*'s attempts to restrict and prohibit activities of the widows, we encounter evidence of one of the major motors of the church's growth in its first two hundred years, which, despite changes, had ongoing power in the third century. The widows are mobile. To the distress of the *Didascalia*'s authors, they go "from house to house." They "wander" to the houses of the unfaithful as well as the faithful. This is unacceptable: an altar should be immobile, "fixed in a single place."[74] In their daily lives, the widows are present to people. They converse with them, eat with them, and fast with them. Some of the people whose homes they visit are pagan; others are believers, occasionally believers who had been "put out of the synagogue."[75] Some of these people provide financial support directly to the widows; this annoys the church's leaders who are attempting to centralize the administration of funds under episcopal control. And the widows engage in spiritual ministry to people—they lay hands on them and pray for them. All this they do without the bishop's or deacons' supervision.[76] They even baptize new converts, which goes against the *Didascalia*'s practice of restricting baptism to the bishop.[77] However connected the widows' ministries are to the life of interested pagans, they are uncoordinated, unauthorized, and out of control. When widows are behaving like this, how can the bishops "shepherd the entire people in peace"?[78]

Even worse, in the perspective of the *Didascalia*'s authors, the widows engage in evangelistic conversation with inquirers, and inevitably, at times these conversations get out of hand. The Christians intrigue people—including no doubt many pagans. Some pagans are interested in Christians' attitudes, values, and lifestyle. Pagans also have questions that range over a variety of important topics, and they are happy to have widows there to discuss things with. Pagans who have been frightened by Christian teaching about the punishment of unbelievers may want to have their fears confirmed or

---

72. Pol. *Phil.* 4.3.
73. *Did. apost.* 3.5.2; 3.7.8.
74. *Did. apost.* 3.6.3 (Stewart-Sykes, 185–86).
75. *Did. apost.* 3.8.3; shortly thereafter (3.8.5) the *Didascalia* refers to those who have been "expelled from the church" (Stewart-Sykes, 189). In the *Didascalia*'s world, "synagogue" and "church" may at times have been words for the same assembly.
76. *Did. apost.* 3.8.1.
77. *Did. apost.* 2.41.2; 3.9.1.
78. *Did. apost.* 2.20.3 (Stewart-Sykes, 137).

dispelled.[79] Pagans who have heard about "the Kingdom of the name of Christ and the divine plan" may be curious and want to know more. Some widows evidently feel ready to talk about these topics, and since in the *Didascalia*'s view they do this "without knowledge," at times they "blaspheme the word." Here they are, these untrained, unaccredited missionaries, disobeying Jesus's command that comes "to widows and all the laity: 'Do not cast your pearls before swine.'"[80] Occasionally the widows stray into the most sensitive of areas—"the incarnation and suffering of Christ." These topics are notoriously difficult. When it is women who speak about them, the pagans (according to the *Didascalia*'s authors) respond by sneering and scoffing.[81] If the essence of mission is imparting correct doctrine instead of forming Christian disciples, this is a missional disaster. The widows shouldn't trespass into this territory, nor should unauthorized laymen. It is all right for the widows to give simple answers to simple questions—about "righteousness and faith in God," the destruction of idols, and "that there is but one God." But other topics are beyond their competence; they should "send those who wish to be instructed to the leader."[82] The widows are too confident. "You desire to know more, and know better, not only than men, but than the presbyters and the bishops."[83] The *Didascalia*'s authors are aware that heresies are spreading;[84] like some other third-century leaders, they are more concerned to instruct candidates in orthodox thinking (the domain of clergymen) than to form candidates in the habitus of Christlike living. The center of gravity in catechesis is shifting. Widows, like other laywomen and men, are caught in this shift. However gifted they are evangelistically and however attuned they are to the pagans' needs and concerns, they are not to subvert this by erring into doctrinal imprecision.

To the authors of the *Didascalia*, who were attempting to construct an ecosystem of peace, the problems associated with the widows were manifest. If the ideal woman is a "passive, obedient instrument of the clergy," the *Didascalia*'s widows were far from that![85] In the course of the third century these problems no doubt dissipated as patterns of episcopal leadership and clerical control became more securely established, as communities became more orderly, and as deaconesses—members of the clergy who were unambiguously under the authority of the male clergy—came into their own. The widows

---

79. For samples of many passages in this work that deal with God's punishment, see *Did. apost.* 1.3.3; 2.17.5; 5.4.4; 5.6.7.
80. Matt. 7:6, in *Did. apost.* 3.5.5 (Stewart-Sykes, 184–85).
81. *Did. apost.* 3.5.6 (Stewart-Sykes, 185).
82. *Did. apost.* 3.5.3 (Stewart-Sykes, 184).
83. *Did. apost.* 3.8.3 (Stewart-Sykes, 189).
84. *Did. apost.* 6.1.1–6.10.5.
85. Penn, "'Bold and Having No Shame,'" 175.

ceased wandering and offering their unbridled, countercultural, grassroots contribution to the church's mission. Somehow potential recruits continued to approach the church through the appropriate channels.

Channels to Belonging

Unlike other church orders, the *Didascalia* does not provide a lot of information about these channels. The outlines of the path to membership in the Christian community are ones we have encountered in earlier chapters. Those who were seriously interested in becoming Christians were brought to the catechists. The *Didascalia* gives only samples of the topics the catechists dealt with. They taught the catechumens to live in a way that would "show forth the fruits of repentance."[86] They prepared the people to face persecution.[87] They gave them instruction about Christ's resurrection and the hope of their own resurrection.[88] They comforted them with the promise of everlasting life and warned them of the consequences of apostasy—"to burn and be tortured endlessly and for ever."[89] No doubt the catechists gave candidates from Jewish families the *Didascalia*'s interpretation of the "second legislation" as it relates to the teaching and way of Christ. Above all, they taught the candidates "to imitate [Christ's] teaching and his patience."[90] The candidates' conduct and character were formed by apprenticeship, by observing the habitus of the community, and by watching the catechists and the bishop, who "copy our Lord, who is master and instructor for us, in what he teaches and in what he does."[91]

Every week in the community's Sunday Eucharist, the candidates, accompanied by the penitents, came into the assembly so they could hear the Word, preached by the bishop who "announces peace to others."[92] They observed the community's order, its solemnity, its habitus. But the bishop dismissed them before the prayers, for their characters were still being formed and they had not yet demonstrated "the fruits of repentance."[93] What kind of character did a candidate ready for baptism have? The *Didascalia* gives a hint when talking

86. *Did. apost.* 2.39.6 (Stewart-Sykes, 161).
87. *Did. apost.* 5.6.4.
88. *Did. apost.* 5.7.11–12.
89. *Did. apost.* 5.6.7 (Stewart-Sykes, 205). The *Didascalia*'s authors' exhilaration that God has called all people was sobered by their belief that people who do not respond will face "the judgment of God through the grievous fire which cannot be quenched and cannot be borne" (*Did. apost.* 2.17.6 [Stewart-Sykes, 132]).
90. *Did. apost.* 5.7.24 (Stewart-Sykes, 210).
91. *Did. apost.* 5.5.2 (Stewart-Sykes, 203).
92. *Did. apost.* 2.54.3 (Stewart-Sykes, 173).
93. *Did. apost.* 2.39.6 (Stewart-Sykes, 161).

about people whom the bishop viewed as trustworthy in giving evidence. The bishop wanted to know

> whether he is humble, and not irascible, and not slanderous, and whether he is kind to widows and to the poor and to strangers, and not a lover of impure profit. And whether he is peaceable, and friendly to all and kind to all, whether he is compassionate and open-handed in his giving, not a glutton, nor greedy, and not rapacious and not a drunkard, and not a prodigal, and not idle . . . and whether he has acted wickedly as does the world, in adultery and fornication.[94]

Those who were formed to be like this, who had embodied the Christian habitus and could say "I believe," came in the baptismal service before the bishop, who exorcised them and immersed them. Then, the *Didascalia* states, "through the imposition of the bishop's hand, the Lord bore witness of each of you, as his holy voice was heard saying, 'You are my son, this day I have begotten you.'"[95] At last, the new believers could join in the community's prayer and Eucharist. They emerged as wise doves, "helpers of God" who by intriguing behavior and appropriate words contributed to the church's primary mode of growth—*attraction*.

94. *Did. apost.* 2.49.2 (Stewart-Sykes, 169).
95. *Did. apost.* 2.32.3 (Stewart-Sykes, 155).

PART 4

THE
TRANSFORMATION
OF PATIENCE

9

THE IMPATIENCE
OF CONSTANTINE

And so we come to Constantine. The church was growing before Constantine, as the *Didascalia apostolorum* makes clear. Throughout the third century the *Didascalia*'s cluster of Syrian congregations was growing. Their growth was not spectacular but patient, a result of their worship of God, which heartened the believers and shaped their way of life. But in the second decade of the fourth century, unanticipated changes took place, and churches throughout the Roman Empire began to grow more rapidly and in new ways. In AD 312 the emperor, Constantine I, who six years earlier in York at the death of his father Constantius had been acclaimed emperor, saw a vision of the cross in the sky and heard the words "in this sign conquer." He then won a military victory on the edges of Rome that secured his dominance over the entire western half of the empire. Constantine ended imperially sponsored persecution of the Christians. Soon he claimed a Christian identity, and by 324 he had defeated his rival Licinius, a victory that made Constantine sole emperor of the entire Roman Empire, the East as well as the West. Throughout his thirty-one year reign (he died in 337), Constantine secured the church's position in society and began to transform the way the churches understood and practiced mission.

In the eighty years between the 230s (when the bulk of the *Didascalia* was written) and the time of Constantine, there were periods when the imperial government made things extremely difficult for Christians. In the 250s the emperors Decius and Valerian instigated two waves of pressure that attempted to force all Romans (except Jews) to placate the gods by sacrificing to them; and from 303 to 312 Diocletian, Maximian, and the other emperors in the Tetrarchy initiated brutal persecution across the empire. But in between these periods of disruption and danger for Christians, there were four decades of relative security for the church. The period from 260 to 300 has been called "forty years of peace."[1] During these decades Christians were able to put down roots, gain confidence, and grow substantially in numbers. By century's end, Christians, whom some people at the beginning of the third century viewed as "discredited and proscribed desperadoes,"[2] had become respected parts of local communities, good neighbors whose idiosyncratic practices were tolerable. As a result, the renewed persecution Christians faced in the years between 303 and Constantine's victory in 312 was traumatic for the believers and their leaders.

In this fifty-year period before Constantine, the church was growing, but it is not easy for us to monitor or explain that growth. Certainly the expansion was more rapid in certain areas than others—for example, it appears to have been especially rapid in Egypt, both rural and urban. But there were places, including much of the rural West, where the church's growth was minimal.[3] In urban areas, where the growth was often appreciable, people in the middle orders of society were beginning to become believers (and leaders), but poor people continued to predominate numerically in the churches. How many Christians were there? It is hard to say. Recognizing that vast swaths of the empire were Christianized little if at all, it seems likely that the church's adherents across the empire totaled less than the widely accepted figure of 10 percent (six million).[4] But this is speculation, because we lack sources that could allow us to be more precise. However, there are places for which sources survive that enable us to be concrete as we examine the church's changing position in society. These give us a sense of what was going on in the peaceful years before Diocletian as well as during the persecution of 303–312.

The sources I have chosen come from upper Egypt—especially from Oxyrhynchus, a city on the Nile a hundred miles south of Cairo. To the delight of archaeologists, Oxyrhynchus's largely rain-free climate enabled thousands of

---

1. W. H. C. Frend, *Martyrdom and Persecution in the Early Church* (Oxford: Blackwell, 1965), 465.

2. Caecilius, in Minucius Felix, *Oct.* 8.4, trans. G. H. Rendall, LCL 250 (1931), 335.

3. Peter Brown, *Through the Eye of the Needle: Wealth, the Fall of Rome, and the Making of Christianity in the West, 350–550 AD* (Princeton: Princeton University Press, 2012), 22, 38.

4. Ramsay MacMullen, *The Second Church: Popular Christianity, A.D. 200–400*, SBL Writings from the Greco-Roman World Supplement Series 1 (Atlanta: Society of Biblical Literature, 2009), 102, 173n18.

papyrus fragments to survive in garbage heaps. The fragments have revealed fascinating details of the activity of varied Christian groups. We also will look at Thmuis, a city in the Nile Delta where articulate Christian leaders emerged. For the Oxyrhynchus papyri I have found AnneMarie Luijendijk to be an illuminating guide.[5]

Luijendijk is careful not to overemphasize the importance of Christians in the Egyptian towns and villages. During the half century preceding Constantine, they were a minority who lived in crowded conditions and rubbed shoulders with their Jewish and pagan neighbors. It didn't concern them that it was impossible to be secretive about their Christian allegiance; they enjoyed a religious environment in which relations among groups were amicable and tolerant.[6] From her reading of the papyri, Luijendijk finds that the Christians melded into society, in large part living "in ways often indistinguishable from their neighbors." Yet she observes that the Christians were in "some ways distinctive."[7] And of course the church would not have been growing if they had been just like everyone else; if Christians were no different, why would anyone join them?

Many of the distinctive traits Luijendijk finds are embedded in the letters of Bishop (Papa) Sotas.[8] Sotas, active in the 270s, may have been the first bishop of Oxyrhynchus and was well known among his non-Christian neighbors as "Sotas the Christian." He wrote letters that reflect his patient character. If he was struggling to find ways to promote his churches' growth, his letters do not reveal this motive. Instead, his letters show Sotas dealing with practical matters—property issues, business transactions, and especially networks with the wider Christian world. Sotas took part in these networks; in 270 he traveled to Antioch to participate in a synod.[9] But it wasn't only the bishop who traveled; many of his fellow Christians traveled long distances as well. Before they left home, Sotas equipped them with letters of recommendation in which he appealed to their host churches to provide hospitality—food, accommodation, and inclusion in eucharistic worship. With his and their congregations' commendations, the believers traveled as "beloved brothers" who confidently expected their hosts to receive them in ways that built familial relationships between the churches.[10] Women were notably present among

---

5. AnneMarie Luijendijk, *Greetings in the Lord: Early Christians and the Oxyrhynchus Papyri*, HTS 60 (Cambridge, MA: Harvard University Press, 2008).

6. Similar good relations were evident in North Africa. See Claude Lepelley, "Chrétiens et païens au temps de la persécution de Dioclétien: Le cas d'Abthugni," StPatr 15 (1984): 226–32.

7. Luijendijk, *Greetings in the Lord*, 188, 228.

8. Ibid., chap. 4.

9. Ibid., 91.

10. Ibid., 111, 114.

the mobile believers, traveling "in a fashion unparalleled in other sources," for reasons including business, health, and education.[11] At times the letters were formulaic. Leaders of other churches modeled their commendations on Sotas's; among the papyri are examples of letters written by a scribe, in which someone else later inserted the name of the traveler.[12]

Sotas was confident that when believers arrived at their destination their hosts would receive them "in peace." According to Luijendijk, this phrase connoted the ritual kiss of peace that was a greeting of familial inclusion as well as a powerful component in their worship services. The peace greeting was a learned reflex, a habitus that expressed the community's deep values. It built community. At the deepest level, the kiss was a sign of family, of being incorporated with "all the sisters and brothers" who belonged to each other in the Lord.[13] To learn the faith and habits of those who live in peace, spiritual and practical formation was necessary. So it is not surprising that Sotas devoted a number of his letters to the operation of the catechumenate in the churches. He wrote about catechumens at their various stages of progress—"catechumens in Genesis," "catechumens in the beginning of the gospel," and "catechumens of the congregation"—and when the catechumens traveled, he urged the congregations to receive them warmly as brothers and sisters. On occasion the letters show catechumens coming from smaller churches to Sotas in Oxyrhynchus for catechesis—"building up."[14] The peace greeting, according to Luijendijk, was a "distinctive trait" of the Christians that shaped their behavior in the world.[15] Nowhere in these letters do we find Sotas evaluating these forms of behavior, calculating how they might have greatest missional success. But one letter refers by name to six catechumens,[16] and all the letters have a tone of hopeful patience. It seems that when pagans looked at their Christian neighbors, some of them were drawn to approach communities that lived "in peace."

If Egyptian Christians behaved with patience in a time of peace, how did they face persecution? In 303 "the great peace" came to an end. Diocletian and his fellow emperors, fearing that the well-being of the empire was being threatened by the god-angering presence of Christians in society, issued a succession of edicts that threatened the Christian communities. Christians across the empire responded in many ways. Our sources from Egypt indicate two approaches: small acts of cunning resistance, and a bold gesture of martyrdom.

11. Ibid., 119–20.
12. Ibid., 112.
13. Ibid., 85.
14. Ibid., 121.
15. Ibid., 123.
16. Ibid., 84.

A sample of reticent resistance is recorded in the Oxyrhynchus papyri. In February 304 the provincial governor of Egypt, Clodius Culcianus, sent three high-ranking imperial officials to visit Chysis, a village on a major trade route outside Oxyrhynchus. Their order was to confiscate the goods of the church there. The papyri do not report where the church's clergy had gone, but the person left on the spot to receive the governor's emissaries was Aurelius Ammonius. In the report that was filed with the authorities, he called himself "reader of the former church of the village of Chysis." Had the "former" church, likely a house, been destroyed, or had it simply reverted to domestic use? Ammonius reports that "the same former church had neither gold nor silver nor money nor clothes nor cattle nor slaves nor lands nor possessions . . . apart from only the bronze matter which was found and given over" to the authorities.[17] What? A church in AD 304 without precious communion vessels and with no clothing to share? In comparison with other churches at this time, this seems most unlikely.[18] It is probable that someone had secreted the silver and left the bronze for the persecuting imperials! At the conclusion of his statement, it is recorded that Aurelius Ammonius swore an oath by "the genius of our lords the emperors," but someone else, Aurelius Serenus, signed it for Ammonius "because he does not know letters."[19] The reader who does not know letters—who knows only Coptic and not Greek? Who does not want to die a martyr, but simultaneously does not want to affix his signature to a document that represents collusion with idolatry and theft? Who, as a Christian, knows that he has been taught "Do not swear at all" (Matt. 5:33)? We do not know Ammonius's reasoning for what he did, but Luijendijk celebrates him as a practitioner of "small negotiations and rebellions around writing and hiding property."[20] We might celebrate Ammonius as a practitioner of ingenious patience.

In the larger city of Thmuis in the Nile Delta, Phileas engaged in a larger form of resistance. We know about him from the *Acts of Phileas*, which report his encounters with the governor Clodius Culcianus—not as in Chysis through intermediaries but face-to-face. Phileas was a big fish. He was bishop of Thmuis and leader of a Christian community that was much larger than

17. Ibid., 193–94.
18. Note the 2 gold chalices, 6 silver chalices, 6 silver urns, 82 women's tunics, and other articles of clothing among the extensive possessions of the church that met in a "house" at Cirta, Numidia, information about which emerged in AD 303 in hearings before Consul Zenophilus. See Mark Edwards, trans. and ed., *Optatus: Against the Donatists*, TTH 27 (Liverpool: Liverpool University Press, 1997), 154, in appendix 1.
19. Ibid., 194.
20. Ibid., 208–10.

that of Oxyrhynchus. According to the *Acts*,[21] when Phileas was summoned for his fifth hearing, he was accompanied by at least twenty other clergy! Phileas was someone whose resolve Culcianus had to break. Already on the occasion of his first defense in Thmuis, Culcianus insulted the bishop and then quickly resorted to torture; he ordered the legionaries to rack him "even beyond the fourth peg."[22] When Phileas refused to sacrifice to the gods, Culcianus moved Phileas to a prison in Alexandria, in chains and bare feet, where he subjected him to more hearings. Apparently the governor was in no hurry to execute the bishop. In these hearings both Culcianus and Phileas show how far things had progressed since earlier encounters between governors and bishops. Culcianus was much better informed than earlier governors; Christianity was now a part of his world of discourse. And Phileas was much more voluble than earlier bishops. So Culcianus, confident that he was well informed, was determined to use his knowledge about Christianity to corner the bishop. Paul "was the one who denied the faith." Jesus was "a common man who spoke Aramaic . . . [and] surely not in the class of Plato." Why did Jesus "not say of himself that he was God"? In response to these gambits Phileas, in contrast to earlier bishops Polycarp and Pothinus, was eager to talk.[23] Jesus did not say he was God because his deeds "performed the works of God in power and actuality. . . . He cleansed lepers, made the blind see."[24] Jesus, said Phileas, was "superior to Plato. . . . [If you wish I shall recite to you some of] his words."[25] In response to the governor's challenge, "I have sworn . . . now you swear," Phileas responded: "We are not permitted to swear. . . . For the holy and divine Scriptures say: *Let your yes be yes and your no no.*"[26] Eventually, when both the governor and bishop were exhausted, Culcianus said, "If you were one of the uncultured . . . who had delivered themselves up out of need, I should not spare you. But now you possess such abundant resources that you can nourish and sustain not only yourself but an entire city. Therefore spare yourself and offer sacrifice." Phileas replied, "I will not."[27] Phileas was not only a Christian bishop; Phileas was rich. He had resources that helped sustain a large Christian community that included many poor

21. In the account that follows of the *Acts of Phileas*, I primarily use the Greek Recension, trans. and ed. Herbert A. Musurillo, *The Acts of the Christian Martyrs* (Oxford: Clarendon, 1972), 328–53.

22. *Acts of Phileas* 1 (Musurillo, 329).

23. Mart. Pol. 10; for Bishop Pothinus of Lyons, see Eusebius, *Hist. eccl.* 5.1.29, trans. Musurillo, *Acts of the Christian Martyrs*, 11, 71.

24. *Acts of Phileas* 6 (Musurillo, 333).

25. *Acts of Phileas* 8 (Musurillo, 339).

26. *Acts of Phileas* 5 (Musurillo, 335).

27. *Acts of Phileas* 11–12 (Musurillo, 343).

members. He had cultural and intellectual confidence. The Latin text of the *Acts* indicates that Culcianus hoped to the end that Phileas would capitulate.[28] When he eventually ordered Phileas's beheading, it was with a sense of defeat. With Phileas, patience, which in early Christian thought had always related to nonviolent suffering, was still alive.

Constantine and Conversion

As the persecution petered out in the fourth century's second decade, we come to the emperor and to the transformation of patience that happened with Constantine's rule. Under Constantine changes took place in the area of patience. Let's see how these played out in the experience of the emperor and his Christian contemporaries.

It's not easy to study Constantine. The sources for his life are complex and contradictory, and historians differ in their views of the emperor. For centuries they have been arguing about him. How many dreams and visions did Constantine have? Were the accounts of them reliable? Did the dreams and visions of 312 make Constantine a Christian? Historian Charles Matson Odahl sees decisive significance in Constantine's reflection on his victory and the signs that accompanied it: "At this moment, Constantine converted to the Christian God."[29] Classicist Timothy Barnes agrees that Constantine's conversion was sudden: it came in a "moment of psychological conviction."[30] Other scholars deny that Constantine was ever a Christian.[31]

In my view, Constantine became a Christian, but not until just before he died. And his conversion did not come in a moment but was the culmination of a process of conversion. Constantine became a Christian when he, like the Christians for centuries before him, submitted himself to catechesis and baptism. Prior to this Constantine was what we might call a liminal Christian who lived on the threshold of Christianity. Constantine was fascinated by Christian theology and became expert at it; he had lots of Christian friends, including clerics; he subsidized the church and its buildings and tried to promote its welfare; he shaped its theology and anathematized its theologians when he

28. *Acts of Phileas* 6–9, Latin Recension (Musurillo, 350–53).
29. Charles Matson Odahl, *Constantine and the Christian Empire* (London: Routledge, 2004), 106.
30. Timothy D. Barnes, *Constantine and Eusebius* (Cambridge, MA: Harvard University Press, 1981), 43.
31. Jakob Burckhardt, *The Age of Constantine the Great* (Garden City, NY: Doubleday Anchor Books, 1956); Alistair Kee, *Constantine versus Christ: The Triumph of Ideology* (London: SCM, 1982).

thought they were wrong. In his own palace parachurch he even engaged in worship. But not until the end of his life did Constantine bow to Christ as Lord. Only then did he allow Christ and his church to limit his options and to free him from his old addictive, reflexive habitus. *Then* he was baptized, then he became a Christian, and then he could worship with Christians at the eucharistic table. Not before.

As Eusebius tells the story, Constantine faced these issues early, in 312, immediately after he had his "amazing vision" and on the eve of the Battle of the Milvian Bridge, in which he fought Maxentius for sole control of Rome and the West. According to Eusebius, Constantine responded to his vision by doing four things.[32] First, he sent for the clergy and asked them questions about his vision and about God. Constantine, we read, was "instructed" in all these matters. Second, he decided to break off study with his Christian instructors. He compared the heavenly vision that he had received on the battlefield with what the theologians told him and "decided personally to apply himself to the divinely inspired writings." As the bishops knew well, in this Constantine was innovating; by choosing to be responsible for his own catechesis, Constantine was parting company from the tradition of the church. But Constantine didn't want to be entirely on his own, so in the third place, according to Eusebius, he took "the priests of God as his advisers." Bishop Hosius of Cordoba was prominent in his entourage, and no doubt other clerics were there as well. Constantine treated the clergy respectfully and soon invited the bishops to have dinner with him in his palace.[33] And fourth, Constantine fostered Christian worship. He wanted the worship of the God "who had appeared to him" to be carried out "with all due rites." So Constantine began to build large Christian buildings and to subsidize the worship that took place in them.[34]

But there was a fifth thing, something that early Christians would have said was indispensable for the journey Constantine was embarking on, that he did not do: Constantine did not become a catechumen preparing for baptism.

---

32. Eusebius, *Vit. Const.* 1.32.3; for Lactantius's account, which differs in significant ways from the later account of Eusebius, see *On the Deaths of the Persecutors* 44. One of the differences has to do with the substance of the vision: Was it, as Lactantius indicates, a simple "Christogram" (with an X bisected by a P)? Or was it, as Eusebius claims, a more elaborate ensemble: a cross with a wreath on top containing the Christogram, accompanied by the Greek words for "by this conquer"? Whatever the vision's substance, it moved Constantine profoundly. For a discussion and drawing of the visions, see Paul Corby Finney, "Labarum," in *Encyclopedia of Early Christianity*, 2nd ed., ed. Everett Ferguson (New York: Garland, 1997), 659–60.

33. Eusebius, *Vit. Const.* 1.42.1.

34. Eusebius, *Vit. Const.* 1.32.3; 1.42.2, trans. and ed. Averil Cameron and Stuart Hall, *Eusebius: Life of Constantine* (Oxford: Clarendon, 1999), 82, 86; Eusebius, *Hist. eccl.* 10.5.

Why not? If Constantine began to identify himself as a Christian in 312, why wasn't he baptized until 337 a few days before he died? Why did he put off baptism for twenty-five years? As emperor, Constantine identified with the church. He called bishops his "beloved brothers"; he built the Lateran Basilica; he gave the clergy subsidies and exemptions from civic duties; he made Sunday a day of rest. Why didn't he become a catechumen? And why didn't this lead to his baptism?

Why Was Constantine Not Baptized?

Did Constantine delay baptism because doing so was a "normal" practice? According to historian Charles Matson Odahl, "it was *normal* for people engaged in dubious professions, e.g., politicians and generals who had to execute capital sentences or conduct military campaigns, . . . [to delay] the rite until they could leave their worldly careers."[35] These baptisms are often called *clinical* baptisms, baptisms on the *klinē* (Greek for "bed"—often the deathbed), and they became common after Constantine. But they were never normal. Before Constantine, deathbed baptisms were not common practice; there are early stories of people who delayed baptism, but only one specific clinical baptism.[36] Nor were delayed baptisms theologically normal. As Gregory of Nazianzus pointed out, there was "great danger" of eternal punishment for someone who died unbaptized.[37] Constantine, who we know feared hell, was playing with fire.[38] Further, a deathbed baptism was not normal because it showed that the candidate was reluctant to submit to the discipline and teaching of the church. People who were baptized on their deathbeds had spent their lives without changing their lifestyles and without making their thinking accountable to the church. Constantine, to be sure, had a profound

---

35. Odahl, *Constantine*, 274.

36. For delays, see Tertullian, *On Penitence* 6; Origen, *Hom. Jos.* 9.9. The example of clinical baptism is that of Novatian, who in the 250s in Rome was baptized on his bed, later recovered, and was ordained a presbyter; many Roman clergy and laity viewed his clinical baptism as an impediment to his ordination: see Everett Ferguson, *Baptism in the Early Church: History, Theology, and Liturgy in the First Five Centuries* (Grand Rapids: Eerdmans, 2009), 382; also F. J. Dölger, "Die Taufe Konstantins und ihre Probleme," in *Konstantin der Grosse und seine Zeit*, ed. F. J. Dölger (Freiburg-im-Breisgau: Herder, 1913), 429–31. Maxwell E. Johnson (*The Rites of Christian Initiation*, rev ed. [Collegeville, MN: Liturgical Press, 2007], 117) says that postponement of baptism became common "in the changed political and social environment *after* Constantine" (with emphasis added).

37. Gregory of Nazianzus, *Oration* 40.14.

38. Constantine, *Oration* 13, "an unquenchable and unceasing fire," trans. and ed. Mark Edwards, *Constantine and Christendom: The Oration to the Saints*, TTH 39 (Liverpool: Liverpool University Press, 2003), 31.

effect on deathbed baptism by making it respectable. People copy monarchs, and in the century after Constantine there were many clinical baptisms, especially of aristocratic men. But the theologians consistently viewed delayed baptisms as a detrimental abnormality.[39]

Or was Constantine not baptized because the bishops refused to admit him to catechesis and baptism? They may have decided that he was not ready to proceed in the normal way and to become a catechumen leading to baptism. If so, this must have been a difficult decision. The bishops had experienced the horrors of the Great Persecution. They were no doubt profoundly grateful to God for Constantine's victories and willing to listen to his accounts of his visions. But they were guardians of a tradition that said that people's words are tested by the way they live. It is possible that the bishops were guided by the *Apostolic Tradition*, which prescribed processes for the reception of new church members. This text, widely used in the third century and with roots in Rome, restated the church's historical opposition to adultery, idolatry, and killing.[40] In light of this commitment, the *Apostolic Tradition* required the catechists to examine the professional behavior of all potential catechumens and to require them to stop wearing the purple and give up wielding the sword.[41] The bishops may have asked Constantine whether he was willing to submit his life to the authority and disciplines of the church. Was he ready to become a catechumen, to allow his character and actions and beliefs to be transformed into the image of Jesus Christ? Was he willing to be formed in community and to participate in the shared journey of seekers (*competentes*) progressing toward baptism? We do not know. But it is possible that the bishops, after they had conversations with Constantine, decided to say no to him.

Or was Constantine not baptized in the years after his visions and victory because the emperor said no to the bishops? Eusebius seems to indicate that Constantine himself decided not to become a catechumen: "[Constantine]

39. Repeatedly the fourth-century Cappadocian fathers bewailed delayed baptism; in numerous sermons Augustine railed against it as well. On the Cappadocians, see Everett Ferguson, "Exhortations to Baptism in the Cappadocians," StPatr 33 (1997): 121–29; Ferguson, "Basil's Protreptic to Baptism," in *Nova et Vetera: Patristic Studies in Honor of Thomas Patrick Halton*, ed. John Petruccione (Washington, DC: Catholic University of America Press, 1998), 74. On Augustine's appeals to catechumens to be baptized, see Alan Kreider, *The Change of Conversion and the Origin of Christendom* (Harrisburg, PA: Trinity Press, 1999; reprint, Eugene, OR: Wipf & Stock, 2006), 57–60.

40. For further discussion of the *Apostolic Tradition*, see chaps. 5–6 above.

41. See *Trad. ap.* 16.9–10 (BJP, 88–90): "A soldier who has authority, let him not kill a man. If he is ordered, let him not go to the task, nor let him swear. If he is not willing, let him be cast out. One who has authority of the sword, or a ruler of a city who wears the purple, let him cease or be cast out [of the group of catechumens]."

decided personally to apply himself to the divinely inspired writings."[42] Constantine may have looked at the bishops and theologians and rightly judged that he was as intellectually able as any of them; he would learn more if he studied on his own! Or he may have concluded that the church's traditions were intrusive and interfered with his work. After all, his business was important for the welfare of the entire populace, not just of the church. Or Constantine may have had concerns about the baptismal rite. Despite the Christians' reticence to talk about their liturgies, he may have heard rumors of baptismal rituals in which exorcists hissed in the faces of the candidates and priests immersed their bodies, submerging the perfumed rich in the same water as the unwashed poor. Or possibly Constantine was hesitant to enter the catechumenate because he sensed that his reflexive inner identity would be exposed and re-formed. Constantine was emperor, and he may have known that he was not ready to develop the habitus of a Christian.[43]

Constantine's Habitus

What was Constantine's habitus? What were his embodied reflexes? Constantine was shaped by the aristocracy, the court, and the army. As a child in an aristocratic family, Constantine would have assumed the value of *dignitas*. As Ramsay MacMullen explains, *dignitas* was embodied in behavior that expressed superiority—"the parade of wealth, the shouting herald who went first in the street, the showy costume and large retinue, the holding of oneself apart, and the limitation of familiar address." And *dignitas* was supported by threat; "it meant the ability to defend one's display by force if need be; to strike back at anyone who offended one or hurt or offended one's dependents; to avenge oneself and others, and to be perceived as capable of all such baneful, alarming conduct."[44] In the court of Emperor Diocletian where Constantine grew up, *dignitas* was an organizing principle. And in the court, Constantine was a special person—the son of Constantius, the western Caesar. As such, his life was in danger. As he grew up, he had to be quick-witted and cautious in order to survive. Constantine's habitus was one of suspicion and reflexive retaliation, not transparency and love. Constantine also grew up in the legions.

42. Eusebius, *Vit. Const.* 1.32.3 (Cameron and Hall, 82).
43. For a definition and discussion of habitus, see the section "Can Humans Change? The Realities of Habitus" in chap. 3 above.
44. Ramsay MacMullen, *Corruption and the Decline of Rome* (New Haven: Yale University Press, 1988), 69.

As a child he celebrated the exploits of military heroes; as a teenager he took part in military expeditions to Egypt and Persia. The habitus that he acquired as a soldier involved quickness, thick-necked manliness, and intimidation, not service of the poor and sick. Of course, the habitus of men brought up in court and army was shaped by pagan worship.[45] Given Constantine's upbringing, it would understandably be a challenge for him to develop the reflexes, the corporeal habitus, of a disciple of Jesus Christ.

Constantine was not unique in facing the challenge of habitus change. It was a challenge common to every potential Christian who wished to grow into the "example of living" of Jesus Christ.[46] Whatever the candidates' backgrounds, in the course of catechesis they engaged in a process in which their habitus was named, understood, unlearned, and transformed. After catechesis some, like Pachomius, chose to follow Christ by leaving their old world for a new life in the desert; others, like Justin's businessman, discovered that it was possible to follow Christ in their everyday world, as new possibilities of faithful discipleship emerged in their professional life. It was possible to be a patient businessman.[47] As candidates journeyed toward baptism, their reflexive responses were reformed so that they embodied the habitus of the Christian church. As Tertullian put it, "Christians are made, not born!"[48]

For whatever reason, Constantine did not become a catechumen. He remained an outsider—but a powerful outsider.

Lactantius Appeals to Constantine: Rule with Patience

Did theologians seriously attempt to engage with Constantine? We know less than we would like. But we do know that in the years immediately after Constantine's victory in Rome, one theologian, Lactantius, was in close contact with the emperor. Lactantius was the writer of the greatest theological work of the era, the seven-volume *Divine Institutes*. Perhaps as early as 310 and certainly by 312 Constantine had invited Lactantius to come to the western capital of Trier, not just to teach rhetoric at the court, but also to tutor the emperor's son and heir Priscus. Further, in Trier Lactantius produced a revised edition of the *Divine Institutes*, which he read aloud at court. At times Constantine, to whom

45. Jan N. Bremmer, "The Vision of Constantine," in *Land of Dreams: Greek and Latin Studies in Honour of A. H. M. Kessels*, ed. A. P. M. H. Lardinois, Marc Van der Poel, and Vincent Hunink (Leiden: Brill, 2006), 70.

46. Cyprian, *Ad Quir.* 3.39, trans E. Wallis, ANF 5:545.

47. *Life of Pachomius*, First Greek Life 3–4; Justin, *1 Apol.* 16.

48. Tertullian, *Apol.* 18.4, trans. T. R. Glover, LCL 250 (1931), 91.

Lactantius dedicated the work, may have attended these lectures.[49] Of course Lactantius was not teaching Constantine as a catechumen, but nevertheless, according to Odahl, the *Divine Institutes* were "a lengthy curriculum for the Christian education of Constantine," and Lactantius may have viewed them as such.[50] Certainly, in the second edition that he completed in 314, Lactantius interpolated dedications that flattered Constantine, the "emperor most great, . . . the first of the Roman emperors to repudiate falsehood."[51] In books 6–7 Lactantius went far beyond flattery to make a direct appeal to Constantine. He urged Constantine to rule as a Christian emperor, a *patient* emperor. And he rooted his appeal in the most basic of early Christian traditions that went back to Moses in Deuteronomy 11:26—the "two ways" tradition. "There are two ways, O Emperor Constantine, along which human life must proceed; one leads to heaven and the other plunges to the underworld."[52] Anticipating the issues and temptations that would face Constantine, Lactantius pointed to two areas in which Constantine must "maintain [his] patience unbroken."[53]

First, the emperor must honor the weak. In this, he must go beyond Cicero, the archetypal Roman political philosopher whose elegant Latin had inspired Lactantius but whose political perspectives had disappointed him. Indeed, the *Divine Institutes* were a dialogue with Cicero about statesmanship. And, with Constantine in mind, Lactantius the Christian constantly went beyond Cicero the Roman. For example, Lactantius pointed to passages in which Cicero inserted words that, from the Christian point of view, spoiled otherwise admirable thoughts. For example, Cicero stated that men should support "suitable people in need." The problem was the insertion of one word—"suitable" (*idoneis*). By directing his readers to give to "suitable" people, people who can reciprocate, Cicero "wiped out" piety and humanity.[54] In contrast to Cicero, Christians repudiated giving calculated to produce reciprocity; in their giving as well as in their praying, they reject a *do ut des* approach. So Lactantius urged Constantine to give uncalculatingly: "Give to the blind, the sick, the lame and the destitute; if you don't, they die. Men may have no use for them, but God has: he keeps them alive, gives them breath and honors them with light. . . . Anyone who can help a

49. Elizabeth DePalma Digeser, "Lactantius and Constantine's Letter to Arles: Dating the *Divine Institutes*," *JECS* 2, no. 1 (1994): 50–52.

50. Odahl, *Constantine*, 127.

51. Lactantius, *Inst.* 1.1.13, trans. Anthony Bowen and Peter Garnsey, *Lactantius: Divine Institutes*, TTH 40 (Liverpool: Liverpool University Press, 2003), 59.

52. Lactantius, *Inst.* 6.3.1 (Bowen and Garnsey, 333).

53. Lactantius, *Inst.* 6.4.11 (Bowen and Garnsey, 336).

54. Lactantius, *Inst.* 6.11.12 (Bowen and Garnsey, 353); S. Brandt, CSEL 19 (1890), 521; cf. Cicero, *Off.* 2.54.

dying man but doesn't is his murderer."[55] This obligation involves providing care for people who are "unsuitable": hospitality for "poor and desperate" people who need accommodation; ransom for captives; support for orphans and widows who are destitute and need to be defended. None of these can reciprocate, but Christians know that acts that help these people are "works [that] are especially ours to do because we have received . . . the words of God himself instructing us."[56] Another distinctive expression of Christian piety was their provision of decent burial for strangers and poor people. Cicero completely ignored this service because he "measured all [his] duties by utility," but Christians believed that in these apparently useless people "the workmanship of God" is evident.[57] If Constantine wanted to obtain the favor of the living God, he must go beyond Cicero and honor "the living images of God"—all of them.[58]

Second, the emperor must deal with evil patiently. Once again Cicero got it wrong, this time by inserting not one word but two. He says that a good man "injures no one *unless provoked by injury* [*lacessitus iniuria*]."[59] These two Latin words, says Lactantius, open the door for vengeance, which is not the Christian way. The distinctive Christian approach to conflict is "invincible patience."[60] Unlike the pagan Cicero who lacks the virtue of patience, in public and private life the patient Christian will not retaliate; he has learned "how to control and reduce his own anger." Lactantius further faults Cicero for advocating retaliation: if Cicero "had kept his patience when provoked," he would have spared himself and the republic great disasters.[61] Ultimately, Lactantius reminds Constantine, the Christian tradition not only rejects retaliation but repudiates killing in all its forms: "Killing a human being is always wrong because it is God's will for man to be a sacred creature." Christians view the killing of newborn babies as "the greatest of impieties," and they equally refuse to engage in killing in the amphitheater, capital punishment, and warfare: "A just man may not be a soldier, since his warfare is justice itself, nor may he put anyone on a capital charge."[62] All forms of killing are shortcuts, signs of impatience that are not appropriate for the Christian, whose tradition views patience as "the supreme virtue."[63]

55. Lactantius, *Inst*. 6.11.18–19 (Bowen and Garnsey, 354).
56. Lactantius, *Inst*. 6.12.22 (Bowen and Garnsey, 357).
57. Lactantius, *Inst*. 6.12.25, 30, trans. W. Fletcher, *ANF* 7:177.
58. Lactantius, *Inst*. 6.13.13 (Bowen and Garnsey, 369).
59. Lactantius, *Inst*. 6.18.15 (Fletcher, 184); Brandt, CSEL 19:549; cf. Cicero, *Off*. 3.76.
60. Lactantius, *Inst*. 6.18.23 (Fletcher, 184).
61. Lactantius, *Inst*. 6.18.27–28 (Bowen and Garnsey, 371).
62. Lactantius, *Inst*. 6.20.16–18 (Bowen and Garnsey, 375).
63. Lactantius, *Inst*. 6.18.30 (Bowen and Garnsey, 371).

Lactantius adds a third concern: religious liberty. In book 5 of the *Divine Institutes*, which he does not directly address to Constantine but which he probably presented at court, Lactantius argues passionately that religion must grow out of people's profound assent, their inner "willingness." Religion cannot be promoted by compulsion. The advocates of a religion must make their case by patience. When people seek to defend a religion by bloodshed and torture, the religion is "polluted and outraged."[64] Instead, advocates of a religion must argue their case. So let the pagans "unsheathe the sharpness of their wits; . . . we [Christians] are ready to listen if they would tell; if they keep silent, we simply cannot believe them." Further, if people use violence against them, the Christians will not yield.[65] Standing in the Christian tradition that goes back to Tertullian, Lactantius affirms a patient approach to religion, an approach that repudiates coercion.[66] "Truth cannot be partnered with violence, nor justice with cruelty. . . . Religion must be defended not by killing but by dying, not by violence but by patience, not by sin but by faith; that is the contrast between bad and good, and in religion the practice must be good, not bad."[67] Lactantius is convinced that what makes a religion persuasive is how it affects people's lives. When people challenge them about their faith, Christians use their unique apologetic—they talk about how they *live*: "We teach, we show, we demonstrate."[68] In this apologetic all believers—not only the literate Christians—are important: "Our old women and our children" also make the case for Christianity.[69] Lactantius is categorical: religions that do not bring vital life to ordinary people will atrophy. Christians know that no amount of force can establish a religion securely and profoundly.

Constantine Responds to Lactantius

Lactantius appealed to Constantine to be a patient emperor. And Constantine, who clearly had read a lot and interacted with Lactantius, pulled back. He had his own theological thoughts and would appropriate from the Christian

64. Lactantius, *Inst.* 5.19.23 (Bowen and Garnsey, 321).
65. Lactantius, *Inst.* 5.19.11 (Bowen and Garnsey, 320).
66. Everett Ferguson, "Voices of Religious Liberty in the Early Church," *Restoration Quarterly* 19 (1976): 13–22; Peter Garnsey, "Religious Toleration in Classical Antiquity," in *Persecution and Toleration*, ed. W. J. Sheils, Studies in Church History 21 (Oxford: Blackwell, 1984), 1–27; Bowen and Garnsey, *Lactantius: Divine Institutes*, 46–48.
67. Lactantius, *Inst.* 5.19.17, 22 (Bowen and Garnsey, 321).
68. Lactantius, *Inst.* 5.19.12 (Bowen and Garnsey, 320).
69. Lactantius, *Inst.* 5.19.14 (Bowen and Garnsey, 321).

tradition what was credible to him and useful. As MacMullen puts it, Constantine was "decidedly a Christian—on his own terms."[70]

How do we learn what his terms were? Supremely by his actions, but also by a speech—his lengthy *Oration to the Assembly of Saints*.[71] Scholars have argued at length about when and where he gave the speech.[72] I follow Mark Edwards, who proposes that Constantine gave the speech in Rome in the Easter season of 314 or 315. I do so in part because the speech seems clearly to be a defense of Constantine's own position as an uncatechized, unbaptized quasi-Christian at a time when this posture would have been new and controversial, and in part because the speech responds to Lactantius, who at that point was resident in this court.[73]

In the speech, Constantine engaged in conventional denunciations of paganism; he attacked polytheism and fate and praised monotheism.[74] More interestingly, he justified himself. He recognized the distance between himself, an uncatechized, unbaptized person, and his Christian audience (the "saints"): "In me . . . no human education ever gave me assistance."[75] Nevertheless, he had something to offer. For him as well as for all Christians the challenge is "to hymn Christ through my way of life"—for Constantine lifestyle mattered.[76] But he was convinced that from Christ he learned less about "the so-called political virtues" than about "paths which lead to the intellectual world."[77] So reason was central to Constantine's approach, but in his view reason would not lead everyone to live in the same way. Constantine differed from many Christians, who believed that everyone must be "of the same

70. Ramsay MacMullen, *Constantine* (London: Croom Helm, 1969), 113.

71. Constantine, *Oration to the Assembly of Saints*, trans. Edwards, *Constantine and Christendom*, 1–62.

72. Robin Lane Fox places the *Oration* on Good Friday 324 in Antioch (*Pagans and Christians* [San Francisco: Harper & Row, 1986], 635); Timothy D. Barnes places it on Easter 325 in Nicomedia ("Constantine's *Speech to the Assembly of the Saints*: Place and Date of Delivery," *JTS* 2/52, no. 1 [2001]: 34); H. A. Drake views it as a "generic or basic speech" that is placeless and timeless, "the type of speech that . . . the emperor was always giving" (*Constantine and the Bishops: The Politics of Intolerance* [Baltimore: Johns Hopkins University Press, 2000], 294).

73. For Mark Edwards's location and dating of the speech, which I accept, see his introduction to *Constantine and Christendom*, xxix; also his "The Constantinian Circle and the Oration to the Saints," in *Apologetics in the Roman Empire: Pagans, Jews, and Christians*, ed. Mark Edwards, Martin Goodman, Simon Price, and Christopher Rowland (Oxford: Oxford University Press, 1999), 268. Edwards states (252) that Constantine's "cardinal aim is . . . to define his own relation to the Church." He also notices that Ivan Heikel, the editor of the Greek text (derived from the original Latin), points out many places in which Constantine is clearly indebted to Lactantius (269 and 269n).

74. Constantine, *Oration* 3, 6, 8.

75. Constantine, *Oration* 11 (Edwards, 20).

76. Constantine, *Oration* 5 (Edwards, 7).

77. Constantine, *Oration* 11 (Edwards, 25).

habits [*homotropos*]. . . . They demand that everything once for all should be of a single form." Constantine found this unreasonable, "utterly ridiculous." People have different habits not only because of the choices they make but also because of their tendency to leave reason behind and "give way to passion."[78]

Constantine wanted to live rationally, dispassionately, in areas that Lactantius had discussed in his writings.

Honoring the weak: Constantine mentioned that Christ emphasized visiting the sick and comforting the extremely poor. But Constantine's passion was aroused, and he denounced people (evidently traditional Christians) who criticized inequality and who found it unjust "that the honorable should rank above the inferior." For Constantine reason dictated a conservative, aristocratic benevolence, in which the rich "share what they have with poorer people by a philanthropic distribution."[79]

A patient approach to enemies: Constantine was astonishingly open to nonviolence. He acknowledged that Jesus in Matthew 26:52 restrained Peter, telling him to put back his sword. Everyone "who initiates unjust acts or undertakes to use the sword against the instigator of unrighteousness will perish by violence." Reflecting Lactantius almost precisely, Constantine added, "This is indeed heavenly wisdom, to choose to be injured rather than to injure, and when it is necessary, to suffer evil rather than to do it."[80] Constantine had had personal experience with violence, and God had rescued him "from the terrors." In the Scriptures Constantine found God performing similar acts of rescue: in the exodus God liberated the Israelites "not by shooting arrows or launching javelins, but just by holy prayer and meek adoration."[81] Recently, like his Roman audience, Constantine had experienced the atrocities brought on by the tyrant Maxentius. You, he said to his audience, "coming forward, gave yourselves up, relying on your faith in God." You struggled valiantly with "executioners and tormentors."[82] But I, in contrast, Constantine said, was there as a warrior. I have seen battles and have observed "God cooperating with our prayers. . . . It is human to lapse sometimes, but God is not to be blamed for human lapses." Constantine looked at his hands, which had been responsible for the shedding of blood, and said, "And all human beings

78. Constantine, *Oration* 13 (Edwards, 30–31); PG 20:1273. Drake (*Constantine and the Bishops*, 303) states that Constantine is arguing against uniformity of belief, "in favor of a broadly inclusive and tolerant monotheism." On the contrary, Constantine is arguing against uniformity of *behavior*. He desires a church in the empire in which not everyone will be "of the same habits," in which there will be various ways of living the faith.

79. Constantine, *Oration* 13, 15 (Edwards, 32, 34).

80. Constantine, *Oration* 15 (Edwards, 35).

81. Constantine, *Oration* 16 (Edwards, 38).

82. Constantine, *Oration* 22 (Edwards, 54–55).

know that the most holy devotion of these hands is owed to God."[83] Human beings, said Constantine, must be allowed to have different habits; and the restraint of these habits will come from God, who honors reason and who "takes his seat in the intellect."[84]

In this oration, Constantine never used the word *patience*. But he came close. As we have seen, he differentiated himself from egalitarian Christians; he remained the *Augustus*. Nevertheless, Constantine was saying to the "saints" that because he wanted life to be governed by reason, there must reasonably be more than one habitual way to be Christian—and that it would be legitimate for some Christians to kill judicially and in battle.[85]

Two kinds of Christian habitus: Constantine anticipates Eusebius of Caesarea, who in the 330s in his *Proof of the Gospel* proposed that there should be "two ways of life," not of Christians and pagans, but of two kinds of Christians: one kind "living the perfect way of life . . . and the other more humble, more human"; the one nonviolent, the other fighting. This arrangement anticipates Christendom and can incorporate emperors and soldiers among the faithful.[86]

83. Constantine, *Oration* 26 (Edwards, 61–62).

84. Constantine, *Oration* 15 (Edwards, 36).

85. Lactantius, probably in the 320s, wrote the *Epitome of the Divine Institutes*, which in 73 brief chapters restates and refines the contents of his huge work—and responds obliquely to Constantine. Louis J. Swift (*The Early Fathers on War and Military Service* [Wilmington, DE: Michael Glazier, 1983], 65–66) has suggested that Lactantius in the *Epitome*, influenced by Constantine, has retreated from his earlier opposition to killing in warfare: e.g., in the passage where the *Divine Institutes* had specified "a just man may not be a soldier," the *Epitome* prohibits suicide. It is possible that this represents a change of thinking on the part of Lactantius. On the other hand, it may be that Lactantius is holding his ground theologically while being diplomatic. Certainly the *Epitome* unapologetically commends a life of practical *patience* that trusts in God's providence. And patience entails abstention from killing and from ordering killing in the cause of the government, applying "the peril of death by word" (capital punishment) (*Epit.* 64, trans. W. Fletcher, ANF 7:249).

86. Eusebius, *Proof of the Gospel* 1.8, trans. and ed. William J. Ferrar, *Eusebius: The Proof of the Gospel* (Grand Rapids: Baker, 1981), 48–49. A two-tiered Christianity that justifies the use of the sword by laymen gradually took hold, despite the reluctance of some theologians and bishops. In the 370s, for example, in his canonical *Ep.* 188.13, St. Basil the Great decreed, as a matter of "concession," that those who have killed in war "only abstain from communion for three years" (trans. B. Jackson, NPNF[2] 8:228). Basil would clearly have liked to make this more stringent. But later Christians, such as the twelfth-century Byzantine canonist Balsamon (*Commentary on the Canons* 13.2.65), viewed Basil as impossibly demanding. Its consequences were clear to Balsamon: if Basil's canon were enforced, it would mean that combatants "who are engaged in successive wars" would "never partake of the divine sanctified Elements." This, according to Balsamon, was "unendurable" and required revision (Patrick Viscusso, "Christian Participation in Warfare: A Byzantine View," in *Peace and War in Byzantium: Essays in Honor of George T. Dennis, SJ*, ed. Timothy S. Miller and John Nesbitt [Washington, DC: Catholic University of America Press, 1995], 33–40).

Christianization of the Law

We have looked at Constantine's ideas. What about his actions? What did Constantine do as a liminal Christian emperor? Although he was not a baptized believer, according to Peter Leithart he was interested in the "Christianization of the law."[87] At his best he was imaginative and courageous. It led him to reform the judicial process so that the law, with bishops as judges, could be available to the "oppressed lower classes."[88] It further led to manumission, the freeing of slaves in church, which Constantine specifically presented as an act pleasing to God.[89] Constantine's Christianizing of the law continued to ripple outward, leading to an outlawing of crucifixion, branding people on the face, and thrusting convicted criminals *ad bestias* in the arena.[90]

And yet Constantine's unreformed habitus kept asserting itself in brutal, violent ways, disfiguring his Christian persona. In 314, at about the time when Constantine was orating to the saints in Rome, he expressed support for the African Catholic bishops as they "exercise[d] patience" in their struggle against the Donatists; but—impatiently—he then told the bishops that he ordered his men "to bring these unspeakable deceivers of religion to my court, so that they may . . . learn that there is something worse than death for them."[91] For the liminal Christian Constantine, torture remains normal. A second example: when a government official publicly shames an indebted woman while distraining her property, what should happen to him? Constantine decreed that

87. Peter J. Leithart, *Defending Constantine: The Twilight of an Empire and the Dawn of Christendom* (Downers Grove, IL: IVP Academic, 2010), 232.

88. Cod. theod. 1.16.4; *Sirmondian Constitution* 1, trans. and ed. Clyde Pharr, *The Theodosian Code and Novels, and the Sirmondian Constitution* [Princeton: Princeton University Press, 1952], 28, 477). See further Drake, *Constantine and the Bishops*, 326–49; Leithart, *Defending Constantine*, 217.

89. Leithart, *Defending Constantine*, 223–24; Cod. theod. 4.7.1.

90. Ramsay MacMullen, "What Difference Did Christianity Make?," *Historia* 35 (1986): 332–34; see also 333n, where MacMullen states that the penalty *ad bestias* was invoked only once in the Theodosian Code (Cod. theod. 9.18.1 [Pharr, 240]), in a letter of 315 to the Vicar of Africa), to punish people who stole the children of others: "If he is a slave or has been presented with his freedom, he shall be thrown to the wild beasts at the first public spectacle." If freeborn, he was to be given to gladiatorial combat with this merciful "general rule" that "before he does anything to defend himself, he shall be destroyed by the sword." On Constantine's discomfort with public spectacles and gladiators by 325, see Cod. theod. 15.12.1 (Pharr, 436), which places criminals in the mines rather than the arena: "Bloody spectacles displease us amid public peace and domestic tranquility. Wherefore, since we wholly forbid the existence of gladiators, you shall cause those persons who, perchance, on account of some crime, customarily sustained that condition and sentence, to serve rather in the mines, so that they will assume the penalty for their crimes without shedding their blood."

91. Constantine to African Catholic Bishops, after the Synod of Arles (314), in Edwards, *Optatus*, 190–91, in appendix 5.

he should "be punished by a capital penalty." Then as an afterthought Constantine added, "Or rather he shall be done to death with exquisite tortures."[92] A third example: if a man incites a young girl to sexual activity against her will, what should be his punishment? Constantine decreed that the man's mouth, which had incited evil, "shall be closed by pouring in molten lead."[93] These examples indicate an emperor with a short fuse and unreconstructed habitus; he was still reflexively in the thrall of *dignitas* and violence. So it's not surprising that in 326, whatever offenses his son Crispus and his wife Fausta may (or may not) have committed, Constantine responded not by forgiving them but by contriving their execution.[94] If Constantine had experienced a conversion of lifestyle and habitus, he could have responded differently to these agonizingly broken relationships—and given a moving Christian witness to the empire.

A Thought Experiment: Constantine the Christian and Patient Mission

I suggest that we do a brief thought experiment—a detour into counterfactual history to see how things might have proceeded throughout Constantine's reign if in 312–14 Constantine had allowed himself to be catechized and baptized as a Christian. We know that Constantine had been influenced by Christians but didn't bow his knees to Christ as Lord until 337. But what if throughout his reign Constantine had been a Christian? What if his convictions and habitus had been changed by his conversion? What if, as a result, he had been a consistently patient emperor? How might his Christian convictions and reflexes have shaped his approach to the church in its mission? Across the centuries there have been many "imaginary Constantines"; I propose to add one more—Constantine the catechized Christian.[95]

92. Cod. theod. 1.22.1, January 316 (Pharr, 30).
93. Cod. theod. 9.24.1, April 320 (Pharr, 245).
94. For various explanations of the behaviors of Crispus and Fausta and the modes of their deaths, see Hans A. Pohlsander, "Crispus: Brilliant Career and Tragic End," *Historia* 33 (1984): 97–106.
95. A. Kazhdan, "'Constantin Imaginaire': Byzantine Legends of the Ninth Century about Constantine the Great," *Byzantion* 57 (1987): 196–250. Garth Fowden ("The Last Days of Constantine: Oppositional Versions and Their Influence," *JRS* 84 [1994]: 169) notes that there is a "newly favorable environment for study of imaginary Constantines." See also Rodney Stark, *One True God: Historical Consequences of Monotheism* (Princeton: Princeton University Press, 2001), 227, who invites his readers to "consider what might have happened had Constantine not given state preference to Christianity and had not supported those who demanded adherence to a universal orthodoxy" and comes up with an intriguing scenario.

Let us recall that Constantine was an educated Roman. In his *Oration to the Assembly of Saints* he impressively demonstrated this education. In his *paideia* (his formation as an aristocrat) he had possibly encountered the letters of Pliny the Younger, written in the early second century, which circulated in aristocratic circles as models of style and public policy. In AD 112 Pliny, then the governor of Pontus, had written a letter to Emperor Trajan that provides a precious early account of Christian church life.[96] Two centuries later this account might have been relevant to Constantine as a Christian emperor. Like all Christians, Constantine would have been repulsed by pagan sacrifice. But what should he do about it?

Reading Pliny's letters, Constantine would have met a Roman governor who in Pontus had encountered something that was new to him—a Christian community that was gaining in strength and local influence. According to information that Pliny had been able to extract, in part by torture, Christians had a lifestyle of sexual purity and truthfulness, they shared economically, and they empowered women, two of whom occupied positions of leadership in the community. Their life centered in gatherings for worship. As a result of the Christian community's influence, local people had ceased attending sacrifices in local pagan temples. Pliny referred to "almost deserted temples." This abandonment of pagan practices enraged local businessmen and farmers, who reported a decline in demand for the sacrificial animals they raised. Paganism was losing strength. People, not finding life in paganism, were voting with their feet.

So, as Constantine read on, what did he find Pliny doing? Pliny thought like a Roman. He was a conventional governor, famous for his conventionality. He used force. When people would not deny that they were Christians, he executed the lower class among them, sent the believers who were Roman citizens to Rome for execution, and restored the practice of sacrifice. For a time Christianity receded in Pontus (although a century and a half later it reemerged strongly under Bishop Gregory the Wonderworker).[97]

Continuing our thought experiment, we imagine that in 312, when Constantine came to sole power in the West, he might have thought back to his upbringing and recalled Pliny's famous epistle, which reported that in Pontus pagan sacrifice had declined when a Christian community had demonstrated an attractive alternative. If Constantine had been on the journey to baptism, he would have thought about what he was learning in his catechesis—that coercion isn't what the Christian tradition teaches. His catechists might have studied Cyprian, whose catechetical document *Ad Quirinum* 3 states: "That the liberty of believing or

96. Pliny the Younger to Trajan, *Ep.* 10.96, trans. J. Stevenson, *A New Eusebius*, rev. ed. (London: SPCK, 1987), 18–20.
97. Raymond Van Dam, *Becoming Christian: The Conversion of Roman Cappadocia* (Philadelphia: University of Pennsylvania Press, 2003), chap. 3.

not believing is placed in free choice."⁹⁸ Certainly Constantine would have been influenced by the teaching of his resident intellectual Lactantius: "Worship cannot be forced; it is something to be achieved by talk rather than blows, so that there is free will in it. . . . We teach, we show, we demonstrate."⁹⁹

So, in our imaginative scenario, Constantine the Christian decided to adopt a policy of mission true to the early Christians' tradition of patience:

- *Regarding paganism*: Constantine would abolish state subsidies for pagan temples and sacrifice. But he would not abolish sacrifice (let the aristocrats pay for it if they want to) or plunder the temples. The many forms of paganism would remain legal.
- *Regarding Christianity*: Constantine would abolish all legal impediments to Christianity, putting the Christians on the same grounds as all religions. The Christians could meet, worship, proselytize, and own property. Christianity was growing, and Constantine would not want to interfere with this patient process, so he would not grant imperial subsidies to Christians or confer privileges on their leaders. He would sense that Christianity's growth is the work of God, and he would intuit that governmental instrumentality could mess this up.
- *Regarding "heretical" Christians*: Constantine would refuse to intervene against the rivals of the orthodox Catholic church that he favors. If the Novatians, Valentinians, Cataphrygians, and others were wrong, Constantine would be confident that their influence would recede.

Where would our imagined Constantine get this confidence? From his belief, shaped by catechesis and shared with the Christians before him, that God is at work and that in Christ and his church there is abundant life.¹⁰⁰ Constantine abhorred pagan sacrifice and hated heresy. In our thought experiment he, as a Christian, would have learned that the way to combat paganism and heresy is to let everyone worship without either subsidy or impediment. When the church worshiped God rightly, the lives of the worshipers became icons of Jesus Christ, and their approaches to urban life, hierarchy, women, burial, and the plague were exemplary and attractive. Our imagined Constantine would determine to give freedom to all religions including the church and to entrust the future to God.

But Constantine did not do these things. Instead, what did he do?

98. Cyprian, *Ad Quir.* 3.52, trans. E. Wallis, *ANF* 5:547.
99. Lactantius, *Inst.* 5.19.11–12 (Bowen and Garnsey, 320).
100. Alan Kreider, *Worship and Evangelism in Pre-Christendom*, Alcuin/GROW Joint Liturgical Studies 32 (Cambridge: Grove Books, 1995), 10–14.

Constantine's Religious Policy

Constantine did not approach religious policy as a baptized believer in the Christian tradition. Instead, he approached it as a traditional Roman with Christian affinities who was convinced that the religious cult played a central role in unifying society. Concord (*homonoia*) in religion was central to his policy; it was the means of securing divine blessing for all of society.[101] To the uncatechized Constantine it was self-evident that the imperial government was duty-bound to use its power, patronage, and wealth to ensure concord. When Constantine identified himself with the church and applied this kind of thinking to the church's mission, he set in motion a transformation in the church's understanding and practice of mission.

Before Constantine, as we have seen, the church was growing steadily, but its leaders gave little thought to the means of its numerical growth. They worshiped God, God changed the worshipers and their communities, and outsiders were attracted to Christians whose lives and communities reflected God's character. Growth was a mystery, the product of God's "invisible power."[102] The Christians' approach to growth was to be patient collaborators with God.

With Constantine we move from mystery to method. The emperor could influence the growth of the correct religion—Christianity—by using means and methods, including the power and manipulation of the state, "in the hope that the human race [may be] enlightened through my instrumentality."[103] Constantine's reflexes were those of a Roman administrator, not of a faithful member in the Christian tradition. Constantine thought impatiently, instrumentally. Under him the state became an instrument of a missional program with two flanks, one flank that fostered and established the correct religion, and the other flank that punished and outlawed the erroneous groups that competed with the correct religion.

Favoring the Acceptable Church

The first flank of Constantine's instrumental approach is evident in his laws and initiatives. Constantine exempted the clergy from taxation and public services *so that* the church's services "may be filled with a great multitude of people" and *so that* local aristocrats would be attracted to the church.[104] He ordered a weekly day of rest for workers *so that* the Lord's day would help "to

101. Eusebius, *Vit. Const.* 3.20.3; MacMullen, *Constantine*, 165.
102. Origen, *Hom. Luc.* 7.7, trans. J. T. Lienhard, FC 94 (1996), 31.
103. Eusebius, *Vit. Const.* 2.28, trans. E. C. Richardson, NPNF² 1:507.
104. Cod. theod. 16.2.10 (in May 320) (Pharr, 442 and 442n).

lead all mankind to the worship of God."[105] He made plentiful provision for the poor *so that* there would be "an incentive to turn to the Saviour's teaching."[106] Instrumental thinking of this sort—aimed at the establishment of the church in society—also underlay his construction of basilicas.[107] To be sure, in all of this there was a risk of producing conformist, careerist "rice Christians"—hypocrites. Both Eusebius and Constantine recognized this risk. As Eusebius put it: "In truth I can myself bear testimony to the scandalous hypocrisy of those who crept into the Church, and assumed the name and character of Christians."[108] This was not new with Constantine: from the book of Acts onward there had been hypocrites in the church. Christian leaders before Constantine had believed that hypocrisy undercut their witness, and they did everything they could to prevent it from nestling in their churches.[109] But under Constantine there was a change. Constantine saw hypocrisy as a necessary by-product of a new form of mission that valued numbers more than lifestyle, rationality more than habitus. And when Constantine used state power to promote the church, from the vantage point of the Christian tradition he was tampering with God's missional work in a way that was both unnecessary and adulterating.

Further, Constantine's use of state power was not to root un-Christian behavior out of the church but rather to root heresy out of society. This was the aim of the council at Nicaea to which Constantine summoned the bishops in 325, and whose creed and canons he backed up by banishings. Constantine's commitment was to a concord that was theological and cultic, and he believed that there should be one entity, the catholic and apostolic church, that would placate God through its proper services. His religious policy and his missional approach involved using the state to promote and protect this church.

105. *Codex Iustinianus* 3.12.2 (ca. 321); Eusebius, *Vit. Const.* 4.18 (Richardson, 544).
106. Eusebius, *Vit. Const.* 3.58.4 (Cameron and Hall, 147).
107. Eusebius, *Vit. Const.* 3.58.3; 3.30–32.
108. Eusebius, *Vit. Const.* 4.54 (*NPNF*² 1:554), which gives Eusebius's perspective; *Vit. Const.* 3.58.4 gives the perspective of Constantine, who expressed himself "almost using the same words as the one [St. Paul, in Phil. 1:18] who said, 'Whether in pretense or in truth let Christ be preached.'"
109. See the scrutinies of lifestyle to which the *Trad. ap.* 15–16 subjected potential catechumens. For an earlier attempt to root out the hypocrisy that damaged Christian witness, see 2 Clem. 13. During the pre-Constantinian persecution, also notice the concern of the church leaders in Cirta in North Africa, whose people's scandalous behavior would "give such an example to the pagans, so that those who believed in God through us may themselves curse us when we come before the public" (*Gesta apud Zenophilum* 9–10, trans. and ed. Ramsay MacMullen and Eugene N. Lane, *Paganism and Christianity, 100–425 CE: A Sourcebook* [Minneapolis: Fortress, 1992], 253). The tradition continues in a post-Constantine text possibly by Athanasius: "Let not the gentiles revile God's name through us" (*Canons of Athanasius 9*, trans. and ed. W. Riedel and E. Crum, *The Canons of Athanasius, Patriarch of Alexandria, ca. 293–373* [Amsterdam: Philo Press, 1973], 18).

Dealing with the Dissidents

The second flank of Constantine's policy had to do with alternatives to catholic Christianity. Constantine did what he could to frustrate these groups—pagans, Donatists, Jews, and heretics. Of these, by far the most numerous were the clusters of practices and beliefs we call paganism. Paganism was deeply embedded in people whose power Constantine had to take account of, notably Roman senators, soldiers, and imperial administrators. Although Constantine (according to Eusebius) banned "every form of sacrifice," some scholars have queried whether this edict existed. If it did, it was not widely enforced; in many places pagans continued to perform sacrifice into the 380s.[110] Constantine clearly was willing to spoil the pagan temples, but he didn't want to punish the pagans.[111] In his *Letter to Eastern Provincials* of 324, Constantine reflected the Christian tradition he had learned from Lactantius: "[Let] no one use what he has received by inner conviction as a means to harm his neighbor. What each has seen and understood, he must use, if possible, to help the other; but if that is impossible, the matter should be dropped. It is one thing to take on willingly the contest for immortality, quite another to enforce it with sanctions."[112]

The "schismatic" Donatists had triggered Constantine's ire in 314. By 321 Constantine had recognized the limitations of his power. Instead of continuing his attempt to repress a movement that was deeply rooted in North African society, he recognized that, lacking a better alternative, he would have to resort to "continual patience." In line with the early Christian tradition, Constantine said, "Let nothing be done to reciprocate an injury; for it is a fool who would usurp the vengeance which we ought to reserve to God."[113] Nine years later nothing had changed, including Constantine's praise of the bishops whose patience imitated "the patience of the Most High God."[114] Traditional Christianity at least applied when Constantine knew that his interventionism was going nowhere.

110. Eusebius, *Vit. Const.* 4.23 (Cameron and Hall, 161). The year of this edict, if in fact the edict existed, is unknown (Cameron and Hall, *Eusebius: Life of Constantine*, 243–44). Alan Cameron (*The Last Pagans of Rome* [Oxford: Oxford University Press, 2011], 45, 61) states that this may not have been a general edict but a response to a local situation.

111. Only six pagan sites are known to have been spoiled during Constantine's reign (Lane Fox, *Pagans and Christians*, 671–72).

112. Eusebius, *Vit. Const.* 2.60.1 (Cameron and Hall, 114).

113. Constantine to the [North African] Catholics, 321, trans. Edwards, *Optatus*, 196–97, in appendix 9.

114. Constantine to Numidian Bishops, February 5, 330, trans. Edwards, *Optatus*, 200, in appendix 10: Constantine, who expressed praise for the bishops' patience, kept up pressure on the Donatists by conferring benefits on the Catholics, such as absolving the Catholic clergy from onerous public duties.

But some of Constantine's language was ominous. Already in 315, when Lactantius's influence was immediate, Constantine railed against the third group, the "feral sect" of the Jews; and in the 320s he impatiently fulminated against the Quartodeciman Christians, who obstinately followed the same calendar as "[that] detestable mob [of Jews] . . . that nation of parricides and Lord-killers."[115] Where might this lead?

And what of the "heretics" who did not fit into the emerging orthodox church? Constantine indicated his approach in two letters. In 330 he wrote a letter addressed to the "Novatians, Valentinians, Marcionites," and the rest, in which he gave unfettered expression to his impatient habitus. According to Constantine, the heretics were full of venomous poison, contagiously infecting people "as with an epidemic disease" and "wounding innocent and pure consciences."[116] Constantine was fed up, out of patience: "Why should I go into detail? . . . Why should we endure such evils any longer?" By his command the authorities were to use "severe public measures" to suppress the heretics, to confiscate the houses in which they meet, and to guide the people into the Catholic church in which they would recover from their "polluted and destructive deviance."[117] Poison, epidemic disease, pollution—all these rhetorical themes show Constantine in disconcerting continuity with Emperor Maximin Daia, who in the recent persecutions had committed outrages against Christians in the eastern part of the empire.[118] In 333 Constantine wrote a second letter, this time to "bishops and people." He informed them that in order to combat the "depraved doctrine" of the heretic Arius, who had been anathematized at Nicaea, all treatises by him were to be burned. If anyone resisted this destruction by hiding a treatise by Arius, that person was to be subject to the death penalty.[119] By burning

---

115. Cod. theod. 16.8.1, from 315, when Lactantius's influence was recent (Pharr, 467); Vit. Const. 3.18.2.

116. Eusebius, Vit. Const. 3.64 (Cameron and Hall, 151–52). For the dating of 330 and comment, see Stuart G. Hall, "The Sects under Constantine," in Voluntary Religion, ed. W. J. Sheils and Diana Wood (Oxford: Blackwell, 1986), 1–13.

117. Eusebius, Vit. Const. 3.65 (Cameron and Hall, 152–53). Constantine had exempted Christian clergy from taxation and onerous public services; then in 326 he issued an edict (Cod. theod. 16.5.1 [Pharr, 450]) clarifying that these benefits must apply only to adherents of the Catholic faith: "Heretics and schismatics shall not only be alien from these privileges but shall also be bound and subjected to various public services."

118. See Maijastina Kahlos, "The Rhetoric of Tolerance and Intolerance: From Lactantius to Firmicus Maternus," in Changes and Continuities in Christian Apologetic, ed. A. Jacobsen, M. Kahlos, and J. Ulrich (Frankfurt: Peter Lang, 2009), 90. Passages from Maximin Daia quoted by Eusebius (Hist. eccl. 9.7.3–12) accuse the Christians of harboring "blinding mists of error" (9.7.3), "severe illness" (9.7.11), and "pollution and impiety" (9.7.12).

119. Socrates, Hist. eccl. 1.9.30, trans. A. C. Zenos, NPNF[2] 2:14.

books, Constantine was flexing his muscles, demonstrating his contempt for the "polluted" religious views of others, and implicitly conceding the impotence of his own views (which could not survive without state force). Book burning was another area in which Constantine established regrettable precedents for later Christian rulers.[120]

Swearing Oaths

A final note concerning Constantine's religious policies has to do with the swearing of oaths. In August 334 Constantine issued the following edict: "We have previously commanded that before they give their testimony, witnesses shall be bound by the sanctity of an oath, and greater trust shall be placed in the witness of more honorable status."[121] So when people, orthodox Christians as well as adherents of other religions, come before courts of law, they shall swear an oath—a "sanctified" oath—that their testimony is true. This may seem unproblematic. But from the perspective of the early Christians, it was deeply troubling. Early Christian theologians and catechists lived in a world in which oaths were sworn on all kinds of occasions, in business as well as in the lawcourts. They were sworn because oaths "were the very foundation of society"; according to Lycurgus, the legendary lawgiver of fourth-century-BC Athens, oaths were "the power" that holds his society together.[122] And yet early Christians dissented from this ancient commonplace, for what they considered good reasons. The pre-Constantinian Christians at times argued that in their experience oath taking didn't lead to a truthful society. Despite the plethora of oaths, perjury was rampant. But more fundamentally, for them Jesus's teaching was authoritative. In the Sermon on the Mount, Jesus had said, "Do not swear at all. . . . Let your yes be yes, and your no be no." Jesus had given this teaching for a reason—so Christians would be people who were truthful and were known to be truthful. As the late second-century martyr Apollonius of Rome put it: "We have been ordered by him never to swear and in all things to tell the truth. It is already considered a great oath when truth is affirmed by a 'yes'; hence it is wicked for a Christian to swear; for from deceit comes distrust, and through distrust in turn comes the oath."[123]

120. Daniel Sarefield, "Bookburning in the Christian Roman Empire: Transforming a Pagan Rite of Purification," in *Violence in Late Antiquity: Perceptions and Practices*, ed. H. A. Drake (Burlington, VT: Ashgate, 2006), 288–89.

121. Cod. theod. 11.39.3 (Pharr, 340).

122. Everett Ferguson, *Backgrounds of Early Christianity* (Grand Rapids: Eerdmans, 1987), 184; Lycurgus, *Against Leocrates* 79, trans. K. J. Maidment, LCL 308 (1941), 71–73.

123. *Martyrdom of Apollonius*, trans. Musurillo, *Acts of the Christian Martyrs*, 91, 93.

Many early Christian writers agreed with Apollonius.[124] Prominent among them was John Chrysostom, who in late fourth-century Antioch made it a central emphasis of his catechesis to help his catechumens break the "wicked habit" of taking oaths.[125] The sense that Jesus's teachings were practicable, expressions of wisdom that enabled new solutions for society's problems, did not disappear suddenly.[126] But in 334, when Constantine as a matter of imperial policy required Christians to swear, he was forcing them—as we have seen the pagan governor Culcianus attempting with Bishop Phileas—to do something in the lawcourts that Jesus said his followers should not do. Is this what the "Christianization of the law" is about?

Of course, like most of Constantine's legislation, his edict about oath taking was not always enforced, and throughout the fourth century many Christians continued to refuse to swear oaths. At the end of the fourth century Augustine of Hippo provided the classical justification of oaths in certain cases of necessity—the "just oath."[127] And throughout the Christendom centuries oaths became omnipresent and unavoidable, functioning in Christian Europe as in pagan Athens as the bond that held society together, and—in the event of someone's refusal to swear—as a potential indicator of heresy.[128]

In his approach to religious dissidents, Constantine showed the limits of his appropriation of Lactantius's teaching. He was not only parting company from Lactantius; he was also jettisoning the early Christians and their practices. Constantine had largely left behind the early Christian convictions that religions flourish when people willingly respond to God, that the very act of forcing religion pollutes religion, and that the difference between true religions and false religions is demonstrated by the way their adherents live. Christianity, said Lactantius, makes its points patiently: "We teach, we show,

124. Justin, *1 Apol.* 16; Irenaeus, *Haer.* 2.22.4; 2.32.1; Tertullian, *Idol.* 23; Origen, *Mart.* 7; *Martyrdom of Potamiaena* (Eusebius, *Hist. eccl.* 6.5); Cyprian, *Mort.* 4; *Ad Quir.* 3.12.

125. John Chrysostom, *Ninth Baptismal Instruction* 38–47, trans. and ed. P. Harkins, *St. John Chrysostom: Baptismal Instructions*, ACW 31 (1963), 143–47; see also Chrysostom, *Against the Judaizers* 1.3.4; *Hom. Gen.* 15.17, trans. R. C. Hill, FC 74 (1986), 205: "There is no call for swearing in just cause or unjust. Accordingly, keep your mouth clean of any oath, and ward off all such from your tongue, your lips, and your mind."

126. Karlmann Beyschlag, "Zur Geschichte der Bergpredigt in der Alten Kirche," *Zeitschrift für Theologie und Kirche* 74 (1977): 291–322.

127. Augustine, *Sermon on the Mount* 1.17.51.

128. Justinian Mandate on Oaths in Lawsuits, *Codex Iustinianus* 2.58.2; Heinrich Bullinger, *Der Widertöufferen ursprung*, 2nd ed. (Zurich: Froschauer, 1561), fol. 181b; trans. Edmund Pries, "Anabaptist Oath Refusal: Basel, Bern, and Strasbourg, 1525–1538" [PhD diss, University of Waterloo, 1995], 266: "The oath is the button, which holds together the authorities and covenants. . . . If you take the oath away from the authorities, behold whether you haven't dissolved the bond which holds together the whole body of the common good and of just government."

we demonstrate."[129] What, we may wonder, did Constantine's behavior teach, show, and demonstrate?

Constantine's Conversion—Nicomedia, 337

In the Easter season of 337 Constantine became ill, and, as Eusebius tells the story, he knew that he must be baptized soon.[130] Constantine did not commonly speak in terms of following the example of Christ, but in this case he thought it would be good to imitate Christ by being baptized in the Jordan River. But he was not well enough to travel to the Jordan, so he returned to home terrain, initially to Helenopolis in Asia Minor. There the aging emperor, failing in strength, knelt on the floor of the *martyrion*. At this the churchmen who received his confession were no doubt astonished and moved; for the first time Constantine experienced the laying on of hands and the prayers of the clergy. Fortified by this, he proceeded to the suburbs of Nicomedia, where he summoned the bishops. He had long "thirsted and yearned to win salvation in God," he informed them, and now he sensed that the time had come to receive "the seal that brings immortality." For twenty-five years he had been an outsider. Could he now be admitted as a catechumen? Constantine longed to be "numbered among the people of God." Further, he was eager to "meet and join in the prayers with them all together." For these to happen, Constantine knew that the Christian tradition required him to be instructed and to change his lifestyle. In his impatient mode Constantine specified that he, and not the bishops, would state how his behavior would change: "I shall now set for myself rules of life which befit God."

The catechesis of this unusual convert followed, preceded by catechesis— "such preliminary instruction as is required"—that must have been as abbreviated as possible. Then, just before Pentecost, Constantine was baptized. "The customary rites" moved Constantine deeply—he was "awestruck at the manifestation of the divinely inspired power" in baptism and, no doubt, in the Eucharist that he finally, at long last, received for the first time. The baptized emperor then promised the tangible expression of his repentance that he had chosen—he would never again wear a purple robe! Why this gesture? Was it because he knew of the church's long-standing rejection of purple clothing as

129. Lactantius, *Inst.* 5.19.12 (Bowen and Garnsey, 330).
130. This account is based on Eusebius, *Vit. Const.* 4.61–64 (Cameron and Hall, 177–79). My interpretation has been influenced by Pierre Batiffol, "Les étapes de la conversion de Constantin," *Bulletin d'ancienne littérature et d'archéologie chrétienne* 3 (1913): 264; and especially by E. J. Yarnold, "The Baptism of Constantine," StPatr 26 (1993): 95–101.

a sign of excess, aristocratic privilege, and imperial power?[131] Was it because of his own sorrow at what he had done as a purple-clad emperor? Constantine then prayed with thanksgiving that now, at long last, he had become a member of the people of God. In this prayer, he used the word *now* three times in one sentence. "I know that *now* I am in the true sense blessed, that *now* I have been shown worthy of immortal life, that *now* I have received divine light."[132] What does this prayer say of Constantine's view of the life he had lived prior to the *now*? Or of the bishops' view of their newly baptized convert? Within days Constantine died.

A Transformation of Patience?

So what have we seen in this chapter? I have said that with Constantine there was a "transformation of patience." In what ways was patience transformed? Let us not exaggerate the changes. Scholars rightly caution against overstating the changes that took place under Constantine.[133] A careful reading of the sources shows that the life of churches in many places continued substantially unchanged in the half century after Constantine's death. Nevertheless, Constantine's reign did offer changes to the Christians that invited them to make decisions. Let us look at five of these changes, particularly as they relate to patience.

First, control. Constantine offered the Christians the attraction of planning their missionary efforts and exercising control over them. Emperors thought instrumentally about everything. Why should Constantine not think instrumentally about Christianity as well? The Christians that Constantine encountered had a long experience of trusting God for the future and were reluctant to engage in strategic thinking about mission. As we have seen, their leaders didn't write about missionary methods; they didn't admonish people to engage in evangelistic activities. Instead, they urged people to worship

131. See, e.g., *Trad. ap.* 16; Minucius Felix, *Oct.* 31.6; 37.10; Cyprian, *Don.* 3.
132. Eusebius, *Vit. Const.* 4.63.1 (Bowen and Garnsey, 178).
133. For an example of the way a great patristics scholar debated this issue in his own head, see two writings of Henry Chadwick. In 1981 he wrote that with Constantine there occurred "one of the many revolutions that in retrospect . . . seem like mild ripples on the water making relatively little difference to what was already happening" ("The Church of the Third Century in the West," in *Roman West in the Third Century*, ed. A. King and M. Henig [London: British Archaeological Reports, 1981], 5). Nine years later, Chadwick concluded an article on "The Early Christian Community" by stating: "The pagan contemporaries of Constantine were not wrong in saying that he had carried through a huge religious and social revolution" (in *The Oxford Illustrated History of Christianity*, ed. J. McManners [Oxford: Oxford University Press, 1990], 61). The debate will go on in other heads.

God and, transformed by catechesis and worship, to obey the teachings of Jesus Christ in communities of peace that were exemplary and that attracted outsiders because they were intriguingly holy and whole. Since the Christians, in patience and hope, saw themselves as collaborators with God, they didn't need to manipulate things.

How different Constantine was! After all, he was shaped by a culture that was starkly different from that of the Christians. His instinctive behavior—shaped by his pagan habitus that he did not allow Christian catechesis to query—reflected an assumption that was self-evident to any pagan aristocrat: in matters of the church, as in all other areas, humans can plan and control events, using whatever means are necessary in order to obtain desired outcomes. Constantine invited Christians to plan and control.

Second, the power of the state. Constantine as emperor used imperial power as an instrument of control. That was his métier! And now he offered to use the power of the state for the best of ends—to promote conversion to Christianity. The early Christians hadn't thought like this. It was not simply that they were excluded from the power of the state. They, in the belief that their task was to live faithfully and patiently, didn't think about using their own power—their *church*'s resources of finance and sacrificial service—as an instrument of conversion. They cared for non-Christian plague victims, not so the victims would become Christians, but because the Christians' behavior reflected the character of the God whom the Christians worshiped. The God who had been infinitely good to them required them to show goodness to others.[134] When the church required a house to meet in or finances to provide burial for the poor and sustenance for widows, the church's members met these needs by giving from their own lives and resources. The believers' generosity probably led to the church's growth, but growth was not the reason for their generosity. So why should the Christians welcome the resources of the state to effect change? And yet that is what Constantine offered them. He issued laws that targeted imperial funds to the relief of poor people as "an incentive to turn to the Saviour's teaching."[135] Further, he allocated money from the imperial treasury to subsidize the construction of massive buildings, whether eucharistic basilicas such as St. John Lateran or funerary basilicas, six of which he constructed around the edges of Rome.[136] Constantine was inviting the Christians to use the state's power responsibly for their own ends.

134. See, e.g., Pontius, *Vit. Cypr.* 9, citing a favorite patience text, Matt. 5:45.
135. Eusebius, *Vit. Const.* 3.58.4 (Cameron and Hall, 147).
136. MacMullen, *Second Church*, 76–89; Richard Krautheimer, "The Ecclesiastical Building Policy of Constantine," in *Constantino il Grande: Dall'antichità all'umanesimo; Colloquio sul Christianesimo nel mondo antico* (Macerata: Università degli studi di Macerata, 1993), 509–52.

Third, religious coercion. Constantine authorized the use of imperial power to crush religious groups he disapproved of. The Christians had not thought like this. Their authors, from Tertullian on, had stated that worship could not be compelled and that "compulsion is not God's way of working."[137] Among the principles that mid-third-century North African Christians memorized was this: "The liberty of believing or of not believing is placed in free choice."[138] Many third-century Christian churches attempted to articulate what their agreed, correct, "orthodox" beliefs were; and at times they excommunicated people whom they viewed as heretics. But they did not run the heretics out of town or attempt to do them in; it was a clearly articulated part of beliefs they considered orthodox to honor the religious liberty of those who departed and, if relations with them were broken, to love them as enemies.[139] From their own experience as a persecuted minority, the Christians knew that many of them under pressure hadn't buckled, and they reasoned that it was useless to try to make other groups buckle. Lactantius spoke for the Christians: "We teach, we show, we demonstrate."[140]

Constantine, on the other hand, never submitted to their values. He was impressed when Lactantius invited him to become a tolerant emperor. And to some extent he was that. He fulminated against the pagans and their sacrifices but gave the pagans a reprieve. He and his successor emperors did not close temples until the 380s, and even then huge numbers of people did not stop engaging in pagan practices.[141] But against heretics Constantine moved more expeditiously. The move to crush illicit Christian groupings was rooted in Constantine's anti-heresy edict of 330, which according to Stuart Hall was "an imperial assault on voluntary Christianity.[142] Lactantius was a bearer of the early Christian tradition—persecution is not God's way of working and ultimately will not be effective.[143] But Constantine had not been catechized, and his hearing of Lactantius was that of an outsider who happened to be emperor. Against the Christian tradition, Constantine assumed that he could use legislation and armed groups to intimidate unacceptable religious groups,

137. *Diogn.* 7.4, trans. E. R. Fairweather et al., *Early Christian Fathers*, ed. C. C. Richardson, LCC 1 (1953), 219.

138. Cyprian, *Ad Quir.* 3.52, trans. E. Wallis, *ANF* 5:547.

139. For different approaches, see Averil Cameron, "The Violence of Orthodoxy," in *Heresy and Identity in Late Antiquity*, ed. Eduard Iricinschi and Holger M. Zelletin (Tübingen: Mohr Siebeck, 2008), 110–12; and Edwards, *Constantine and Christendom*, xiii: "We waive the dubious premiss that a religion must be intolerant because it is exclusive."

140. Lactantius, *Inst.* 5.19.11–12.

141. Cameron, *Last Pagans*, 45–46, 382.

142. Eusebius, *Vit. Const.* 3.64.1–65.3; Hall, "Sects under Constantine," 5.

143. Lactantius, *Inst.* 5.19.17, 22.

to shut them down, and to force their adherents into the church. Constantine was inviting the Christians to be realistic. Or was he simply being impatient?[144]

Fourth, speed. For the early Christians patience meant much more than an unhurried approach to life; trusting in God's goodness, they seem to have been astonishingly relaxed and laid back. In contrast, Constantine was in a hurry. He offered the Christians a faster tempo. Of course in all periods of Christian history there is "development," but in the century after Constantine the pace of development sped up markedly. The triumph of the church under Constantine led to a standardization of liturgies, the church year, and hymnody in a process that Paul Bradshaw calls "homogenization"—with all the glories and problems this entailed.[145] Some of the liturgical changes are evident in catechesis and baptism, which relate specifically to Constantine himself.

As we have seen, when Constantine first encountered the church, he was too impatient to submit to catechesis and baptism, so he deferred these until just before his death. By doing this, Constantine truncated his catechesis drastically. He also by implication expressed a theological idea that would have a huge future—that baptism is necessary not, as in the past, to enter into abundant, faithful life as a disciple of Jesus Christ but rather to avert eternal damnation. As was often the case, Constantine was a model. In the century after his death, many people deferred catechesis and baptism until the end of their lives. Many of those who proceeded to receive catechesis before they were on their deathbeds discovered that catechesis had changed. Surviving fourth-century catechetical homilies are numerous and lengthy, but they no longer involve the conscious, unhurried formation of believers who unlearn the reflexes of the world and are formed in the habitus of followers of Jesus Christ.[146] After Constantine, catechists largely avoided teaching behavior; instead they focused on belief, shaping the thinking of believers whose theology would be orthodox. Often catechetical programs were considerably shorter than they had been before Constantine.[147] Was this a consequence of Constantine's invitation to speed things up?

---

144. Realism requires us to note that, despite threatening imperial laws, unorthodox Christian groups continued to exist for centuries. For one example, the Montanists, see Christine Trevett, *Montanism: Gender, Authority and the New Prophecy* (Cambridge: Cambridge University Press, 1996), 223–32.

145. Paul F. Bradshaw, "The Homogenization of Christian Liturgy—Ancient and Modern," *SL* 26 (1996): 1–15.

146. For comment on Cyril of Jerusalem's famous catechetical homilies, see Alan Kreider, *The Change of Conversion and the Origin of Christendom* (Harrisburg, PA: Trinity Press International, 1999), 43–47.

147. On this point, which requires further research, see Maxwell E. Johnson, *The Rites of Christian Initiation*, rev. ed. (Collegeville, MN: Liturgical Press, 2007), 118–19.

Finally, conversion. Under Constantine a fascinating double conversion occurred. On the one hand, ambitious people "converted," approaching the churches with the intention of becoming members.[148] They were often in a hurry. The second canon of Nicaea of 325 was concerned "that men just converted from heathenism to the faith, and who have been instructed but a little while, are straightway brought to the spiritual laver, and as soon as they have been baptized, are advanced to the episcopate or the presbyterate."[149] From the perspective of the council fathers, speedy, superficial conversion was inappropriate, and the council opposed it. But it is unsurprising that this was taking place. The emperor's allure attracted adherents to convert to the emperor's religion—even when the emperor himself had not fully submitted to it.

On the other hand, the emperor "converted" the behavior of Christians in many areas, of which I cite two. One is killing. Constantine adhered to a faith whose disciplinary documents forbade the taking of human life.[150] He himself had deep reservations about this restriction and spoke clearly in favor of a Christianity in which not all believers are "of the same habits."[151] In the course of time Constantine's two-tier approach won out: in Christendom it came to be assumed that lay Christians and clerical Christians would have different habits about the taking of life. But it is interesting to observe signs in the fourth and fifth centuries that indicate that the early Christians' nonviolent habits were resilient.[152]

A second area has to do with the clothing of the clergy. This changed more rapidly than Christian approaches to killing. Soon after his victory over Maxentius, Constantine honored the ministers of God by inviting them to his table. One observer noted that their "appearance was *euteleis* (modest, thrifty, cheap) as to style of dress."[153] Some years later, when Constantine invited the bishops to a banquet in Nicaea at the time of his Vicennalia, the standard of living had escalated.

---

148. Cameron, *Last Pagans*, 174; Mark Edwards, "The Beginnings of Christianization," in *The Cambridge Companion to the Age of Constantine*, ed. Noel Lenski (Cambridge: Cambridge University Press, 2006), 139.

149. Council of Nicaea, canon 2, trans. H. R. Percival, *NPNF*² 15:10.

150. See *Trad. ap.* 16.9–11; *Canons of Hippolytus* 13. For an overview of the Christians' comprehensive repudiation of killing, see Ronald J. Sider, ed., *The Early Church on Killing: A Comprehensive Sourcebook on War, Abortion, and Capital Punishment* (Grand Rapids: Baker Academic, 2012).

151. Constantine, *Oration* 13 (Edwards, 30).

152. See *Trad. ap.* 16; Basil of Caesarea, *Ep.* 188.13; Socrates, *Hist. eccl.* 3.13 (regarding Julian the Apostate); Augustine, *Ep.* 136 and 138 (regarding Volusian).

153. Eusebius, *Vit. Const.* 1.42.1 (Cameron and Hall, 86); PG 20:956.

Not one of the bishops was missing. . . . The event was beyond all description. Guards and soldiers ringed the entrance to the palace, guarding it with drawn swords, and between these the men of God passed fearlessly, and entered the innermost royal courts. Some then reclined with him, others relaxed nearby on couches on either side. It might have been supposed that it was an imaginary representation of the Kingdom of Christ, and that what was happening was "dream, not fact."[154]

Eusebius does not tell us how the bishops were dressed on this occasion, but we can imagine. They were on a journey toward sartorial splendor that pagans scorned and sensitive Christians bewailed; the bishops, courted by the court, found it hard to keep their values or their habitus intact.[155] Given their changed context it was also a challenge, one imagines, to keep their biblical exegesis sound and their theological thinking straight. As theologian Reinhold Niebuhr once observed, "It is wonderful what a simple White House invitation will do to dull the critical faculties."[156]

154. Eusebius, *Vit. Const.* 3.15.1–2 (Cameron and Hall, 127).

155. Ammianus Marcellinus, *Res gestae* 27.3.14–15; for comment, see Léon Cristiani, "Essai sur les origines du costume ecclésiastique," in *Miscellanea Guillaume de Jerphanion* (Rome: Pontificium Institutum Orientalium Studiorum, 1947), 69–79.

156. Reinhold Niebuhr, "The King's Chapel and the King's Court," in *Christianity and Crisis*, August 4, 1969, http://www.religion-online.org/showarticle.asp?title=454; cited by Rebekah Miles, "Uncredited: Was Ursula Niebuhr Reinhold's Coauthor?," *Christian Century*, January 25, 2012, 30.

——— 10 ———

AUGUSTINE
AND THE JUST IMPATIENCE

In 337 Constantine I, whom we have seen in dialogue with the patience of the church, was baptized and died. Eighty years later, in 417, Bishop Augustine of Hippo wrote *On Patience*, the third of the three treatises on patience by Christian authors in antiquity. In this little-known treatise, Augustine articulated an understanding of patience that was novel in the life and thought of the church, and that justified a missional revolution that was taking place, of which he was becoming the primary spokesman.

These eighty years encompassed an exceptionally eventful period in Christian history. In this chapter we cannot tell the entire story of the Christian churches as they grew during these years of post-Constantinian opportunity and turbulence. An account of this period should be leisurely and give due attention to two periods of forty years—the first in which churches by and large grew steadily, unspectacularly, in continuation with patient approaches; and the second, after 380, in which rapid numerical growth occurred, as churchmen and emperors collaborated to crush paganism and to force the "schismatic" Donatist Christians into the Catholic church. But we must look ahead to Augustine's *On Patience*, because we do not want to conclude this book without listening to his contributions to the theme that has permeated the entire study. Augustine, of course, was an ecclesiastical lion, the preeminent North African churchman of his era, and we will look at him in dialogue with an earlier North African lion, Bishop Cyprian of Carthage, who in 256 had written the second of the three treatises on patience—*On the Good of Patience*—and whose ongoing influence was great.

In 417 Augustine was at home in Hippo Regius, the city of which he was bishop. For two years he had been engaged in a campaign to crush the "pestiferous virus" of Pelagianism.[1] According to Peter Brown, this had led him to engage in "maneuvers that were unprecedented in the history of Latin Christianity."[2] Councils of African bishops had determined Pelagius to be a heretic; episcopal delegations had hurried to Italy to make representations at the papal curia in Rome and the imperial court in Ravenna; eighty African stallions had made the journey to Ravenna as bribes to courtiers.[3] In all this, Augustine strategized and organized, corresponded and preached.[4] And yet in 417 both the papacy and the imperial court seemed wobbly. Despite the expenditure of African prestige and treasure, their response to Pelagius was unclear. Augustine's patience grew thin; he felt out of control.

Augustine's *On Patience*

At about this time, very possibly while he was waiting, Augustine wrote *On Patience*.[5] Why, we may wonder, did he write it? Was it therapeutic for him? Were the two previous treatises on patience, by Tertullian and Cyprian, insufficient? And if so, in what way was their insufficiency so dire that Augustine—perpetually overstretched and ever attuned to politically sensitive controversy—chose to write about patience rather than something else?[6] Let us look at his *On Patience* to see what we can learn.[7]

---

1. Rescript of Honorius and Theodosius II, in 418, in *Roman State and Christian Church: A Collection of Legal Documents to A.D. 535*, ed. P. R. Coleman-Norton (London: SPCK, 1966), 2:583.

2. Peter Brown, *Through the Eye of a Needle: Wealth, the Fall of Rome, and the Making of Christianity in the West* (Princeton: Princeton University Press, 2012), 369.

3. Ibid., 371.

4. Peter Brown, *Augustine of Hippo: A Biography*, rev. ed. (Berkeley: University of California Press, 2000), 358–63.

5. Kossi Adiavu Ayedze, "Tertullian, Cyprian, and Augustine on Patience: A Comparative and Critical Study of Three Treatises on a Stoic-Christian Virtue in Early North African Christianity" (PhD diss., Princeton Theological Seminary, 2000), 264.

6. Augustine's *De Patientia* has been of little interest to scholars, including Augustinian experts (Gerald W. Schlabach, *For the Joy Set before Us: Augustine and Self-Denying Love* [Notre Dame, IN: University of Notre Dame Press, 2000], 64, 87). The only extensive study is by Ayedze, "Tertullian, Cyprian, and Augustine," 220–76.

7. Augustine, *On Patience*, trans. Luanne Meagher, FC 16 (1952), 237–64.

Patience, according to Augustine, is an attribute of God, who is "extremely patient" (1). And God calls forth from humans a patient response that deserves the name of virtue. Patience bears wrongs rather than committing them; it endures the insults and attacks of adversaries (2). As exemplars of patience Augustine points to David, who used his royal power to forbid vengeance rather than exercise it; to Jesus, who taught patience (the farmer in the parable lets the weeds grow until harvest) and who lived patiently (allowing Judas to kiss him) (9); and especially to "holy Job," to whom Augustine devotes two chapters (11–12).

Augustine cautions his readers to beware of the many guises in which false patience presents itself. "All who suffer are not sharers in patience," but only those who suffer for the right cause in the right way.[8] He dismisses the schismatic Donatists, beaten down but still evidently a threat, as impatient; their deaths for their cause were unnecessary and therefore were self-inflicted suicides, the worst of sins.[9] He also rebuffs the heretical Pelagians, his antagonists of the moment, as bearers of false patience. Why false? Because they are proud, asserting that they can attain patience by sheer willpower, "without any help of God."[10]

How then can people discern "the true patience of the just"? Not by looking at people's overt actions but by discerning their inner motivations. Their sufferings, persecutions, and good works are beside the point. What matters is the source of their behavior—it is true patience only when it is rooted in the love that God has poured into the hearts of his elect through the Holy Spirit and is united to the Catholic church in the bond of peace. Love, indeed, is the primary gift. "Our patience is from him from whom our love comes."[11] So patience, for all its beauty, has its limits; it must never stand in the way of actions that love deems necessary. When "the lust of the world" brings about calamities that people fail to resist, and when pride leads people to put up with "what seems intolerable," then what is at work is "not patience but madness."[12] Augustine concludes by urging his readers: "Let us be liberal in love, not patient with a servile fear."[13] For earlier Christians patience had been the "highest virtue"; for Augustine it has become an ambivalent virtue: it "might be bad—if not directed to a just cause—or good, if it was."[14]

8. *Pat.* 6 (Meagher, 241).
9. *Pat.* 13 (Meagher, 246–47).
10. *Pat.* 15–16 (Meagher, 250).
11. *Pat.* 23 (Meagher, 258).
12. *Pat.* 23 (Meagher, 258).
13. *Pat.* 29 (Meagher, 263).
14. Tertullian, *Pat.* 1.7; Brent D. Shaw, *Sacred Violence: African Christians and Sectarian Hatred in the Age of Augustine* (Cambridge: Cambridge University Press, 2011), 608.

Augustine's careful, casuistic approach to the patience of his tradition is pastorally defensible. In a way that Cyprian and his other predecessors had not acknowledged, Augustine could see that when patience is an unqualified virtue, it can lead vulnerable people and groups to be uncreatively servile in the face of their oppressors. Further, Augustine's approach is theologically comprehensible. Certainly patience, like all virtues, must be subordinate to a larger purpose about which Augustine was passionately clear—the love of God and neighbor.[15] But what opened the way for his legitimate arguments to become dubious rationalizations was his social location. Augustine was at the apex of African society, an ally of imperial administrators and a participant in negotiations with the papal and imperial courts. In such a position he could not see that his arguments could serve, not the vulnerable, but the imperial status quo in which his own church now had a stake—and, inevitably, his own self-interest.

On Patience may be one of Augustine's treatises that few people read today, but it has many of his characteristic strengths. It is subtle and profoundly attuned to his readers' inner dispositions. Yet whatever pastoral sensitivities may have informed the treatise, one must suspect additional motives. To Augustine the Christian tradition of patience as taught by Cyprian—emphasizing a life that trusts God and therefore does not control things, is not in a hurry, and does not use violence—must have seemed anachronistic. Conceived in a time of persecution, it seemed out of touch with a world in which emperors served the Lord.[16] And it was standing in his way. Here he was, confronting yet another urgent reality—the threat of Pelagian "heresy" to orthodoxy as he conceived it. Like the Donatists in earlier decades, the Pelagians were impatient! In their elitist sort of way, they couldn't understand the struggles of ordinary Christians.[17] From Augustine's perspective their elitist impatience grew naturally out of their convictions that were inimical to the doctrine of grace that had come to be central to his theology.

In 417 Augustine was an old man. He was tired of having to confront repeatedly the expressions of what he considered prideful theological error. So it is plausible that Augustine wrote *On Patience* to justify his own impatience. His likely intent was to provide justification for his and the other African bishops' *Realpolitik*—firm, unschismatic, paradoxically self-confident that their position was not proud or impatient, and certain that it was loving in the proper sense of the term. It is also possible that Augustine had in mind local

15. Schlabach, *For the Joy*, chap. 1.
16. This is an argument that Augustine developed in *Ep.* 93.3.9 and *Ep.* 185.5.19–20.
17. Augustine saw a continuity between the Donatists and the Pelagians in their negative assessment of ordinary Christians; see Brown, *Augustine of Hippo*, 348–49.

believers who, shaped in their understandings by Cyprian's writings, viewed the bishops' machinations in Rome and Ravenna with horror. How could local believers construe the attempt to arouse imperial power to proscribe and banish their ecclesiastical opponents as anything other than impatience? And impatience, even a *just impatience*, was against the tradition of the African church that Cyprian had articulated and catechized faithfully. Building on the tradition of Tertullian, Cyprian had burned patience into the habitus of the people. A century and a half later it was still there.

Augustine and the Patient Tradition

Augustine gave no indication that the church had a tradition concerning patience. He wrote as if he were beginning de novo. Why did he not cite Cyprian's *On the Good of Patience*? We know that Augustine knew of it. In 405, in his treatise *On Baptism*, Augustine reported that he had "read and reread again and again" *Epistle* 73 that Cyprian had written in 256; he quoted the letter at length, including the passage in which Cyprian refers to a treatise, *On the Good of Patience*, which he had just written.[18] But elsewhere Augustine never mentioned the treatise. Unencumbered by tradition, he was free to write his own treatise on patience that differed strikingly from Cyprian's. It is fascinating to set the two treatises side by side.

The treatises are of similar length, and both Cyprian and Augustine cited Scripture with similar frequency. But the treatises differ in their use of the Bible. Of the seventy-seven biblical texts that Cyprian thought worthy of mention, Augustine cited only three.[19] Their ratio of New Testament to Old Testament is similar—two to one. But what they saw in the testaments was different. Cyprian saw the world through the Gospel of Matthew (twenty-four citations, compared to three in Augustine), whereas Augustine's window on reality is Paul's Letter to the Romans (twenty-two citations, compared to two in Cyprian). Like Tertullian, Cyprian began his treatise by underscoring the patient character of God, who "bestows his rains without distinction on the just and the unjust" (Matt. 5:45); Augustine began with "the sufferings of our present time" (Rom. 8:18).[20] In explaining the patient character of God, Cyprian quoted Jesus, who urges his disciples to be like God by loving their

18. Augustine, *Bapt.* 5.17.22, trans. C. D. Hartranft, *NPNF*[1] 4:471, regarding Cyprian, *Ep.* 73.26.1.

19. There is much greater continuity between Cyprian and Tertullian in their writings on patience: Cyprian cites 12 of Tertullian's 61 biblical texts; and both cite the Gospel of Matthew more often than any other biblical book (Tertullian, 17×; Cyprian, 24×).

20. Cyprian, *Pat.* 4, trans E. G. Conway, FC 36 (1958), 265; Augustine, *Pat.* 2 (Meagher, 238).

enemies and praying for their persecutors; and he devoted three chapters to the narrative of Jesus, in whose "salutary footsteps" Cyprian urged his "beloved brethren" to walk.[21] Augustine, who told the story of Job, did not tell the story of Jesus or urge his readers to follow him.[22]

According to Cyprian, the patient precepts of Christ prohibit certain behavior for Christians.[23] In contrast, Augustine's ethic is situational. In his view patient actions can take many forms if their cause is true and their inner motivation is love. These are matters of personal judgment that manifest themselves in different ways in different contexts. At times Augustine's approach could lead to a limitation of violence. In *On Patience* he cited King David as an example of patience that used power to forbid vengeance; in his life Augustine used his influence on Roman authorities to condemn the use of torture and capital punishment on the Donatists.[24] So Augustine's ethic is elastic. But he seems to have been uncomfortably aware of the strong spine of the African patient tradition.

In *On Patience* Augustine cites 1 Corinthians 13, Paul's love chapter, three times; is it accidental that he never cites the obvious verse, "Love is patient" (13:4)? Would that have made love less elastic, infusing it with Cyprianic patience? By leaving the tradition of Tertullian and Cyprian behind, in his conflicts with the pagans, Donatists, and Pelagians, Augustine was able to deploy "love" to justify strong-armed policies—state-imposed fines, confiscation, and exile—that seemed urgently necessary to him. To Cyprian and other earlier Christians these behaviors would have seemed acts of impatience, inappropriate for believers in the God whose patient work in Christ relativized urgency and necessity. Indeed, for Cyprian, Augustine's thinking would very likely have seemed pagan—and perhaps that is not accidental. Like the Christians who preceded him, Augustine was engaging in inculturation, in which he embodied and sanctioned behavior characteristic of influential Romans, which may have seemed necessary, especially after 380, as Christians were beginning to be successful in courting aristocrats.[25] But, as we have seen, the balance between "indigenizing" and being "pilgrim" required constant monitoring. Who was in a position to monitor Augustine?

---

21. Cyprian, *Pat.* 6–8 (the story of Jesus), 9 (on following Jesus) (Conway, 268–71).

22. The one teaching of Jesus that Augustine mentions in *On Patience* is Matt. 5:10, in which he reiterates one of his favorite points: persecution is only blessed when it is "for righteousness' sake" (10).

23. Cyprian (*Pat.* 14 [Conway, 14]) labels adultery, deceit, and homicide as mortal sins; he denies the Eucharist to people whose hands are "sullied by the blood-stained sword."

24. Augustine, *Pat.* 9; *Ep.* 185.3.14; 185.7.26; *Ep.* 93.5.19; *Ep.* 133; *Ep.* 134.

25. Brown, *Through the Eye*, 528; Michele Renee Salzman, *The Making of a Christian Aristocracy* (Cambridge, MA: Harvard University Press, 2002), 80.

Augustine did not lightly depart from the approach of earlier Christians. The understanding that Christians should attract nonbelievers by loving behavior was deeply engrained in him. As he put it at the close of a sermon of 404, after the catechumens had left, "[I] am always begging you to win over those who haven't yet believed by leading good lives." Augustine knew that this takes time: "If you all live in a manner worthy of God, the time will very soon come when none of those who have not believed will remain in unbelief." This was a classic mission strategy.[26]

Early on, Augustine had had reservations about more interventionist strategies. After all, Christians are followers of Jesus who "did nothing by force, but everything by persuasion and admonition."[27] The secular power should not coerce people into communion, but "we should act with words, fight with arguments, and conquer with reason." Forced conversion leads to "false Catholics"—hypocrites.[28] In thinking in this way, the early Augustine followed in the well-established tradition of Cyprian. After Constantine Christianity had been a privileged, triumphant minority that coexisted with other religions; it was growing, but probably not very rapidly. In the middle of the fourth century a few discordant voices—Firmicus Maternus in Sicily and Optatus of Milevis in North Africa—called for the urgent, immediate, imperial imposition of Catholic Christianity, but most Catholic Christians disagreed with them.[29] The patient tradition persisted.

In the 380s this began to change. Activist bishops such as Ambrose worked together with Theodosius I and other compliant "orthodox" emperors to secure legislation that stripped paganism of its shrines and moved against

26. Augustine, *Serm.* 360B.28 (in F. Dolbeau, *Augustine: Vingt-six sermons au peuple d'Afrique* [Paris: Institut d'études augustiniennes, 1996], 25), trans. E. Hill, *Saint Augustine: Newly Discovered Sermons*, vol. 11 in part 3 of *The Works of Saint Augustine: A Translation for the 21st Century*, ed. J. E. Rotelle (Hyde Park, NY: New City Press, 1997), 383. See also *Serm.* 149.16–18 of 412, in which Augustine shows he had attended to Cyprian. He urges his hearers to love their enemies, in whom God's patience is at work, so that their repentance will ensue.

27. Augustine, *Retractions* 1.12.6, citing his early *True Religion* 16.31. He corrected himself: "I forgot that he [Jesus] casts out the sellers and buyers from the Temple by flogging" (trans. M. I. Bogan, FC 60 [1968], 54).

28. Augustine, *Ep.* 93.5.17, trans. R. J. Teske, *Saint Augustine: Letters 1–99*, vol. 1 in part 2 of *Works of Saint Augustine* (Hyde Park, NY: New City Press, 2001), 387; Peter Brown, "St. Augustine's Attitude to Religious Coercion," in *Religion and Society in the Age of Saint Augustine* (New York: Harper & Row, 1972), 268–69.

29. On Firmicus, see Maijastina Kahlos, "The Rhetoric of Tolerance and Intolerance: From Lactantius to Firmicus Maternus," in *Changes and Continuities in Christian Apologetic*, ed. Anders-Christian Jacobsen, Maijastina Kahlos, and Jörg Ulrich (Frankfurt: Peter Lang, 2009), 79–95. On Optatus, see Émilien Lamirande, *Church, State, and Toleration: An Intriguing Change of Mind in Augustine* (Philadelphia: Villanova University Press, 1974), 58–66. On disagreement, see Brown, *Augustine of Hippo*, 460.

"heretics"; beginning in 405 imperial authorities took action to suppress the Donatists, whom the authorities now called heretics.[30]

In the first decade of the fifth century, Augustine articulated a vision for this new activism. It was breathtakingly novel. According to Peter Brown, "More than any other Latin Christian of his age, [Augustine] dared to think the unthinkable thought that Christianity could be the faith of an entire society."[31] Augustine's thinking was unthinkable not only about the goal, a uniformly Christian society; it was even more so about the missional means he advocated to reach the goal. For Augustine this shift entailed a radical reassessment of the Christian tradition and a demotion of patience within it. According to Émilien Lamirande, by 405 Augustine had lost his illusions. "[Augustine] knew well that truth does not infallibly attract, and that the sweet appeal of charity is not always effective. So was he gradually brought to take another path, not against his will, but certainly in contrast with earlier more idealistic views."[32] This observation misses the point. The earlier views that refused to place highest value on urgency and effectiveness were not idealistic; they were the church's tradition, its seasoned wisdom. Further, they were the teachings of the hard-bitten martyr Cyprian. When Augustine displaced these teachings, advocating methods that Cyprian would have considered impatient, he entered into conflict with his great predecessor.

Augustine and Cyprian

In North Africa in Augustine's day, Cyprian's influence was omnipresent. He was not only the iconic leader of the third-century African church; he was a martyr whose story was told in *Acta* and celebrated on his anniversary in countless churches. His influence was imposing in the Catholic churches and "overwhelming" in the Donatist churches.[33] The Donatists assembled a collection of his letters, but Augustine also read the letters closely. He cited Cyprian's work as giving "the canonical meaning" of biblical passages and constituting the "foundations of the church," indicating what the church

---

30. Cod. theod. 16.1.2; 16.5.12; 16.6.4; Shaw, *Sacred Violence*, 551–52.

31. Brown, *Augustine of Hippo*, 461.

32. Lamirande, *Church, State, and Toleration*, 23. On 58–59 Lamirande observes that Augustine was "perhaps a very lonely figure" who had to work out his positions on his own. His distant forerunner was Optatus of Milevis, "the only great exponent of the Catholic position we know for the fourth century." On the contrary, in North Africa the Catholic position of the fourth century was still that of Tertullian, Cyprian, and their successors, which is why Augustine needed to unlearn things and write both his *Retractions* and *On Patience*.

33. Shaw, *Sacred Violence*, 420.

had always held. Under pressure regarding the baptism of infants, Augustine took a book of Cyprian into his hand and waved it at the congregation: "Listen for a moment to what [Cyprian] . . . demonstrated that the Church had always held."[34] According to Augustine, Cyprian's writings were potent: "What region in all the lands can be found . . . where his eloquent words are not read, his teaching not praised, his charity not loved, his life not extolled?"[35] Even more potent than his writings were his bones. Preaching in 403 on the anniversary of Cyprian's death, in the Mappalia basilica in Carthage where Cyprian was buried and where people gathered at his *mensa* tomb to celebrate in their inimitable ways, Augustine declaimed: "Many people everywhere have the great corpus of his works. But let us, here, give more thanks than ever to God, because we have been found worthy to have with us the holy corpus of his body."[36] Even in his bodily death Cyprian was powerful.

Cyprian's story also was powerful. In 405, preaching in Carthage on the anniversary of Cyprian's martyrdom, Augustine retold the story that Cyprian wrote of his conversion in his *To Donatus*. But he nuanced it so that he suppressed Cyprian's conversion issues—his addictions to wealth, elaborate food, luxurious clothing, sycophants' adulation—and replaced them with unilluminating generalities: "[Cyprian] testifies himself to the sort of life he led once, how profane, how godless, how reprehensible, and how detestable."[37] Augustine's praise of Cyprian suppressed Cyprian's Christian radicalism and enlisted him into Augustine's campaign: Cyprian was "the teacher of the peoples of the world, the smasher of idols, the unmasker of demons."[38] Cyprian a smasher of idols? As Augustine preached his sermons, always open to dialogue, the people repeatedly interjected "their usual cry, 'One is free to believe or not to believe. With whom did Christ use force? Whom does he compel?'" Augustine knew how to respond to this usual cry. He pointed to Christ who used force, who coerced Paul into conversion by blinding him, as a result of which "the Church, then, imitates its Lord in forcing the Donatists." But Augustine may have been uncomfortable with

34. Augustine, *Serm.* 294.18, trans. E. Hill, *Augustine: Sermons on the saints, 273–305A,* vol. 8 in part 3 of *Works of Saint Augustine* (1994), 193.

35. Augustine, *Serm.* 313C.2, trans. E. Hill, *Augustine: Sermons on the Saints, 306–340A,* vol. 9 in part 3 of *Works of Saint Augustine* (1994), 102.

36. Augustine, *Serm.* 313C.2; for Augustine's preaching at Cyprian's *mensa,* see Ramsay MacMullen, *The Second Church: Popular Christianity, A.D. 200–400,* SBL Writings from the Greco-Roman World Supplement Series 1 (Atlanta: Society of Biblical Literature, 2009), 63.

37. Augustine, *Serm.* 311.7, trans. Hill, *Augustine, Sermons on the Saints, 306–340A,* 74. For an account of Cyprian's struggle with his conversion issues, see pp. 136–39 above.

38. Augustine, *Serm.* 313B.2, trans. Shaw, *Sacred Violence,* 439.

the people's objection, because their words closely resembled Cyprian's cat-echetical teaching.[39]

Augustine knew that he was innovating. Late in life, when his position was secure and he, at least in North Africa, had redefined the Catholic tradition, he was able to admit it. One of his early writings that he now retracted con-tained this statement: "I am displeased that schismatics are violently coerced to communion by the force of any secular power."[40] In a letter of 407, soon after he had repented his earlier stance, Augustine wrote to Vincentius, a Donatist leader: "My opinion originally was that no one should be forced to the unity of Christ."[41] When he returned to North Africa after his conversion in Milan, Augustine had clearly been schooled in the Cyprianic tradition that shaped his original opinion.[42] But now, because of conflicts with Donatists and Pelagians, Augustine had drawn lines in new places and enforced them with new severity.

Augustine and the Future of Patience

In this new situation, what future was there for patience? The words for patience (*hypomonē* and *patientia*) clearly would be less important in the vocabulary of the church of the Christendom centuries than they had been in the early church's vocabulary. In his voluminous writings Augustine used *patientia* often, and he emphasized its rooting in grace, its primarily super-natural character, and its orientation toward life after death.[43] As we have seen, he placed patience within a larger ethical framework—indeed, a meta-physic—*caritas*, love. One unfortunate result was that patience figured less centrally in his thinking than it did in the thought of his Latin predecessors. This did not have to be so. As Gerald Schlabach has reminded us, Augustine in

39. Augustine, *Ep.* 185.6.22–23, trans. R. J. Teske, *Augustine: Letters 156–210*, vol. 3 in part 2 of *Works of Saint Augustine* (2004), 192. The words of Augustine's objectors (PL 33:803): "Liberum est credere, vel non credere"; cf. the words in Cyprian's catechesis (*Ad Quir.* 3.52; CCL 3.139; Wallis, 547): "Credendi vel non credendi libertatem in arbitrio positam."

40. Augustine, *Retractions* 31 (Bogan, 129), citing two books titled *Against the Party of Donatus* (both lost; written between 397 and 400); in contrast, his corrected position: "I had not yet learned either how much evil their impunity would dare or to what extent the applica-tion of discipline could bring about their improvement."

41. Augustine, *Ep.* 93.5.17 (Teske, *Augustine: Letters 1–99*, 387).

42. For a view that sees Augustine as continuing in "the African tradition" and mentions Cyprian frequently, see Robert A. Markus, *Saeculum: History and Society in the Theology of Augustine* (Cambridge: Cambridge University Press, 1970), chap. 5, esp. 115. In contrast, in chap. 6, which deals with religious coercion, Markus never looks prior to Augustine to find an African tradition and, strikingly, never mentions Cyprian.

43. Michel Spanneut, "Geduld," *RAC* 9 (1976): 267–68.

his conversion had experienced a reordering of his loves and desires through the grace of continence (self-control and self-denial).[44] And continence did much to shape his doctrine of Christian love that was essential to his theology. As such, continence might have synergized well with patience, reinforcing the outward habitus of patience by nourishing its inner resources. But this could go wrong. According to Schlabach, Augustine's search for the good of church unity went awry when he grasped for it desperately, incontinently; and something similar happened in his approach to patience. In his desperate politicking to ensure that the empire would repudiate Pelagian heresy, Augustine wrote about the interior conditions of Christian faithfulness. But he took his eyes off the places that patience could "bite"—patience's exterior, behavioral conditions. He exposed patience to his own impatience, and it withered.

As a result, patience no longer functioned—as it had in Cyprian's community, for example—as a countercultural habitus to be formed by catechesis. Augustine was aware that people were bound to Donatist schism by the "heavy chain of inveterate habit," which needed to be broken. However, he never conceded that a habitus of impatience lurked darkly in the Roman culture and that Christian catechesis could correct this, re-forming converts so they would behave with patience.[45]

Why was Augustine unworried about a habitus of impatience? For two reasons. First, his primary concern was with inner motivation and not outward habitus. For Augustine, unlike the African Christian tradition in which he stood, patience had to do with attitudes, not with physical reflexes or actions. It was about thinking and possibly feeling, not about behavior. Augustine stated his ideas in an indirect correspondence that he was carrying on with a Roman aristocrat. Volusian was exploring Christianity but was put off by its reputation for countercultural practices that "are contrary to the practices of the state."[46] Augustine wrote to reassure him, communicating via an intermediary—his and Volusian's mutual friend Marcellinus, the imperial commissioner for Africa, no less. Augustine conceded that everyone ("even someone apart from [the Christian] religion") knows that the churches regularly read "the great commandments of harmonious unity"—Jesus's Sermon on the Mount instructions to turn the other cheek, share what you have, go the second mile. But Augustine soothed Volusian's uneasiness. What these teachings seek to do, he said, is to free people from "an inner evil . . . [which] ravages more seriously and more destructively than . . . the cruelty of

---

44. Augustine, *Conf.* 8.8.19–8.12.30; Schlabach, *For the Joy*, 61, 84–85.
45. Augustine, *Ep.* 93.5.17 (Teske, *Augustine: Letters 1–99*, 387).
46. Augustine, *Ep.* 136.2, trans. R. J. Teske, *Augustine, Letters 100–155*, vol. 2 in part 2 of *Works of St. Augustine* (Hyde Park, NY: New City Press, 2003), 211.

an enemy from outside." Patience is important; "we should value [it] more than everything that an enemy can take."[47] But Jesus's commandments on patience "pertain to the disposition of the heart, which is something *interior*, rather than to action, which is something *exterior*. In that way we maintain patience along with goodwill in the secret of our soul while we do openly what is thought to be able to benefit those for whom we ought to do good."[48]

In this passage Augustine parted company from Cyprian. He was alert to Jesus's emphasis upon interior intention in his Sermon on the Mount (e.g., Matt. 5:22, 28); he was more introspective, more profound psychologically than Cyprian. This is a welcome contribution; later writers on spirituality would be the poorer without Augustine's moral psychology and his testimony in his *Confessions* to prayerful self-examination. Alas, however, Augustine not only added intention to the tradition; he also subtracted from the tradition the exterior action that had been central to it and central to Cyprian. Christians had always maintained that actions matter! Their witness depended on their actions. As Cyprian put it in his catechesis, "We must labor with deeds, not with words." He justified this by appealing to Jesus's peroration in the Sermon on the Mount, in which Jesus speaks of the disaster that will come to people who "hear my words and do them not" (Matt. 7:24–27).[49] The tradition loses actions rooted in Jesus's words at its own grave peril. Without distinctive actions, Christian witness will rely on force.

Of course, the shift from action to intention was useful to Augustine's immediate missional objective. Augustine wanted the aristocrat Volusian to know that he could take the plunge without hesitating. He could become a Christian without changing his habitus. After all, love (whatever in his estimation does good for other people) trumps patience, and the Christian can execute punishment with "a certain kind harshness" if his interiority, his inner disposition, is loving.[50] The implications of this for the history of mission are weighty.

Second, Augustine was not worried about a habitus of impatience because patience was a matter for monks and clerics, not laypeople. As we saw in chapter 9, a century earlier Constantine had responded to Lactantius by suggesting a two-level ethic, and now we encounter Augustine tending in the same direction. Late in his life he wrote to the abbot of the monastery in Hadrumetum, 170 miles southeast of Hippo. Monks from the monastery had made their way to Hippo to spend time with Augustine, who had instructed

47. Augustine, *Ep.* 138.11–12 (Teske, *Augustine: Letters 100–155*, 231).
48. Augustine, *Ep.* 138.13 (Teske, *Augustine: Letters 100–155*, 232).
49. Cyprian, *Ad Quir.* 3.96, trans. E. Wallis, ANF 5:554.
50. Augustine, *Ep.* 138.14 (Teske, *Augustine: Letters 100–155*, 232).

them concerning the danger of the Pelagian heresy. Augustine informed the abbot that "we" (Augustine and others) had read Cyprian's book *On the Lord's Prayer* to the monks so they would know that moral conduct is rooted not in free choice but in God's grace. However, "we also demonstrated how the same most glorious martyr [Cyprian] warned us that we ought to pray even for our enemies who have not yet believed in Christ, so that they may come to believe." The monks who had withdrawn from the world would realize that God's grace can convert "even the evil and unbelieving wills of human beings."[51] Evidently Augustine thought this would be an inspiring vision for monks.

But how about Christians who were not monks? What was the relevance of patience to the laypeople who remain in the world? Will they live a distinctive life, embodying patience in their daily pursuits so that their enemies will see this and come to believe? In his *Questions on the Gospels* (dated around 400), Augustine emphasizes the importance of believers who "do the things that pertain to the world [*saeculum*]." These believers live "among the peoples," who watch them and observe their lives. They are taught how to live by the church's teachers; they are "ruled by those with knowledge." In their work the laypeople do things that are necessary for the functioning of society. The image that Augustine chooses for their work is grinding in a mill (Luke 17:34–36), keeping the mill wheels turning, demonstrating the importance of "the constant round of temporal occupations." Their work is vital for the church, for their earnings enable them to "contribute to the needs of the church."[52] But the importance of laypeople is not in their distinctiveness. For them distinctiveness would be proud, self-vaunting. Instead, their calling is to live with what historian Robert Markus calls "mediocrity." It is to maintain the *saeculum*, to keep the mill wheels going round and round, not to imagine how the teachings and way of Jesus could transform the workers and their mill so that others may come to believe.[53]

---

51. Augustine, *Ep.* 215.3, trans. R. J. Teske, *Augustine: Letters 211–270*, vol. 4 in part 2 of *Works of St. Augustine* (Hyde Park, NY: New City Press, 2005), 41. Cyprian, in *On the Lord's Prayer*, uses the word *patientia* only once (15); but in its chap. 17, which Augustine read to the monks, Cyprian develops his patience themes and fully quotes Matt. 5:45, about God who sends rain on the just and the unjust.

52. Augustine, *Questions on the Gospels* 2.44.1, trans. R. J. Teske, *Augustine: New Testament I and II*, in *Works of St. Augustine* (Hyde Park, NY: New City Press, 2014), 408–9. For comment, see Henry Chadwick, "Augustine on Pagans and Christians: Reflections on Religious and Social Change," in *History, Society and the Churches: Essays in Honour of Owen Chadwick*, ed. Derek Beales and Geoffrey Best (Cambridge: Cambridge University Press, 1985), 26.

53. Robert Markus, *The End of Ancient Christianity* (Cambridge: Cambridge University Press, 1990), chap. 4.

Augustine does not wholly withdraw Jesus's teachings from laypeople and the public square; as late as 417 in a sermon he eloquently states that Christ's call to self-denying discipleship is for more than monks: "The universal Church, the whole body, all its members . . . they all ought to follow Christ."[54] Nevertheless, in this sermon Augustine's appeals to discipleship are largely generic. Unlike earlier preachers such as Cyprian, he does not attempt to apply Jesus's teachings to specific situations and professions. Augustine's millworkers were different from the business people whom Justin mentioned in his *First Apology*. Justin's friends had turned to Christianity "from the ways of violence and tyranny, overcome by observing the consistent lives of their [Christian] neighbors, or noting the *strange patience* of their injured acquaintances, or experiencing the way they did business with them."[55] Justin contended that christocentric patience was potent. It didn't merely change people's attitudes, and it didn't take people out of the world. It formed people who made a difference in the world, including the business world, and they attracted people to the faith because their patience made them different enough to be intriguing, and because they held out hope.

Of course, Justin had written 250 years earlier and in Greek; there is no indication that Augustine read him. But Augustine had read Lactantius, whose *Divine Institutes* were much more recent and said similar things in elegant Latin. As we have seen in our previous chapter, Lactantius in the tradition of Cyprian was convinced that patience could offer distinctive possibilities to any profession—even that of the emperor! To Constantine, whom Lactantius knew and addressed personally, he dared to say that even *you* can "maintain [your] patience unbroken."[56] Not if you have a loving interiority, but if you act Christianly—honoring the weak, ruling without vengeance and killing, and refusing to arm-twist people into the right religion.[57] Constantine was intrigued but didn't take the bait. Others did. Whatever their jobs, people in the fourth century were still becoming Christians because of believers whose patient behavior they watched and gossiped about.[58]

Augustine's Missional Revolution

What if Augustine had listened to Cyprian and Lactantius and incorporated the tradition they represented into the understandings of mission that he

---

54. Augustine, *Serm.* 96.9, trans. E. Hill, *Augustine: Sermons on the New Testament* 94A–174A, vol. 4 in part 3 of *Works of St. Augustine* (Hyde Park, NY: New City Press, 1992), 33.
　　55. Justin, *1 Apol.* 16.4, trans. E. R. Hardy, LCC 1 (1953), 252, with emphasis added.
　　56. Lactantius, *Inst.* 6.4.11 (Bowen and Garnsey, 336).
　　57. Lactantius, *Inst.* 6.12.18–19; 6.18.27–28; 5.19.17, 22.
　　58. Lactantius, *Inst.* 5.19.12–13; 5.23.

was developing? Augustine had a more expansive vision of mission than most of his contemporaries. God, he was convinced, wanted to reach all the people of the Roman Empire. Some other Christians shared this vision, but Augustine was more definite than they. And he went further. In his view God also wanted to bring good news to people beyond the empire.[59] As Augustine told the story, this vision came to him as he met slaves whom Roman troops had captured while "pacifying" their lands and Romanizing their territories. These slaves had never heard the gospel, and they told Augustine about other people "further inland . . . not under Roman power" who had never had contact with Christianity. "It is by no means correct to say," Augustine was convinced, "that God's promise does not pertain to them." The tradition of Christians in the West had been too narrow; their vision had been too small. Augustine did not counteract this smallness by reclaiming the Matthean "Great Commission" (Matt. 28:19–20) to justify mission as a calling to his era; like many early Christians he continued to use that passage primarily as a trinitarian proof text.[60] But Acts 1:8 had seized his imagination: "You will be my witnesses in Jerusalem, in all Judea and Samaria, and to the ends of the earth." Unlike many earlier Christians Augustine was "completely certain" that Jesus did not limit these words to the twelve apostles. Jesus's sending is a task for "the whole Church . . . and will last here until the end of the world."[61]

But what happened when those sent from Augustine's Catholic West began to approach un-Christian peoples? Thanks to Augustine's missional revolution, the carriers brought a gospel in which impatient, forceful actions—animated of course by loving intentions—replaced patient actions. The earlier Christian tradition was based on an understanding of God's work as manifested in the life, teaching, death, and resurrection of Jesus. The word that summed this up for them was *patientia* (*hypomonē* in Greek). In their patience-shaped perspective, history is safe in God's generous hands. So people who worship God and follow Jesus do not need to control things; they do not rely on the power of the state to vindicate their point of view; they do not fret their brows or hurry; and they never ever impose their views by coercion and force. And somehow, spontaneously, carriers of the gospel show up—slave women, business people, people of no account—and the church grows, spottily, unsystematically, and by

59. Norbert Brox, "Zur christlichen Mission in der Spätantike," in *Mission im Neuen Testament*, ed. Karl Kertelge, Questiones Disputatae 93 (Freiburg-im-Breisgau: Herder, 1982), 200–205. Origen had shared the larger vision, anticipating the gospel spreading "everywhere," to "the ends of the earth" (*Cels.* 1.11; *Hom. Gen.* 9.2).

60. Augustine, *Ep.* 55.16.30 (Teske, *Augustine: Letters 1–99*, 232).

61. Augustine, *Ep.* 199.46, 49 (Teske, *Augustine: Letters 156–210*, 350–51).

ferment.[62] In his own pre-baptismal catechesis in Milan, Augustine probably did not encounter catechists who sought to change his habitus or challenge him with the vision of patience.[63] However, when he returned to his native North Africa, he encountered the patience of the African tradition, and his mind understood it.

But patience apparently never became embodied in his habitus. In the early years of the fifth century Augustine turned a corner. He changed his mind, his way of thinking about life and mission. He became anxious—concerned to control things, eager to micromanage them. He devoted countless hours to politicking, mobilizing colleagues, beleaguering emperors, and pestering popes. He wanted to rally the local aristocrats and deploy the powers of state, and he wanted these rulers to use appropriate force. And when he turned beyond the empire, he gave to monarchs the vision of finding their eternal salvation by doing what they did naturally, using top-down methods for Christian ends. As Augustine put it, rulers were to make "their power a servant to the divine Majesty, to spread the worship of God far and wide."[64] He did all of these things for what he considered the best of ends: to glorify God by destroying pagan religions and achieving Christian unity and orthodoxy. Most of the time he was able to suppress his fears that his intentions were unloving, directed to self-praise rather than the ultimate well-being of others.[65] Augustine confronted the apparent effectiveness of force; what he repeatedly called *exempla*—experiences, facts—demonstrated that a just impatience works![66] In light of the evidence, Augustine was convinced that he should turn away from the traditional Christian missional approach that was saturated in patience. His *On Patience* rationalized his turning.

---

62. See chap. 4 above and esp. two articles by Andrea Sterk: "'Representing' Mission from Below: Historians as Interpreters and Agents of Christianization," *Church History* 79, no. 2 (2010): 271–304; "Mission from Below: Captive Women and Conversion on the East Roman Frontiers," *Church History* 79, no. 1 (2010): 1–39; and one by Cornelia Horn: "St. Nino and the Christianization of Pagan Georgia," *Medieval Encounters* 4 (1998): 242–64.

63. At least there is no hint of such challenge in William Harmless, *Augustine and the Catechumenate* (Collegeville, MN: Liturgical Press, 1995), 82–98.

64. Augustine, *City of God* 5.24, trans. W. M. Green, LCL 6 (1963), 263.

65. In *Conf.* 10.36.59, Augustine confesses his capacity to pollute his love for the other with the "temptation . . . to wish to be feared or loved for . . . the joy derived from such power, which is no joy at all" (Schlabach, *For the Joy*, 141).

66. Augustine, *Ep.* 93.17 (Teske, *Augustine: Letters 100–155*, 387). Augustine, the rationalizer of the just impatience, is also the rationalizer of the just war and the just oath—all permissible variants of behavior that the earlier church had viewed as impermissible. All the justified actions grow out of practical necessities that seem to Augustine and other fourth- and fifth-century Christians to be exceptionally urgent; all the actions are utilized by people who rationalize their exceptional departure from an earlier norm by the justice of their cause and the love of their motivation; and all the actions cease to be exceptional and (in the culture of Christian Europe) become reflexive—habitus. The variants become the norm.

The Future of Patient Ferment

In this book we have traveled from patient ferment to impatient force. This was a slow journey that gained speed in the missional revolution of the late fourth and early fifth centuries. The revolution succeeded in part because impatience dovetailed neatly with the habitus of surrounding non-Christian religions. This impatience shaped the Christianity that conquered Europe, sent crusaders to the Middle East, and spread the faith to many parts of the world. It also led to an assumption that has seemed self-evident to many people, especially since the Enlightenment in the eighteenth century: that in its essence Christianity is violent, and that Christian mission—however loving its professed intentions—is essentially an exercise in imperialism. Historian of late antiquity Ramsay MacMullen expresses this in a significant aside about Constantine's behavior, describing it as "a more truly Christian posture of active aggression."[67] This observation stings because there is truth in it; there are many *exempla*—experiences, facts—that substantiate the violence of Christianity.

Twenty-first-century Christians must live with this heritage. Of course we can point to other *exempla*. We can point to sacrificial Christian missionaries from many peoples who poured out their lives in loving service; we can point to the witness of minority Christian traditions, and to saints and trailblazers among the majority traditions. And we can point to the *patientia* of the Christians of the early centuries, a witness that utters a reticent protest against all subsequent expressions of violence, strident or honeyed.

If we Christians today wish to embody this patience and to claim that our faith is not intrinsically violent,[68] we may find it helpful to converse with the early Christians whom we have studied. We will not do things precisely as the early Christians did, but the early believers may give us new perspectives and point us to a "lost bequest."[69] As we rediscover this bequest, we will not make facile generalizations or construct how-to formulas—those would be impatient responses! Instead, consciously seeking the reformation of our habitus by the work of the Holy Spirit and by catechesis rooted in the teaching and way of Jesus, we will begin to live in new ways in today's *saeculum*. We will discover that we are in a good tradition. And we will say with Cyprian and other early Christians: "We do not speak great things but we live them."[70]

---

67. Ramsay MacMullen, *Christianizing the Roman Empire (A.D. 100–400)* (New Haven: Yale University Press, 1984), 50.

68. For comment on the "intrinsic violence" of Christianity, see H. A. Drake, *Constantine and the Bishops: The Politics of Intolerance* (Baltimore: Johns Hopkins University Press, 2000), 22–28.

69. Roger Dowley, *Towards the Recovery of a Lost Bequest* (London: Evangelical Coalition for Urban Mission, 1984).

70. Cyprian, *Pat.* 3, trans. G. E. Conway, FC 36 (1958), 265.

BIBLIOGRAPHY

Adams, Edward. *The Earliest Christian Meeting Places: Almost Exclusively Houses?* Library of New Testament Studies 450. London: Bloomsbury T&T Clark, 2013.

Alexis-Baker, Andy. "*Ad Quirinum* Book Three and Cyprian's Catechumenate." *Journal of Early Christian Studies* 17, no. 3 (2009): 357–80.

Ameling, Walter. "The Christian *Lapsi* in Smyrna, 250 A.D. (*Martyrium Pionii* 12–14)." *Vigiliae Christianae* 62 (2008): 133–60.

———. "*Femina Liberaliter Instituta*—Some Thoughts on a Martyr's Liberal Education." In *Perpetua's Passions: Multidisciplinary Approaches to the "Passio Perpetuae et Felicitatis,"* edited by Jan N. Bremmer and Marco Formisano, 78–102. Oxford: Oxford University Press, 2012.

Ascough, Richard S., Philip A. Harland, and John A. Kloppenborg, eds. *Associations in the Greco-Roman World: A Sourcebook*. Waco: Baylor University Press, 2012.

Ayedze, Kossi Adiavu. "Tertullian, Cyprian, and Augustine on Patience: A Comparative and Critical Study of Three Treatises on a Stoic-Christian Virtue in Early North African Christianity." PhD diss., Princeton Theological Seminary, 2000.

Baldovin, John F. *The Urban Character of Christian Worship: The Origins, Development and Meaning of Stational Liturgy*. Orientalia Christiana Analecta 228. Rome: Pontificio Instituto Orientale, 1987.

Bardy, Gustave. *La conversion au Christianisme durant les premiers siècles*. Paris: Aubier, 1949.

Barnes, Timothy D. *Constantine and Eusebius*. Cambridge, MA: Harvard University Press, 1981.

———. "Constantine's *Speech to the Assembly of the Saints*: Place and Date of Delivery." *Journal of Theological Studies* 2/52, no. 1 (2001): 26–36.

Barrett-Lennard, R. J. S. *Christian Healing after the New Testament: Some Approaches to Illness in the Second, Third, and Fourth Centuries.* Lanham, MD: University Press of America, 1994.

Batiffol, Pierre. "Les étapes de la conversion de Constantin." *Bulletin d'ancienne littérature et d'archéologie chrétienne* 3 (1913): 178–88, 241–464.

Bazzana, Giovanni Battista. "Early Christian Missionaries as Physicians: Healing and Its Cultural Value in the Greco-Roman Context." *Novum Testamentum* 51 (2009): 232–51.

Beard, Mary, John North, and Simon Price, compilers. *A Sourcebook.* Vol. 2 of *Religions of Rome.* Cambridge: Cambridge University Press, 1998.

Beck, Roger. "The Religious Market of the Roman Empire: Rodney Stark and Christianity's Pagan Competition." In *Religious Rivalries in the Early Roman Empire and the Rise of Christianity,* edited by Leif E. Vaage, 232–51. Waterloo, ON: Wilfred Laurier University Press, 2006.

Bediako, Kwame. *Theology and Identity: The Impact of Culture upon Christian Thought in the Second Century and in Modern Africa.* Oxford: Regnum Books, 1992.

Beskow, Per. "Mission, Trade and Emigration in the Second Century." *Svensk Exegetisk Årskbok* 35 (1970): 104–14.

Beyschlag, Karlmann. "Zur Geschichte der Bergpredigt in der Alten Kirche." *Zeitschrift für Theologie und Kirche* 74 (1977): 291–322.

Bobertz, Charles A. "An Analysis of *Vita Cypriani* 3.6–10 and the Attribution of *Ad Quirinum* to Cyprian of Carthage." *Vigiliae Christianae* 46 (1992): 112–28.

Bodel, John. "Dealing with the Dead: Undertakers, Executioners and Potter's Fields in Ancient Rome." In *Death and Disease in the Ancient City,* edited by Valerie M. Hope and Eireann Marshall, 128–51. London: Routledge, 2000.

Bouley, Allen. *From Freedom to Formula: The Evolution of the Eucharistic Prayer from Oral Improvisation to Written Texts.* Studies in Christian Antiquity 21. Washington, DC: Catholic University of America Press, 1981.

Bourdieu, Pierre. *The Logic of Practice.* Translated by Richard Nice. Stanford, CA: Stanford University Press, 1980.

———. *Pascalian Meditations.* Translated by Richard Nice. Stanford, CA: Stanford University Press, 2000.

Bowen, Anthony, and Peter Garnsey, eds. *Lactantius: Divine Institutes.* Translated Texts for Historians 40. Liverpool: Liverpool University Press, 2003.

Bowes, Kim. "Early Christian Archaeology: A State of the Field." *Religion Compass* 2, no. 4 (2008): 431–41.

Boyarin, Daniel. *Dying for God: Martyrdom and the Making of Christianity and Judaism.* Stanford, CA: Stanford University Press, 1999.

Bradshaw, Paul F. *Eucharistic Origins.* New York: Oxford University Press, 2004.

———. "The Gospel and the Catechumenate in the Third Century." *Journal of Theological Studies* 2/49, no. 1 (1998): 143–52.

———. "The Homogenization of Christian Liturgy—Ancient and Modern." *Studia Liturgica* 26 (1996): 1–15.

———. "The Profession of Faith in Early Christian Baptism." *Evangelical Quarterly* 78, no. 2 (2006): 101–15.

———. "The Reception of Communion in Early Christianity." *Studia Liturgica* 37 (2007): 164–80.

———. *Reconstructing Early Christian Worship*. Collegeville, MN: Liturgical Press, 2010.

———. *The Search for the Origins of Christian Worship: Sources and Methods for the Study of Early Liturgy*. Rev. ed. London: SPCK; New York: Oxford University Press, 2002.

———. "Women and Baptism in the *Didascalia Apostolorum*." *Journal of Early Christian Studies* 20, no. 4 (2012): 641–45.

Bradshaw, Paul F., and Maxwell E. Johnson. *The Eucharistic Liturgies: Their Evolution and Interpretation*. Collegeville, MN: Liturgical Press, 2012.

Bradshaw, Paul F., Maxwell E. Johnson, and L. Edward Phillips. *The Apostolic Tradition: A Commentary*. Hermeneia. Minneapolis: Fortress, 2002.

Bremmer, Jan N. "'Christianus sum': The Early Christian Martyrs and Christ." In *Eulogia: Mélanges offert à Antoon A.R. Bastiaensen à l'occasion de son soixante-cinquième anniversaire*, edited by G. J. M. Bartelink, A. Hilhorst, and C. J. Kneepkens, 11–20. Instrumenta Patristica 24. The Hague: Nijhoff, 1991.

———. "Felicitas: The Martyrdom of a Young African Woman." In *Perpetua's Passions: Multidisciplinary Approaches to the "Passio Perpetuae et Felicitatis,"* edited by Jan N. Bremmer and Marco Formisano. Oxford: Oxford University Press, 2012.

———. "Pauper or Patroness: The Widow in the Early Christian Church." In *Between Poverty and the Pyre: Moments in the History of Widowhood*, edited by Jan N. Bremmer and L. P. Van den Bosch, 31–57. London: Routledge, 1995.

———. *The Rise of Christianity through the Eyes of Gibbon, Harnack and Rodney Stark*. Groningen: Barkhuis, 2010.

———. "The Vision of Constantine." In *Land of Dreams: Greek and Latin Studies in Honour of A. H. M. Kessels*, edited by A. P. M. H. Lardinois, Marc Van der Poel, and Vincent Hunink, 57–79. Leiden: Brill, 2006.

Brenneman, Robert. *Homies and Hermanos: God and Gangs in Central America*. New York: Oxford University Press, 2012.

Brent, Allen. *Cyprian and Roman Carthage*. Cambridge: Cambridge University Press, 2010.

Brown, Peter. *Augustine of Hippo: A Biography*. Rev. ed. Berkeley: University of California Press, 2000.

———. "St. Augustine's Attitude to Religious Coercion." In his *Religion and Society in the Age of Saint Augustine*, 260–78. New York: Harper & Row, 1972.

———. *Through the Eye of a Needle: Wealth, the Fall of Rome, and the Making of Christianity in the West, 350–550 AD*. Princeton: Princeton University Press, 2012.

———. *The World of Late Antiquity*. London: Thames & Hudson, 1971.

Brox, Norbert. "Zur christlichen Mission in der Spätantike." In *Mission im Neuen Testament*, edited by Karl Kertelge, 190–237. Quaestiones Disputatae 93. Freiburg-im-Breisgau: Herder, 1982.

Bruun, Christer. "The Antonine Plague and the 'Third-Century Crisis.'" In *Crises and the Roman Empire: Proceedings of the Seventh Workshop of the International Network Impact of Empire (Nijmegen, June 20–24, 2006)*, edited by Olivier Heckster, Gerda de Kleijn, and Danielle Slootjes, 201–17. Leiden: Brill, 2007.

Budde, Achim. "Improvisation im Eucharistiegebet: Zur Technik freien Betens in der Alten Kirche." *Jahrbuch für Antike und Christentum* 44 (2001): 127–41.

Cagnet, R., G. Lafaye, et al., eds. *Inscriptiones graecae ad res romanas pertinentes*. Vol. 4, *Inscriptiones Asiae II*. Paris: E. Leroux, 1927. Reprint, Chicago: Aries, 1975.

Cameron, Alan. *The Last Pagans of Rome*. Oxford: Oxford University Press, 2011.

Cameron, Averil. "The Violence of Orthodoxy." In *Heresy and Identity in Late Antiquity*, edited by Eduard Iricinschi and Holger M. Zelletin, 102–14. Tübingen: Mohr Siebeck, 2008.

Cameron, Averil, and Stuart G. Hall, trans. and eds. *Eusebius: Life of Constantine*. Oxford: Oxford University Press, 1999.

Carroll, Scott T. "An Early Church Sermon against Gambling (*CPL* 60)." *Second Century* 8 (1991): 83–95.

Carruthers, Mary. *The Craft of Thought: Meditation, Rhetoric, and the Making of Images, 400–1200*. Cambridge: Cambridge University Press, 1998.

Castagno, Adele Monaci. "Origen the Scholar and Pastor." In *Preacher and Audience: Studies in Early Christian and Byzantine Homiletics*, edited by Mary B. Cunningham and Pauline Allen, 65–89. Leiden: Brill, 1998.

Chadwick, Henry. "Augustine on Pagans and Christians: Reflections on Religious and Social Change." In *History, Society and the Churches: Essays in Honour of Owen Chadwick*, edited by Derek Beales and Geoffrey Best, 9–28. Cambridge: Cambridge University Press, 1985.

———. "The Church of the Third Century in the West." In *Roman West in the Third Century*, edited by A. King and M. Henig. London: British Archaeological Reports, 1981.

———. *The Early Church*. Harmondsworth, Middlesex: Penguin Books, 1967.

Chadwick, Henry, and Peter Brown. "Prayer." In *Late Antiquity: A Guide to the Postclassical World*, edited by G. W. Bowersock, Peter Brown, and Oleg Grabar, 648–51. Cambridge, MA: Harvard University Press, 1999.

Clark, Elizabeth A. "'Devil's Gateway and Bride of Christ': Women in the Early Christian World." In *Ascetic Piety and Women's Faith: Essays on Late Christian Antiquity*, edited by Elizabeth A. Clark. Studies in Women and Religion 20. Lewiston, NY: Edwin Mellen, 1986.

———. "Thinking with Women: The Uses of the Appeal to 'Woman' in Pre-Nicene Christian Propaganda Literature." In *The Spread of Christianity in the First Four Centuries: Essays in Explanation*, edited by W. V. Harris, 43–51. Leiden: Brill, 2005.

Congar, Yves. "Souci du salut des païens et conscience missionaire dans le Christianisme postapostolique et préconstantinien." In *Kyriakon: Festschrift Johannes Quasten*, edited by Patrick Granfield and Josef A. Jungmann, 3–11. Münster: Aschendorff, 1970.

Cooper, Kate. "Christianity, Private Power, and the Law from Decius to Constantine: The Minimalist View." *Journal of Early Christian Studies* 19, no. 3 (2011): 327–43.

———. "Closely Watched Households: Visibility, Exposure, and Private Power in the Roman *Domus*." *Past and Present* 197 (2007): 3–33.

———. "A Father, a Daughter, and a Procurator: Authority and Resistance in the Prison Diary of Perpetua of Carthage." *Gender and History* 23, no. 1 (2011): 685–702.

———. "Insinuations of Womanly Influence: An Aspect of the Christianization of the Roman Aristocracy." *Journal of Roman Studies* 82 (1992): 150–64.

———. *The Virgin and the Bride: Idealized Womanhood in Late Antiquity*. Cambridge, MA: Harvard University Press, 1996.

Crouzel, Henri. "Gregor I (Gregor der Wundertäter)." In *Reallexikon für Antike und Christentum*, 12:779–93. Stuttgart: Anton Hiersemann, 1983.

———. *Origen*. Translated by A. S. Worrall. Edinburgh: T&T Clark, 1989.

Cunningham, Mary B. "Preaching and the Community." In *Church and People in Byzantium*, edited by Rosemary Morris, 29–47. Birmingham: University of Birmingham, 1990.

Daniélou, Jean. "L'histoire du salut dans la catéchèse." *La Maison-Dieu* 30 (1952): 19–35.

Digeser, Elizabeth DePalma. "Lactantius and Constantine's Letter to Arles: Dating the *Divine Institutes*." *Journal of Early Christian Studies* 2, no. 1 (1994): 33–52.

Dölger, F. J. "Die Taufe Konstantins und ihre Probleme." In *Konstantin der Grosse und seine Zeit*, edited by F. J. Dölger, 377–447. Freiburg-im- Breisgau: Herder, 1913.

Downs, David J. "Redemptive Almsgiving and Economic Stratification in 2 Clement." *Journal of Early Christian Studies* 19, no. 4 (2011): 493–517.

Drake, H. A. *Constantine and the Bishops: The Politics of Intolerance*. Baltimore: Johns Hopkins University Press, 2000.

———. "Models of Christian Expansion." In *The Spread of Christianity in the First Four Centuries: Essays in Explanation*, edited by W. V. Harris, 1–13. Leiden: Brill, 2005.

Dujarier, Michel. *A History of the Catechumenate: The First Six Centuries.* Translated by Edward J. Haasl. New York: Sadlier, 1979.

Eisen, Ute. *Women Officeholders in Early Christianity.* Collegeville: Liturgical Press, 2000.

Edwards, Mark. "The Beginnings of Christianization." In *The Cambridge Companion to the Age of Constantine,* edited by Noel Lenski, 137–58. Cambridge: Cambridge University Press, 2006.

————, trans. and ed. *Constantine and Christendom: The Oration to the Saints; The Greek and Latin Accounts of the Discovery of the Cross; The Edict of Constantine to Pope Silvester.* Translated Texts for Historians 39. Liverpool: Liverpool University Press, 2003.

————. "The Constantinian Circle and the Oration to the Saints." In *Apologetics in the Roman Empire: Pagans, Jews, and Christians,* edited by Mark Edwards, Martin Goodman, Simon Price, and Christopher Rowland, 251–77. Oxford: Oxford University Press, 1999.

————, trans. and ed. *Optatus: Against the Donatists.* Translated Texts for Historians 27. Liverpool: Liverpool University Press, 1997.

Ekenberg, Anders. "Evidence for Jewish Believers in 'Church Orders' and Liturgical Texts." In *Jewish Believers in Jesus: The Early Centuries,* edited by Oskar Skarsaune and Reidar Hvalvik, 640–58. Peabody, MA: Hendrickson, 2007.

Ferguson, Everett. *Backgrounds of Early Christianity.* Grand Rapids: Eerdmans, 1987.

————. *Baptism in the Early Church: History, Theology, and Liturgy in the First Five Centuries.* Grand Rapids: Eerdmans, 2009.

————. "Basil's Protreptic to Baptism." In *Nova et Vetera: Patristic Studies in Honor of Thomas Patrick Halton,* edited by John Petruccione, 70–83. Washington, DC: Catholic University of America Press, 1998.

————. "Catechesis and Initiation." In *The Origins of Christendom in the West,* edited by Alan Kreider, 229–68. Edinburgh: T&T Clark, 2001.

————. *Demonology of the Early Christian World.* Symposium Series 12. New York: Edwin Mellen, 1984.

————. "Early Christian Martyrdom and Civil Disobedience." *Journal of Early Christian Studies* 1, no. 1 (1993): 73–83.

————, ed. *Early Christians Speak: Faith and Life in the First Three Centuries.* 2 vols. vol. 1, rev. ed. Abilene, Texas: ACU Press, 1987; vol. 2. Abilene, Texas: ACU Press, 2002.

————. "Exhortations to Baptism in the Cappadocians." *Studia Patristica* 33 (1997): 121–29.

————. "Irenaeus' *Proof of the Apostolic Preaching* and Early Catechetical Tradition." *Studia Patristica* 18, no. 3 (1989): 119–40.

———. "Some Factors in the Growth of the Early Church." *Restoration Quarterly* 16 (1973): 32–52.

———. "Voices of Religious Liberty in the Early Church." *Restoration Quarterly* 19 (1976): 13–22.

Ferngren, Gary B. *Medicine and Health Care in Early Christianity*. Baltimore: Johns Hopkins University Press, 2009.

Fink-Dendorfer, Elisabeth. *Conversio: Motive und Motivierung zur Bekehrung in der Alten Kirche*. Regensburger Studien zur Theologie 33. Frankfurt-am-Main: Peter Lang, 1986.

Finn, Thomas M. *Early Christian Baptism and the Catechumenate: Italy, North Africa and Egypt*. Message of the Fathers of the Church 6. Collegeville, MN: Liturgical Press, 1992.

Finney, Paul Corby. "Images on Finger Rings and Early Christian Art." In *Studies on Art and Archaeology in Honor of Ernst Kitzinger on His Seventy-Fifth Birthday*, edited by William Tronzo and Irving Lavin. *Dumbarton Oaks Papers* 41 (1987): 181–86. Washington, DC: Dumbarton Oaks Research Library and Collection, 1987.

———. "Labarum." In *Encyclopedia of Early Christianity*, edited by Everett Ferguson, 2:659–60. 2nd ed. New York: Garland, 1997.

Fonrobert, Charlotte Elisheva. "The *Didascalia Apostolorum*: A Mishnah for the Disciples of Jesus." *Journal of Early Christian Studies* 9, no. 4 (2001): 483–509.

Fowden, Garth. "The Last Days of Constantine: Oppositional Versions and Their Influence." *Journal of Roman Studies* 84 (1994): 146–70.

Frend, W. H. C. "Blandina and Perpetua: Two Early Christian Heroines." In *Les Martyrs de Lyon (177)*, 167–75. Colloques internationaux du Centre national de la recherche scientifique 575. Paris: Éditions CNRS, 1978.

———. *Martyrdom and Persecution in the Early Church*. Oxford: Blackwell, 1965.

———. "A Note on the Influence of Greek Immigrants on the Spread of Christianity in the West." In *Mullus: Festschrift Theodor Klauser*, edited by Alfred Stuiber and Alfred Hermann, 125–29. Münster: Aschendorff, 1964.

Gamble, Harry Y. *Books and Readers in the Early Church*. New Haven: Yale University Press, 1995.

Garnsey, Peter. "Religious Toleration in Classical Antiquity." In *Persecution and Toleration*, edited by W. J. Sheils, 1–27. Studies in Church History 21. Oxford: Blackwell, 1984.

Glancy, Jennifer A. *Corporal Knowledge: Early Christian Bodies*. Oxford: Oxford University Press, 2010.

Goodman, Martin. *Mission and Conversion: Proselytizing in the Religious History of the Roman Empire*. Oxford: Clarendon, 1994.

Green, Michael. *Evangelism in the Early Church*. London: Hodder & Stoughton, 1970. Rev. ed., Grand Rapids: Eerdmans, 2002.

Hall, Stuart G. "The Sects under Constantine." In *Voluntary Religion*, edited by W. J. Sheils and Diana Wood, 1–13. Studies in Church History 23. Oxford: Blackwell, 1986.

Hamman, Adalbert-G. *La prière*. Vol. 2, *Les trois premiers siècles*. Tournai: Desclée, 1963.

Hanson, R. P. C. "The Liberty of the Bishop to Improvise Prayer." In *Studies in Christian Antiquity*, 113–16. Edinburgh: T&T Clark, 1985.

Harmless, William. *Augustine and the Catechumenate*. Collegeville, MN: Liturgical Press, 1995.

Harnack, Adolf. *The Mission and Expansion of Christianity in the First Three Centuries*. Translated by James Moffatt. 2 vols. New York: G. P. Putnam's Sons, 1908.

Harris, W. V. *Ancient Literacy*. Cambridge, MA: Harvard University Press, 1989.

Hebert, Laura. "Pagans and Christians in Late Antique Aphrodisias." In *Conversion to Christianity from Late Antiquity to the Modern Age*, edited by Calvin B. Kendall, Oliver Nicholson, William D. Phillips Jr., and Marguerite Ragnow, 85–114. Minneapolis: Center for Early Modern History, University of Minnesota, 2009.

Horn, Cornelia B. "St. Nino and the Christianization of Pagan Georgia." *Medieval Encounters* 4 (1998): 242–64.

Horn, Cornelia B., and John W. Martens. *"Let the Little Children Come to Me": Childhood and Children in Early Christianity*. Washington, DC: Catholic University of America Press, 2009.

Hornus, Jean-Michel. *It Is Not Lawful for Me to Fight: Early Christian Attitudes toward War, Violence, and the State*. Translated by Alan Kreider and Oliver Coburn. Scottdale, PA: Herald Press, 1980.

Hvalvik, Reidar. "In Word and Deed: The Expansion of the Church in the Pre-Constantinian Era." In *The Mission of the Early Church to Jews and Gentiles*, edited by Jostein Ådna and Hans Kvalbein, 265–87. Tübingen: Mohr Siebeck, 2000.

Jefferson, Lee M. *Christ the Miracle Worker in Early Christian Art*. Minneapolis: Fortress, 2014.

Jenkins, Philip. *The New Faces of Christianity: Believing the Bible in the Global South*. New York: Oxford University Press, 2006.

Jensen, Robin Margaret. *Understanding Early Christian Art*. London and New York: Routledge, 2000.

Johnson, Maxwell E. "Christian Initiation of Fourth-Century Jerusalem and Recent Developments in the Study of the Sources." *Ecclesia Orans* 26 (2009): 143–61.

———. *Praying and Believing in Early Christianity: The Interplay between Christian Worship and Doctrine*. Collegeville, MN: Liturgical Press, 2013.

———. *The Rites of Christian Initiation*. Rev. ed. Collegeville, MN: Liturgical Press, 2007.

Kahlos, Maijastina. "The Rhetoric of Tolerance and Intolerance: From Lactantius to Firmicus Maternus." In *Changes and Continuities in Christian Apologetic*, edited by A. Jacobsen, Maijestina Kahlos, and J. Ulrich, 79–95. Frankfurt: Peter Lang, 2009.

Kalantzis, George. *Caesar and the Lamb: Early Christian Attitudes on War and Military Service*. Eugene, OR: Cascade Books, 2012.

Kaster, Robert A. "The Taxonomy of Patience, or When Is *Patientia* Not a Virtue?" *Classical Philology* 97, no. 2 (2002): 135–38.

Kazhdan, A. "'Constantin Imaginaire': Byzantine Legends of the Ninth Century about Constantine the Great." *Byzantion* 57 (1987): 196–250.

Kelly, Henry Ansgar. *The Devil at Baptism: Ritual, Theology, and Drama*. Ithaca: Cornell University Press, 1985.

Kenneson, Philip. "Gathering: Worship, Imagination, and Formation." In *The Blackwell Companion to Christian Ethics*, edited by Stanley Hauerwas and Philip Wells, 53–67. Malden, MA: Blackwell, 2004.

Klassen, William. "The Sacred Kiss in the New Testament: An Example of Social Boundary Lines." *New Testament Studies* 39 (1993): 122–35.

Koskenniemi, Erkki. *The Exposure of Infants among Jews and Christians in Antiquity*. Social World of Biblical Antiquity 2/4. Sheffield: Sheffield Phoenix, 2009.

Krautheimer, Richard. "The Ecclesiastical Building Policy of Constantine." In *Constantino il Grande: Dall'antichità all'Umanesimo; Colloquio sul Christianesimo nel mondo antico*, 509–52. Macerata: Università degli studi di Macerata, 1993.

———. *Rome, Profile of a City, 312–1308*. Princeton: Princeton University Press, 1980.

Kreider, Alan. *The Change of Conversion and the Origin of Christendom*. Harrisburg, PA: Trinity Press International, 1999. Reprint, Eugene, OR: Wipf & Stock, 2006.

———. "Military Service in the Church Orders." *Journal of Religious Ethics* 31, no. 3 (2003): 415–42.

———. "Peacemaking in Worship in the Syrian Church Orders." *Studia Liturgica* 34, no. 2 (2004): 177–90.

———. *Worship and Evangelism in Pre-Christendom*. Alcuin/GROW Joint Liturgical Studies 32. Cambridge: Grove Books, 1995.

———, ed. *The Origins of Christendom in the West*. Edinburgh: T&T Clark, 2001.

Kreider, Eleanor. "Let the Faithful Greet Each Other: The Kiss of Peace." *Conrad Grebel Review* 5 (1987): 29–49.

Kretschmar, Georg. "Das christliche Leben und die Mission in der frühen Kirche." In *Kirchengeschichte als Missionsgeschichte*, vol. 1, *Die alte Kirche*, edited by Heinzgünter Frohnes and Uwe W. Knorr, 94–128. Munich: Chr. Kaiser, 1974.

Labriolle, Pierre de. "Paroecia." *Bulletin du Cange (Archivum Latinitatis Medii Aevi)* 3 (1927): 196–207.

Laeuchli, Samuel. *Power and Sexuality: The Emergence of Canon Law at the Synod of Elvira*. Philadelphia: Temple University Press, 1972.

Lamirande, Émilien. *Church, State, and Toleration: An Intriguing Change of Mind in Augustine.* Philadelphia: Villanova University Press, 1974.

Lampe, Peter. *From Paul to Valentinus: Christians in Rome in the First Two Centuries.* Minneapolis: Fortress, 2003.

Land, Steven J. *Pentecostal Spirituality: A Passion for the Kingdom.* Sheffield: Sheffield Academic Press, 1993.

Lane, Anthony N. S. "Did the Apostolic Church Baptise Babies? A Seismological Approach." *Tyndale Bulletin* 55, no. 1 (2004): 109–30.

Lane Fox, Robin. "Literacy and Power in Early Christianity." In *Literacy and Power in the Ancient World*, edited by Alan K. Bowman and Greg Woolf, 126–48. Cambridge: Cambridge University Press, 1994.

———. *Pagans and Christians.* San Francisco: Harper & Row, 1986.

Lathrop, Gordon W. *Holy Things: A Liturgical Theology.* Minneapolis: Fortress, 1993.

Leithart, Peter J. *Defending Constantine: The Twilight of an Empire and the Dawn of Christendom.* Downers Grove, IL: IVP Academic, 2010.

Lepelley, C. "Chrétiens et païens au temps de la persécution de Dioclétien: Le cas d'Abthugni." *Studia Patristica* 15 (1984): 226–32.

Leyerle, Blake. "Meal Customs in the Greco-Roman World." In *Passover and Easter: Origin and History to Modern Times*, edited by Paul F. Bradshaw and Lawrence A. Hoffman, 29–61. Notre Dame, IN: University of Notre Dame Press, 1999.

Lienhard, Joseph T. "Origen as Homilist." In *Preaching in the Patristic Age: Studies in Honor of Walter J. Burghardt, S.J.*, edited by David G. Hunter, 36–52. New York: Paulist Press, 1989.

Lieu, Judith M. *Neither Jew nor Greek? Constructing Early Christianity.* New York: T&T Clark, 2003.

Lindsay, Hugh. "Eating with the Dead: The Roman Funerary Banquet." In *Meals in a Social Context: Aspects of the Communal Meal in the Hellenistic and Roman World*, edited by Inge Nielsen and Hanne Sigismund Nielsen, 67–80. Aarhus: Aarhus University Press, 2001.

Lofland, John, and Rodney Stark. "Becoming a World-Saver: A Theory of Conversion to a Deviant Perspective." *American Sociological Review* 30 (1965): 862–75.

Lohfink, Gerhard. *Does God Need the Church? Toward a Theology of the People of God.* Translated by Linda M. Maloney. Collegeville, MN: Liturgical Press, 1999.

———. "'Schwerter zu Pflugscharen': Die Rezeption von Jes 2, 1–5 par Mi 4, 1–5 in der Alten Kirche und im Neuen Testament." *Theologische Quartalschrift* 166 (1986): 184–209.

Longenecker, Bruce W. "Socio-Economic Profiling of the First Urban Christians." In *After the First Urban Christians: The Socio-Scientific Study of Pauline Christianity Twenty-Five Years Later*, edited by Todd D. Still and David G. Horrell, 36–59. London: T&T Clark, 2009.

Luijendijk, AnneMarie. *Greetings in the Lord: Early Christians and the Oxyrhynchus Papyri*. Harvard Theological Studies 60. Cambridge, MA: Harvard University Press, 2008.

Lysaught, M. Therese. "Witnessing Christ in Their Bodies: Martyrs and Ascetics as Doxological Disciples." *Annual of the Society of Christian Ethics* 20 (2000): 239–62.

MacDonald, Margaret Y. *Early Christian Women and Pagan Opinion: The Power of the Hysterical Woman*. Cambridge: Cambridge University Press, 1996.

———. "Was Celsus Right? The Role of Women in the Expansion of Early Christianity." In *Early Christian Families in Context: An Interdisciplinary Dialogue*, ed. David L. Balch and Carolyn Osiek, 157–84. Grand Rapids: Eerdmans, 2003.

MacMullen, Ramsay. *Christianizing the Roman Empire (A.D. 100–400)*. New Haven: Yale University Press, 1984.

———. *Constantine*. London: Croom Helm, 1969.

———. *Corruption and the Decline of Rome*. New Haven: Yale University Press, 1988.

———. *Paganism in the Roman Empire*. New Haven: Yale University Press, 1981.

———. *Roman Social Relations, 50 B.C. to A.D. 284*. New Haven: Yale University Press, 1974.

———. *The Second Church: Popular Christianity, A.D. 200–400*. SBL Writings from the Greco-Roman World Supplement Series 1. Atlanta: Society of Biblical Literature, 2009.

———. "Two Types of Conversion to Early Christianity." *Vigiliae Christianae* 37 (1983): 174–92.

———. "What Difference Did Christianity Make?" *Historia* 35 (1986): 322–43.

MacMullen, Ramsay, and Eugene N. Lane, eds. *Paganism and Christianity, 100–425 C.E.: A Sourcebook*. Minneapolis: Fortress, 1992.

Madigan, Kevin, and Carolyn Osiek, eds. *Ordained Women in the Early Church*. Baltimore: Johns Hopkins University Press, 2005.

Markus, Robert. *The End of Ancient Christianity*. Cambridge: Cambridge University Press, 1990.

———. *Saeculum: History and Society in the Theology of Augustine*. Cambridge: Cambridge University Press, 1970.

McGowan, Andrew B. "Food, Ritual, and Power." In *Late Ancient Christianity*, edited by Virginia Burrus, 145–64. A People's History of Christianity 2. Minneapolis: Fortress, 2005.

———. "Rethinking Agape and Eucharist in Early North African Christianity." *Studia Liturgica* 34 (2004): 133–46.

McGuckin, John. "The Life of Origen (c. 186–255)." In *The Westminster Handbook to Origen*, edited by John McGuckin, 1–23. Westminster Handbooks to Christian Theology. Louisville: Westminster John Knox, 2004.

Meeks, Wayne. *The Origins of Christian Morality: The First Two Centuries.* New Haven: Yale University Press, 1993.

Methuen, Charlotte. "'For Pagans Laugh to Hear Women Teach': Gender Stereotypes in the *Didascalia Apostolorum.*" In *Gender and Christian Religion,* edited by R. N. Swanson, 23–35. Woodbridge, Suffolk: Boydell Press, 1998.

———. "Widows, Bishops and the Struggle for Authority in the *Didascalia Apostolorum.*" *Journal of Ecclesiastical History* 46 (1995): 197–213.

Metzger, Marcel, Wolfram Drews, and Heinzgerd Brakmann. "Katechumenat." In *Reallexikon für Antike und Christentum,* 20:497–574. Stuttgart: Anton Hiersemann, 2001.

Milavec, Aaron. *The Didache: Faith, Hope, and Life of the Earliest Christian Communities, 50–70 C.E.* New York: Newman, 2003.

———, ed. *Didache: Text, Translation, Analysis, and Commentary.* Collegeville, MN: Liturgical Press, 2003.

Miles, Margaret R. *Carnal Knowing: Female Nakedness and Religious Meaning in the Christian West.* Boston: Beacon Press, 1989.

Molland, Einar. "Besass die Alte Kirche ein Missionsprogramm und bewusste Missionsmethoden?" In *Kirchengeschichte als Missionsgeschichte,* vol. 1, *Die Alte Kirche,* edited by Heinzgünter Frohnes and Uwe W. Knorr, 51–67. Munich: Chr. Kaiser, 1974.

Moss, Candida. *Ancient Christian Martyrdom: Diverse Practices, Theologies, and Tradition.* New Haven: Yale University Press, 2012.

———. *The Myth of Persecution: How the Early Christians Invented a Story of Martyrdom.* New York: Harper One, 2013.

Muir, Steven C. "'Look How They Love One Another': Early Christian and Pagan Care for the Sick and Other Charity." In *Religious Rivalries in the Early Roman Empire and the Rise of Christianity,* edited by Leif E. Vaage, 213–31. Waterloo, ON: Wilfred Laurier University Press, 2006.

Musurillo, Herbert A., trans. and ed. *The Acts of the Christian Martyrs.* Oxford: Clarendon, 1972.

Neymeyr, Ulrich. *Die christlichen Lehrer im zweiten Jahrhundert: Ihre Lehrtätigkeit, ihr Selbstverständnis und ihre Geschichte.* Supplements to Vigiliae Christianae 4. Leiden: Brill, 1989.

North, John A. "Pagans, Polytheists and the Pendulum." In *The Spread of Christianity in the First Four Centuries: Essays in Explanation,* edited by W. V. Harris, 126–43. Leiden: Brill, 2005.

Oakes, Peter. *Reading Romans in Pompeii: Paul's Letter at Ground Level.* Minneapolis: Fortress, 2009.

Odahl, Charles Matson. *Constantine and the Christian Empire.* London: Routledge, 2004.

O'Loughlin, Thomas. *The Didache: A Window on the Earliest Christians*. Grand Rapids: Baker Academic, 2010.

———. "From a Damp Floor to a New Vision of Church: Footwashing as a Challenge to Liturgy and Discipleship." *Worship* 88, no. 2 (2014): 137–50.

———. "The Missionary Strategy of the Didache." *Transformation: An International Journal of Holistic Mission Studies* 28, no. 2 (2011): 77–92.

Osiek, Carolyn. "Roman and Christian Burial Practices." In *Commemorating the Dead: Texts and Artifacts in Context; Studies of Roman, Jewish, and Christian Burials*, edited by Laurie Brink and Deborah Green, 243–72. Berlin and New York: de Gruyter, 2008.

Osiek, Carolyn, and Margaret Y. MacDonald. *A Woman's Place: House Churches in Earliest Christianity*. Minneapolis: Fortress, 2006.

Penn, Michael Philip. "'Bold and Having No Shame': Ambiguous Widows, Controlling Clergy and Early Syrian Communities." *Hugoye: Journal of Syriac Studies* 4, no. 2 (2001): 159–85.

———. *Kissing Christians: Ritual and Community in the Late Ancient Church*. Philadelphia: University of Pennsylvania Press, 2005.

Pharr, Clyde, trans. and ed. *The Theodosian Code and Novels, and the Sirmondian Constitution*. Princeton: Princeton University Press, 1952.

Phillips, L. Edward. "The Ritual Kiss in Early Christian Worship." PhD diss., University of Notre Dame, 1992.

———. *The Ritual Kiss in Early Christian Worship*. Alcuin/GROW Joint Liturgical Studies 36. Cambridge: Grove Books, 1996.

Pohlsander, Hans A. "Crispus: Brilliant Career and Tragic End." *Historia* 33 (1984): 79–106.

Price, Simon. "Latin Christian Apologetics: Minucius Felix, Tertullian, and Cyprian." In *Apologetics in the Roman Empire: Pagans, Jews and Christians*, ed. Mark Edwards, Martin Goodman, Simon Price, and Christopher Rowland, 105–29. Oxford: Oxford University Press, 1999.

Quasten, Johannes, ed., *Patrology*, vol. 2, *The Ante-Nicene Literature after Irenaeus*. Westminster, MD: Christian Classics, 1950.

Reinbold, Wolfgang. *Propaganda und Mission im ältesten Christentum: Eine Untersuchung zu den Modalitäten der Ausbreitung der frühen Kirche*. Forschungen zur Religion und Literatur des Alten und Neuen Testaments 188. Göttingen: Vandenhoek & Ruprecht, 2000.

Richardson, Cyril C., ed. *Early Christian Fathers*. Philadelphia: Westminster, 1953.

Rives, James B. *Religion in the Roman Empire*. Malden, MA: Blackwell, 2007.

Robeck, Cecil M., Jr. *Prophecy in Carthage: Perpetua, Tertullian, and Cyprian*. Cleveland: Pilgrim Press, 1992.

Robert, Dana L. "World Christianity as a Women's Movement." *International Bulletin of Missionary Research* 30, no. 4 (2006): 180–88.

Robert, Dana L., and M. L. Daneel. "Worship among Apostles and Zionists in Southern Africa, Zimbabwe." In *Christian Worship Worldwide: Expanding Horizons, Deepening Practices*, edited by Charles Farhadian, 43–70. Grand Rapids: Eerdmans, 2007.

Rohr, Richard. *Simplicity: The Art of Living*. New York: Crossroad, 1991.

Rouwhorst, Gerard. "The Reading of Scripture in Early Christian Liturgy." In *What Athens Has to Do with Jerusalem: Essays on Classical, Jewish, and Early Christian Art and Archaeology in Honor of Gideon Foerster*, edited by Leonard V. Rutgers, 305–31. Leuven: Peeters, 2002.

———. "The Roots of the Early Christian Eucharist: Jewish Blessings or Hellenistic Symposia?" In *Jewish and Christian Liturgy and Worship: New Insights into Its History and Interaction*, edited by Albert Gerhards and Clemens Leonhard, 295–307. Leiden: Brill, 2007.

Sage, Michael M. *Cyprian*. Cambridge, MA: Philadelphia Patristic Foundation, 1975.

Salzman, Michele Renee. *The Making of a Christian Aristocracy*. Cambridge, MA: Harvard University Press, 2002.

Sarefield, Daniel. "Bookburning in the Christian Roman Empire: Transforming a Pagan Rite of Purification." In *Violence in Late Antiquity: Perceptions and Practices*, edited by H. A. Drake, 287–96. Burlington, VT: Ashgate, 2006.

Scheidel, Walter C. "A Model of Demographic and Economic Change in Roman Egypt after the Antonine Plague." *Journal of Roman Archaeology* 15 (2002): 97–114.

Scheidel, Walter C., and Steven J. Friesen. "The Size of the Economy and the Distribution of Income." *Journal of Roman Studies* 99 (2009): 61–91.

Schlabach, Gerald W. *For the Joy Set before Us: Augustine and Self-Denying Love*. Notre Dame, IN: University of Notre Dame Press, 2000.

Schöllgen, Georg. *Die Anfänge der Professionalisierung des Klerus und das kirchliche Amt in der Syrischen Didaskalie*. Jahrbuch für Antike und Christentum, Ergänzungsband 26. Münster: Aschendorff, 1998.

———. *Ecclesia Sordida? Zur Frage der sozialen Schichtung frühchristlicher Gemeinden am Beispiel Karthagos zur Zeit Tertullians*. Münster: Aschendorff, 1984.

———. "From Monepiscopate to Monarchical Episcopate: The Emergence of a New Relationship between Bishop and Community in the Third Century." *The Jurist* 66 (2006): 114–28.

Schreiter, Robert. "Inculturation of Faith or Identification with Culture?" In *Christianity and Cultures: A Mutual Enrichment*, edited by Norbert Greinacher and Norbert Mette, 15–24. Maryknoll, NY: Orbis Books, 1994.

Secrétan, H. F. "Le Christianisme des premiers siècles et le service militaire." *Revue de Théologie et de Philosophie* 2 (1914): 345–65.

Shaw, Brent D. "The Passion of Perpetua." *Past and Present* 139 (1993): 3–45.

————. *Sacred Violence: African Christians and Sectarian Hatred in the Age of Augustine*. Cambridge: Cambridge University Press, 2011.

Sider, Ronald J., ed. *The Early Church on Killing: A Comprehensive Sourcebook on War, Abortion, and Capital Punishment*. Grand Rapids: Baker Academic, 2012.

Smith, James K. A. *Imagining the Kingdom: How Worship Works*. Grand Rapids: Baker Academic, 2013.

Snyder, Graydon F. *Ante Pacem: Archaeological Evidence of Church Life before Constantine*. Macon, GA: Mercer University Press, 1985.

Snyder, Harlow Gregory. "'Above the Baths of Myrtinus': Justin Martyr's 'School' in the City of Rome." *Harvard Theological Review* 100, no. 3 (2007): 335–62.

Spanneut, Michel. "Geduld." In *Reallexikon für Antike und Christentum*, 9:243–94. Stuttgart: Anton Hiersemann, 1976.

————. "La Nonviolence chez les pères Africaines avant Constantin." In *Kyriakon: Festschrift Johannes Quasten*, edited by Patrick Granfield and Josef A. Jungmann, 1:36–39. Münster: Aschendorff, 1970.

Stark, Rodney. *One True God: Historical Consequences of Monotheism*. Princeton: Princeton University Press, 2001.

————. "Physiology and Faith: Addressing the 'Universal' Gender Difference in Religious Commitment." *Journal for the Scientific Study of Religion* 41, no. 3 (2002): 495–507.

————. *The Rise of Christianity: A Sociologist Reconsiders History*. Princeton: Princeton University Press, 1996.

Stark, Rodney, and William Sims Bainbridge. "Networks of Faith: Interpersonal Bonds and Recruitment to Cults and Sects." *American Journal of Sociology* 85 (1980): 1376–95.

Sterk, Andrea. "Mission from Below: Captive Women and Conversion on the East Roman Frontiers." *Church History* 79, no. 1 (2010): 1–39.

————. "'Representing' Mission from Below: Historians as Interpreters and Agents of Christianization." *Church History* 79, no. 2 (2010): 271–304.

Stevenson, J. *A New Eusebius: Documents Illustrating the History of the Church to AD 337*. Revised ed. W.H.C. Frend. London: SPCK, 1987.

Stevenson, Kenneth W. *The Lord's Prayer: A Text in Tradition*. London: SCM, 2004.

Stewart-Sykes, Alistair. "Catechumenate and Contra-Culture: The Social Process of Catechumenate in Third-Century Africa and Its Development." *St. Vladimir's Theological Quarterly* 47, nos. 3–4 (2003): 289–306.

————, trans. and ed. *The Didascalia Apostolorum*. Studia Traditionis Theologiae 1. Turnhout: Brepols, 2009.

————. "Hermas the Prophet and Hippolytus the Preacher: The Roman Homily and Its Social Context." In *Preacher and Audience: Studies in Early Christian and*

Byzantine Homiletics, edited by Mary B. Cunningham and Pauline Allen, 33–65. Leiden: Brill, 1998.

————, trans. and ed. *Hippolytus: On the Apostolic Tradition*. Crestwood, NY: St. Vladimir's Seminary Press, 2001.

————. *From Prophecy to Preaching: A Search for the Origins of the Christian Homily*. Supplements to the *Vigiliae Christianae* 59. Boston: Brill, 2001.

————, trans. and ed. *Tertullian, Cyprian, Origen: On the Lord's Prayer*. Crestwood, NY: St. Vladimir's Seminary Press, 2004.

Swift, Louis J. *The Early Fathers on War and Military Service*. Message of the Fathers of the Church 19. Wilmington, DE: Michael Glazier, 1983.

Taubes, Jacob. *The Political Thought of Paul*. Translated by Diana Hollander. Stanford, CA: Stanford University Press, 2004.

Thraede, Klaus. "Kuss." In *Reallexikon für Antike und Christentum*, 22:546–76. Stuttgart: Anton Hiersemann, 2007.

Thurston, Bonnie B. *The Widows: A Women's Ministry in the Early Church*. Minneapolis: Fortress, 1989.

Tilley, Maureen A. "The Ascetic Body and the (Un)Making of the World of the Martyr." *Journal of the American Academy of Religion* 59, no. 3 (1991): 467–79.

————, trans. and ed. *Donatist Martyr Stories: The Church in Conflict in Roman North Africa*. Translated Texts for Historians 24. Liverpool: Liverpool University Press, 1996.

Toner, Jerry. *Popular Culture in Ancient Rome*. Cambridge: Polity Press, 2009.

Trevett, Christine. *Christian Women and the Time of the Apostolic Fathers (AD c. 80–160): Corinth, Rome and Asia Minor*. Cardiff: University of Wales Press, 2006.

————. *Montanism: Gender, Authority and the New Prophecy*. Cambridge: Cambridge University Press, 1996.

Vaage, Leif E., ed. *Religious Rivalries in the Early Roman Empire and the Rise of Christianity*. Waterloo, ON: Wilfred Laurier University Press, 2006.

Van Dam, Raymond. *Becoming Christian: The Conversion of Roman Cappadocia*. Philadelphia: University of Pennsylvania Press, 2003.

Veilleux, Armand. *Pachomian Koinonia*. Vol. 1, *The Life of Saint Pachomius and His Disciples*. Kalamazoo, MI: Cistercian Publications, Inc., 1980.

Viscusso, Patrick. "Christian Participation in Warfare: A Byzantine View." In *Peace and War in Byzantium: Essays in Honor of George T. Dennis, SJ*, edited by Timothy S. Miller and John Nesbitt, 33–40. Washington, DC: Catholic University of America Press, 1995.

Walls, Andrew F. *The Missionary Movement in Christian History: Studies in the Transmission of Faith*. Maryknoll, NY: Orbis Books, 1996.

Walter, Tony, and Grace Davie. "The Religiosity of Women in the Modern West." *British Journal of Sociology* 49, no. 4 (1998): 640–60.

Whitaker, Charles. "Baptism." In *Essays on Hippolytus*, edited by Geoffrey J. Cuming, 52–60. Grove Liturgical Study 15. Bramcote, Notts: Grove Books, 1978.

Wiles, Maurice F. "The Theological Legacy of St. Cyprian." *Journal of Ecclesiastical History* 14, no. 2 (1963): 139–49.

Wilken, Robert L. "Alexandria: A School of Training in Virtue." In *Schools of Thought in the Christian Tradition*, edited by Patrick Henry, 15–30. Philadelphia: Fortress, 1984.

———. *The Christians as the Romans Saw Them*. New Haven: Yale University Press, 1984.

———. "*In novissimis diebus*: Biblical Promises, Jewish Hopes and Early Christian Exegesis." *Journal of Early Christian Studies* 1, no. 1 (1993): 1–9.

———. *Remembering the Christian Past*. Grand Rapids: Eerdmans, 1995.

———. *The Spirit of Early Christian Thought: Seeking the Face of God*. New Haven: Yale University Press, 2003.

Willimon, William H. *Peculiar Speech: Preaching to the Baptized*. Grand Rapids: Eerdmans, 1992.

Wischmeyer, Wolfgang. *Von Golgatha zum Ponte Molle: Studien zur Sozialgeschichte der Kirche im dritten Jahrhundert*. Forschungen zur Kirchen- und Dogmengeschichte 49. Göttingen: Vandenhoek & Ruprecht, 1992.

Wright, David F. "At What Ages Were People Baptized in the Early Centuries?" *Studia Patristica* 30 (1997): 389–94.

———. "Infant Dedication in the Early Church." In *Baptism, the New Testament and the Church: Historical and Contemporary Studies in Honour of R. E. O. White*, edited by Stanley E. Porter and Anthony R. Cross, 352–78. Journal for the Study of the New Testament Supplement Series 171. Sheffield: Sheffield Academic Press, 1999.

Yarnold, Edward J. *The Awe-Inspiring Rites of Initiation: Baptismal Homilies of the Fourth Century*. Slough, UK: St. Paul Publications, 1971.

———. "The Baptism of Constantine." *Studia Patristica* 26 (1993): 95–101.

Yoder, John Howard. "As You Go: The Old Mission in a New Day (1961)." In Yoder, *Theology of Mission: A Believers Church Perspective*, edited by Gayle Gerber Koontz and Andy Alexis-Baker, 399–421. Downers Grove, IL: IVP Academic, 2014.

Young, Robin Darling. *In Procession before the World: Martyrdom as Public Liturgy in Early Christianity*. Milwaukee: Marquette University Press, 2001.

Index